What They Say about Us

"One organization with a long record of success
in helping people find jobs is The Five O'Clock Club."

FORTUNE

"Many managers left to fend for themselves are turning to the camaraderie offered by [The Five O'Clock Club]. Members share tips and advice, and hear experts."

The Wall Street Journal

"If you have been out of work for some time . . . consider The Five O'Clock Club."

The New York Times

"Wendleton has reinvented the historic gentlemen's fraternal oasis and built it into a chain of strategy clubs for job seekers."

The Philadelphia Inquirer

"Organizations such as The Five O'Clock Club are building . . . an extended professional family."

Jessica Lipnack, author, *Professional Teams*

"[The Five O'Clock Club] will ask not what you do, but 'What do you want to do?' . . . [And] don't expect to get any great happy hour drink specials at this joint. The seminars are all business."

The Washington Times

"The Five O'Clock Club's proven philosophy is that job hunting is a learned skill like any other. The Five O'Clock Club becomes the engine that drives [your] search."

Black Enterprise

"Job hunting is a science at The Five O'Clock Club. [Members] find the discipline, direction and much-needed support that keeps a job search on track."

Modern Maturity

"Wendleton tells you how to beat the odds—even in an economy where pink slips are more common than perks. Her savvy and practical guide[s] are chockablock with sample résumés, cover letters, worksheets, negotiating tips, networking suggestions and inspirational quotes from such far-flung achievers as Abraham Lincoln, Malcolm Forbes, and Lily Tomlin."

Working Woman

What Job Hunters Say

"During the time I was looking for a job, I kept Kate's books by my bed. I read a little every night, a little every morning. Her common-sense advice, methodical approach, and hints for keeping the spirits up were extremely useful."

Harold Levine, coordinator, Yale Alumni Career Resource Network

"I've just been going over the books with my daughter, who is 23 and finally starting to think she ought to have a career. She won't listen to anything I say, but you she believes."

Newspaper columnist

"Thank you, Kate, for all your help. I ended up with four offers and at least 15 compliments in two months. Thanks!"

President and CEO, large banking organization

"I have doubled my salary during the past five years by using The Five O'Clock Club techniques. Now I earn what I deserve. I think everyone needs The Five O'Clock Club."

M. S., attorney, entertainment industry

"I dragged myself to my first meeting, totally demoralized. Ten weeks later, I chose from among job offers and started a new life. Bless You!

Senior editor, not-for-profit

"I'm an artistic person, and I don't think about business. Kate provided the disciplined business approach so I could practice my art. After adopting her system, I landed a role on Broadway in Hamlet."

Bruce Faulk, actor

"I've referred at least a dozen people to The Five O'Clock Club since I was there. The Club was a major factor in getting my dream job, which I am now in."

B. R., research head

"My Five O'Clock Club coach was a God-Send!!! She is truly one of the most dynamic and qualified people I've ever met. Without her understanding and guidance, I wouldn't have made the steps I've made toward my goals."

Operating room nurse

"The Five O'Clock Club has been a fantastic experience for my job search. I couldn't have done it without you. Keep up the good work."

Former restaurant owner, who found his dream job with
an organization that advises small businesses

What Human Resources Executives Say about
The Five O'Clock Club Outplacement

"**This thing works.** *I saw a structured, yet nurturing, environment where individuals searching for jobs positioned themselves for success. I saw 'accountability' in a nonintimidating environment. I was struck by the support and willingness to encourage those who had just started the process by the group members who had been there for a while.*"

Employee relations officer, financial services organization

"**Wow! I was immediately struck by the electric atmosphere** *and people's commitment to following the program. Job hunters reported on where they were in their searches and what they had accomplished the previous week. The overall environment fosters sharing and mutual learning.*"

Head of human resources, major law firm

"*The Five O'Clock Club program is* **far more effective** *than conventional outplacement. Excellent materials, effective coaching and nanosecond responsiveness combine to get people focused on the central tasks of the job search. Selecting The Five O'Clock Outplacement Program was one of my best decisions this year.*"

Sr. vice president, human resources, manufacturing company

"**You have made me look like a real genius** *in recommending The Five O'Clock Club [to our divisions around the country]!*"

Sr. vice president, human resources, major publishing firm

Go to our website
www.fiveoclockclub.com
Join our mailing list and receive FREE periodic
emailings on job search or career development.

The Five O'Clock Club®

Find your personal path in job search and career success

Shortcut Your Job Search

Get Meetings That Get You The Job

KATE WENDLETON

CENGAGE
Learning®

Professional • Technical • Reference

Australia • Canada • Mexico • Singapore • Spain • United Kingdom • United States

CENGAGE Learning®

Professional • Technical • Reference

Shortcut Your Job Search: Get Meetings That Get You the Job
Kate Wendleton

Vice President, Career Education SBU: Dawn Gerrain
Director of Editorial: Sherry Gomoll
Publisher and General Manager,
Cengage Learning PTR: Stacy L. Hiquet
Associate Director of Marketing: Sarah Panella
Manager of Editorial Services: Heather Talbot
Senior Marketing Manager: Mark Hughes
Acquisitions Editors: Martine Edwards and Mitzi Koontz
Developmental Editor: Kristen Shenfield
Editorial Assistant: Jennifer Anderson
Director of Production: Wendy A. Troeger
Production Manager: J.P. Henkel
Production Editor: Rebecca Goldthwaite
Technology Project Manager: Sandy Charette
Director of Marketing: Wendy E. Mapstone
Channel Manager: Gerard McAvey
Marketing Coordinator: Erica Conley
Cover Design: TDB Publishing Services
Text Design: Bookwrights

For product information and technology assistance, contact us at
Cengage Learning Customer & Sales Support, 1-800-354-9706
For permission to use material from this text or product, submit all requests online at cengage.com/permissions Further permissions questions can be emailed to permissionrequest@cengage.com

Cengage Learning PTR
20 Channel Center Street
Boston, MA 02210
USA
Cengage Learning is a leading provider of customized learning solutions with office locations around the globe, including Singapore, the United Kingdom, Australia, Mexico, Brazil, and Japan. Locate your local office at:
international.cengage.com/region
Cengage Learning products are represented in Canada by Nelson Education, Ltd.
For your lifelong learning solutions, visit **cengageptr.com**
Visit our corporate website at **cengage.com**

For information, please contact: The Five O'Clock Club®
300 East 40th Street
New York, New York 10016 www.fiveoclockclub.com
Library of Congress Cataloging-in-Publication Data
Shortcut Your Job Search/ Kate Wendleton.
p. cm.
"The Five O'Clock Club."
Includes index.
ISBN 978-1-285-75346-1

2013937127

For the thousands of members of The Five O'Clock Club—
These stories are theirs.

*Without effort we cannot attain any of
our goals in life, no matter what the
advertisements may claim to the contrary.
Anyone who fears effort, anyone who backs off
from frustration . . . will never get anywhere.*
Erich Fromm, *For the Love of Life*

Preface

Dear Member or Prospective Member of The Five O'Clock Club:

You probably think there is only one best way to get meetings in your target market. You may personally believe ads are best for you, or search firms or networking. You are probably incorrect. Chances are, the technique that helped you get your last job will not be the best technique for you this time around. The situation has changed. You are older now and have more to offer, the kind of job you want next may have changed, and the job market has certainly changed.

Luckily, we have spent the last 25-plus years researching and keeping up-to-date on job-search techniques that work. You can benefit from our efforts on your behalf. It is very difficult for job searchers themselves to know which techniques will work best this time around. Therefore, we suggest you take an organized, methodical *research* approach to your own search. Observe what is working for you and what is not—and do more of whatever is working. We'll show you how.

There are four basic techniques for getting meetings in your target market: search firms, ads (in print and online), networking, and contacting companies directly. We urge you to consider all four techniques—and their variations—for your search. The best searches rely on two or more techniques for getting meetings.

Chances are, you are going after published job *openings* rather than unpublished job *possibilities*. If you chase advertised openings, you will automatically have competition for those openings. We suggest that you develop more *possibilities*. This means contacting hiring managers who do not happen to have an opening right now, but would *love* to have someone like you on board. Then we'll want you to keep in touch with those managers (we'll tell you how), and develop 6 to 10 similar contacts.

This may sound like a lot of work, but it's a lot less work than applying for openings and continually being rejected. As a matter of course, Five O'Clock Clubbers regularly develop 6 to 10 leads—and more. We want them to wind up with three concurrent job offers so they will have a choice. You can do this, too.

Chances are, you are not contacting enough organizations. Be sure to read "Measuring Your Targets" and "Current List of Stage-1, Stage-2, and Stage-3 Contacts." In our research, we have found these worksheets to be the most effective ways to make sure you are on the right path in your search.

Believe it or not, a successful search hinges on *having an effective Stage 2*. I know you don't understand what I'm saying right now, but soon you will be glad that there is actually a *methodology* you can follow, a way to measure the effectiveness of your job search—in good economic times and bad.

We found that there is no one job-hunting technique that always works. Job-hunting formulas hold true in the aggregate, but may not for a specific situation. The techniques that work depend, to a large extent, on the industry being pursued, the kind of job you want within that industry, and your own style and personality.

This book series gives you guidelines, but also offers flexibility in deciding which job-hunting approach is right for you. When you understand what is happening and why, you will be in a better position to plan your own job-hunting campaign, and rely less on chance or on what a specific expert tells you.

Job hunting can be thought of as a project—much like any project you might handle in your regular job. Most of the approaches in this book are businesslike rather than intensely psychological. Thinking of job hunting in a business-type way allows you to use the problem-solving skills you might use at work.

I feel duty-bound to address the issue of career planning. Most people are interested in job-hunting techniques but don't want to give much thought to what they should do with their *lives*. So be sure to read our book, *Targeting a Great Career,* to make sure your career is heading in the right direction. When you uncover what it is you want to do long term, then you can look for a job that will take you in that direction.

These books are the result of years of research into how successful job hunters land the best jobs at the best pay. This series replaces the very successful and popular *Through the Brick Wall* series, and, with the addition of new material, takes job search to an even higher level of sophistication. Together, these books provide the most detailed explanation of the search process:

- *Targeting a Great Career* shows you *what kind* of job you should look for. It is a relatively painless way to think about the career-planning process. In addition, it contains the most comprehensive job-search bibliography available anywhere.

- *Packaging Yourself: The Targeted Résumé* is quite simply the best résumé book on the market. It uses the résumés of real people and tells you their stories. It refers to more than 100 industries and professions.

- *Shortcut Your Job Search: Get Meetings That Get You The Job* (this book) tells you *how* to get job leads—part-time or full-time, freelance or consulting. In addition, it contains worksheets that you may copy for your own use.

- *Mastering the Job Interview and Winning the Money Game* tells you how to interview, get the offer, and negotiate using proven Five O'Clock Club techniques.

- *Navigating Your Career* and *WorkSmarts* tell you how to do well in your job and manage your career.

Welcome to the exciting world of managing your own career. And thank you for supporting The Five O'Clock Club through your purchase of this book. Because of people like you, we can keep the program going so we'll be there when you need us. Our goal is, and always has been, to provide the best affordable career advice. And—with you as our partners—we will continue to do this.

Cheers, God bless, and good luck!

Kate Wendleton
New York City, 2013
www.fiveoclockclub.com

Contents

Introduction

People can be divided into three groups: those who make things happen, those who watch things happen— and those who wonder, What happened?

ANONYMOUS

The Five O'Clock Club is a research-based organization working with job hunters across the country both individually and in small groups.

In the small-group strategy sessions, members report on their searches every week, and coaches report on client cases at Coach Guild meetings. We transcribe the "graduation speeches" of successful job hunters, and these reports are often published in our newsletter, *The Five O'Clock News*. Because we have done this continuously since 1978, we have monitored job-market changes and have kept up-to-date with what works in today's market.

For example, we know that:

- It takes an average of eight follow-up phone calls to get a meeting. The chapter "How to Handle the Phone: A Life Skill" will help you increase your success rate.
- The average job hunter who comes to The Five O'Clock Club is not targeting enough *positions*. A job hunter must target 200 positions to get a job within a reasonable time frame (*positions*, not openings and not companies). See the section "Measuring Your Targets."
- Job hunters who rely on only one technique for getting meetings (networking, search firms, print or online ads, or contacting companies directly) have weaker searches. Those who consider all four techniques do better.

- The only way to measure the effectiveness of these techniques is not whether they result in job offers, but whether they result in *meetings*.
- Networkers should contact anyone at any level to get information on a field, but they are unlikely to get a job unless they contact those who are one or two levels higher than they are.
- To maintain momentum, job hunters must have 6 to 10 things in the works at all times: five will fall away through no fault of their own!
- The key to the job search process is Stage 2: meet with at least 6 to 10 people who are the right people at the right level in the right organizations. It's okay (or even better) if they do not have a job opening right now. The question to ask is this: "If you had an opening, would you consider bringing someone like me on board?"

  If the answer is yes, just keep in touch with them. Do this with enough companies and you will hear about openings before your competitors do. You are more likely to get offers this way.
- The Internet is great—especially for research. Definitely answer ads on the web, but also use the Internet to develop your target list of companies to contact (your Targeting Map of 200 Positions), to research companies before you go in for a meeting, and to research the information you need to develop an excellent follow-up piece.

Ah! A Process I Can Follow

When job hunters have been looking for a while and finally find The Five O'Clock Club, they are relieved that:

- There is a methodology they can follow.
- They can tell right away where they are in their searches.
- They can measure the effectiveness of their job search.

Most books tell you simply to network to get meetings. But networking is spotty (i.e., you get meetings only at the places where someone you know knows someone) and networking alone is too slow for most people. Use all four techniques highlighted in this book.

As you will see, these techniques work at all levels—and for all types of people. They have even been used successfully by actors and actresses, and at least one orchestra conductor. Whatever your field, this book will give you the inside track.

When job hunters find jobs, they report to the group. Last week, a man reported that he had been unemployed for three years. His wife had a good job, he spent time with his kids, and he found a few temporary assignments, but he was essentially unemployed, and was trying very hard to get a job. After only four Five O'Clock Club sessions, he found a great one.

The week before, a woman spoke who had been unemployed for a year and a half; she had come to six sessions. Her first session had been a full year earlier, and she had decided to search on her own. After a year, she came back, attended five more sessions, and got a great job.

The week before that, a man who had been unemployed for six months before joining The Five O'Clock Club found a great job. In his four months with the Club, the group helped him see how he was coming across in meetings (very stiff and preachy) and how to expand his job targets. Some people take longer because they are at the beginning of their search or because they have not searched in many years and need to learn this new skill.

Many job hunters think they have to lower their salary expectations because they are unemployed or have been job searching for a long time. You may have to lower your salary expectations for other reasons but, if you position yourself well, not because of being unemployed—none of these three people did. Their unemployment did not affect their salary negotiations. In our book, *Mastering the Job Interview and Winning the Money Game*, you will learn how to negotiate properly and increase your chances of getting what you deserve—whether you are employed or not.

The Five O'Clock Club techniques work whether a job hunter is employed or unemployed. Most job hunters try to get meetings and then try to do well in them. They are skipping two important parts of the process that come before interviewing, and are therefore probably not doing the two remaining parts very well. At The Five O'Clock Club, we stress that all four parts are important. They are:

- **Assessment:** Deciding what you really want results in better job targets. (See our book *Targeting a Great Career* and Part Two of this book for an introduction to the process.) Assessment also results in better résumés. (See our book *Packaging Yourself: The Targeted Résumé.*)

- **Campaign Preparation and Getting Meetings:** Planning your campaign results in lots of meetings in each job target (this book).

- **Interviewing:** Meetings result in an assessment of the company's needs. (See our book *Mastering the Job Interview and Winning the Money Game.*)

- **Interview Follow-Up:** Proactive steps taken after the interview result in job offers. (See our book *Mastering the Job Interview and Winning the Money Game.*)

As you can see, job hunters who think that job interviews lead to offers have skipped a step. Interviews lead to a better understanding of what the company wants. What you do *after* the interview leads to an offer.

Here are a few quick stories to get you started. They were written by David Madison on our staff.

CASE STUDY *Pierre*
Getting a Career Back on Track

Pierre had been away from his chosen field of urban planning for almost a decade, and he knew he was fighting an uphill battle. He found that The Five O'Clock Club approach to correct positioning and research played a major role helping him overcome objections and get back in. He decided to respond to three jobs posted on a website; working with his Five O'Clock Club small group and coach, he crafted cover letters to show that his experience was a match for the stated requirements, relying heavily on the language of the ad itself to describe his background.

> **Pierre found jobs listed on the Internet, but so did thousands of others. So he networked to find people who knew the hiring manager.**

But once the letter and résumés were on the way, he went into high gear to outclass the competition; since it was an Internet ad, he knew there would be plenty of competition—and he could assume that most of the other candidates would have current experience. He networked heavily to find out as much as he could about the company and the key players. He was able to reach people who knew the hiring manager and he called the president of an industry association to get suggestions and insights about the company. By the time he went on the interview, it was hard for the hiring manager to see him as unconnected or out of touch—and he landed the job.

He attended the Club for two months.

CASE STUDY *Natalie*
Learning the Price of Networking without Positioning

Natalie is one of the leaders in her field, but is the first to admit that her job-search skills left something to be desired. Her position was eliminated in a corporate merger and she found herself in the job market for the first time in 13 years. "I have a stellar résumé," she said. "I had this completely unrealistic expectation that, when I told people I would be available, they would be clamoring to have me." She set out to network on a massive scale, and because of her position and reputation, many doors were opened. A year later, she confesses, "I had an incredible collection of business cards."

But she still didn't have a job, although a few teaching and writing assignments had come her way. Her networking had put her on the trail of The Five O'Clock Club, and she began attending sessions. She credits The Five O'Clock Club, especially the books, with giving her crucial insights about strategy and positioning. She learned that people wouldn't be "clamoring" to have her until she helped them grasp what she could do for them. "The Five O'Clock Club gave me a different way of approaching job interviews: trying to identify company needs, positioning myself in terms of their needs." She credits the Club with giving her "heightened awareness" that turned the situation around—and she acknowledges the role of her coach in inspiring her to listen more carefully. On the interviews, she says, "I could hear his voice in the back of my head!"

Natalie credits the weekly contact with her coach for "keeping me motivated. The Five O'Clock Club gave me strategy. I'm just sorry that I didn't find the Club sooner." She attended the Club for almost two months.

People are always blaming their circumstances for what they are. I don't believe in circumstances. The people who get on in this world are the people who get up and look for the circumstances they want, and if they can't find them, make them.

GEORGE BERNARD SHAW,
"MRS. WARREN'S PROFESSION" (1893)

CASE STUDY *Tanya*
Relying on the Two-Minute Pitch

Tanya also credits The Five O'Clock Club with helping her engineer a major career change. She had been a manager at a not-for-profit organization, and just a year later managed to land where she wanted: as an in-house corporate trainer. As one of the first steps, she followed her coach's suggestion to join the American Society for Training and Development, and soon after accepted a committee assignment—and began the process of meeting the right people.

> **Never make a call unless your
> Two-Minute Pitch is ready.**

But she forged ahead on other fronts as well: She spent a lot of time on self-assessment, especially the Seven Stories, and took classes to learn the Internet, Excel, and PowerPoint. Having been in the not-for-profit environment only, she wanted to experience the corporate world before going on interviews in her new chosen field. She signed up for temp jobs to get assignments at major corporations, including American Express and Merrill Lynch. So she got her feet wet in the world of business—and her ego got a nice boost when some of the firms wanted her to come on board full-time.

Tanya accomplished her career change after 11 sessions at The Five O'Clock Club, and is pleased with her new role in a new industry. She is a firm believer in positioning and in always being prepared. The Five O'Clock Club teaches that the follow-up calls are critical in the process, and Tanya warns, "Never make calls unless your Two-Minute Pitch is ready—unless you have your résumé in front of you."

CASE STUDY *Chandler*
Well Positioned . . . to Hire Himself

Chandler came to The Five O'Clock Club intent on finding a new job. After 13 sessions, however, he was able to say, "I hired myself." "I really found that coming here helped me a lot because it helped pull a lot of things together that I couldn't have done on my own." He praised the Seven Stories (see our book *Targeting a Great Career*) especially for confirming his interest in training and teaching, but also for helping him realize that he prizes his independence. Hence he came to see that he didn't want a new job in the sense of being hired by someone. He realized he was giving such signals when an interviewer commented: "I know you can do this job. The question is, Do you want to do it?"

Chandler met a woman at the Club who helped him hook up with an assignment that proved to be a valuable foundation for launching his own consulting practice. He felt that his small group was helpful in keeping him focused, and he credits regular attendance with "keeping me on track." Chandler's experience illustrates the truth that The Five O'Clock Club methodology is valid for consultants as well as traditional employees—it is about life management as well as job-search and career skills. After his 13 sessions at the Club, Chandler said, "I don't see myself being retired. I want to work close to things that are important to me. I feel like I've taken this really giant step forward toward doing that."

A New Definition of Job Hunting

Job hunting in our changing economy is a *continuous* process and requires a new definition. Job hunting now means continually becoming aware of market conditions both inside and outside your present organization, and learning what you have to offer—to both markets. This new definition means you must develop new attitudes about your work life, and new skills for doing well in a changing economy.

Today's economy requires job hunters to be more proactive, more sophisticated, and more willing to go through brick walls to get what they want. Employers don't plan your career for you. You must look after yourself, know what you want, and know how to get it.

Understanding How the Job-Hunting Market Works

Knowing why things work the way they do will give you flexibility and control over your job hunt. Knowing how the hiring system works will help you understand why things go right and why they go wrong—why certain things work and others don't. Then you can modify the system to fit your own needs, temperament, and the workings of the job market you are interested in.

It is simplistic to say that only one job-hunting system works. The job-selection process is more complicated than that. Employers can do what they want. You need to understand the process from their point of view. Then you can plan your own job hunt in your own industry. You will learn how to compete in this market.

Always remember, the best jobs don't necessarily go to the most qualified people, but to the people who are the best job hunters. You'll increase your chances of finding the job you want by using a methodical job-hunting approach.

The Five O'Clock Club Coaching Approach

Our approach is methodical. Our coaches are the best. The Five O'Clock Club coaches are full-time career coaches. Each one has met with hundreds of job hunters. Often within minutes we can pin-point what is wrong with a person's search and turn it around. In this book, you will get that same information. Like our Five O'Clock Club job hunters, you will learn the techniques and hear the stories of other people so you can job hunt more effectively.

It is other people's experience that makes the older man wiser than the younger man.

Yoruba Proverb

PART ONE

Finding Good Jobs

THE CHANGING JOB-HUNTING PROCESS

11 Hints for Job Hunting in a Tight Market

If you haven't the strength to impose your own terms upon life, then you must accept the terms it offers you.

T. S. ELIOT, *THE CONFIDENTIAL CLERK*

The global economy and general economic turmoil have, indeed, put pressure on all of us, especially job hunters. Looking for a job The Five O'Clock Club way can ease the pressure and get you a job more quickly and at a higher salary. Here is a summary of 11 tips to keep in mind during your search.

1. Expand Your Job-Hunting Targets

A critical mistake that job hunters often make is limiting their search to one specific geographic area. The job market may be over-saturated in your current city, but there may be openings in your area of expertise elsewhere. Widening your job-search horizon may help you to find a job more quickly than if you restrict your search to one particular area or company structure. So, if you are looking only in large public corporations, consider small or private companies. If you are looking for a certain kind of position, investigate what other kinds of work you could also do.

2. Expect to be Searching for the Long Haul.

These days it's taking longer than many of us suspect to get a new job. While it's possible that you may find something right away, it's best that you develop a long-term financial backup plan.

What kind of side work could you do now to ensure that you still have money flowing in? How could you reduce your expenses? A time-tested way to resolve these issues and to get advice on how to handle being out of a job is to join The Five O'Clock Club for support, ideas, and feedback.

When you meet someone who doesn't "have" anything for you right now, that's okay. Plan to get in touch with that person again. In fact, you may meet dozens of people who don't have anything right now. Get to know them and their needs better, and tell them about yourself. Build relationships so you can contact them later.

3. Keep Your Spirits Up.

An alarming number of job hunters are becoming discouraged and dropping out of the job market. Don't let yourself become one of them. Read the next section, "When You've Lost the Spirit to Job Hunt." Be aware that what you are going through is not easy, and that many of the things you are experiencing are being experienced by just about everybody else. Our country is seeing its highest unemployment rate in years.

Be aware that what you are going through is not easy, and that many of the things you are experiencing are being experienced by just about everybody else. Hang in there, get a fresh start, and eventually you will find something.

4. Develop New Skills.

If you suspect that your old skills are out-of-date, use your time to develop new ones. If you're being told that you aren't being hired because you don't have the right experience, get the experience. Depending on your area of expertise, there are lots of great ways to hone and expand your skills. Take a class. Do volunteer work to gain expertise that you can later market. Or join an association related to your new skill area.

If you need to earn money immediately, try to do something that will enhance your job search. For example, if you decide to do temporary work, and you want a job in the airline industry, consider doing your temporary work with an airline.

Consider doing something for little or no money simply because it would improve your résumé. A Five O'Clock Clubber got a 12-week assignment with a Sears consignee during the Christmas rush. The pay was terrible but the job title was Regional Manager. He needed something to do, and the job looked great on his résumé.

5. Become a Skilled Job Hunter.

Being good at your job does not necessarily mean that you will be good at *getting* a job. Good job hunters know what they want, what the market wants, and how to present themselves. Having a well-written résumé and cover letter are keys to being competitive when job hunting.

A poorly crafted résumé or cover letter can prevent you from ever getting your foot in the door at most businesses, particularly in an economy that is flooded with people looking for jobs. Work with your Five O'Clock Club coach to develop a winning résumé. Follow the guidance in *Packaging Yourself: The Targeted Résumé* to make your résumé stand out above the rest. Learn how to job hunt like an expert. Your future depends on it.

6. Look for Opportunities

In this economy, opportunities probably will not come knocking on your door. You have to look for them—both inside and outside your present company. Chances are, your present company and

even the industry you are in are going to change. So rather than just doing the same old job, think of how you can take on new assignments so you are at the forefront of the changes. Put out feelers to find out whether you are marketable outside your company. Continually test the waters.

When you are on an interview, try to negotiate a job that suits both you and the hiring manager. For example, if the job is for an administrator, and you would like to do some writing, see if they will allow you to do that too.

Don't passively expect to be told where you could fit in. Actively think about your place in their organization. Create a job for yourself.

7. Target What You Want

As Lily Tomlin said, "I always wanted to be somebody, but I should have been more specific." Be sure you select specific geographic areas, specific industries, and specific positions within those industries.

For example, you may want to be a writer in publishing or advertising in Manhattan or Chicago. Find the names of the people to contact in those cities and industries—or people who know people in those targets. If you target, you have a better chance of finding the job you want.

8. Learn How to Get Meetings

There are a lot of techniques for generating meetings. The basic ones are: answering ads, using search firms, contacting companies directly, and networking. Only 10 percent of all jobs are filled through ads and search firms, so it is wise to learn how to contact companies directly and how to network properly.

Identify all of the companies you need to contact, and then contact them as quickly as possible. Make sure you consider every technique for getting meetings in your target area. Don't focus on getting a job: Focus on getting meetings.

9. See People Two Levels Higher than You Are

When you are in the initial stages of exploring a target area, you will want to do some library research and contact people at your level to find out about that area and see how well your skills match up.

But after you have decided to conduct a full campaign in a target area, contact people who are at a higher level than you are. They are the ones who are in a position to hire you or recommend that you be hired.

Make sure you talk to lots of people. It will give you practice and actually relax you. You will find out how much in demand you are, and how much you can charge.

10. Work at Your Job Hunt the Same Way You Would Work at a Job

Plan your job-hunting campaign. Work at it 35 hours a week if you are unemployed, and 15 hours a week if you are employed. It's only when you are devoting a certain number of hours a week to your search that you can get some momentum built up. Of course, you also need to be concerned about the quality of your campaign. You can have an organized and methodical search by carefully following the process in this book.

11. Follow-Up, Follow-Up, Follow-Up

After you meet with someone who has no job for you, keep in touch with that person by letting him or her know how your search is going or by sending a magazine article that would be of interest, for example. After a job interview, consider what they liked about you and what they didn't, and how you could influence their hiring decision. Follow-up is the main opportunity you have to turn a job interview into a job offer.

You think you understand the situation, but what you don't understand is that the situation just changed.

PUTNAM INVESTMENTS ADVERTISEMENT AS QUOTED IN
"THE WORKPLACE OF THE FUTURE,"
Alabama Connection, 2007

When You've Lost the Spirit to Job Hunt

"I can't explain myself, I'm afraid, Sir," said Alice,
"because I'm not myself, you see."
"I don't see," said the Caterpillar.

LEWIS CARROLL, *Alice in Wonderland*

They're all doing terrific! You're not. You're barely hanging on. You used to be a winner, but now you're not so sure. How can you pull yourself out of this?

I've felt like that. Everyone in New York had a job except me. I would never work again. I was ruining interviews although I knew better— I had run The Five O'Clock Club for years in Philadelphia. Yet I was unable to job hunt properly. I was relatively new to New York and divorced. Even going to my country house depressed me: A woman wanted me to sell it, join her cult, and have a 71-year-old as my roommate. It seemed to be my fate.

Then I got a call from my father—a hurricane was about to hit New York. When I told him my situation, he directed me to get rid of the cult lady and take the next train out. I got out just as the hurricane blew in, and he and I spent three beautiful days alone at my parents' ocean place. He encouraged me, even playing 10 motivational tapes on "being a winner"! One tape taught me:

The winners in life think constantly in terms of I can, I will and I am. Losers, on the other hand, concentrate their waking thoughts on what they should have or would have done, or what they can't do.

DR. DENNIS WAITLEY, *The Psychology of Winning*

My father wined and dined and took care of me. We watched a six-hour tape of my family history—the births, and birthdays, Christmases past, marriages, and parties. We talked about life and the big picture. I had no strength. He nurtured me and gave me strength.

What can *you* do if you can't get this kind of nurturing? Perhaps I've learned a few lessons that may help you.

> **There seem to be phases and cycles in a job hunt—there is the initial rush, the long haul, the drought, followed by the first poor job offer and the later better offers.**

---

1. Put Things in Perspective

A depressing and difficult passage has prefaced every new page I have turned in life.

CHARLOTTE BRONTË, *Villette*

You've worked 10 or 20 years, and you'll probably work 10 or 20 more. In the grand scheme of things, this moment will be a blip: an aberration in the past.

Focusing on the present will make you depressed and will also make you a poor interviewee. You will find it difficult to brag about your past or see the future. You will provide too much information about what put you in this situation.

Interviewers don't care. They want to hear what you can do for *them.* When they ask why you are looking, give a brief, light, logical explanation, and then drop it.

Focus on what you have done in the past, and what you can do in the future. You *do* have a future, you know, although you may feel locked into your present situation. Even some young people say it is too late for them. But a lot can happen in 10 years—and *most* of what happens is up to you.

My life seems like one long obstacle course,
with me as the chief obstacle.

JACK PAAR, AMERICAN ENTERTAINER

Woe to him that is alone when he falleth, for he hath
not another to help him up.

THE WISDOM OF SOLOMON (BIBLE)

2. Get Support

The old support systems—extended families and even nuclear families—are disappearing. And we no longer look to our community for support.

Today, we are more alone; we are supposed to be tougher and take care of ourselves. But relying solely on yourself is not the answer. How can you fill yourself up when you are emotionally and spiritually empty?

Job hunters often need some kind of emotional and spiritual support because this is a trying time. Our egos are at stake. We feel vulnerable and uncared for. We need realistic support from people who know what we are going through.

There is no such thing as a self-made man. I've had
much help and have found that if you are willing to
work, many people are willing to help you.

O. WAYNE ROLLINS

Join a job-hunting support group to be with others who know what you're going through.

Many places of worship have job-hunting groups open to anyone. During a later job hunt when I was employed, I reported my progress weekly to my group at The Five O'Clock Club. It kept me going.

Statistics show that job hunters with regular career-coaching support get jobs faster and at higher rates of pay. A job-hunting group gives emotional support, concrete advice, and feedback. Often, however, these are not enough for those who are at their lowest.

The more lasting a man's ultimate work, the more sure
he is to pass through a time, and perhaps a very long
one, in which there seems to be very little hope for him.

SAMUEL BUTLER, *The Way of All Flesh*
(SIMON & BROWN)

- If possible, rely on your friends and family. I could count on a call from my former husband most mornings after I returned from breakfast—just so we could both make sure I was really job hunting. I scheduled lunches with friends and gave them an honest report or practiced my job-hunting lines with them.
- Don't abuse your relationships by relying on one or two people. Find lots of sources of support. Consider joining a church, synagogue, or mosque (they're supposed to be nice to you).

3. Remember That This Is Part of a Bigger Picture

We, ignorant of ourselves, Beg often our own harms,
Which the Wise Power Denies us for our own good;
so we find profit by losing of our prayers.

SHAKESPEARE, *Antony and Cleopatra*

. . . so are My ways higher than your ways and My thoughts than your thoughts.

Isaiah 55:9

You are a child of the universe no less than the trees and the stars; you have a right to be here. And whether or not it is clear to you, no doubt the universe is unfolding as it should.

MAX EHRMANN, *The Desiderata of Happiness,* RANDOM HOUSE (1995)

Why me? Why now? Shakespeare thought there might be someone bigger than ourselves watching over everything—a Wise Power. My mother (and probably yours, too) always said "everything happens for the best."

We know that in all things God works for the good of those who love Him.

ROMANS 8:28

If you can believe that things happen for a purpose, *think about the good in your own situation.* What was the *purpose* of my own unemployment? Because of it:

- I experienced a closeness with my father that still affects me;
- I became a better coach; and
- I stopped working 12-hour days.

Though shattered when they lose their jobs, many say in retrospect it was the best thing that could have happened to them. Some say this time of transition was the most rewarding experience of their lives.

Every adversity has the seed of an equivalent or greater benefit.

W. CLEMENT STONE

Perhaps you, too, can learn from this experience and also make some sense of it. This is a time when people often:

- decide what they *really* should be doing with their careers—I had resisted full-time career coaching because I liked the prestige of the jobs I had held;
- better their situations, taking off on another upward drive in their careers;
- develop their personalities; learn skills that will last their entire lives, and
- Reexamine their values and decide what is now important to them.

For what shall it profit a man, if he shall gain the whole world, and lose his own soul?

MARK 8:36

The trouble with the rat race is that if you win, you're still a rat.

LILY TOMLIN

4. Continue to Do Your Job

When you were in your old job, there were days you didn't feel like doing it, but you did it anyway because it was your responsibility. *Job hunting is your job right now.* Some days you don't feel like doing it, but you must. Make a phone call. Write a proposal. Research a company. Do your best every day. No matter how you feel. Somehow it will get done, as any job gets done. Some practical suggestions:

- Make your job hunting professional. Organize it. Get a special calendar to use exclusively to record what you are doing. Use The Five O'Clock Club's Interview Record in this book to track more professionally your efforts and results.
- Set goals. Don't think of whether or not you want to make calls and write letters. Of course you don't. Just do them anyway. Spend most of your time interviewing— that's how you get a job.
- Depression → Inactivity → Depression.

- If you're at the three-month mark or beyond, you may be at a low point. It's hard to push on. Get a fresh start. Pretend you're starting all over again.
- Finding a job is your responsibility. Don't depend on anyone else (search firms, friends) to find it for you.
- Watch your drinking, eating, smoking. They can get out of hand. Take care of yourself physically. Get dressed. Look good. Get some exercise. Eat healthful foods. You may need a few days off to recharge.
- Don't postpone having fun until you get a job. If you are unemployed, schedule at least three hours of fun a week. Do something you normally are unable to do when you are working. I went out to breakfast every morning, indulged in reading the Times, and then went back to my apartment to job hunt. I also went to the auction houses, and bought a beautiful desk at Sotheby's when I sold my country house.
- Assess your financial situation. What is your backup plan if your unemployment goes on for a certain number of months? If need be, I planned to get a roommate, sell furniture, and take out a loan. It turned out not to be necessary, but by planning ahead, I knew I would not wind up on the street.
- Remember: You are distracted. Job hunters get mugged, walk into walls, lose things. This is not an ordinary situation, and extraordinary things happen. Be on your guard.

- Observe the results of what you do in your job hunt. Results are indicators of the correctness of your actions and can help refine your techniques.

All's well that ends well.

SHAKESPEARE

- Become a good job hunter so you can compete in this market. It takes practice, but the better you are, the less anxious you will be.

In nature there are neither rewards nor punishments—there are consequences.

ROBERT GREEN INGERSOLL, *Some Reasons Why* (1895)

In the depths of winter I discovered that there was in me an invincible summer.

ALBERT CAMUS AS QUOTED IN *Albert Camus: The Invisible Summer* (1958) BY ALBERT MAQUET

Finally, two sayings especially helped me when I was unemployed:

> *You don't get what you want.*
> *You get what you need.*

and

> *When God closes a door, He opens a window.*

Good luck.
—Kate

An Overview of the Job-Search Process

If you only care enough for a result you will almost certainly obtain it. If you wish to be rich, you will be rich; if you wish to be learned, you will be learned; if you wish to be good, you will be good.

WILLIAM JAMES

The following chart outlines each part of the process. It's best to do every part, however quickly you may do it. Experienced job hunters pay attention to the details and do not skip a step.

The first part of the process is **assessment** (or evaluation). You evaluate yourself by doing the exercises in *Targeting a Great Career*, and you evaluate your prospects by doing some preliminary research in the library or by talking to people.

Assessment consists of the following exercises:

The Seven Stories Exercise
- Interests
- Values
- Satisfiers and Dissatisfiers
- Your Forty-Year Vision

If you are working privately with a career coach, he or she may ask you to do a few additional exercises, such as a personality test.

Assessment results in:

- a listing of all the targets you think are worth exploring; and
- a résumé that makes you look appropriate to your first target (and may work with other targets as well).

Even if you don't do the entire assessment, the Seven Stories Exercise is especially important because it will help you develop an interesting résumé. Therefore, we have included that exercise in this book.

Research will help you figure out which of your targets:
- are a good fit for you; and
- offer hope in terms of being a good market.

You can't have too many targets as long as you rank them. Then, *for each one*, conduct a campaign to get meetings in that target area.

The circumstances that surround a man's life are not important. How that man responds to those circumstances is important. His response is the ultimate determining factor between success and failure.

BOOKER T. WASHINGTON

Step I: Campaign Preparation

- Conduct research to develop a list of all the companies in your first target. Find out the names of people you should contact in appropriate departments in those companies.
- Write your cover letter. (Paragraph 1 is the opening; Paragraph 2 is a summary about yourself appropriate for this target; Paragraph 3 contains your bulleted accomplishments ("You may be interested in some of the things I've done"); Paragraph 4 is the close. (Sample letters are included in this book.)
- Develop your plan for getting **lots of meetings in this target**. You have four basic choices:
- Networking,

- Direct contact,
- Search firms, and
- Ads (print and Internet).

You will read more about these methods for getting meetings later in this book.

Sometimes it's best if a man just spends a moment or two thinking. It is one of the toughest things he will ever do, and that's probably why so few bother to do it.

ALONZO HERNDON, BORN A SLAVE; DIED A MILLIONAIRE; FOUNDER, ATLANTA LIFE INSURANCE COMPANY

Step II: Interviewing

Most people think interviews result in job offers. But there are usually a few intervening steps before a final offer is made. Interviews should result in getting and giving information.

Did you learn the issues important to each person with whom you met? What did they think were your strongest positives? Where are they in the hiring process? How many other people are they considering? How do you compare with those people? Why might they be reluctant to bring you on board, compared with the other candidates? How can you overcome the decision makers 'objections?

One of the most important, yet most overlooked parts of the job-search process, this is covered in extensive detail in this book.

Step III: Follow-Up

Now that you have analyzed the interview, you can figure out how to follow up with each person with whom you interviewed. Aim to follow up with 6 to 10 companies. Five job possibilities will fall away through no fault of your own.

What's more, with 6 to 10 possibilities, you increase your chances of having three good offers to choose from. You would be surprised: even in

a tight market, job hunters are able to develop multiple offers.

When you are in the Interview Step of Target 1, it's time to start Step I of Target 2. This will give you more momentum and ensure that you do not let things dry up. Keep both targets going, and then start Target 3.

You ain't goin' nowhere . . . son. You ought to go back to driving a truck.

JIM DENNY, GRAND OLE OPRY MANAGER, FIRING ELVIS PRESLEY AFTER ONE PERFORMANCE. AN INTERVIEW ON OCTOBER 2, 1954.

Develop Your Unique Résumé

Read all the case studies in *Packaging Yourself: The Targeted Résumé*. You will learn a powerful new way of thinking about how to position yourself for the kinds of jobs you want. Each of the résumés in that book is for a unique person aiming at a specific target. Seeing how other people position themselves will help you think about what you want a prospective employer to know about you.

Now, it is best to go back to the first part of the process, assessment. In *Targeting a Great Career*, you will read actual case studies that will show you how real people benefited from doing the assessment, including the Forty-Year Vision.

However, if you have already done the Seven Stories Exercise and the Forty-Year Vision, just keep reading.

Everyone should learn to do one thing supremely well because he likes it, and one thing supremely well because he detests it.

B. W. M. YOUNG, HEADMASTER, CHARTERHOUSE SCHOOL

Life never leaves you stranded. If life hands you a problem, it also hands you the ability to overcome that problem. Are you ever tempted to blame the world for your failures and shortcomings? If so, I suggest you pause and reconsider. Does the problem lie with the world, or with you? Dare to dream.

DENNIS KIMBRO, *Think and Grow Rich: A Black Choice*

ASSESSMENT

Consists of:

- The Seven Stories Exercise
- Interests
- Values
- Satisfiers and Dissatisfiers
- Your Fifteen- or Forty-Year Vision

Results in:

- As many targets as you can think of
- A ranking of your targets
- A résumé that makes you look appropriate to your first target
- A plan for conducting your search

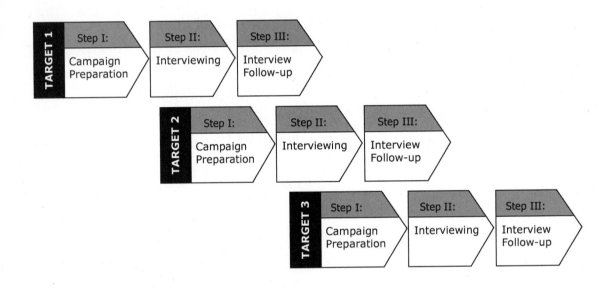

RESULTS

Step I: Campaign Preparation. Results in:	Step II: Interviewing. Results in:	Step III: Follow-Up. Results in:

❏ Research (list of companies)
❏ Résumé
❏ Cover letter
❏ Plan for getting interviews
  - networking
  - direct contact
  - search firms
  - ads
	❏ Giving them information to keep them interested in you
	❏ Getting information so you can "move it along"
	❏ Plan for follow-up (You may do several in-depth follow-ups with each person)
		❏ Aiming to have 6 to 10 things in the works, and
		
		Job Offers!

A Systematic Job Hunt

*Man is not born to solve the problems of the universe,
but to find out what he has to do; and to restrain
himself within the limits of his comprehension.*

GOETHE

Successful Job Hunting Is a System

Working the system increases your chances of getting the job you want—faster. Working the system also helps relieve your natural anxiety about what you should do next.

The system is the same whether you are employed or unemployed, and even if you are not interested in changing jobs now. The system is the same whether you are looking for full-or part-time employment, consulting, or freelance work.

That's because job hunting in a changing economy means: **continuously becoming aware of market conditions inside as well as outside your present company. And learning what you have to offer—both inside and outside your company**.

The time to become aware of your opportunities is *not* when the pressure is on to find a new job, but *now*.

The Job-Hunting Process

You select or target a job market by selecting a geographic area you'd be willing to work in, an industry or company size (small, medium, or large company), and a job or function within that industry. For example, you may want to be a salesperson in the medical industry in New Hampshire. That's your target market.

Then conduct a campaign for the sole purpose of getting meetings in your target area. A number of those meetings might eventually lead to acceptable job offers.

Job hunting seems to have dozens of equally important steps. There are résumés and cover letters to write, personal contacts to make, search firms to contact, ads to answer, notes to write, and so on. You can lose sight of what is most important.

There are only four main parts in a job-hunting campaign: targeting, getting meetings in each target, interviewing, and following up. Do your best and put your effort into those areas. Everything you do in a job hunt grows out of your targets, which lead to meetings and then to offers. If you have targeted well, can get meetings, are well prepared for them, and know how to turn interviews into offers, you will be focused and less affected by mistakes in other areas of your search.

How Long Will a Job Search Take?

The length of each step in your search can vary considerably. For example, selecting the area in which you want to work (see *Targeting a Great Career*) can be as simple as saying, "I want to be a controller in a small firm." Or, it can be as complex as saying, "I want a position of leadership in a growing computer services business in any major U.S. city, where I can run my part of the operation, working with fast-paced but ethical people who are imaginative and leaders in their field. The job should lead to the position of partner."

The entire campaign can be very short. Let's say, for example, that:

- You have focused on a specific, realizable target.
- There are openings in the area that interests you.
- You know of someone in a position to hire you.
- You and the hiring manager "strike sparks" during the interview, which progresses naturally.

Start to finish could take several months.

The average job hunt takes longer. Statistics show that it takes an average of six months or more for professionals and middle managers to find the jobs they want. *Career changes generally take longer.* People who are already employed usually take longer to find a new job because they often don't work as hard at the hunt.

It could take you longer than a month or two because, among other things:

- You may not be clear about what you want.
- What you want may not be realistic.
- Maybe what you want is realistic, but there are no immediate openings.
- There may be openings, but you may not know where they are.
- You may hear of openings, but may not know anyone in a position to hire you.
- You may meet someone in a position to hire you, but the two of you don't hit it off.

> **Devote a large amount of time and energy to your search if you seriously intend to find a suitable job. A thorough search is so much work that the job you finally land will seem easy by comparison!**

On the other hand, job hunting is like any other skill: You get better at it with practice. You'll learn the techniques and what's right for you. You'll become aware of what's happening in your chosen field, so when you start a formal search it won't take so long.

Make it a rule of life never to regret and never to look back. Regret is an appalling waste of energy; you can't build on it; it's only good for wallowing in.

KATHERINE MANSFIELD, *Bliss and Other Stories* (1920)

The New Approach to Job Hunting

Keep up with changes in your company and your target area. To compete in today's market, you must know:

- yourself,
- the market, both inside and outside your company, and
- how to compete against trained job hunters.

Job Hunting—An Everyday Affair

Job hunting is no longer something that happens only when you want to change jobs. Do it informally *all the time* to stay sharp in your present position.

You should always be aware of what may adversely affect your present security. Don't expect your employer to tell you that the company or your department is heading in a different direction. Be ready when the time for change comes. Take advantage of changes so you can move your career in the direction you want it to go. Take control and "impose your own terms upon life."

In today's world, many people job hunt virtually all the time. Years ago, when organizations were more stable, I met an executive at a major pharmaceutical company. He had been with that company 30 years, and planned to stay there until retirement.

Yet, while I was talking to him, he reached into his bottom drawer and pulled out an up-to-date résumé. He was not starting a new job hunt; he believed he should always have an up-to-date résumé and keep on looking—even though he had been working at the same company for 30 years! A good number of his job hunts were "successful" since his outside exploration got him to his high position in the same company.

Job hunting does not necessarily mean you want to change jobs now. Maybe you'll make your next job change a few years down the road. Or maybe someone will change your job for you, without asking. When are you going to start thinking about your next move?

Few things are impossible to diligence and skill.
SAMUEL JOHNSON (1709-1784)

Plan Your Next Move

Plan your career transitions—your moves from one job to the next—don't have them thrust upon you. First, know which job is right for you: a job in which you will excel and feel satisfied doing. Then see how well your present job fits those desires. Don't leave your job for another one that is equally unsatisfying. On the other hand, don't remain in your current job out of inertia.

Career transitions are prompted by changes in a company—such as when it cuts back or introduces major technological or strategic changes—or by a change in you and your goals for your life. Be alert for a coming transition.

If You're Thinking about Changing Jobs

If you don't like your present job, don't leave yet...a good job hunt starts at home. Try to enrich your present job or move elsewhere in the company. Leave only after you are convinced there is nothing there for you.

Whether you want to stay or leave, find out your options and your marketable skills. Figure out what would be a good growth move for you.

One way to find out is to talk informally with people in other companies who are at least two levels higher than you are. They have an overview of the broad spectrum of job possibilities and are also in a position to hire you, or know others who might.

Another way to find out what is marketable is to look at newspaper and Internet ads. This can

also give you ideas for growing in your present position.

Let me give you an example. As soon as I accepted the job of vice president of operations for an advertising agency, I started saving ads for vice president of personnel, controller, vice president of finance, general manager—anything that would apply, even remotely, to my new position. The ads gave me ideas that neither my new employer nor I would have thought of.

I expanded the job and organized the categories of work I should be concentrating on.

These ads also told me the likelihood of being able to get one of those jobs. Even though I saved lots of ads for vice president of finance, I would never qualify because those positions required skills I did not have and was not interested in acquiring.

Ads also let you see who is hiring and what is in demand. Ads teach you the buzzwords of certain professions, and indicate how to tailor your résumé—just in case.

Your constant job hunt can only be good for your present employer. It motivates you to do better, keeping your company more competitive than if you were not aware of what was happening outside.

Practicing Job-Hunting Techniques

Job hunting is a specialized skill just like public speaking or gourmet cooking. You probably wouldn't, for example, get up to speak before an important audience without preparation and practice.

Job hunting takes planning to decide on your message; conduct research; consider your audience and how your message will sound to them; write and rewrite résumés, letters, and interview presentations; and then practice to hear how it all sounds.

Successful job hunting is a formal process. But once you know the basics, you can and should put your own personality into your presentations, just as you would in public speaking.

Follow the "rules" for job hunting the same

What a Job Hunt Looks Like

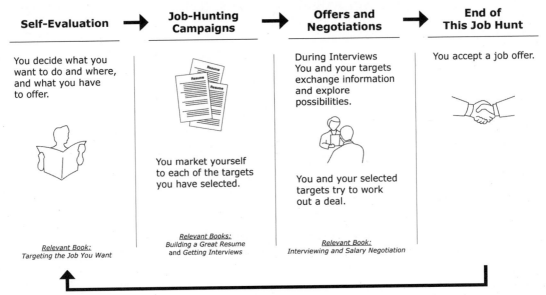

| **Self-Evaluation** → | **Job-Hunting Campaigns** → | **Offers and Negotiations** → | **End of This Job Hunt** |

You decide what you want to do and where, and what you have to offer.

You market yourself to each of the targets you have selected.

During Interviews You and your targets exchange information and explore possibilities.

You and your selected targets try to work out a deal.

You accept a job offer.

Relevant Book:
Targeting the Job You Want

Relevant Books:
Building a Great Resume and Getting Interviews

Relevant Book:
Interviewing and Salary Negotiation

Note: After you are in your new job for a while (such as six months, one year, two years), you will want to reevaluate your situation and make sure you are still on track. That's why this chart points back to the beginning after you've landed your job.

© Kate Wendleton, The Five O'Clock Club®

way you would follow the "rules" for public speaking or cooking. A wise beginner does everything by the book. After you become skilled, you can deviate a bit because you have mastered the basics. You will do what is right for you and the situation you are in. You can exercise sound judgment.

You will then be at the point where it flows. You will find you are operating from an inner strength, and you'll feel what is and is not important. It is *your* job hunt, and you are the one calling the shots. You will feel sure enough to do what is appropriate regardless of what some expert says. You will know when it is to your advantage to break the rules.

Don't develop a siege mentality. Practice job hunting now, even if you happen to enjoy what

you're doing, and even if you want to continue in your present job. In fact, you will be more effective in your job if you become sharper about what is happening in the world.

The rules of the game keep changing and that's part of the game. Only those who change along with the rules will be allowed to continue to play.

Our rate of progress is such that an individual human being, of ordinary length of life, will be called on to face novel situations which find no parallel in his past. The fixed person, for the fixed duties, who, in older societies was such a godsend, in the future will be a public danger.

ALFRED NORTH WHITEHEAD, *Process and Reality,* FREE PRESS (1979)

What to Do If You Are about to Be Fired

*I don't deserve this, but I have arthritis
and I don't deserve that either.*

Jack Benny

When people get fired, many say to themselves, "I'm good at what I do. I won't have trouble finding a job." Or, "The market is terrible. I'll never work again." Neither thought process is helpful. Unfortunately, job hunting calls for special skills. If you get fired, ask for outplacement help as part of your separation agreement. You cannot purchase the services of an outplacement firm yourself. Your company pays The Five O'Clock Club or other outplacement firm directly. You will get far more and your employer will pay far less if they choose The Five O'Clock Club as their outplacement provider.

On the home page of our website (www. fiveoclockclub.com), go to both the "For Employers" and "For Individuals" sections. You will find extensive information there on negotiating severance for yourself and. Information on how Five O'Clock Club outplacement packages are so much more helpful to you, just as these books are.

Five O'Clock Club outplacement help can make all the difference in finding new employment quickly and confidently. Most corporate outplacement packages last for one to three months, sometimes just a few days! You are then left to fend for yourself. Many months later, the job hunter may wish he or she had more help.

Five O'Clock Club outplacement packages *all* last for one a minimum of one full year—even if you land a job quickly—a great benefit. Our one-year package means we will continue working with you even if you decide to do consulting work for a while, lose your next job, or need help handling the political situation in a new job.

You will receive a guaranteed number of hours of private coaching, one full year in the small group, a set of books, a boxed set of 16 40-minute Five O'Clock Club audio presentations on CD-ROMs, and other benefits. Check our website for the latest offering.

If you are currently employed, or outplacement is not available to you, consider your options. A seminar is fine but will not see you through the job-hunting process. Job-coaching firms often charge from $4,000 to $6,000 or more up front, and some have been known to lose interest once the fee is paid.

You need advice and support. Job hunting is stressful and lonely. You may feel you are the only one going through what you are going through. You may even feel as though you will never work again.

The Five O'Clock Club was founded to provide "outplacement" help to individuals. More and more organizations are paying for their former employees to receive The Five O'Clock Club's services. However, most of our attendees pay their own way. Those who are already in traditional outplacement often pay to come to the Club on their own. They appreciate the superior coaching at the Club and also enjoy the healthy environment of being in groups with employed, as well as unemployed, people. The small groups are full of proactive, intelligent people who want to move ahead with their searches—and have fun while doing so.

Join The Five O'Clock Club. We offer job-search training and coaching from professional career coaches. You can also meet with a coach privately (in person or by phone) to help you figure out your job targets, prepare your résumé, or get individualized help on specific parts of your campaign. You will be with others who are trying to accomplish the same things. See the back of this book for more information on the Club.

Unemployed people are sometimes embarrassed by their situation and pretend they are not looking, which is the worst thing they can do. *When you are unemployed and looking for a job, the more people who know what you are looking for, the better.* Spend time regularly with other job hunters, and also with a professional career coach who can give you solid advice.

How to Negotiate Your Severance Package

You may want a career coach to help you during this difficult and sensitive time. Here are some things to consider:

- **Explore your options.**

  During the negotiation, be pleasantly persistent as you explore the options available to you. The situation may be more flexible than it originally appears to be.

- **Deal with each compensation issue separately.**

  A severance package is made up of many items. These may include an actual cash settlement, outplacement help, health care and other benefits, and other items, depending on the industry and

company. You need to look at each component individually. A large cash settlement, for example, will evaporate quickly if you end up paying for outplacement help and benefits.

- **Push to continue your benefits.**

  It costs a company very little to carry employees on its medical plan. But if you tried to duplicate coverage on your own, it would cost a small fortune.

- **Develop a mantra.**

  Find one that succinctly describes your feelings. The phrase will keep you focused and give your overall campaign consistency. Use a phrase such as, "I simply want what is fair."

- **Ask for career-coaching help for a year.**

  You should never underestimate the amount of time it will take you—or the help you will need—to find another comparable position. Depending on the complexity of your situation and your own psychological makeup, your search may last a long time—some tough searches have taken more than a year. If your company only grants you three months' outplacement assistance, you could find yourself cut off in the middle of your job search. Therefore, ask them to consider using The Five O'Clock Club as their outplacement provider.

- **Don't take money over outplacement.**

  A cash settlement of $3,000—or even $30,000—sounds like a lot, but on your own you will not be able to replicate what you could get with top-of-the-line outplacement services.

The fact is that people who get ongoing Five O'Clock Club career coaching throughout their searches get better jobs faster, and at higher rates of pay.

- **Select the outplacement services yourself.**

Although your employer may have a relationship with an outplacement firm, many companies will allow you to select the outplacement firm with which you want to work. Call The Five O'Clock Club (1-800-538-6645) for referral to one of our coaches for help with your severance negotiation. The coach will charge you on a per-hour basis.

• **Use outplacement help to launch your own business.**

You may dream of going out on your own, and be tempted to take a cash settlement, believing money is the most important ingredient you need to form your new company from scratch. However, a good outplacement firm can help you write a business plan, talk with venture capitalists and merchant bankers, and serve as valued advisors until you are on your feet. This is advice you could never afford on your own. In fact, it costs an outplacement firm more to help someone launch a business than to do a traditional job search. The time involved is longer, and the services required are more complex.

• **You can start outplacement coaching even though you have not completely come to terms with your employer.**

You can be looking for another job at the same time you are asking your company for a better settlement. But bear in mind: Traditional outplacement firms cannot help you with negotiations with your employer.

• **Find out what other employees have walked away with.**

Use this information to further your own case. Remember: Every situation is unique. Get help while you are negotiating your severance package. The amount you spend on a little bit of coaching, even over the phone, will convince you that you did your very best to get what you deserve and need.

For far more advice about negotiating your severance, be sure to go to our website, www.fiveoclockclub.com.

It is work, work that one delights in, that is the surest guarantor of happiness.

ASHLEY MONTAGU, *The American Way of Life*

The Five O'Clock Club®

How Long Will It Take to Find a Job?

Nothing in the world can take the place of persistence. Talent will not; nothing is more common than unsuccessful men with talent. Genius will not; the world is full of educated derelicts. Persistence and determination alone are omnipotent. The slogan "press on" has solved and always will solve the problems of the human race.

CALVIN COOLIDGE

Most of the factors influencing the length of a job hunt are under your control. Scan the following topics and read the ones of interest to you now. Read the others later.

Factor #1: Career Continuation vs. Career Change

All things being equal, changing careers takes two to three months longer than looking for a job in the field you are in now. If you want to head your career in a new direction, do it—but realize that it may take longer. However, if your present field is dying, it may be futile to try to stay in it. (See the chapter: "How to Change Careers.")

Factor #2: A Clear Target

You dramatically reduce your chances of finding the job you want if you don't have clearly defined targets.

A job target is a clearly selected geographic area, industry or organization size (small, medium, or large organization), and function within that industry. For example, a job hunter may target the advertising industry in New York or

Chicago, and aim at positions in the account management area. That's one target. That same job hunter may target media sales positions in the publishing industry, also in New York or Chicago. That's a second target. They are related, but require quite different campaigns.

You may feel you are willing to take any job that comes along, but attaining results with such an approach takes longer than with a targeted approach. When you target, your campaign is focused and more convincing to hiring managers. Your pitch is more polished, and you'll find it easier to network. Serendipitous leads can certainly be worthwhile, but the core of your campaign should be targeted.

Factor #3: A Clear Positioning Statement or Pitch within That Target

You are selling an expensive product—yourself— and you cost many thousands of dollars. To sell this product, know what the *customer* (your prospective employer) wants, what you have to offer, and why the customer would want to buy this product. As you position yourself, figure out what to say about yourself in light of what your customer needs. Know how you fit in.

Factor #4: Favorable Conditions within Your Target Market

If your target area is growing or desperately needs what you are offering, or if there are plenty of jobs for which you would qualify, your job hunt will not take as long.

20

Courtesy of Jerry King, Cartoons, Inc.

"Take me to the first office building that's hiring."

On the other hand, if you decide to go for a tough target, expect to work hard to overcome the difficulties. Find out how to get in, and then do it.

Factor #5: True Desire to Find a Job

The people most likely to succeed are the ones who sincerely want to find a job, and work hard at getting it.

Job hunting is a job in itself. If you are unemployed, work at it full-time (with time off for a little fun). If you are employed, treat job hunting as a serious part-time job.

Many job hunters do not treat finding a job as their top priority. Some spend time suing their former employer. Others work hard at a job hunt doing the wrong things: When choosing between doing two things, they seem to choose the one less likely to result in job-hunting progress. Some people spend months on the Internet getting ready, for example, when they know they should be out meeting people. They may consciously or unconsciously sabotage their own efforts because they were recently fired and are afraid of getting

fired again. If you find everything is going wrong all the time, ask yourself if you may be afraid of the future.

Factor #6: Attitude, Attitude, Attitude

You may have the right target, the perfect market, and be the perfect match for an organization, but if your attitude is wrong, you'll have a hard time. The worst attitude is expecting someone else to find a job for you. Successful job hunters are those who take responsibility for their own success or failure rather than blaming the career coach or the system when things go wrong.

Attitude includes:
- taking responsibility for your own job hunt,
- the self-confidence you portray,
- being able to think and act like a winner even if you don't feel like it (who wants to hire a loser?), and
- your drive and energy level.

Your attitude is as important as the actual job-hunting techniques you use. Flawless technique is worthless with a bad attitude.

Life shrinks or expands in proportion to one's courage.

Anais Nin, *The Diary of Anais Nin, Volume 4,* 1944-1947

Factor #7: Working The Five O'Clock Club System

In addition to being willing to work hard, you must be willing to work the system. Those most likely to find a job quickly are those who go through every step, even if they go through certain steps quickly or find other steps distasteful.

A job hunt is going to take time. The time you think you're saving by skipping a Step will haunt you later. Do not bypass the system. *There are no shortcuts.*

Factor #8: Good Interviewing and Follow-Up Skills

Some people get lots of job interviews but no job offers.

You cannot get a job without an interview, in which you'll have to do well. Interviewing is a skill that requires preparation, practice, and an ability to notice what is important to the interviewer so you can take whatever next steps are required.

Factor #9: Support and Encouragement from Friends and Family/Absence of Personal Disruptions

Recently divorced people, for example, tend to do less well in their jobs and job-hunting efforts. If you have other things on your mind, they may adversely affect your job hunt. Try to be effective despite these problems.

Job hunters usually need emotional support because this can be a trying experience. Our egos are at stake. Job hunting is not an easy thing to do.

Sometimes the support of family and friends is not enough because they are not going through what you are going through. That's why people join job-hunting groups or get outplacement coaching. You need realistic, honest support from people who know what you are going through. Studies have proved that *those who get ongoing coaching during their searches (especially in strategy groups) get more satisfying jobs faster and at higher rates of pay than those who simply take a course or decide to search on their own.*

Factor #10: Previous Job-Hunting Experience

If you haven't job hunted in a while, you're probably rusty. People will ask questions you're not used to answering and you may not sound polished. The process requires skills we don't use in our everyday work lives. Inexperienced job hunters usually take longer than those who are used to marketing themselves. You need to develop the skills that will land the right job for you.

It is only by risking our persons from one hour to another that we live at all. And often enough our faith beforehand in an uncertified result is the only thing that makes the result come true.

WILLIAM JAMES, *The Will to Believe*

Everyone has a mass of bad work in him which he will have to work off and get rid of before he can do better.

SAMUEL BUTLER, *The Way of All Flesh*

Think excitement, talk excitement, act out excitement, and you are bound to become an excited person. Life will take on a new zest, deeper interest and greater meaning. You can think, talk and act yourself into dullness or into monotony or into unhappiness. By the same process you can build up inspiration, excitement and a surging depth of joy.

NORMAN VINCENT PEALE, MINISTER AND AUTHOR, *The Power of Positive Thinking*

The Five O'Clock Club®

PART TWO

Deciding What You Want

HOW TO SELECT YOUR JOB TARGETS

The Five O'Clock Club®

Targeting the Job You Want:
An Introduction to the
Assessment Process

There will be many turnings along the way. It will be easy to get lost in attractive bypaths that lead nowhere. Resist deflections.

MAHATMA GANDHI

The Five O'Clock Club is a serious program for those who want to work hard at developing a plan and then achieving it. Right now, you probably think of a job search in terms of, "Do I have an offer or don't I?" That is not a helpful way to measure the effectiveness of a job search.

At The Five O'Clock Club, we like it when people have 6 to 10 things in the works. It's our magic range. Five of those will fall away through no fault of your own. We like it when people have three offers to choose from, so they can select the job that positions them best for the long term. That's our mantra. We want you to think two jobs out. Your next job will probably not be your last. So take a job that will position you for the job after that.

We have a shorthand way of talking about our methodology. You will find our lexicon in the back of each of our books. When a coach asks, "How are you doing in your search?" you'll say something like "I have four things in Stage Two and two in Stage Three." That tells us where you stand. Our lexicon helps us understand each other clearly without having to go into extreme detail. After all, each person in the group has only a short time in which to talk about his or her search.

> **Study our books as if you were in graduate school. Mark them up, take notes, and constantly reread them. Most people read a little every morning and a little every night. Most people listen many times over to our audio lectures.**

Growing vs. Retrenching Industries

The crux of the problem for many people is selecting the fields and industries they want to target. That's what we cover in *Targeting a Great Career*. For now, remember this: If you don't target growing industries, you will have to job hunt more often and will have a more difficult time finding the next position.

At The Five O'Clock Club, we track trends, so we can tell you what is happening in certain industries. For example, the majority of people in banking who lose their jobs leave that industry. The number varies over time, but it is still better if someone in that industry knows the facts at the beginning of his or her search. Otherwise, someone will come into The Five O'Clock Club, say they've been in banking for 12 years, and everyone they know is in banking, so of course it makes sense for them to target banks. Three months later, they may be still looking for a job.

But if they had known the market situation at the beginning of their search, they might have selected other targets in addition to banking, and would have had a much shorter search.

If your industry is retrenching, and if you decide you want to stay in it, you are more likely to have to relocate with each job move. In addition, you are more likely to have to search more often—it's like the game of musical chairs where they keep taking the chairs away. You become less marketable with each move because the industry is becoming smaller. This happens at every level in the hierarchy—not just the senior levels.

If an industry is retrenching, it is usually not as profitable as high-growth industries. It becomes less fun because it attracts less new blood. Those who remain have to do the mundane, core work, which is not as exciting as new developments. There's no money and no movement.

How many more years do you think you will work? If you want to work only a few more years, it's okay if you land a job in a retrenching industry. But if you want to work more than five years or so, you will probably have to search again. Even if you're over 60, you will probably be working longer than you think. The average American today is living 29 years longer than the average American lived at the turn of the twentieth century. Those years are being tacked on to middle age, not old age. Most of us will be working a lot longer than our predecessors did.

The good news is that you are marketable. If you think your industry is retrenching, brainstorm as many targets as you can at the beginning of your search. When a specific target does not work out, you will have others to fall back on. If you decide to stay in this field, learn some of the new technologies, such as the Internet, that will affect it in the future.

What Successful People Do

When Steven Jobs, the founder of Apple Computers, was fired by John Sculley, the man he brought in to run the company, he felt as though he had lost everything. Apple had been his life. Now he had lost not only his job, but his company. People no longer felt the need to return his phone calls. He did what a lot of us would do. He got depressed. But then:

Confused about what to do next...he [Jobs] put himself through an exercise that management psychologists employ with clients unsure about their life goals. It was a little thing, really. It was just a list. A list of all the things that mattered most to Jobs during his ten years at Apple."Three things jumped off that piece of paper, three things that were really important to me," says Jobs.

Michael Meyer, The Alexander Complex

The exercise Steven Jobs went through is essentially what you will do in the Seven Stories Exercise. The threads that ran through his stories formed the impetus for his next great drive: the formation of NeXT computers. If the Seven Stories Exercise is good enough for Steven Jobs, maybe it's good enough for you.

"Successful managers," says Charles Garfield, head of Performance Services, Inc., in Berkeley, California, "go with their preferences." They search for work that is important to them, and when they find it, they pursue it with a passion.

Lester Korn, Chairman of Korn, Ferry, notes in his book The Success Profile: "Few executives know, or can know, exactly what they aspire to until they have been in the work force for a couple of years. It takes that long to learn enough about yourself to know what you can do well and what will make you happy. The trick is to merge the two into a goal, then set off in pursuit of it."

I've tried relaxing, but—I don't know—I feel more comfortable tense.

Hamilton cartoon caption

The Results of Assessment: Job Targets—Then a Résumé

A job target contains three elements:
- industry or organization size (small, medium, or large organization)
- position or function
- geographic location

If a change is required, a change in any one of these may be enough.

Looking Ahead—A Career Instead of a Job

Assessment will help you decide what you want to do in your next job as well as in the long run. You will select job targets.

Through your Fifteen- and Forty-Year Visions (found in *Targeting a Great Career*), you will have the opportunity to look ahead to see whether a hidden dream may dramatically influence what you will want to do in both the short and long run. I did my own Forty-Year Vision many years ago, and the vision I had of my future still drives me today, even though it was rather vague at the time. Knowing where you would like to wind up in 10, 20, 30, or 40 years can broaden your ideas about the kinds of jobs you would be interested in today.

The Forty-Year Vision is a powerful exercise. It will help you think long-term and put things into perspective.

The Seven Stories Exercise is equally powerful. Without it, many job hunters develop stilted descriptions of what they have accomplished. But the exercise frees you up to brag a little and express things very differently. The results will add life to your résumé and your meetings, and also dramatically increase your self-confidence.

Here's Looking at You

Go through the exercises in *Targeting a Great Career*. Most Five O'Clock Clubbers are glad they did—even if they thought they already knew what kind of job they wanted.

It's a dangerous business, Frodo, going out your door. You step onto the road, and if you don't keep your feet, there's no knowing where you might be swept off to.

J.R.R. TOLKIEN (*The Lord of the Rings*)

Whenever we're afraid, it's because we don't know enough. If we understood enough, we would never be afraid.

EARL NIGHTINGALE, AMERICAN MOTIVATIONAL SPEAKER

The Five O'Clock Club®

Preliminary Target Investigation: Jobs/Industries Worth Exploring

How many things have been looked upon as quite impossible until they have been actually effected?

PLINY THE ELDER

You got a dream... You gotta protect it. People can't do somethin' themselves, they wanna tell you you can't do it. If you want somethin', go get it. Period.

THE CHARACTER PLAYED BY WILL SMITH, SPEAKING TO HIS SON, IN THE MOVIE *PURSUIT OF HAPPYNESS,* 2006

Although it takes up only a few paragraphs in this book, Preliminary Target Investigation is essential.

Your Preliminary Target Investigation may take only a few weeks if you have high energy and can devote yourself to it full-time. You have to test your ideas for targets in the marketplace to see which ones are worth pursuing. As you research at the library, on the web, and by meeting with people in your fields of choice, you will refine those targets and perhaps develop others. Then you will know where to focus your job search, and the search will be completed much more quickly than if you had skipped this important step.

People who conduct a Preliminary Target Investigation while employed sometimes take a year to explore various fields while they continue in their old jobs. If you are not at all familiar with some of the job targets you have selected, do some Preliminary Target Investigation *now* through Internet and library research (be sure to read this section) and network-

ing. You will find that some targets are not right for you. Eliminate them and conduct a full campaign in areas that both seem right for you and offer some reasonable hope of success.

Whether you are employed or between jobs, Preliminary Target Investigation is well worth your time and a lot of fun. It is the difference between blindly continuing in your old career path because it is the only thing you know, and finding out what is really happening in the world so you can latch on to a field that may carry you forward for many years. This is a wonderful time to explore and find out what the world offers. Most job hunters narrow their targets down too quickly, and wind up later with not much to go after. It is better for you emotionally, as well as practically, to develop now more targets than you need so you will have them when you are actively campaigning. If, on the other hand, you do not have the inclination or time to explore, you can move on. *Just remember, you can come back to this point if your search dries up and you need more targets.*

Most job hunters target only one job type or industry, take a very long time to find out that this target is not working, get depressed, try to think of other things they can do with their lives, pick themselves up, and start on one more target.

The will to persevere is often the difference between failure and success.

DAVID SARNOFF

Instead, **brainstorm as many targets as possible before you begin your real job search**. Then you can overlap your campaigns, going after a number of targets at once. If some targets do not seem to work as well for you as others, you can drop the targets in which you are no longer interested. And when things don't seem to be going well, you have other targets to fall back on.

1. **List below all of the jobs/industries of interest to you.**
2. If you are not familiar with some targets you have selected, do some Preliminary Target Investigation now through library or web research or networking. You will find that some targets are not right for you. Eliminate them and conduct a full campaign in those areas which both seem right for you and offer some reasonable hope of success.

   As you find out what is happening in the world, new fields will open up for you. Things are changing so fast that if you conduct a serious search without exploration, you are probably missing the most exciting developments in an area.

Spend some time exploring. Don't narrow your targets down too quickly; you will wind up later with not much to go after. It is better for you emotionally, as well as practically, to develop now more targets than you need so you will have them when you are actively campaigning. If you do not have the time or inclination to explore, you can move on to the next step. **Just remember: You can come back to this point if your search dries up and you need more targets.** An easy way to find targets is to complete the worksheet below:

JOBS/INDUSTRIES OF INTEREST TO ME AT THIS POINT:

(Conduct a Preliminary Target Investigation to determine what is really going on in each of them.)

_____

_____

_____

_____

_____

_____

_____

_____

_____

_____

_____

_____

Targeting: The Start of an Organized Search

Dream. Dream big dreams! Others may deprive you of your material wealth and cheat you in a thousand ways, but no man can deprive you of the control and use of your imagination. Men may deal with you unfairly, as men often do; they may deprive you of your liberty; but they cannot take from you the privilege of using your imagination. In your imagination, you always win!

JESSE JACKSON, *Brother's Keeper: Words of Inspiration for African-American Men*, RODERICK TERRY, ED. (1996)

To organize your targeting:

1. Brainstorm as many job targets as possible. You will not conduct a campaign aimed at all of them, but will have backup targets in case certain ones do not work out.

2. Identify a number of targets worthy of preliminary research. (If they are large targets and represent a lot of job possibilities, you will need fewer targets.)

3. Research each one enough—through the Internet, the library, and a few networking meetings—to determine whether it is worth a full job-search campaign. This is your Preliminary Target Investigation.

4. If your research shows that a target now seems inappropriate, cross it off your list, and concentrate on the remaining targets. **As you continue to network and research, keep open to other possibilities that may be targets for you. Add those to your list of targets to research.**

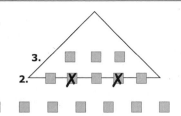

The boxes above represent different job targets. The triangle represents your job search. As you investigate targets, you will eliminate certain ones and spend more time on the remaining targets. You may research your targets by reading or by talking to people. The more you find out, the clearer your directions will become.

During Targeting Step 1 you brainstormed lots of possible job targets, not caring whether or not they made sense.

During Targeting Step 2 you conducted preliminary research to determine whether or not you should mount a full campaign aimed at these targets.

During Targeting Step 3 you will focus on the targets that warrant a full campaign. This means you will do full research on each target, and consider using all of the techniques for getting meetings: networking, direct contact, search firms, and ads.

As you add new targets, reprioritize your list so you are concentrating first on the targets that should be explored first. Do *not* haphazardly go after everything that comes your way.

5. If you decide the target is worth pursuing, conduct a full campaign to get meetings:
    * Develop your pitch.
    * Develop your résumé.
    * Develop a list of all the companies in the target area and the name of the person you want to contact in each organization.
6. Then contact each organization through networking, direct contact, ads, or search firms.

Serendipitous Leads

Make a methodical approach the basis of your search, but also keep yourself open to serendipitous *lucky leads* outside your target areas. In general, it is a waste of your energy to go after single serendipitous leads. It is better to ask yourself if this lead warrants a new target. If it does, then decide where it should be ranked in your list of targets, and research it as you would any serious target.

Target Selection

After you have done some preliminary research, select the targets that you think deserve a full campaign. List first the one you will focus on in your first campaign. If you are currently employed and have time to explore, you may want to select as your first target the most unlikely one, but the one that is the job of your dreams. Then you can concentrate on it and find out for sure whether you are still interested and what your prospects are.

On the other hand, if you must find a job quickly, you will first want to concentrate on the area where you stand the best chance of getting a job—probably the area where you are now working. After you get that job, you can explore your other targets. (To expand your targets quickly, consider broadening your search geographically.)

If you are targeting a geographic area different from where you are now, be sure to conduct a serious, complete campaign aimed at that target. For example, you will want to contact search firms in that area, do Internet or library research, perhaps conduct a direct-mail campaign, and network.

Target 1: Industry or organization size: _____

Position/function: _____

Geographic area: _____

Target 2: Industry or organization size: _____

Position/function: _____

Geographic area: _____

Target 3: Industry or organization size: _____

Position/function: _____

Geographic area: _____

Target 4: Industry or organization size: _____

Position/function: _____

Geographic area: _____

Target 5: Industry or organization size: _____

Position/function: _____

Geographic area: _____

Measuring Your Targets

You've selected one to five (or more) targets on which to focus. Will this be enough to get you an appropriate job?

Let's say, for example, that your first target aims at a small industry (10 organizations) having only a few positions that would be appropriate for you.

Chances are, those jobs are filled right now. In fact, chances are there may be no opening for a year or two. The numbers are working against you. Now, if you have targeted 20 small industries, each of which has 10 organizations with a few positions appropriate for you, the numbers are more in your favor.

On the other hand, if one of your targets is large and has a lot of positions that may be right for you, the numbers are again on your side. Let's analyze your search and see whether the numbers are working for you or against you.

Fill out the following on your own target markets. You will probably have to make an educated guess about the number. A ballpark figure is all you need to get a feel for where you stand.

Target 1: Industry or organization size: _____

     Position/function: _____

     Geographic area: _____

How big is the market for my service in this target?
A. Number of organizations in this target market: _____
B. Number of probable positions suitable for me in the average organization in this target: _____
A x B = Total number of probable positions appropriate for me in this target market: _____

For Target 2: Industry or organization size: _____

     Position/function: _____

     Geographic area: _____

How big is the market for my service in this target?
A. Number of organizations in this target market: _____
B. Number of probable positions suitable for me in the average organization in this target: _____
A x B = Total number of probable positions appropriate for me in this target market: _____

For Target 3: Industry or organization size: _____

     Position/function: _____

     Geographic area: _____

How big is the market for my service in this target?
A. Number of organizations in this target market: _____
B. Number of probable positions suitable for me in the average organization in this target: _____
A x B = Total number of probable positions appropriate for me in this target market: _____

Rule of thumb:

A target list of 200 positions in a healthy market results in seven interviews, which result in one job offer. Therefore, if there are fewer than 200 potential positions in your targets, develop additional targets or expand the ones you already have. Remember: When aiming at a target of less than 200 potential positions, a more concentrated effort is required.

How to Change Careers

And so with the sunshine and the great bursts of leaves growing on the trees, just as things grow in fast movies, I had that familiar conviction that life was beginning over again with the summer.

F. Scott Fitzgerald, *The Great Gatsby*

Ted had spent 10 years in marketing and finance with a large cosmetics company. His dream was to work in the casino industry. He selected two job targets: one aimed at the cosmetics industry, and one aimed at his dream.

All things being equal, finding a job similar to your old one is quicker. A career change will probably take more time. What's more, the job-hunting techniques are different for both.

Let's take Ted's case. The casino industry was small, focused in Atlantic City and Las Vegas. Everyone knew everyone else. The industry had its special jargon and personality. What chance did Ted have of breaking in?

Ted had another obstacle. His marketing and finance background made him difficult to categorize. His hard-won business skills became a problem.

It's Not Easy to Categorize Career Changers

The easier it is to categorize you, the easier it is for others to see where you fit in their organizations, and for you to find a job. Search firms, for example, generally will not handle career changers. They can more easily market those who want to stay in the same function in the same industry. Search firms that handled the casino industry would not handle Ted.

You Must Offer Proof of Your Interest and Competence

Many job changers essentially say to a prospective employer, "Give me a chance. You won't be sorry." They expect the employer to hire them on faith, and that's unrealistic. The employer has a lot to lose. First, you may lose interest in the new area after you are hired. Second, you may know so little about the new area that it turns out not to be what you had imagined. Third, you may not bring enough knowledge and skill to the job and fail— even though your desire may be sincere.

The hiring manager should not have to take those risks. It is the job hunter's obligation to prove that he or she is truly interested and capable.

How You as a Career Changer Can Prove Your Interest and Capability

- Read the industry's trade journals.
- Get to know the people in that industry or field.
- Join its organizations; attend the meetings.
- Be persistent.
- Show how your skills can be transferred.
- Write proposals.
- Be persistent.

- Take relevant courses, part-time jobs, or do volunteer work related to the new industry or skill area.
- Be persistent.

The thing is to never deal yourself out . . . Opt for the best possible hand. Play with verve and sometimes with abandon, but at all times with calculation.

L. DOUGLAS WILDER, FIRST ELECTED AFRICAN AMERICAN GOVERNOR IN UNITED STATES HISTORY

Ted, as a career changer, had to offer proof to make up for his lack of experience. One proof was that he had read the industry's trade newspapers for more than 10 years. When he met people in his search, he could truthfully tell them that he had followed their careers. He could also say he had hope for himself because he knew that so many of them had come from outside the industry.

Another proof of his interest was that he had sought out so many casino management people in Atlantic City and Las Vegas. After a while, he ran into people he had met on previous occasions. Employers want people who are sincerely interested in their industry, their organization, and the function the new hire will fill. Sincerity and persistence count, but they are usually not enough.

Another proof Ted offered was that he figured out how to apply his experience to the casino industry and its problems. Writing proposals to show how you would handle the job is one way to prove you are knowledgeable and interested in an area new to you. Some people prove their interest by taking courses, finding part-time jobs, or doing volunteer work to learn the new area and build marketable skills.

Ted initially decided to "wing it," and took trips to Atlantic City and Las Vegas hoping someone would hire him on the spot. That didn't work and took two months and some money. Then he began a serious job hunt—following the system explained in the following pages. He felt he was doing fine, but the hunt was taking many months and he was not sure it would result in an offer.

After searching in the casino industry for six months, Ted began a campaign in his old field—the cosmetics industry. Predictably, he landed a job there quickly. Ted took this as a sign that he didn't have a chance in the new field. He lost sight of the fact that a career change is more difficult and takes longer.

Ted accepted the cosmetics position, but his friends encouraged him to continue his pursuit of a career in the casino industry—a small industry with relatively few openings compared with the larger cosmetics industry.

Shortly after he accepted the new position, someone from Las Vegas called him for an interview, and he got the job of his dreams. His efforts paid off because he had done a thorough campaign in the casino industry. It just took time.

Ted was not unusual in giving up on a career change. It can take a long time, and sometimes the pressure to get a paycheck will force people to take inappropriate jobs. That's life. Sometimes we have to do things we don't want to do. There's nothing wrong with that.

What *is* wrong is forgetting that you had a dream. What is wrong is expecting people to hire you on faith and hope, when what they deserve is proof that you're sincere and that hiring you has a good chance of working. *What is wrong is underestimating the effort it takes to make a career change.*

Most people will have to change careers. Your future may hold an involuntary career change, as new technologies make old skills obsolete. Those same new technologies open up new career fields for those who are prepared and ready to change. Know what you're up against. Don't take shortcuts. And don't give up too early. Major career changes are normal today and may prove desirable or essential tomorrow.

Keep in mind that there is no harder work than thinking—really thinking—about who you are and what you want out of your life. Figuring out where your goals and your skills match up is a painful, time-consuming process. . . . But unless you make the effort you are no more likely to be happy in your next career than you have been in your current one. In fact, you're likely to be a good deal less happy.

JULIE CONNELLY, *"Fortune"* MAGAZINE

For Other Techniques to Help You Change Careers, Take a Look at the Following Chapters in . . .

. . . this book:

- Repositioning Yourself for a Job Change

. . . our book *Mastering the Job Interview and Winning the Money Game*:

- Salary Negotiation: Power and Positioning (see especially "Case Study: Charlie—Negotiating a Career Change")
- Your Two-Minute Pitch: The Keystone of Your Search

. . . our book *Targeting a Great Career*:

- Targeting the Jobs of the Future
- Case Studies: targeting the Future

. . . our book *Packaging Yourself: The Targeted Résumé*:

- Résumés for Making a Career Change (also see résumés and summaries for the industry or profession you are targeting)

I would recut something maybe five times in a night and run it again and again and again.
I just knew it was sweat. I had no special touch or anything like that.
ROBERT PARRISH, AWARD-WINNING FILM EDITOR-DIRECTOR QUOTED IN *The New York Times*

Repositioning Yourself for a Job Change

Greatness is not measured by what a man or woman accomplishes, but by the opposition he or she has overcome....

Dr. Dorothy Height, president,
National Council of Negro Women

Feel stuck in your present position? Peel off your old label, slap on a new one, and position yourself for something different.

Whether you're an accountant who wants to go into sales, or an operations person who dreams of being a trainer, the challenge you face is the same: You have to convince people that even though you don't have experience you can handle the new position.

It's a little like show biz: You play the same role for years and then you get typecast. It can be difficult for people to believe that you can play a different role. To move on to new challenges, you have to negotiate into the new job by offering seemingly unrelated skills as an added benefit to the employer. The key to these negotiations is positioning yourself.

Positioning

Simply put, positioning yourself means stating your skills and qualities in a way that makes it easy for the prospective employer to see you in the open position or in other positions down the road.

You may want to stay in your present organization, in which case you are positioning yourself to the person in charge of hiring for the particular department you want to enter. Or, you may want to go to a new organization or even a new industry. In this case, you are positioning yourself to a new employer. Either way, the steps are the same:

1. Determine what skills and qualities your prospective employer wants.
2. Search your background to see where you have demonstrated skills and qualities that would apply.
3. Write a summary at the top of your résumé to position yourself.
4. Use the same summary on your LinkedIn page and to sell yourself in an interview.

Your summary says it all. It should sell your ability, experience, and personality. It brings together all your accomplishments.

The rest of your résumé should support your summary. For example, if the summary says that you're a top-notch marketer, the résumé should support that. It's completely within your control to tell whatever story you want to tell. You can emphasize certain parts of your background and de-emphasize others.

> You can get typecast. To move on, you have to negotiate into the new job... by *positioning* yourself.

Thinking through your summary is not easy, but it focuses your entire job hunt. It forces you to clarify the sales pitch you will use in meetings.

However, many people *don't* put a summary that positions them on their résumés or on their LinkedIn page. They say they want "a challenging job in a progressive and growth-oriented organization that uses all my strengths and abilities." That doesn't say anything at all, and it doesn't do you any good.

Résumé: Your Written Pitch

Make sure the first words on your résumé position you for the kind of job you want next, such as *Accounting Manager*. Line two of your résumé, also centered, should separate you from all those other accounting managers. For example, it could say, "specializing in the publishing industry." These headlines in your summary could then be followed by bulleted accomplishments that would be of interest to your target market.

Most people write boring résumés. To avoid this, keep in mind to *whom you are pitching*. Tell readers the most important things you want them to know about you. List your most important accomplishments right there in your summary.

It all starts with the Seven Stories Exercise. After you have done this exercise, you will talk about your accomplishments very differently than if you just sit down and try to write a résumé. The Seven Stories Exercise is the foundation for your résumé. Write out your work-related stories in a way that is *expressive* of you as an individual. Brag about yourself the way you would brag to the people in your family or your friends. Put *those* words at the top of your résumé to make it much more compelling.

Let's consider a few examples of summaries that will work for you:

Pursuing the Dream Job

Jane, a client-relationship manager at a major bank, has handled high-net-worth clients for more than 20 years. She is taking early retirement and thinking about a second career. Two directions are of interest to her: a job similar to what she has done but in a smaller bank; or, the job of her dreams—working as one of the top administrative people for a high-net-worth family (such as the Rockefellers), handling their business office and perhaps doing things that involve her interests: staffing and decorating.

If Jane were to continue on her current career path and go for a position as a relationship manager at a smaller bank, she would highlight the years she has worked at the bank. Her summary, if used in her résumé, would look like this:

> More than 20 years handling all aspects of fiduciary relationships for PremierBank's private banking clients. Successfully increased revenue through new business efforts, client cultivation, and account assessment. Consistently achieved fee increases. Received regular bonus awards.

However, to pursue her dream job, Jane's regular résumé won't do. She has to reposition herself to show that her experience fits what her prospective employer needs. Her summary would read like this:

Administrative manager
with broad experience in running operations

- In-depth work with accountants, lawyers, agents, and others.
- More than 20 years' experience handling all aspects of fiduciary relationships for bank's private banking clients (overall net worth of $800 million).
- Expert in all financial arrangements (trust and estate accounts, asset management, nonprofits, and tenant shareholder negotiations).

Her résumé would also focus on her work *outside* PremierBank because these activities would interest her prospective employer: first, her work on the board of the luxury apartment building of which she was president for 14 years, and then the post she held for 10 years as treasurer of a nonprofit organization. Finally, Jane would highlight accomplishments at Premier-Bank that would be of interest to a prospective employer, such as saving a client $300,000 in taxes.

Ready to Take Charge

Robert had worked in every area of benefits administration. Now he would like to head up the entire benefits administration area—a move to management. His summary:

14 years in the design and administration of all areas of employee benefit plans

- 5 years with Borgash Benefits Consultants
- Advised some of the largest, most prestigious companies in the country
- Excellent training and communications skills
- MBA in finance

From Supporting to Selling

Jack wants to move into sales after being in marketing support. His prior résumé lacked a summary. Therefore people saw him as a marketing support person rather than as a salesperson—because his most recent job was in marketing support. He has been an executive in the sales promotion area, so his summary stresses his internal sales and marketing, as well as his management, experience:

Sales and marketing professional with strong managerial experience

- Devise superior marketing strategies through qualitative analysis and product repositioning
- Skillful at completing the difficult internal sale, coupled with the ability to attract business and retain clients
- Built strong relationships with the top consulting firms
- A team player with an enthusiastic approach to top-level challenges

Notice how he packages his experience running a marketing department as sales. His pitch will be, "It's even more difficult to sell inside because, in order to keep my job, I have to get other people in my company to use my marketing services. I have to do a good job, or they won't use me again."

If you do not have a summary, then, by default, you are positioned by the last job you held. In Jack's case, the employer would receive the new résumé with the new summary and say, "Ah-ha! Just what we need—a salesperson!"

Sophisticated Positioning

Here are how some people repositioned their backgrounds in a sophisticated way. Jeff had been in loan-processing operations in a bank. Outside of financial services, not many organizations do loan processing. To position himself to work in a hospital, Jeff changed his positioning to say transaction processing because hospitals process a large numbers of *transactions*, but not loans. Otherwise, they would look at his résumé and say, "We don't need to have loans processed."

In fact, many people who work in banking see themselves as working for information services companies. Money is sent via computer networks and wire transfers. They are passing information, not currency.

Nydia had worked at both banks and pharmaceutical companies. Because of her target, she positioned herself as having worked in *regulated industries*.

David saw himself as an international human resources generalist, but was having difficulty with his search. Since there were no international jobs in his field, he should not have positioned himself as *international*.

Now, think about *your* target market and how you should position your background for your target.

Making a Career Change

Elliott had been in sports marketing years ago, and had enjoyed it tremendously. However, he had spent the past four years in the mortgage industry, and was having a hard time getting back into sports marketing.

The sports people saw him as a career changer and a mortgage man. Even when he explained how marketing mortgages is the same as marketing sports, people did not believe him. He was being positioned by his most recent experience, which was derailing his search.

When job hunters want to change industries— or go back to an old industry—they cannot let their most recent positions act as a handicap.

For example, if a person has always been in pharmaceuticals marketing, and now wants to do marketing in another industry, his or her résumé should be rewritten to highlight generic marketing, with most references to pharmaceuticals removed.

In Elliott's case, the summary in his new résumé helps a great deal to bring his old work experience right to the top of the résumé. In addition, Elliott removed the word "mortgage" from the description of his most recent job; his title at the mortgage company now stands out more than the company name. And he removed company and industry jargon, such as the job title *segment director*, which is not easily understood outside his company. He also updated his Linkedin profile to represent his new positioning of himself as a sports marketing person.

Notice that Elliott's description of what he did for the mortgage business is now written generically—it can apply to the marketing of any product. With his new résumé, Elliott had no trouble speaking to people in the sports industry. They no longer saw his most recent experience as a handicap, and he soon had a terrific job as head of marketing for a prestigious sporting-goods company.

If you want to move into a new industry or profession, state what you did generically so people will not see you as tied to the old.

Bring Something to the Party

When it comes down to negotiating yourself into a new position, seemingly unrelated skills from former positions may actually help you get the job.

For example, some of my background had been in accounting and computers when I decided to go into coaching and my CFO (chief financial officer) experience helped me ease into this new career. I agreed to be CFO at a 90-person career-coaching company provided I was also assigned clients to coach. My ability to create a cost-accounting system for them was what I "brought to the party." I was willing to give the company something they wanted (my business expertise) in exchange for doing something I really wanted to do (coaching executives).

Combining the new with the old, rather than jumping feet first into something completely new is often the best way to move your career in a different direction. You gain the experience you need in the new field without having to come in at the entry level. Equally important, it is less stressful because you are using some of your old strengths while you build new ones.

Coming from a background different from the field you are targeting can also give you a bargaining chip. If you are looking at an area where you have no experience, you will almost certainly be competing with people who do have experience. You can separate yourself from the competition by saying, "I'm different. I have the skills to do this job, and I can also do other things these people can't do." It works!

Our résumé book contains dozens of additional positioning (summary) statements. In addition, you will see how the positioning statements are used to set the tone for the rest of the résumé.

Elliott's positioning (summary) statement is on the next page.

ELLIOTT JONES
421 Morton Street Chase   Fortune, KY 23097

SEARS MORTGAGE COMPANY   2012-present
Vice President, Segment Director, Shelter Business
- Director of $4.6 billion residential mortgage business for largest mortgage lender
- Organized and established regional marketing division for largest mortgage lender, including first and second mortgages and mortgage life insurance

SportsLife Magazine   2009-2012
Publisher and Editor
- Published and edited largest health/fitness magazine. Increased circulation by 175%. and so on...

ELLIOTT JONES
421 Morton Street, Chase Fortune, KY 23097   ejones@yahoo.com

Fifteen years: domestic and international marketing management in the leisure/sporting goods industry

- Multibrand expertise specializing in marketing, new business development, strategic planning, and market research.
- Identified customer segments, developed differentiable product platforms, implemented communication strategies, managed sales, oversaw share growth, and generated profit.

SEARS MORTGAGE COMPANY   2012-present
VICE PRESIDENT, BUSINESS DIRECTOR
Residential Real Estate Business

- Business Director of a $4.6 billion business. **Managed strategic planning, marketing, product development, and compliance**.
- Consolidated four regional business entities into one; doubled product offerings. Grew market share 150 basis points and solidified #1 market position.
- **Developed and executed nationally recognized consumer and trade advertising, public relations, and direct-response programs**.
- Structured a product-development process, integrating product introductions into the operations and sales segments of the business.
- Organized and established regional marketing division.

SPORTSLIFE MAGAZINE   2009-2012
Publisher and Editor
- Published and edited largest health/fitness magazine. Increased circulation by 175%.

and so on...

Summary of What I Have/Want to Offer—Target 1

To Help Me Develop My Written Pitch to That Target

You must know:
- to whom you are pitching; you have to know something about them.
- what they ideally want in a candidate.
- what they are interested in.
- who your likely competitors are.
- what you bring to the party that your competitors do not.

For Target 1:   Geographic area: _____

Industry or organization size: _____

Positionfunction: _____

1. What is the most important thing I want this target to know about me? (This is where you position yourself. If they know nothing else about you, this is what you want them to know.) _____

_____

2. What is the second most important thing I want this target to know about me? (This could support and/or broaden your introductory statement.) _____

_____

3. Key selling points: statements/accomplishments that support/**prove** the first two statements:

a. _____

b. _____

c. _____

d. _____

e. _____

4. Statement of why they should be interested in me/what separates me from my competition: _____

_____

_____

_____

5. Other key selling points that may apply even indirectly to this industry or position: _____

_____

_____

_____

6. Any objection I'm afraid the interviewer may bring up, and how I will handle it: _____

_____

Summary of What I Have/Want to Offer—Target 2

To Help Me Develop My Written Pitch to That Target

You must know:
- to whom you are pitching; you have to know something about them.
- what they ideally want in a candidate.
- what they are interested in.
- who your likely competitors are.
- what you bring to the party that your competitors do not.

For Target 1: Geographic area: _____

Industry or organization size: _____

Positionfunction: _____

1. What is the most important thing I want this target to know about me? (This is where you position yourself. If they know nothing else about you, this is what you want them to know.) _____

_____

2. What is the second most important thing I want this target to know about me? (This could support and/or broaden your introductory statement.) _____

_____

3. Key selling points: statements/accomplishments that support/**prove** the first two statements:

a. _____

b. _____

c. _____

d. _____

e. _____

4. Statement of why they should be interested in me/what separates me from my competition: _____

_____

_____

_____

5. Other key selling points that may apply even indirectly to this industry or position: _____

_____

_____

_____

6. Any objection I'm afraid the interviewer may bring up, and how I will handle it: _____

_____

_____

Summary of What I Have/Want to Offer—Target 3

To Help Me Develop My Written Pitch to That Target

You must know:
- to whom you are pitching; you have to know something about them.
- what they ideally want in a candidate.
- what they are interested in.
- who your likely competitors are.
- what you bring to the party that your competitors do not.

For Target 1:   Geographic area: _____
Industry or organization size: _____
Positionfunction: _____

1. What is the most important thing I want this target to know about me? (This is where you position yourself. If they know nothing else about you, this is what you want them to know.) _____

_____

2. What is the second most important thing I want this target to know about me? (This could support and/or broaden your introductory statement.) _____

_____

3. Key selling points: statements/accomplishments that support/**prove** the first two statements:

a. _____

b. _____

c. _____

d. _____

e. _____

4. Statement of why they should be interested in me/what separates me from my competition: _____

_____

_____

_____

5. Other key selling points that may apply even indirectly to this industry or position: _____

_____

_____

_____

6. Any objection I'm afraid the interviewer may bring up, and how I will handle it: _____

_____

The Five O'Clock Club®

PART THREE

Knowing the Right People

HOW TO GET MEETINGS IN YOUR TARGET AREAS

The Five O'Clock Club®

Precampaign Planning

It is circumstance and proper timing that give an action its character and make it either good or bad.

AGESILAUS II

You certainly have done a lot of work so far! You completed your self-assessment (using the exercises in *Targeting a Great Career*), selected three or four targets after conducting a Preliminary Target Investigation, and ranked them so you know which one you want as your first campaign, your second, third, and fourth. You have also developed a preliminary résumé for the first campaign. Now you will plan your *entire* job hunt, just as you would plan any other project. A planned job search will save you time. You will be able to tell what is working and what is not, and change what you are doing accordingly.

Take a look at the chart below. It is a conceptual view of the job-hunting process. There are no time frames for a Step. The time each step takes depends on you and the situation you face.

Do every step, spending the length of time on them required for your situation. This time is not wasted. It will save time later because your effort will be organized.

Your campaigns aimed at each target (Target 1, Target 2) will overlap. You will start one campaign, and when it is in full swing, you will start campaign number two. Each campaign will be condensed, and your total job search will be *shorter* if you follow this approach than if you conducted all of the campaigns together.

As you can see in the chart below, each campaign has three Steps. The first Step is Preparation; the second is Interviewing; and the third is Follow-Up. **Each Step should be given equal weight.**

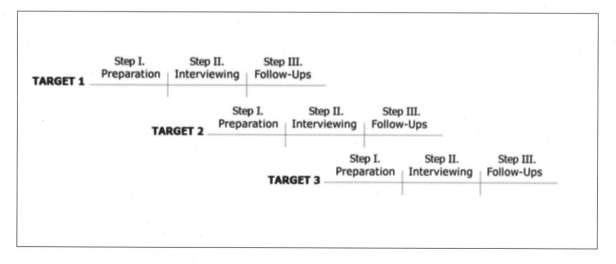

During the Preparation Step, you:

- Research and make a list of the companies you want to contact.
- Develop your Two-Minute Pitch and your cover letters.
- Make sure your résumé (and Linkedin page) make you look appropriate to your target.
- Plan your strategy for getting meetings (through networking, direct contact, search firms, and ads).

When you are in the Interview Step of campaign one, you may start campaign two.

CASE STUDY *Jim*
An Organized Approach

Jim, a marketing manager, had targeted four industries: environmental, noise abatement, shipping, and corporate America, which was a backup target in case the other three did not work. Jim had selected 30 companies in the environmental area, and began to contact them. When he met with an environmental company, he could mention that he had "just met yesterday with another environmental company, and this is what we discussed. What do you think?" *Focusing* on one target at a time can give you credibility and information. Jim can mention other companies with which he is speaking, and let a prospective employer know he is truly interested in the industry. Focus also saves him time. It takes so much time to develop a good pitch, cover letter, and résumé that it only makes sense to sell yourself to a *number* of companies. It's too difficult to try one pitch one day and then a completely different pitch the next. It's better to completely test one pitch and have it down pat. That's why you can start your second campaign when you are in the interview Step of the first campaign.

Furthermore, a condensed campaign allows you to test what is wrong and drop what is not working. Job hunters who go after lots of different targets at the same time usually do not develop a great pitch for any of them, and cannot tell what is working and what is not.

Jim dropped his first target—the environmental industry—except for following up on two possibilities that seemed promising. He also came up with a number of possibilities from his second and third targets. In the end, he got one job offer from each target, and never started his fourth campaign, corporate America, which he was not interested in anyway. In addition, Jim followed up on serendipitous leads, which also could have yielded something. But a focused search was the core of his campaign, with serendipitous leads on the side.

A focused campaign is shorter, even though you're zeroing in on only one target at a time (until you are in the follow-up stage, in which you are following up on *all* of your targets, and generating more leads in each of them). Many executives who follow a targeted approach can cover four good-sized targets in depth in two months. And many executives have that next position within two-and-a-half to four months!

The distance doesn't matter.
Only the first step is difficult.

MME. DUDEFFAND

The Timing of Your Campaigns

In the next chapter, you will plan the strategy for getting meetings in your first campaign, which you should implement right away. When you are midway through it, start your second campaign—even if you do not think you will need it.

When you start your first campaign, you will be full of hope. Your résumé will be great, and you will be talking to lots of people. Some will tell you that you should have no problem finding a job. They are being sincere. But job offers dry up. What once seemed like a sure thing does not materialize.

There seem to be phases and cycles in each campaign—there is the initial rush, the long haul, the drought, followed by the first poor job offer and the later better offers. After a letdown, job hunters can lose momentum. They sometimes think they will *never* find a job.

If, however, you have already started that second campaign, you will know that those cover letters are in the mail working for you. You stand a chance of getting some response from the second campaign. You will do better in the interviews from your first campaign because you will not feel so desperate. Your second campaign backs you up.

Your second campaign could include additional people in the same target market as the first. (Do more research and get more names.) It could be a variation of your first target market (a related field or industry) or a new target.

I have had clients start a second campaign even when they were in the final negotiation stages of the first. Those negotiations went better, and helped them land the job because they had the comfort of knowing that the second campaign was in the mail.

If, perchance, your first campaign does *not* work, you will not lose momentum if you are already in the midst of your second—or perhaps even preparing to start your third. It is better not to lose momentum.

Customize Your Campaign

Think of yourself as a corporation. Given equal economic conditions, certain corporations thrive while others fail. Successful companies adjust their approaches to the changes in the economy. And even when the economy is at its worst, certain companies come up winners.

In many respects, job-hunting management resembles the management of an organization. The economy has changed dramatically over the past several years; times are more competitive— for companies and for job hunters. Whether you are managing a company or managing your own career, adjust the techniques you use.

Statistics show that certain techniques work better than others in the aggregate. But consider what might be best for you *and* your situation.

The hiring system works differently in different industries and companies. Remain flexible: Do what works in the industry and profession in which you are interested.

In addition, do what works for your personality. For example, certain job hunters phone company executives rather than using the written approach of a direct-mail campaign. What if you find it difficult (as I do) to make calls to people with whom you have had no contact? Or what if you are currently employed and find that heavy use of the phone is out of the question? Or it may be that the industry you are approaching considers this technique an arrogant way to do business.

This same rule applies to the techniques you will find in this book. Use what you want. Do what works for *you*.

Everything comes to him who hustles while he waits.

Thomas A. Edison

A Campaign to Promote Yourself— Just like Promoting a Product or Service

In soloing—as in other activities—it is far easier to start something than it is to finish it.

Amelia Earhart

Airlines run promotional campaigns to get passengers to fly with them. Computer software companies use their promotional efforts to get people to buy their software. You will conduct a promotional campaign to generate interest in your "service."

You and an airline go through the same steps to market your respective services:

- *An airline analyzes the market to determine the kinds of people who are interested in its service, the number of potential customers, and how much need there is for the service.* Analyze your market to determine the kinds of companies that could be interested in you, and the number of companies and positions in your field of interest. Find out how much demand there is for your services in your target market.

- *An airline defines itself by its features*, such as the kind of seating it has, the cities to which it flies, and so on—and it also defines its personality or style. For example, an airline may say it represents the "friendly skies" or is the "only way to fly." Or it may define itself as a bargain or an exclusive carrier.

  Define yourself not only in terms of your skills and experience but also in terms of your style and personality. There are many qualified people for each position, just as there are a number of airlines offering the same kinds of planes going to the same cities. The differences among airlines is not in their basic service, but in their personality and the way they go about their business.

  You and your competition will often be equally well qualified. The differences will lie in your style and the way you go about your business. For example, a person who ran a department and doubled productivity could have done it in a nasty, threatening way, or could have motivated people to do more, instituted training programs, and encouraged workers to come up with suggestions for improving productivity. Let *your* personality come through.

- *An airline test-markets what it has decided to offer.* If the test results are poor, the airline changes either its basic product (such as its number of seats) or offers the same product in a way that is more attractive to the target market. It could also decide to withdraw from that target market.

  Test what you have decided to offer. If it is not of interest to your target market, change what you are offering, the way you are offering it, or the image you are projecting. For example, you can change what you are offering by getting more ex-

perience or training in a certain area. You can change your image by looking different or by highlighting a certain aspect of your personality that is of interest to your target market. Or you can change your promotional techniques.

On the other hand, you may decide to with draw from a particular market. Perhaps it is inappropriate for you. An example is when your target market is in the middle of major layoffs. If you can help turn the company around, you have a chance. If you are comparable to the people it is laying off, consider a different target.

Some people pick a target and stick with it no matter what. But you need flexibility and common sense to figure out what may be going wrong in your campaign. You may need more experience or you may need to present yourself differently. Or it may be there is no hope of obtaining an offer in certain markets. No matter how much you may want to work for a foundation, for example, there may not be many positions available. Then even the best job-hunting techniques will not help you. Change your target.

- *An airline assesses its competition, and so will you.* Who is your competition and how well do you stack up in your basic qualifications? What can you offer that is different?

- *An airline asks itself if the timing is right for a campaign it may be planning.* Consider if the timing is right for what you want to offer a particular market. Sometimes there is great demand for lawyers or engineers, for example, and at other times there is a glut in the market. When the oil business was booming, there was a demand for people in that field. Aerospace engineers could once name their price. You can easily find out the level of demand by testing what you want.

- *An airline asks itself if it is worth it*—if it can afford to do what it would take to offer its product to a certain market. It decides if its return will be adequate, and it makes sure this venture will satisfy other company needs and support company objectives.

Ask yourself if it is worth it. You may find that a field is not what you thought it was: Perhaps the pay is too low or the hours too long. Or the field may not fit with your long-term goals. Or it may run contrary to your motivated skills or values or what you want in an organization or a position. You can lower your expectations or you can look elsewhere.

There is one major difference between what you and the airline have to offer: The airline has a lot of planes and seats, but there is only one of you. Be particular about to whom you sell your services. Get a couple of potential offers so you can make a comparison and select what is best for you.

We are here to be excited from youth to old age, to have an insatiable curiosity about the world.... We are also here to help others by practicing a friendly attitude. And every person is born for a purpose. Everyone has a God-given potential, in essence, built into them. And if we are to live life to its fullest, we must realize that potential.

NORMAN VINCENT PEALE, *Positive Thinking: The Norman Vincent Peale Story*
(PUBLIC BROADCASTING DOCUMENTARY)

Weekly Group Meetings

Throughout life our internal lives are enriched by the people we have permitted to touch us.

GEORGE E. VAILLANT, *Adaptation to Life*

Not everything can be covered in a book. Meeting every week in a Five O'Clock Club small group with people like yourself can be a tremen-

dous help. They will become familiar with your job search and can give you feedback on your efforts. The experiences of other people can teach you what to do when the same things happen to you. In the group, you can trade stories and techniques, and network with one another.

Believe it or not, weekly group meetings are *fun* and a respite from the discouraging job of job hunting. They can spark you on: Your own situation seems less hopeless. You feel if they can do it, you can too.

During the job search itself (as opposed to assessment), being in a group with your peers can be more effective than one-on-one coaching with a *pro.* A group can take risks that a coach cannot. For example, even if you have been unemployed for a while, the group may suggest that you not take a position because it is not right for you. You can easily ignore the advice of the group if you want. A coach has to be more careful about giving advice that could adversely affect a person's financial situation. Your peers have more freedom to discuss your needs and to give a variety of *free* advice.

In one of my groups, there was a dynamic public relations man who had been unemployed for two months. The group came to know him well. He received a job offer to do public relations work for a conservative dental firm. When he told us about the offer, the look on his face clearly showed how unhappy he felt about it. Everyone knew that this would not be the right job for him, and the group discouraged him from taking it.

A few weeks later, he received another job offer—this one from a dynamic company in San Francisco. The company had been searching to fill this position for more than six months, and it was thrilled to find him. So was he: For him, the job was the chance of a lifetime.

There is no music in a "rest," Katie that I know of: but there's the making of music in it. And people are always missing that part of life—melody.

JOHN RUSKIN

Time for Personal Development

If you happen to be unemployed, welcome to the club. Some unemployed people think they don't deserve any fun at all. But it is difficult to job hunt for a full 40 hours a week.

If you have only 30 hours of work to do, you may spread it out to fill 40 hours. With too much time on your hands, you may take longer than usual to write a memo or make a phone call or appointment. You may stretch things out so you will always have "something to look forward to." You will wind up stretching out your search.

Wasting time is itself not the bad part. The bad part is losing your flow of adrenaline. Better to spend 35 or 37 hours a week searching for a job and make those hours *intense*—just as you would in a real job—and then reward yourself with three hours of fun that week.

During a period of unemployment, I indulged myself by going to auction houses and spending the time it takes to study furniture. Auctions aren't crowded during the day when everyone else is working. I never regretted the time I spent there. I felt I would never have such a luxury again. I worked hard at my job hunt and felt I deserved a break. So do you.

But you don't deserve *too* much of a break. One of the worst things a person can do is start off his or her unemployment with a "well-deserved" vacation. Sometimes the job hunt never gets started. The momentum never builds. Instead, why not look for a job and take two weeks off after you have landed it? If you are unemployed, don't punish yourself, but don't overindulge yourself, either.

Job hunting is a job in itself, hard work that can be discouraging. But since you have to do it, you might as well have fun. You will meet interesting people who may become new friends. And you will learn a lot. That's not so bad.

We can define "purpose" in several ways. For one, when we know our purpose, we have an anchor—a device of the mind to provide some stability, to keep the surprises of a creative universe from tossing us to and fro, from inflicting constant seasickness on us. Or we can think of our purpose as being a master nautical chart marking shoals and rocks, sandbars, and derelicts, something to guide us and keep us on course. Perhaps the most profound thing we can say about being "on purpose" is that when that is our status, our condition, and our comfort, we find our lives have meaning, and when we are "off purpose," we are confused about meanings and motives.

DUDLEY LYNCH AND PAUL L. KORDIS, *Strategy of the Dolphin: Scoring a Win in a Chaotic World*

The world presents enough problems if you believe it to be a world of law and order; do not add to them by believing it to be a world of miracles.

LOUIS BRANDEIS, BRANDEIS UNIVERSITY WEBSITE

The Five O'Clock Club®

Conducting a Campaign to Get Meetings in Your Target Market

The codfish lays ten thousand eggs,
The homely hen lays one.
The codfish never cackles
To tell you what she's done.
And so we scorn the codfish,
While the humble hen we prize,
Which only goes to show you
That it pays to advertise.

ANONYMOUS

An Overview of the Strategy for Your First Campaign

If the only tool you have is a hammer, you tend to
see every problem as a nail.

ABRAHAM MASLOW

By now, you have developed preliminary job targets and conducted a Preliminary Target Investigation (through networking, the Internet, and the library) to see which targets are worth pursuing.

Then you selected those you think are worth a full campaign and ranked them in the order in which you want to conduct those campaigns. You are ready to conduct a campaign to contact every organization in your first target. When you are busy meeting with people in Target 1, you will start the campaign preparation for Target 2.

A Targeting Map of 200 Positions, which you may show to your networking contacts, contains your list of targets, including the organizations in each of those targets. This plan forms the overview of your search.

Do not expect to get a job through:
- **Networking**
- **Direct contact**
- **Search firms**
- **Ads (even on the Internet)**

These are techniques for getting *meetings*, not jobs.

After you get the meeting, you can think about what to do next to perhaps turn it into a job. (See the chapters on Follow-Up in our book *Mastering the Job Interview and Winning the Money Game*.

For Target 1 you will now:
1. **Research to develop a list of all the organizations**, if you have not already done so. Find out—through networking, the Internet, or other research—the names of the people you should contact in the appropriate departments in each of those organizations.
2. **Develop your cover letter**. Paragraph 1 is the opening; Paragraph 2 is a summary about yourself appropriate for this target;

Paragraph 3 contains your bulleted accomplishments ("You may be interested in some of the things I've done"); Paragraph 4 is the close. (Many sample letters appear later in this book.)

3. **Develop your plan for getting a large number of meetings in this target**. There are four basic techniques for meeting people in each of the areas you have targeted for a full campaign. In the following chapters, you will learn more about them. They are:

   Do not think of these as techniques for getting *jobs*, but as techniques for getting *meetings*. After the meeting, think about what to do next to keep the relationship going or perhaps to turn the interview into a job offer.

Organize the names of the people you want to contact, and develop strategies for contacting them:

Only 5 to 10 percent of all job leads are through search firms, and another 5 to 10 percent are through ads. You do not have much control over these leads: you have to *wait* for an ad to appear, and *wait* for a search firm to send you on an interview. Both networking and direct contact are *proactive* techniques you can use to get meetings in your target market. In networking, you contact someone simply by using someone else's name. In direct contact, you contact someone directly—usually after you have done some research and know something about him or her. Networking and direct contact complement each other and gain added effectiveness when used together. You may start your campaign either with direct contact (if you know your target area very well) or with networking (to research an area you don't know well or find a way to contact people), and introduce the other technique as your campaign progresses.

Consider all four techniques for getting meetings, but spend most of your energy and brainpower on networking and direct contact.

Selecting the Techniques

Do not be too timid and squeamish about your actions. All life is an experiment.

RALPH WALDO EMERSON

Select the techniques most appropriate for the industry or profession you are targeting, as well as for your own personality. Each technique can work, but the strength of your campaign lies in your ability to use what is best for your particular situation. Contact as many potential employers as possible and then *campaign* to keep your name in front of them.

Use all of the techniques to:

- Learn more about your target area.
- Test what you are offering.
- Let people know you are looking.
- Contact people in a position to hire you.

Opportunities are multiplied as they are seized.

SUN TZU, *The Art of War*

The Myth of How to Get Meetings: Consider Contacting Organizations Directly

Search firms. Ads. Networking. Ask most people how to get interviews, and they'll mention those ways. But The Five O'Clock Club wanted to find out what really works. Its survey of professionals, managers, and executives clearly shows that *job hunters get more meetings for the time spent through "direct contact" than through any other single technique.*

Articles abound to prove the importance of networking. However, Five O'Clock Club research shows that direct contact is a more efficient way to generate meetings.

Networking means using someone else's name to get a meeting. *Direct contact* means aggressively pursuing people whom you may have known in the past or people you have never

met. These might include association members or people identified on the Internet, through newspaper or magazine articles, or from library research. (For entry-level people, direct contact even includes going from one human resources office to another in an office center.) Here are the survey results:

- **Direct contact is the most time-efficient way to get meetings.** Surveyed job hunters spent 45 percent of their time networking, yet networking accounted for only 35 percent of their meetings. On the other hand, surveyed job hunters spent 24 percent of their time on direct contact, resulting in 27 percent of their meetings. Networking is very time-consuming. You have to find people who are willing to let you use their names. With direct contact, there is no middle person.

- **Even executives got almost 1/3 of their meetings through direct contact.** It's a myth that executives must rely on networking to get in to see people more senior than they are. Our surveyed senior executives did in fact get 62 percent of their meetings through networking, but almost 30 percent of their meetings resulted from their contacting executives to whom they had not been referred. Executives should not overlook direct contact.

- **People making a career continuation relied on direct contact even more than networking.** People looking to stay in the same industry or field got about one-third of their meetings through direct contact and a little less by using someone else's name to get a meeting. The job searchers contacted strangers, and got meetings because of their accomplishments—and their discipline in working follow-up phone calls.

- **Even career changers (42 percent of those surveyed) got 20 percent of their meetings through direct contact**. Career changers often feel they should network to meet people in new fields or industries.

However, direct contact can also result in meetings.

- **Search firms accounted for only 8 percent of meetings; newspaper ads accounted for 7 percent; online job boards accounted for 13 percent.** Everyone makes the mistake of placing too much emphasis on published openings. Contact organizations that don't publicize openings now, and stay in touch with them. This increases the chance they'll hire *you*, rather than post the job, when they need help.

We want our job hunters to consider all four techniques for getting meetings in their target markets. See what's working for you.

Using Search Firms

If you are looking for a position that naturally follows your most recent one, you can immediately contact search firms. As I've mentioned, only about 5 to 10 percent of all professional and managerial positions are filled by search firms, so it would seem logical to spend only 5 percent of your effort on them. However, certain professions use search firms more than others do.

Contact reputable search firms that handle positions in your target area. If you don't already have relationships with search firms, find the good ones by asking managers which search firms they use or recommend. Remember, search firms are rarely able to help career changers.

Answering Ads

Five to 10 percent of all jobs are filled through ads—both print and Internet. The odds are against you, so don't spend too much thought or energy on them. And don't sit home hoping for a response. Just answer the ad—as long as it sounds close to what you have to offer—and get on with your search. Maybe you'll hear from them— maybe you won't. (See the chapters in this book on "How to Answer Ads" and "What to Do When You Know There's a Job Opening.")

You must call each thing by its proper name, or that which must get done will not.

A. HARVEY BLOCK, PRESIDENT, BOKENON SYSTEMS

Networking

Studies show that about 60 to 70 percent of all positions are filled through networking. This is partly because most job hunters mistakenly refer to talking to people as "networking," no matter how they wound up talking to them. For example, Pete just found a job. I asked how he got the initial meeting. He said, "Through networking." When I asked him to tell me more, he said, "I'm an accountant, originally from Australia. There is an association here of accountants from Australia. I sent for a list of all the members, and wrote to all of them. That's how I got the job."

Pete got the job lead through a direct-mail campaign, *not* through networking. That's why the survey numbers are off, and that's why you should consider using every technique for getting meetings in your target market. You never know where your leads will come from.

Networking simply means getting to see someone by using another person's name. You are using a contact to get in. You want to see the person *whether or not they have a job for you.* This technique is essential if you want to change careers, because you can get in to see people even if you are not qualified in the traditional sense. To stay in the same field, you can network to get information on which organizations are hiring, which are the best ones to work for, and so on.

Networking can lead you in directions you had not considered and can open up new targets to pursue. You can network to explore even if you are not sure you want to change jobs right now. What's more, it's a technique you can use after you land that new job, whenever you get stuck and need advice.

Networking is more popular today than ever before and it is effective when used properly. But, depending on your target, it is not always the most *efficient* way to get meetings. Furthermore, it

sometimes gets a bad name because even though people are constantly networking, they often are doing it incorrectly. Learn how to network correctly (see the chapters on networking), but combine targeted mailings (a direct-contact technique) with your networking when you are aiming at small organizations or ones with very few jobs appropriate for you. Networking your way into all of them could take forever. Also, directly contact other people when you would have great trouble getting a networking contact. If the direct contact doesn't work, you can always network in later.

When you combine direct mailing with networking, you can cover the market with a direct-mail campaign and then network certain sections of that market. Or you can network in to see someone, and then perhaps get a list of names you can use for further networking or a direct-mail campaign.

If you do not cover your market, you risk losing out. You may find out later that they "just filled a job a few months ago—too bad we didn't know you were looking." Be thorough. Let everyone in your target market know that you are looking.

The beginning of wis dom is to call things by their right names.

CHINESE PROVERB

Direct-Contact Campaigns

Writing directly to executives is a consistently effective technique for generating meetings.

Twenty to 40 percent of all jobs are found this way and more jobs would result from this technique if more job hunters knew about it. You can write to lots of organizations (direct mail) or a few (targeted mail). The techniques are quite different.

Direct contact can save time. You can quickly test your target to see if there are job possibilities for someone like you. If you are familiar with your target area, you can develop your list, compose your letter, send it out, and start on your next target, all within a matter of weeks. Most job hunters contact larger corporations, ignoring smaller firms. Yet new jobs are being created in smaller organizations, so don't overlook them.

Direct contact is also the only technique that allows you to quickly contact every employer in the area of interest to you. You are essentially blanketing the market. Networking, on the other hand, is spotty by nature: You get to see only those organizations where your contact knows someone. Direct contact is effective for an out-of-town job search. And this technique works whether you are employed or unemployed. It works for all job levels.

This technique is an effective one for career changers. You can state all the positive things you offer and leave out anything not helpful to your case. Those things can be handled at the meeting.

Direct contact can help you get in to see someone you know you cannot network in to see. Shelli, for example, wanted to see someone very senior in an industry in which she had no experience. But she knew the field would be a good fit for her—she researched the industry and figured out how her background could fit in. She targeted six organizations and was able to network into two of them. She knew she would not be able to network into the other four organizations within a reasonable time frame: It would take her months to find someone who could only *possibly* help her get in to see the people she'd need to see.

Instead of networking, she researched each of the four organizations, wrote to the senior people she was targeting at each one, and followed up with a phone call. Because of her presentation, three of the executives agreed to see her. This saved her many months in her search. Sometimes a targeted mailing can be *more* effective than networking in getting in to see important people. It takes more brainpower than networking, but you already have that.

Direct contact primarily involves targeted and direct mailing, but a junior person can also go from organization to organization to talk to personnel departments or store managers. As long as job hunters follow up, this technique can work. An executive client of mine used this technique ef-

fectively by walking into a small, privately owned, prestigious store, speaking with the store manager to find out the name of the president, and then calling the president. It led to an executive position with that company. This was "direct contact" because he did not use someone's name to get in to see the store manager or the president. Even when I was very young, I used direct contact to get in to see virtually anyone I wanted.

Sometimes I had trouble getting in, but people eventually saw me because I usually had a good reason, did my homework, didn't waste their time, was sincere about why I wanted to see them, and was gently persistent. It suits my personality because I am shy about using someone else's name for the core of my effort, I am comfortable about putting my effort into research and writing, and I don't have the time it takes to see a lot of people who may not be right on target for me. As I go along, I network when appropriate.

Direct contact also includes cold calls, which can work for some personalities in some industries.

We will now focus on targeted mail and direct mail:

Targeted mailings are similar to networking. You target a relatively small number of people (e.g., fewer than 20 or 30) and try to see all of them, *whether or not they have a job for you.* Instead of already having a person to contact, you *establish* your own contact through the research you do. The meeting is handled exactly the same as a networking meeting.

Direct mail is used when you have a large number of organizations to contact (e.g., 200 or more). You mail a brilliant package to all of them and expect seven or eight meetings from the mailing.

If I had eight hou rs to chop down a tree,
I'd spend six sharpening my ax.

ABRAHAM LINCOLN

The difference between direct mail and targeted mail:

- **Direct Mail**: No follow up required; You can contact 100 or more people with a slightly tailored cover letter.

- **Targeted Mail**: Follow-up is required. Because it takes an average of eight follow-up phone calls to get a meeting, most people can handle no more than 20—or possibly 30—targeted mailings.

Using All of the Techniques

A good campaign usually relies on more than one technique to get meetings. Think of how you can divide up your target list. For example, if you have a list of 200 organizations in your target area, you may decide you can network into 20 of them, do a targeted mailing (with follow-up phone calls) to another 20 or 30, and do a direct-mail campaign to the rest. This way you have both blanketed your market and used the most appropriate technique to reach each organization in your target area. In addition, you could also contact search firms and answer ads.

Networking vs. Direct Mail

Let's use the banking industry as an example.

You could easily network your way into a large bank. You could find someone who knew someone at a number of them. Each contact you'd make at a large bank could refer you to other people within the same bank, which would increase your chances of getting a job there. Since one person knows others within that organization, networking is efficient. You can meet many potential hiring managers within one organization.

On the other hand, it may be difficult to network into smaller banks. Fewer of your friends are likely to know someone there, because each small bank has far fewer employees. Each networking meeting would represent fewer jobs and fewer referrals within each bank. Referrals to other small banks would also generally represent fewer jobs than the larger banks have. It could take forever to network to the same number of potential jobs at hundreds of small banks that could easily be covered by networking at large banks. Networking can be inefficient with smaller organizations and you may find that you can't put a dent in the market.

You could contact smaller banks directly. They do not expect you to know someone who works there, so they are more open to intelligent mailings. They tend to get fewer contacts from job hunters. You could categorize the smaller banks in a way that makes sense to you—those strong in international banking, for example, or those strong in lending. Or you could categorize banks by nationality—grouping the Japanese banks, European banks, South American banks, and so on. Then you could *target each segment with a cover letter customized for that market*.

Decide which techniques are best for you. Think about how people tend to get hired within your target industry and profession. Also consider your own circumstances, such as whether you are currently employed, how much freedom you have to go on networking meetings, how much use you can make of the phone, and so on. You can always network your way into a few specific organizations, but networking into a great number is sometimes not possible.

Remember, networking requires a great deal of time and travel. Direct mail is often appealing to those who are working and must ration their meeting and travel time.

A word of caution to very senior executives: Because of your extensive networks, you may be tempted to rely exclusively on them to find your next position. As extensive as they are, your contacts are probably spotty. You may be reluctant to do research because you are used to having others do such things for you. Do your research anyway. Define your targets. List all of the organizations in your target areas that are appropriate for you and the names of the people you need to see in each of these organizations. Most very senior executives skip this step and get their next position serendipitously. That's just fine—if the position is right for you. But many senior executives in their eagerness to land something quickly may land something inappropriate, beneath what they deserve, or nothing at all. If you have listed all of the people you should see in your target areas, you increase your chances of having a thorough campaign and you will not miss out on a good possibility for yourself.

If you can network in to see the people you should see in your target market, fine. But if you can think of no way to network in, contact them directly. You will get plenty of serendipitous leads and meet plenty of people who have business ideas and want to form partnerships with you. These opportunities may be fine, but they are better if you can compare them with those you uncover through an organized search.

Things which matter most must never be at the mercy of things which matter least.

Goethe

In Summary

Make a list of all the people you should meet in *each* of your target areas or, at the very least, make a list of all the organizations in your target areas. Intend to contact all of them. Get meetings with people in your target area through networking, direct contact, search firms, and ads (print and online). Do not think of these as techniques for getting *jobs*, but as techniques for getting *meetings*. Plan how you can contact or meet the *right* people in *every* organization in each of your target areas as quickly as possible.

After the meeting, either keep in touch with networking-type contacts (regardless of how you met them) or think about what you can do next to *perhaps* turn the interview into a job offer.

Getting Polished for a Full Campaign

Although action is typical of the American style, thought and planning are not; it is considered heresy to state that some problems are not immediately or easily solvable.

Daniel Bell, sociologist, *Daedalus*

Before the meeting, be prepared: know exactly what you want and what you have to offer. In the next chapter, you will prepare your pitch to organizations. Have your pitch ready even *before* you contact anyone—just so you are prepared. Read the chapters on interviewing in our book *Mastering the Job Interview and Winning the Money Game*, and practice. Be a polished interviewer. Remember the cliché; "You don't get a second chance to make a good first impression."

After you have practiced interviewing, contact the people on your "hit list." Start with those who are less important to you, so you can practice and learn more about your target area. You will want to know, for example, your chances in that market and how you should position yourself.

After you have met with someone, follow up. This method works. Read the chapters on following up. Once you have contacted a target area, contact it again a few months later. Keep following up with the people you meet.

Read magazines and newspapers. Attend organizational meetings. Keep abreast of what is happening in the field. Keep on networking.

Begin at the beginning . . . and go on till you come to the end: then stop.

Lewis Carroll

A Promotional Campaign to Get Meetings

Sometimes I say to a client who is shy, "So far, you and I are the only ones who know you are looking for a job." Get your name out there. Get on the inside track. You must conduct a promotional campaign to contact as many potential employers as possible. *Campaign* to make sure they remember you.

Make a lot of contacts with people in a position to hire or recommend you. If there are sparks between you, and if you help them remember you, you will be the one they call when a job comes up. Or they can give you the names of others to contact. They may even create a job for you if it makes sense.

The goal of your promotional campaign is to let the *right* people know what you are seeking. Some discussions will become job interviews, which will lead to offers. Get a lot of meetings so you will have a number of offers to consider. You want options.

Focus on getting *meetings* in your target area. People who focus on *getting a job* can get uptight when they have a meeting. They do not think of themselves as *looking around* or *finding out what is out there*. They act as if they are in a display case hoping someone will buy them. They may accept the first offer that comes along—even when they know it is inappropriate—because they think they will never get another one.

If you aim to make lots of contacts and get lots of meetings, you are more likely to keep your perspective. If you are an inexperienced job hunter, talk to some people who are not in a position to hire you. Practice your lines and your techniques. Get experience in talking about yourself, and learn more about your target market. Then you will be more relaxed in important meetings and will be able to let your personality come through.

Labor not as one who is wretched, nor yet as one who would be pitied or admired. Direct yourself to one thing only, to put yourself in motion and to check yourself at all times.

Marcus Aurelius Antonius, *Meditations*

May the Force be with you.

The character of Han Solo played by Harrison Ford in *Star Wars*, 1977

You Are the Manager of This Campaign

You are in control of this promotional campaign. After reading this book you will know what to say, how to say it, and to whom. You will select which promotional techniques to use and when and learn how to measure the effectiveness of your campaign.

You will also decide on your image. You can present any picture of yourself you like. You present your image and credentials in your written communications—résumé, cover letters, LinkedIn write-up and follow-up notes. You have *complete* control over what you put in them and how you present yourself.

How you act and dress are also important to your image. Look like you're worth the money you would like. Watch your posture—sit up straight. **Smile!** Decide to feel good and to feel confident. Smile some more. Smile again. Smiling makes you look confident and competent and gives you extra energy. It is difficult to smile and continue being down. Even when you are at home working on your search, smile every once in a while to give yourself energy and the right attitude to help you move ahead. This is true no matter what your level. Even executives are better off doing this as they go through their searches. The ones who cannot do this tend to do less well than those who can.

Whether direct contact or networking, search firms or ads, choose techniques most likely to result in a good response from your target—techniques appropriate to your situation. When you become an expert, change a technique to suit yourself.

Modify your approach or even abandon an effort that is ineffective. You want a good response from your promotional efforts. A *response* is a meeting. A polite rejection letter (if you're lucky enough to get one) does not count as a response. Some organizations have a policy of sending letters and some have a policy against them. Rejection letters have nothing to do with you. They do not count. Only meetings count.

This is a campaign to generate meetings. Your competition is likely to have polished presentations. Decide on the message you want to get across in the meeting, and practice it. There are two kinds of meetings: information-gathering (networking) meetings and actual job interviews. Do not try to turn every meeting into a job interview. You will turn people off—and lessen the chances of getting a job. *In the beginning, you are aiming for contact or networking meetings.* (See the chapters on networking meetings, as well as information on handling the job interview, in our book *Mastering the Job Interview and Winning the Money Game.*)

When things do not work, there is a reason. Be aware and correct the situation. There is no point in continuing an unsuccessful campaign. Remember, when things go wrong—as they will—it is not personal. This is strictly business. It is a project. With experience, you will become better at managing your promotional campaigns to get meetings.

Why Stagger Your Campaigns?

Why is it unwise to start all of your campaigns at once? Let's pretend your first target is the telephone industry, and your second target is the environmental industry. If one day you talk to a telephone company and the next day you talk to an environmental organization, you will not sound credible. When you meet with the environmental organization, it does you no good to mention that you met with the telephone company.

If, however, you talk to someone in a telephone company, and then another person in the same or another telephone company, you can say, "I'm talking to four different divisions of your firm right now and I'm also talking to other phone companies." Then it sounds as if you really want to work in their industry.

Similarly, when you want to talk to an environmental organization, you can mention you are talking to a lot of environmental organizations. The information you learn at one organization will make you sound smarter with the next.

As you research and meet with people in a target area, the target becomes richer and less superficial. In the beginning of a search, for example, you may be interested in health care, which is too broad a target. Later, however, you may find that the field is more complex than you thought and learn that people's jobs are not at all what an outsider would expect.

You are an insider when you give back non-proprietary information, such as: "Do you know that Southern Bell has a fulfillment system very similar to yours?"

Or you can say to an environmental organization: "I've been talking to a lot of environmental organizations and it seems that a trend in this industry right now is _____. Do you agree?"

This methodical search is the only smart way to do it because you gain momentum. Most job hunters simply "go on interviews," but that's not enough in this economy. Organizations expect you to know something about them.

On the following page is one Club member's Targeting Map of 200 Positions. There are additional plans in our book *Targeting a Great Career.* You may want to use them as a model for your own.

Sample Targeting Map

Targeting Map: Joe Doakes

TARGET FUNCTIONS: VICE PRESIDENT/DIRECTOR/MANAGER

- Management Information Services
- Applications Development
- Information Systems
- Information Systems Technology
- Systems Development
- Business Reengineering

RESPONSIBILITIES:

- Identification of new information systems technologies and how they could affect the profitability of a company.
- Management of projects for the implementation of information systems or new technologies.
- Providing for and managing a business partner relationship between the information systems department and the internal company departments that use their services.
- Implementing and managing a business partner relationship among the company and its primary vendors and its customers using systems technologies, such as EDI (Electronic Data Interchange).

TARGET COMPANIES:

Attributes
- People oriented
- Growth minded through increased sales, acquisitions, or new products
- Committed to quality customer service
- Receptive to new ideas on how to do business use new technologies

Location
- Primary—Northern New Jersey or Westchester/Orange/Rockland Counties in New York
- Secondary—New York City, Central New Jersey, or Southern Connecticut, Eastern Pennsylvania
- Other—anywhere along the Eastern Seaboard

TARGET INDUSTRIES:

Consumer Products:	Pharmaceuticals:	Food/Beverage:	Chemicals	Other:
Unilever Kimberly-Clark	Merck	Pepsico	Castrol	Medco
Avon	Schering-Plough	T.J. Lipton	Witco	Toys-R-Us
Carter Wallace	Warner-Lambert	Kraft/General Foods	Allied Chemical Olin	Computer Associates
Sony Products	American Home	Nabisco	Corp.	Becton Dickinson
Minolta	Bristol-Myers Squibb	Hartz Mountain	Union Carbide	Siemens
Boyle Midway	Pfizer	Continental Baking	Air Products	Dialogic
Revlon	Jannsen Pharmaceutica	Nestlé	General Chemical	Automatic Data Proc.
L&F Products	Hoffmann-LaRoche	Haagen-Dazs	Englehard Corp.	Vital Signs
Houbigant	Ciba-Geigy	Tuscan Dairies	BASF Corp.	Benjamin Moore
Mem	Sandoz	Dannon Co.	Degussa Corp.	
Chanel	A.L. Laboratories	BSN Foods	GAF Corp.	
Airwick	Smith Kline Beecham	Campbell Soup	Lonza Inc.	
Church & Dwight	American Cyanamid	Cadbury Beverages	Sun Chemical	
Johnson & Johnson	Boeringer Ingelheim	Labatt		
Reckitt & Colman	Roberts Pharmaceuticals	Arnold Foods		
Philip Morris	Glaxo	S. B. Thomas		
Clairol	Block Drug	Sunshine Biscuits		
Estee Lauder	Hoechst Celanese			
Cosmair	Ethicon			
	Winthrop Pharmaceuticals			

Research: Developing Your List of Organizations to Contact

Wisdom is the principal thing; therefore get wisdom: and with all thy getting get understanding. Exalt her, and she shall promote thee: she shall bring thee to honour, when thou dost embrace her.

PROVERBS 4: 7-8

The entire job search process is a research process. After all, if you knew exactly the *right* organization and the *right* person and the *right* job for you, you would not be reading this book, and you would not go to The Five O'Clock Club. You would simply go to the organization that had the right job for you—and get hired!

But that's not the way it is. You'll conduct research throughout your *entire* search. Research will help you *home* in on the right place for you: the right industry, the right *organization*, and the right *kinds* of positions—those where you stand a good chance of getting a job right now. Research will also help you pick the right *job*—the one suiting you best for the long term.

If you've been having little luck answering ads and talking with search firms, you may *now* be ready for an organized, methodical search instead. This means you must conduct research. Once you develop your target list, which we also call your Targeting Map of 200 Positions, the rest of your search will be routine. Then you "simply" contact those organizations, arrange to have meetings, and follow up.

> **Looking for a place to start your research? Read this chapter and then study the bibliography at the back of this book. Once you have your list of organizations to contact, the rest of your search is clear.**

<u>Your Targeting Map of 200 Positions</u> will guide you in your search, and it will make your search more efficient. You can directly contact people listed in your plan, and use your list in networking meetings. You'll be able to show people your plan and ask them, "Are you familiar with any of the organizations on this list? What do you think of them? Who do you think I should contact at each organization? May I use your name?"

If you started with our book, *Targeting a Great Career*, during the assessment step, you accomplished the following:

- You **brainstormed** *all* of the **targets** that you thought might be of interest to you. Later on, when things seem to be drying up, you'll be glad you did this.
- You conducted your ***Preliminary* Target Investigation** to check out each one. At this point, you were not trying to get a job; instead, you were conducting a little research to see if it made sense to mount a full campaign aimed at each of those

targets. You talked to people to see what they thought, and you conducted research at the library and on the Internet. This helped you eliminate some targets.

- Then you **ranked your targets**, and decided which targets to go after first, second, third, and fourth. If you are desperate for a job, you decided to focus first on the target where you were most likely to get hired. If you have time to explore— maybe you're employed right now—maybe your first target is the dream job you've always wanted to explore

- Then you *measured* **your targets**. If the total number of positions you're going after is fewer than 200, that's not good. Remember that we are not totaling job openings, but positions. And it does not matter if the positions are filled right now. You are trying to avoid having a search that is too small. Those searches are doomed from the start.

For example, if you want to be a writer in the corporate communications department of a large corporation, you would ask yourself: "How is this large company *organized*? I wonder to whom *corporate communications* reports. I wonder how many *writers* they have in corporate communications." You'd estimate the number of writers you *think* they have. Just take a guess. They certainly have more than one writer in corporate communications! Might they have 5? Or 10? Just take a guess. Of course, a smaller organization would have fewer writers in corporate communications.

Estimate the number of positions each organization might have and add up all of the positions for the organizations on your target list. If in all of your targets the number does not add up to 200 positions (not *openings* but positions), then brainstorm more targets or more organizations within those targets. If you don't follow

this strategy, you're going to have a longer search.

- Next, you *segmented* **your targets**, and segmented *again* if that was reasonable. In the publishing industry, for example, segments could include book publishing, magazine publishing, and publishing online. Magazine publishing is still too big a target, so you would segment it to better manage your campaign. Within magazine publishing, you would list the kinds of magazines of most interest to you— for example, sports magazines, health magazines, women's magazines, men's magazines, and so on. And within each of those, you might target print as well as online. You'll find much more on targeting and segmenting in *Targeting a Great Career*.

Successful people often experience more failures than failures do. But they manage to press on. One good failure can teach you more about success than four years at the best university. Failure just might be the best thing that ever happens to you.

HERB TRUE, SUPER-SALESMAN, AS QUOTED BY ROBERT ALLEN IN *Creating Wealth*

Most people generally target the well-known organizations—the *top* magazines to work for, the *top* museums, the most prestigious hospitals. They target the organizations that *everybody* has heard of and at which everyone wants to work. It's a better idea to research *lesser-known* organizations. These may be even *better* places to work than some of the top-tier organizations. In the second-tier organizations, you may get to do more, have a chance of being a star, and advance more easily. So don't overlook the second-tier organizations.

Your Targeting Map of 200 Positions allows you to *survey all this at a glance*. It lists the industries you're targeting and the organizations within those industries. Your Targeting Map of 200 Positions is so important that it is one of *three key documents* you should share with your small group, in addition to your résumé and cover letter. Show it to your coach and small-group members even when you have just a rudimentary plan, that is, a *tentative* list of industries and sub industries and perhaps a few organizations within each. You will *refine* your Targeting Map as you move along in your search. Chances are you will change your mind about your most important targets and the most important organizations within each target.

If your small-group members (or your parents or friends) recognize the names of most of the organizations on your list, *you have not yet begun your research!* Dig in more. You'll have to think hard and do your research to uncover organizations that may be *better* places to work.

Job search is just like any other worthwhile project in life. You *make* your plan and then you *execute* it. At the beginning of your search, you'll have a *tentative* Targeting Map of 200 Positions. As you search—and conduct more research—you'll add more organizations to your list. Your Targeting Map doesn't have to be 100 percent correct before you start contacting prospective employers.

As you move forward, it's best to divide each target into an A-list, B-list and C-list. The A-list includes companies where you would love to work. The companies you would consider okay go on the B-list, and the C-list companies are of no interest to you.

Contact your C-list companies first to get your feet wet and use them for practice. Because you don't care that much about them, you will probably be more relaxed and confident and will interview well. You are *practicing*. You will also be testing your market to see if you get a good response from these C-list companies.

> **To get a job within a reasonable time... target 200 positions—not openings—positions.**

It's important for you to know if the companies on your C-list are *not* interested in you. You need to talk to the people in your small group to find out what you're doing wrong. However, if you are well received by the companies on your C-list, then you can contact the companies on your B-list. You could say something like, "I am already talking to a number of companies in your industry [which is true], but I didn't want to accept a job with any of them [which is also true] until I had a chance to talk with you." This script is just one approach. Be sure to talk to your small group about the right things to say to those on your B-list.

> - **Your A-list: You'd love to work there.**
> - **Your B-list: They're okay.**
> - **Your C-list: They don't interest you.**

Using your Targeting Map of 200 Positions and your A-, B-, and C-Lists together is the search: It's a search for organizations to contact and the names of people within each of those organizations. This is a vastly superior approach to what you might have done in the past. Your competitors, on the other hand, are out there contacting search firms, scanning ads, and hitting the "send" button on job-search websites. But *you'll* get in to see hiring managers before they even post their jobs. You'll have less competition and you'll find that a job may be created just for you!

This part of your search *must* be combined with the assessment you did in *Targeting a Great Career*. Review that book again and again during your job-search process. You don't want just a job; you want a career. This means you want a job *that positions you best for the long run*; you can achieve this only if you *know* what your long-run vision is.

Now, let's develop your Targeting Map of 200 Positions. This chapter will give you some ideas and your coach and small group will give you others. In addition, you can use the bibliography at the back of this book or the even more extensive bibliography in the Members Only section of our website (www.fiveoclockclub.com).

The choice of a career, a spouse, a place to live; we make them casually, at times, because we do not know how to articulate the choices... I believe that people often persuade themselves that their decisions do not matter, because they feel powerless to make the best decision. Some of us feel that, no matter what we do, our decisions won't matter much... But I believe that we know at heart that decisions do matter.

PETER SCHWARTZ, *The Art of the Long View*

Few things are impossible to diligence and skill.

SAMUEL JOHNSON, *A Dissertation on the Art of Flying*

Using Search Engines to Develop Your List

Many job hunters use Google or Yahoo for industry information, even if they're going after esoteric industries such as social service agencies, ethics, education policy, and think tanks. Key any industry name into Google or Yahoo and see what comes up. You may have to look through a few pages of information, but there will probably be a site that lists what's going on in that industry, or lists other sites for that industry; one or two of those sites will probably list *organizations* in that industry. Luckily, most organizations have a website and contact information, making it much easier to develop your list right from your own home.

It might be helpful to see how a few people have progressed through this process. Let's start with something that is not as easy as it appears. I'll give you a few examples of *junior-level job searchers* because they can have a more difficult time uncovering the names of people to contact: It's usually easier to find the names of senior people in organizations.

Dan had experience as a computer operator, line assembler (computers), data controller, and mailroom clerk. He lived in Magnolia, Texas. Where could Dan find prospective employers without simply responding to ads? To develop a list of companies where Dan could work, I went

into Google and simply keyed in "Magnolia, TX businesses." More than 75 *pages* of company listings came up—company name, address, phone number, and distance from Magnolia, TX. Those are a *lot* of companies for Dan to contact. Since Dan's skills are applicable to many industries, he could think about a few industries in which he would enjoy working and focus on those, which would make his job more interesting. How Dan would *contact* those companies is another matter covered in great detail elsewhere in this book.

Jon, a manufacturing engineer/supervisor, had been unemployed quite a while. Manufacturing in Arizona was in a downturn and there were very few jobs. But *some* people were getting hired for jobs that were not advertised. How could Jon find the names of companies to contact so he could become proactive in his search rather than wait for openings? Again, I went into Google. I entered "manufacturers Arizona." It took me to **Manta.com**, which returned 1002 company names. If I keyed in "manufacturers Scottsdale, Arizona," I got 85 names and places that were closer to where Jon lived. Then I went to company websites to start my research. The first company I looked up was Allied Tool and Die. It's probably too small for Jon, so he could then go on to the next one. Or he could scan the list to see which companies he recognized or found appealing.

Research is the process of going up alleys to see if they are blind.

MARSTON BATES, *American Zoologist*

CASE STUDY *Julie*
Targeting Professional Services Firms

Let's take it one step further. The Internet can be a great way to develop your target list and also *contact* hundreds of people within a few hours. This technique works when you want to contact small—to mid-sized professional service firms, such as accounting, architecture, or law firms. It also works if you want to contact small businesses in general. It can work for job hunters at all levels—from college students to executives who want to work for a small business.

Julie had just finished her sophomore year at a small college and was having a problem finding a summer job related to her major, which was architecture. If Julie had gone to a major school such as the University of Michigan, she could have contacted alumni who were in her field, used the job-posting boards on the University of Michigan website, or gone to on-campus job fairs where the employers come to the students. But those options were not open to her. Julie's school was small and not especially geared to helping students get placed.

Here's what it took for Julia to get *four terrific concurrent offers.*

Julie lived in a rural area and there were no architectural firms in her town. So she targeted the major metropolitan area that was closest to her (90 minutes away) because that's where most of the firms were located. She also targeted the suburban areas nearer her home.

Julie would be glad to do administrative work in an architectural firm and also work in CAD, a computer program for architects. She had taken a CAD course and worked on CAD a little at a previous job. But she didn't want to get stuck as a CAD operator. Instead, she wanted to learn more about the way small architectural firms work. Doing some administrative work would help her get a feel for the firm. So **Julie had defined her targets The Five O'Clock Club way**:

- Industry: architectural firms
- Position: administration or CAD operator
- Geographic area: large metropolitan area and the suburbs near her home.

A basic Five O'Clock Club tenet is that a job hunter must go after 200 job possibilities to get one good offer! This holds true for students as well as for the most senior executives. So it is important to pay attention to the response rate to your emailing. Notice how many people ask you to come in for a meeting. If you send 200 emails and get only two calls for meetings you must send out 200 *additional* emails. Two meetings are not enough!

Architectural firms are generally small, perhaps employing only one student per firm, so Julie would probably need to contact 200 of them. How could Julie come up with the names of 200 architectural firms—and quickly? She was only a week away from the end of the term and had not yet tried to contact many firms.

Julie contacted 200 small firms in less than 10 hours.

Julie used job-posting sites to make a start on her contact list of 200 firms. First, she went into *www.monster.com*, and selected job postings for *architects* in the major metropolitan area near her. Then she selected job postings for architects in the nearby suburban areas. Julie selected only architectural jobs at *firms* as opposed to jobs in the government or major organizations such as hospitals and hotel chains.

Then Julie clicked on the companies she was interested in—*as if* she were responding to the ad. After all, those organizations were hiring! Her approach was to reach out to the person in each small firm who was likely to handle hiring. (This works for students who want to work in a small firm. A more senior person would need to contact the department or division head in a larger firm, which can require making a phone call or looking at the company's website.)

When ads are answered automatically like this—through a job-posting site—the "subject" line contains the ad number so the organization will know which ad a person is responding to. Julie changed the subject line to read (see example on the next page):

Administrator/CAD Drafter— Architecture-related—Employment for top student.

Julie contacted about 50 firms this way, but this was not enough. She needed to find at least 150 additional firms.

> **Julie responded to ads for senior architects, but asked for a junior-level job instead. Let them know what *you* want.**

Next she tried the search engines. Julie went into Google and keyed in the word *architect* and the two geographic areas she was interested in one at a time. The American Institute of Architects was one of the results and is a good source, but she also found lots of individual architectural firms listed. In most cases, Julie had to go to the company website to get an appropriate email address. One by one, she came up with 155 additional organizations to contact, bringing her total to 205 firms (including the 50 from *monster.com*).

This is the email Julie sent to 205 architectural firms. Her Five O'Clock Club résumé was an attachment.

To: julieangelo@udallas.edu
Subject: **Administrator/CAD Drafter—Architecture-Related—Employment for Top Student**.

May 11, 201x

Dear Sir or Madam:

I am writing to you because yours is a prestigious firm in the architecture industry and I am an architectural student interested in summer work at a firm such as yours. I'd like to meet with you or someone else in your firm to find out more about your company and to tell you about myself. Even if you have no openings right now, you never know when you may need someone like me.

I have 10 months' experience with a civil engineering firm. You may be interested in some of the specific things I have done:

Served as an **assistant office manager**, organizing client proposals and setting up manuals. I also answered an 8-line phone.

Because of my **basic autoCAD experience**, engineers turned to me when they wanted routine things done.

As an architectural studies major, I tend to **be among the best in my class**, winning contests and doing excellent work. I enjoy client contact, helping architects get ready for meetings, putting proposals together, and assisting with autoCAD work. I would appreciate a meeting and look forward to hearing from you.

With thanks,
Julie Angelo

julieangelo@udallas.edu, University of Dallas Box #3124, 76 North Churchill Rd., Irving, TX 99999, 555-666-4693
angelo555@hotmail.com, 863 Erie Avenue, Brewster, TX 99945
Attachment: JAngelo résumé

She sent a mass email. To save time, she stopped emailing the firms individually. Instead, she captured the email addresses in a Word document, with one email address per line. After she had gathered 20 or 30 email addresses, Julie sent a "mass email." She didn't put the addresses in the "To" field. She copied all the email addresses into the "bcc" field so the recipients would not be able to tell to which or to how many firms she had mailed. She put the same "subject" as she had for her earlier emails, attached her résumé as before, and addressed the email to herself. She did this until she had sent out all 205 emails. Then she took her last final exam.

Julie had spent a total of about 10 hours on her research and emailing.

Using a mass email technique, Julie was able to contact 20 to 30 firms at a time using the "bcc" field.

Then the calls came in. Within two days, Julie received nine calls for meetings. Interestingly, eight of the calls were from the suburban area and only one call was from the major metropolitan area.

Julie had sent 75 percent of her emails to firms in the major metropolitan area—that's where most of the firms were. The major metropolitan area was the obvious place to look for architectural jobs. That means, of course, that she had far more competitors and, accordingly, lower response.

Firms in the suburban area were more responsive to her because most job hunters were ignoring the suburbs.

The results of *your* search may surprise you. That's why you have to contact so many places. You never know who will respond.

Julie scheduled seven job interviews (she immediately ruled out two firms because the travel would have been more than two hours from home, something she would have found acceptable if she had gotten only a few calls).

Julia was thrilled to have seven meetings lined up because a key Five O'Clock Club maxim is to have 6 to 10 job possibilities in the works. It

increases the chances of landing something appropriate for you.

Another Five O'Clock Club maxim is, "Don't chase jobs—chase companies." Contact organizations whether or not they have an opening right now. If your search is solely from postings, you will have competition for the jobs you go after. Everyone is chasing those same job openings. So too, most people target the top-tier firms in major metropolitan areas. If Julie had done that, she would have been discouraged by the results, since she got only *one* call from a firm in the major metropolitan area.

Even though 75 percent of her emails went to firms in the major metropolitan area, Julie received almost no response from them.

---

aHowever, Julie did schedule five job interviews over three days' time.

The Five O'Clock Club wants you to line up 6 to 10 meetings. Julie lined up 7.

Julie prepared for the interview; the full scope of that process is covered in our book, *Mastering the Job Interview and Winning the Money Game*. At the very least, we can say here: **Go to each organization's website** before the interview so you know something about the organization. Even managers at small companies will ask applicants, "So, have you seen our website? How much do you know about us?" Because of the web, companies expect you to know something about them.

Her offers poured in. In the end, Julie went on **four interviews and got four offers**. As she got offers, she became pickier about the remaining firms on her list, ruling out those requiring more than an hour and a half of travel. In her last job, Julie earned $10 an hour. Her first offer was at $11, two were at $12.50, and one offer had not yet come in.

Julie seemed very desirable *because* she had so many possibilities in the works. Companies were essentially in a bidding war for her. Remember that you need to **see 6 to 10 organizations concurrently to have a good search**.

When Julie interviewed at the last firm, she told them about her other offers, hoping for another offer at $12.50 per hour. They wooed her by promising her she would be able to learn a lot about architecture on the job: She would visit some of the sites where the architects were building, go to client meetings, "shadow" an architect to see what was done all day. They said they would email her an offer later that evening.

Julie would have found it difficult to resist their offer almost regardless of the salary they offered: The experience would have been so extraordinary compared with the others and Julie was trying to keep her long-range future in mind.

However, Julie did not have to choose content over salary. The email came that evening with an offer of $15 per hour!

The last firm knew what it was up against: three other offers. The hiring manager also knew it was difficult to recruit architects in their neck of the woods. But for Julie, the location was perfect: only 45 minutes from her home.

> **Julie increased her pay by 50 percent because she had so many offers and she contacted companies that other job hunters ignored.**

Research is to see what everybody has seen and to think what nobody else has thought.

ALBERT SZENT-GYORGYI, AMERICAN BIOCHEMIST

CASE STUDY *Jack*
A Marketing Executive

You, too, can use search engines to develop your list. Large or even mid-sized organizations are generally easier to research. For example, Jack, a marketing executive, got *all* of the information for his job search online. His targets were pharma-ceutical, biotech, and biotech marketing organizations. Jack made lists of companies in all three areas appropriate for him in his geographic area.

You're trying to do the same as Jack. You're trying to make a list of the organizations to contact in each of your targets and find out whom to contact at each organization. *Then* Jack started networking and contacting organizations directly. He shortly ended up with four offers—right close to home.

The Internet changes over time. The sites job hunters love and depend on can go out of business or start charging huge fees. So you'll have to find out what's current. Ask your small-group members what they use or check the Members Only area of our website.

However you do it, you'll need a preliminary list of organizations to contact. You'll learn other helpful techniques as you develop your list. Just remember: The list is your search. Throughout your search, you refine your target list. That's why they call it a *search*. You have to *search* for the names of people to contact.

For what a business needs the most for its decisions— especially its strategic ones—are data about what goes on outside of it. It is only outside the business where there are results, opportunities and threats.

PETER F. DRUCKER, "BE DATA LITERATE—KNOW WHAT TO KNOW," *The Wall Street Journal*

Associations

Associations are an important source of information. If you don't know anything at all about an industry or field, associations are often the place to start. Attending their meetings will assist you in getting the jargon down so you can use the language of the trade. If you are interested in the rug business, there's a related association.

Maria, a Five O'Clock Club member, was interested in competitive intelligence. Maria simply went to Google and keyed in "competitive intelligence association." (Or she could have gone to her local library to consult the massive *Encyclopedia of Associations* (EOA).) There seems to be an association for almost everything, and, believe it or not, she found the Society of Competitive Intelligence Professionals. She called the headquarters, found out about the local chapter, and went to a meeting. She met a lot of people in the field. She also read the association trade journal and learned enough to sound like an "insider." One of these new contacts led her to the job she later accepted.

You can do what Maria did. Google and see what you find, or go to *your* library and ***ask for the Encyclopedia of Associations***. Chances are, you'll find one or more associations related to your field of interest. The EOA usually provides information on the national headquarters of associations (many of which are located in or near Washington, DC). Call and ask for information on the **local chapter.** Then call the local chapter and say that you'd like to attend a meeting as a guest. Associations usually *love* to have guests! You'll meet people in the field, hear lectures that will bring you up-to-date, and find copies of their journals, magazines, or newsletters.

Networking is expected at association meetings. When you meet someone you think may help you, ask if you can meet on a more formal basis for about half an hour. If there is no local chapter in your area, the national office may still be willing to send you information.

Associations usually have **membership directories**, which you will have access to when you join. This directory can become the keystone of your search. You can *contact members directly.* You can write, "As a fellow member of the American Rug Association, I thought you could give me some information that would help me in my search." Fellow members are a great source of information.

Associations often publish **trade magazines and newspapers** you can read to stay up-to-date on the business. By reading these, you'll learn about the important issues facing the industry and find out who's been hired and who's moving; you should try to talk to the people you read about. If

an association is large enough, it may even have a library or research department, or a public relations person you can talk to. Associations often sell books related to the field.

An association's **annual convention** is a very quick way to become educated about a field. These conventions are not cheap (they run from hundreds to thousands of dollars), but you will hear speakers on the urgent topics in the field, pick up literature, and meet lots of people. You can network at the conference and later.

If you spend a couple of days at a conference, you'll know more about an industry than many people who are *in* the field right now. You can contact people in the industry (many of whom were *not* at the conference) and say, "Were you at the conference? No? Well, I was and maybe I can give you some of the information that I learned there." This is a chance for you to become an insider! A Five O'Clock Club maxim is, "Only insiders get hired." So share the information you pick up.

Since the EOA is the most complete source of association information, we recommend you use it if you can get to your library. A few websites are also helpful. **Associations on the Net** http://www.ipl.org/ref/aon/ lists more than 2000 associations. Simply key in a profession. If you put in "accounting," for instance, you'll find 22 organizations. Also try http://www.business.com; under each business category, there's a link to "associations." (There are additional sources for associations at the back of this book. Some are in print; some are online.)

On these sites, you'll find links to well-known sites like the one for the National Association of Fund Raising Executives and the Association of Legal Administrators. Or just go to Google, key in the word "association" and an industry or field name (e.g., "accounting"), and you'll come up with leads. But as of this writing, nothing beats the EOA.

Few Americans would lay a large wager that they will be in the same job, working for the same company, ten years hence.

Michael Mandel, *The High-Risk Society*

Alumni Associations

If you went to a prestigious school, you have an advantage over other job hunters because those schools often have great alumni associations. Martin, a graduate of Stanford University, wanted to start a job search. He thought he wanted to target some of the hot technology areas, such as radio frequency identification technology. I told him that his alumni database would be his entire search, and it was. He got a copy of the alumni directory and looked for the names of people who were working in the companies he was interested in. He sent 40 emails (which were opened because he put his school's name in the "subject" line) and got responses from 12 alumni who were glad to talk to him about the new technologies and the organizations for which they worked. Martin asked each alumnus about the field, but he also asked for the names of the right person he should contact in each organization. Then he used the alumnus's name when he contacted the appropriate manager. To keep up momentum, Martin sent out 40 more emails. Needless to say, all his hard work paid off. Martin accepted a one-year assignment in London with his present employer. He plans to stay in touch with his new Stanford network through email to ensure he will be able to find a job quickly when he returns to the United States.

Network with Five O'Clock Club Alumni

Thousands of successful Five O'Clock Club graduates have volunteered to help current job hunters who are attending the Club. The profile of our alumni is impressive: 40 percent of our attendees earn more than $100,000 per year and a growing number earn in excess of $200,000 (60 percent earn under $100,000 a year).

If you have attended four small group sessions at the Club (so we're sure you know how to network properly, The Five O'Clock Club way), you can join our LinkedIn group yourself. Here is the way it works right now (although the Internet changes all the time):

- Go to www.linkedin.com. Sign in or join.
- The menu on the left of the page has "home" followed by "groups." Click on "groups."
- At the top of the Groups page, there are tabs. The second one says "Groups Directory."
- On the right-hand side, it says, "Search Groups." Enter "Five O'Clock Club".
- You will be taken to the Five O'Clock Club main page. Click on "Join this group." If you are eligible, you request to join will be accepted.

After you join, you will not have to go through all of this. Instead, **The Five O'Clock Club will be listed as one of the groups you belong to and you will be able to simply click on our group.**

LinkedIn.com

Linkedin.com is a network of professional job seekers. Since members refer each other, it is a network of "trusted professionals." Service is free and people join by being referred online (via email) by a classmate, coworker, colleague, or other professional. Members fill out a profile, which allows them to search the network for contacts by such things as job title, job function, location, etc.; it also allows others to contact them. Members can access via these searches those who are not in their own network, but in the overall database. There are more than 300,000 job listings from more than 1,000 employers worldwide. Jobs are posted directly on the employers' own sites. This network allows users to get needed introductions to a hiring manager or recruiter. For example, a member can call a hiring manager and say, "Joan Smith of Exco recommended that I call you," even if he or she only knows Joan via a network search.

Linkedin.com has been getting rave reviews at The Five O'Clock Club as of this writing. Says one member, "Linkedin is a terrific web-based tool that can help extend a person's network and simplify the process of identifying members of your network in target companies. It's free to join so I've tried to recruit lots of other Five O'Clock Clubbers. As a quick anecdote, I received a cold call this morning from a distant contact in my Linkedin network who is looking for help on a number of his projects. I was the perfect fit. A perfect lead! Good luck. And pass it on. If you join, make sure to connect to me; the bigger your network, the more effective it will be."

Other Sources

First, go to the bibliography in this book (and in our Members Only area). This is a great resource . Sometimes I meet with a client who says, "I don't know how I can find out the names of organizations in this target area" or "How can I find out about these industries?" I just reach for the *bibliography* at the back of the book and look up the industries in which they're interested. I can point out, "Well, here are five or six sources you might consider—just to find out what's going on in that industry."

The press (in print or on the Web). Read newspapers and magazines *with your target in mind*, and you will see all kinds of things you would not otherwise have seen. And don't be afraid to contact the author of an article in a trade magazine or someone who writes a blog on a subject of interest to you. Tell him or her how much you enjoyed the article, what you are trying to do, and ask to connect just to chat. I've made many friends this way. And don't be afraid to contact someone quoted or mentioned in an article.

The Internet Public Library (http://ipl.org/). ipl2 is a public service organization and a learning/teaching environment. To date, thousands of students and volunteer library and information science professionals have been involved in answering reference questions for their *Ask an ipl2* Librarian service and in designing, building, creating and maintaining the ipl2's collections. It is through the efforts of these students and volunteers that the ipl2 continues to thrive to this day.

In January 2010, the website "ipl2: information you can trust" was launched, merging the collections of resources from the Internet Public Library (IPL) and the Librarians' Internet Index (LII) websites.

Chambers of Commerce. If you are doing an out-of-town job search, call the local chamber of commerce for a list of organizations in their area. Local business publications can be very helpful as well. In Chicago and New York, for example, Crain's Business is a great resource; it publishes annual lists for every industry in the geographic area.

Universities have libraries or research centers on fields of interest. Your research may turn up the name of a professor who is an expert in a field that interests you. Contact him or her.

Networking is a great research tool. At the beginning of your search, network with peers to find out about a field or industry. When you are really ready to get a job, network with people two levels higher than you are.

Databases at your library. A CD-ROM database organizes data on a compact disk. This is important because:

1. One disk can hold several volumes' worth of printed material. For example, the *Encyclopedia of Associations* comprises 13 volumes, which would fill a couple of bookshelves. However, all 13 of these volumes are contained on *one* CD!

2. Information can be updated much more frequently on a CD. Publishers can and do release current information on a quarterly basis that is simply "downloaded" onto a disk. Contrast this with print volumes, which can take years to be reprinted and republished. By this time, the new information is often already out of date.

3. You can access and retrieve desired information in a fraction of a second when using CD technology. You simply type the keyword you want to look up. Any information containing the keyword is presented to you almost instantly. When you use printed works, searching for specific pieces of information can be very time consuming.

Libraries. Do not rely only on the Internet for your information. Google cannot replace your local librarian. Libraries have been very enthusiastic adopters of technology. The trend is to continue moving to remote self-service. For example, QuestionPoint is 24-hour live library assistance offered by 1,500 libraries worldwide. Technology inside the libraries themselves is a tremendous source of information for your search, so you may just have to pick yourself up and go there to get the really useful data.

Libraries can often provide you with lists of contacts that will form the basis for your entire search. Many Five O'Clock Clubbers have come into the small-group meetings with disks or computer-printed lists of organizations obtained at the library. See what *your* library has. Many libraries have a system where you can key in the zip codes by which you want to search, the SIC or NAICS codes, and size of the organization. You type, "I'm interested in organizations from $5 million to $10 million in sales," and/or "I want organizations in my geographic area that have between 60 and 200 employees." The system will download or print out the name of the organization, the address, all of the principals (the president, vice president, and other officers), the type of organization (i.e., the product or service), and other information. This could be your entire job-search list! You can look at that list and do some weeding, "Oh, I'm not interested in this organization. Yes, I'm interested in that one." And you'd refine your target list.

Contacting the Company or Organization To Find the Name of the Right Person To Contact

Obviously, it's easier to build lists of *organizations*, but the names of the right people can be more elusive. So, sometimes you just *have* to call the organization and *probe* to find the right person to contact. For example, if you're in customer service, you can call up an organization and say, "May I have the name of the head of customer service?" or "I have to send some correspondence to your head of customer service. Who would that be?" Sometimes you can call and ask for the right person, but sometimes you need to *write* to someone asking for the correct name. (See the chapter, "Handling the Telephone: A Life Skill.")

This can be tough, so brainstorm with your small group to see how you can get the information you need for developing your target list. Make sure you get your group to help you. That's why we *have* small groups. You need *other* people's brains to help you in your search. And it's not just enough to get advice from your friends.

Job Postings

Many websites, such as Monster.com as well as many field- and industry-specific sites, list job postings. These sites help you find out who is hiring—even if the postings are not right for you. You don't necessarily need to apply for those jobs, but these sites do give you an idea of what's happening.

Many job hunters place false hopes on job postings. We know most good jobs are never listed in the ads and you'll face stiff competitors when you do answer ads. However, studying the ads can be useful. Look at the ads to see who's hiring. It doesn't matter whether they list jobs that are appropriate for you. If they're hiring and you're interested in the organization, add them to your target list. A Five O'Clock Club maxim is to aim for organizations, not just the jobs. If that industry is not currently on your Targeting Map of 200 Positions, perhaps it's time for you to start a new category.

And no grown-up will ever understand that this is a matter of so much importance!

Antoine de Saint-Exupéry, *The Little Prince*

Two Kinds of Research

There are two kinds of research. *Primary* research means talking to people who are doing the kind of work you're interested in or people who know something about those industries or organizations. You can get in touch with such people through networking or by contacting them directly. *Primary research simply means talking to people.*

Secondary research is reading materials in print, at the library, or online. In a sense, secondary research is *removed* from the source—it is information written by and about people and organizations.

It is vital to conduct *both* primary and secondary research and keep a balance between the two. Some job hunters would rather spend their time talking with people during their job search. Others prefer to spend their time in the library or working at their computers. But whichever one you *prefer*, do more of the other. You need balanced sources of information in your search.

So, if you like to stay at home or in the library, get out more and talk to people. If you're a person who *loves* the Internet, don't kid yourself that you'll get hired online! And don't *waste* time online and claim you've spent *hours* on job search! Be careful how you spend your time online. Or if you're the type who likes to meet people and press the flesh, spend some time at your computer or in the library so you will sound intelligent and well informed when you have meetings.

Primary research—talking to people—doesn't just happen in offices. You're researching when you're talking to people on a bus or a plane or at a coffee shop. They ask, "What do *you* do for a living?" You say, "Well, this is what I do and this is what I am interested in doing next." They may be able to tell you something about the industry you're interested in. That's research—and it does happen!

You're researching when you go to an *association* meeting, talk to people there, and find out more about what is happening in the industry. You can research while you're at a *party*. These are all examples of primary research—talking to people.

Time to Move On

If you've researched smartly and thoroughly, your Targeting Map of 200 Positions should have taken shape nicely—at least a rudimentary version of it. Now it's time to start contacting the companies and organizations on your target lists. Maybe you've been itching to do this all along, but it was better to spend time *planning* first. Now you're on your way!

In this high-risk society, each person's main asset will be his or her willingness and ability to take intelligent risks. Those people best able to cope with uncertainty—whether by temperament, by talent, or by initial endowment of wealth—will fare better in the long run than those who cling to security.

MICHAEL MANDEL, *The High-Risk Society*

The greatest obstacle to discovery is not ignorance— it is the illusion of knowledge.

EDWARD BOND, *Washington Post*

Campaign Checklist

Aim for a critical mass of activity that will make things happen, help you determine your true place in this market, and give you a strong bargaining position.

I plan to approach this target using the following techniques:

1. Do research (gather information at the library and through the Internet).
2. Network (gather information through people).
3. Conduct a direct-mail or targeted-mail campaign.
4. Contact selected search firms.
5. Join one or two relevant trade organizations.
6. Regularly read trade magazines and newspapers.
7. Follow up with "influence" notes.
8. Follow up with key contacts on a monthly basis.
9. Answer ads.
10. Aim to give out as much information as I get.

The best techniques for you to use to get meetings depend on your personality and your target market.

For certain targets, search firms may be the most important technique for getting meetings. In other fields, my own for example, people rarely get job leads through search firms. When you are networking in your target market, ask people: "Are there certain search firms you tend to use? How do you go about hiring people?"

If I insist that my work be rewarding, that it mustn't be tedious or monotonous, I'm in trouble....Time after time it fails to become so. So I get more agitated about it, I fight with people about it, I make more demands about it.... It's ridiculous to demand that work always be pleasurable, because work is not necessarily pleasing; sometimes it is, sometimes it isn't. If we're detached and simply pick up the job we have to do and go ahead and do it, it's usually fairly satisfying. Even jobs that are repugnant or dull or tedious tend to be quite satisfying, once we get right down to doing them.... One of the routine jobs I get every once in a while comes from putting out a little magazine. You have to sort the pages. It's a simple, routine, mechanical sort of job.... I never realized that this would be one of the most satisfying parts of the whole thing, just standing there sorting pages. This happens when we just do what we have to do.

THOMAS MERTON, *The Springs of Contemplation*

Information on Research:
Before you go any further, take a look at the huge bibliography in the back of this book.

Getting Meetings and Building Relationships

Four ways to get interviews in your target market

1. Search Firms
2. Ads
3. Networking
4. Direct Contact:
   - *Targeted Mailing*
   - *Direct Mail Campaign*
   - *Cold Calls*

Plan to contact or meet the *right* people in *every* company in each of your target areas—as quickly as possible.

Get meetings with people in your target areas through:
- Search Firms
- Ads
- Networking
- Direct Contact

Do not think of these as techniques for getting *jobs*, but as techniques for getting *meetings*.

- After a networking meeting, be sure to keep in touch with the person you met.
- After a job interview, think about what you can do next to turn the situation into a job offer.

COMPANIES IN THIS TARGET MARKET	BUILD RELATIONSHIPS	FOLLOW-UP
Company	Contact(s)	✍ ☎ ✍ ☎ ✍ ☎
Company	Contact(s)	✍ ☎ ✍ ☎ ✍ ☎
Company	Contact(s)	✍ ☎ ✍ ☎ ✍ ☎
Company	Contact(s)	✍ ☎ ✍ ☎ ✍ ☎
Company	Contact(s)	✍ ☎ ✍ ☎ ✍ ☎
Company	Contact(s)	✍ ☎ ✍ ☎ ✍ ☎
Company	Contact(s)	✍ ☎ ✍ ☎ ✍ ☎
Company	Contact(s)	✍ ☎ ✍ ☎ ✍ ☎
and so on ...	Contact(s)	✍ ☎ ✍ ☎ ✍ ☎

When you have a meeting, build a relationship: — find out about them; let them know about you.

Figure out how to move each of them along.

PLAN how you can contact or meet the *right* people in *every* company in each of your target areas —as quickly as possible.

How to Network Your Way In

I use not only all the brains I have,
but all I can borrow.

WOODROW WILSON

In the old days, networking was a great technique. We job hunters were appreciative of the help we got and treated those we met with respect and courtesy. We targeted a field and then used networking to meet people, form lifelong relationships with them, and gather information about the area. We called it "information gathering," but it also often led to jobs.

Today, stressed-out, aggressive, demanding job hunters want a job quickly and expect their "contacts" to hire them, refer them to someone important (obviously not the person with whom they are speaking), or tell them where the jobs are. The old way worked; this new attitude does not. This chapter tells you how to network correctly.

Network informally by talking to acquaintances who may know something about your target area. **Network formally** by contacting people at their jobs to get information about their organization or industry. Networking is one way to find out what skills are needed where, what jobs may be opening up, and where you might be able to fit in. Use the networking—or information-gathering—process to *gather information and to build new relationships.*

Gather Information

Networking is one way to find out what skills are needed where, what jobs may be opening up, and where you may be able to fit in. Talking to people because "they might know of something for me" rarely works.

Build Lifelong Relationships

You are also trying to build lifelong relationships. If a target area interests you, get to know the people in it and let them get to know you. It is unreasonable to expect them to have something for you just because you decided to contact them right now. Some of the most important people in your search may provide you with information and no contacts. Be sincerely grateful for the help you get, form a relationship that will last a lifetime, and plan to **recontact regularly the people you meet**.

Remember, you are not talking to people assuming they have heard of job openings. That approach rarely works. For example, if someone asked you if you happen to know of a position in the purchasing department in your old organization, your answer would be no. But if they said, "I'm really interested in your former organization. Do you happen to know anyone I could talk to there?" you could certainly give them the name of someone.

This is how people find jobs through networking. As time passes, the people you've met hear of things or develop needs themselves. If you keep in touch, they will tell you what's happening. It is a long-term process, but an effective one.

As you talk to more and more people, you will gather more and more information about business situations and careers in which you think you are interested. And the more people you meet and tell about your career search, the more people are out there to consider you for a job or a referral to a job when they know of one. But, remember, they have to know you first. Networking allows you to meet people without asking them for a job and putting them on the spot. And the fact is, **if they like you and happen to have a job that's appropriate for you, they will tell you about it—you will not have to ask**.

People *like* to talk to sincere, bright people and send on those who impress them. People will not send you on if you are not skilled at presenting yourself or asking good questions.

CASE STUDY *Monica*
Networking when You Don't Know Anyone

Monica moved to Manhattan from a rural area because she wanted to work in publishing. She found a temporary job and then thought of ways to network in a city where she knew no one. She told everyone she had always wanted to work in publishing and would like to meet with people who worked in that industry. She told people at bus stops, church, and restaurants. She read *Publishers Weekly*, the publishing trade magazine, to find out who was doing what in the industry and contacted some people directly. She also joined an association of people in the publishing industry. At meetings, she asked for people's business cards and said she would contact them later. She then wrote to them and met with them at their offices.

Monica found that one of the best contacts she made during her search was a man close to retirement who was on a special assignment with no staff. There was no possibility of her ever working for him, but he gave her great insights into the industry and told her the best people to work for. He saved her from wasting many hours of her time and she felt free to call him to ask about specific people she was meeting.

Over time, lots of people got to know Monica and Monica got to know the publishing industry. She eventually heard of a number of openings and was able to tell which ones were better than others. Monica is off to a good start in her new profession because she made lifelong friends she can contact *after* she is in her new job.

Using the networking technique correctly takes:

- time (because setting up meetings, going on them, and following up takes time),
- a sincere desire for information and building long-term relationships, and
- Preparation.

You Are the Interviewer

In an information-gathering meeting, you are conducting the meeting. The worst thing you can do is to sit, expecting to be interviewed. The manager, thinking you honestly wanted information, agreed to see you. Have your questions ready. After all, you called the meeting.

Our plans miscarry because they have no aim. When a man does not know what harbor he is making for, no wind is the right wind.

Seneca the Younger, Roman statesman

Questions You May Want to Ask

To repeat: People will be more willing to help you than you think *if* you are sincere about your interest in getting information from them and if you are asking them appropriate questions to which you could not get answers through library research or from lower-level people.

If what you really want from them is a job, you will not do as well. At this point, you don't want a job, you want a meeting. You want to **develop a relationship with them**, ask them for information, tell them about yourself, see if they can recommend others for you to talk to, and build a basis for contacting them later.

Before each meeting, write down the questions you sincerely want to ask *this specific person*. (If you find you are asking each person exactly the same thing, you are not using this technique properly.) Some examples:

The Industry

- How large is this industry?
- How is the industry changing? What are the most important trends or problems? Which parts of the industry will probably grow (or decline) at what rates over the next few years?
- What are the industry's most important traits?
- What do you see as the future of this industry 5 or 10 years from now?
- What do you think of the organizations I have listed on this sheet? Which ones are you familiar with? Who are the major players in this industry? Which are the better organizations?

The Company or Organization

- How old is the organization and what are the most important events in its history? How large is the organization? What goods and services does it produce? How does it produce these goods and services?
- Does the organization have any particular clients, customers, regulators, etc.? If so, what are they like and what is their relationship to the organization?

- Who are your major competitors?
- How is the company organized? What are the growing areas? The problem areas? Which areas do you think would be good for me given my background?
- What important technologies does this organization use?
- What is the organizational culture like? Who tends to get ahead here?
- What important challenges is the organization facing right now or in the near future?

The Job or Function

- What are the major tasks involved in this job? What skills are needed to perform these tasks?
- How is this department structured? Who reports to whom? Who interacts with whom?
- What is it like to work here? What is the organization's reputation?
- What kinds of people are normally hired for this kind of position?
- What kind of salary and other rewards would a new hire usually get for this kind of job?
- What are the advancement opportunities?
- What skills are absolutely essential for a person in this field?

The Person with Whom You Are Meeting

- Could you tell me a little about what you do in your job?
- How does your position relate to the bottom line?
- What is the most challenging aspect of your job?
- What is the most frustrating aspect of your job?
- What advice would you give to someone in my position?
- What are some of the intermediate steps necessary for a person to reach your position?
- What do you like or dislike about your job?
- How did you get into this profession or industry?
- What major problems are you facing right now in this department or position?

The Information-Gathering or Networking Process

1. **Determine your purpose.** Decide what information you want or what contacts you want to build. Early on in your job search, networking with people at your own level helps you research the field you have targeted. At this point in your search, you are not trying to get hired. Later, meet with more senior people. *They* are in a position to hire you someday.

2. **Make a list of people you know**. In the research step, you made a list of the organizations you thought you should contact in each of your target areas. You need lists of important people or organizations you want to contact. Then, when you meet someone who tends to know people, you can ask if he or she knows anyone on your list.

   Now make a list of all the people you already know (relatives, former bosses and coworkers, your dentist, people at your church or synagogue, former classmates, those with whom you play baseball). Don't say you do not know enough appropriate people. If you know one person, that's enough for a start.

   Don't discard the names of potential contacts because they are not in a position to hire you. Remember, you are not going to meet people to ask for a job, but to ask for information. These contacts can be helpful, provide information, and most likely have other friends or contacts who will move you closer and closer to your targets.

People to Contact in Each Target Area

   In the chapter, "Research: Developing Your List of Organizations to Contact," you made a list of organizations you want to contact in each of your target areas. Then you used the "Sample Targeting Map" as a model for your own complete list. Now you want to get in to see the people at these and other organizations.

   For each target, list on the following page the names of people you know, or know of, or even generic names (such as "lawyers who deal with emerging businesses") who can help you in each target. Whether you contact them through networking or a targeted mailing, the meetings will all be networking meetings.

   You will not be idly chatting with these people. Instead, you will have your pitch ready (see the chapter on the Two-Minute Pitch in our book *Mastering the Job Interview and Winning the Money Game*) and will tell them the target you have in mind. The target will include the industry or organization size, the kind of position you would like, and the geographic area. For example:

   "I'm interested in entrepreneurially driven, medium-sized private organizations in the Chicago area. I would do well as a chief financial or chief administrative officer in that kind of organization. Can you suggest the names of people who might have contact with those kinds of organizations or do you know anyone who works at such an organization or an organization on my list?"

   Tell *everyone* the target you are going after—including people you meet on the train and at the barbershop or beauty salon. You never know who knows somebody.

If you have always done it that way, it is probably wrong.

CHARLES KETTERING

3. **Contact the people you want to meet**. Chances are, you will simply call (rather than write to) people you already know—those on your "People to Contact" list. In the beginning of your search, practice on people who know you well. If you say a few things wrong, it won't matter. You can see them again later.

   But as you progress in your search, most of the people you meet should not be people you know well. Extend your network beyond those people with whom you are comfortable. (See the worksheet on the next page.)

People to Contact in Each Target Area

You made a list of organizations to contact in each of your target areas. Now you will show your list to those with whom you network because you want to get in to see those on your list and other organizations as well.

For each target, list below the names of people you know, or know of, or even generic names, such as "lawyers who deal with emerging businesses." You will contact them through networking or a targeted mailing. The meetings you set up will be networking meetings. However, you will not be idly chatting with people. Instead, you will have your "pitch" ready (See Two-Minute Pitch in our book *Mastering the Job Interview and Winning the Money Game*) and will tell them the target you have in mind. The target will contain the industry or organization size, the kind of position you would like, and the geographic area. For example:

"I'm interested in entrepreneurially driven, medium-sized private organizations in the Chicago area. I would do well as a chief financial or chief administrative officer in such an organization. Can you suggest the names of people who might have contact with those kinds of organizations, or do you know anyone who works at such an organization?"

You will tell *everyone* the target you are going after—including people you meet on the train and at the barbershop or beauty salon. You never know who knows somebody.

Target 1	Target2	Target 3	Target 4	Other Names
				such as:
				dentist
				hairdresser
				neighbors

As you build your network of contacts (people you know refer you to people you don't know and they refer you to others), you will get further away from those people with whom you originally began. But as you go further out, you are generally getting closer to where the jobs are. Be willing to go to even further networking levels. Many people report that they got their jobs through someone six or seven levels removed from where they started.

You will probably want to contact people you do not know personally by letter. Force yourself to write that letter and then follow up. People who are busy are more likely to spend time with you if you have put some effort into your attempt to see them. Busy people can read your note when they want rather than having to be dragged away from their jobs to receive your phone call. Often, people who receive your note will schedule an appointment for you through their administrative assistant and you will get in to see them without ever having spoken to them. (On the other hand, some job hunters are in fields where people are used to picking up the phone. "Cold calling" can work for them.)

- Identify the link between you and the person you wish to meet; state why you are interested in talking to her or him.

- Give your summary and two short examples of achievements of possible interest to him or her.
- Indicate that you will call in a few days to see when you can meet briefly.

Courtesy of Jerry King, Cartoons, Inc.

"I'm sorry, but Mr. Roberts no longer takes meetings, phone calls, cell calls, faxes, snail mail, e-mail, messages, notes or appointments. Is there anything else we can do for you?"

A Sample Note for Information Gathering

Dear Mr. Brown:

Penny Webb suggested I contact you because she thought you could give me the information I need.

I'm interested in heading my career in a different direction. I have been with Acme Corporation for seven years and I could stay here forever, but the growth possibilities in the areas of interest to me are extremely limited. I want to make a move during the next year, but I want it to be the right move. Penny thought you could give me some ideas.

I'm interested in human resources management. My seven years' experience includes the development of an executive compensation system that measures complex human resource variables. For the past two years, I have been the main liaison with our unions and am now the head of the labor relations section. In this position, I managed the negotiation of six union contracts—and accomplished that feat in only 90 days.

I'd like some solid information from you on the job possibilities for someone like me. I'd greatly appreciate a half hour of your time and insight. I'll call you in a few days to see when you can spare the time.

Sincerely,

Levels of Networking Contacts

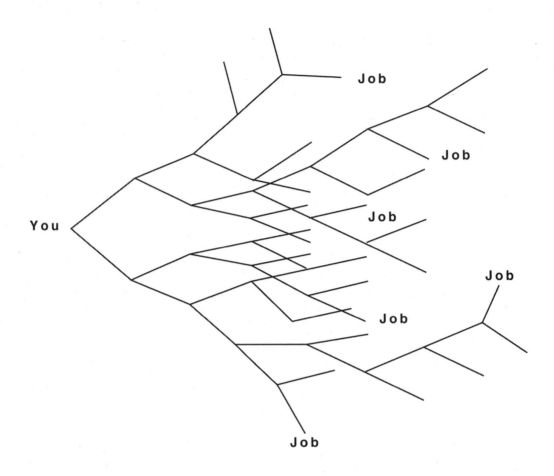

As you build your network of contacts (people you know refer you to people you don't know and they refer you to others), you will get further away from those people you originally knew personally. But as you go further out, you are generally getting closer to where the jobs are.

Be willing to go to further networking levels. Many people report that they got their jobs six or seven levels removed from where they started.

If there are obstacles, the shortest line between two points may be the crooked line.

BERTOLT BRECHT, *Galileo*

> **Enclose your résumé if it supports your case. Do not enclose it if your letter is enough or if your résumé hurts your case.**

. . . we know that suffering produces perseverance; perseverance character; and character hope.

ROMANS 5: 3-4

4. **Call to set up the appointment** (first, build up your courage). When you call, you will probably have to start at the beginning. Do not expect the person to remember anything in your letter. Don't even expect him to remember that you wrote at all. Say, for example, "I sent you a letter recently. Did you receive it?"

   Remind him of the reason you wrote. Have your letter in front of you—to serve as your script—because you may again have to summarize your background and state some of your accomplishments.

   If the person says the organization has no openings at this time, that is okay with you— you were not necessarily looking for a job; you were looking for information or advice about the job possibilities for someone like you or you wanted to know what is happening in the profession, organization, or industry.

   If the person says he is busy, say, "I'd like to accommodate your schedule. If you like, I could meet you in the early morning or late evening." If he or she is still too busy, say, "Is it okay if we set something up for a month from now? I would call you to confirm so you could reschedule our meeting if it's still not a good time for you. And I assure you I won't take up more than 20 minutes of your time." Do your best to get on his calendar—even if the date is a month away. (Remember: You are trying to form lifelong relationships. Don't force yourself on people, but do get in to see them.)

Don't let the manager interview you over the phone. You want to meet in person. You need face-to-face contact to build the relationship and be remembered by the manager.

Rather than leave a message, keep calling back to maintain control. If no one returns your call, you will feel rejected. But be friendly with the administrative assistant; apologize for calling so often. An example: "Hello, Joan. This is Louise DiSclafani again. I'm sorry to bother you, but is Mr. Johnson free now?"

"No, Ms.DiSclafani, he hasn't returned yet. May I have him call you?"

"Thanks, Joan, but that will be difficult. I'll be in and out a lot, so I'll have to call him back. When is a good time to call?"

Expect to call 7 or 8 times. Accept it as normal business. It is not personal. (See the section, "How to Use the Telephone.")

5. **Prepare for the meeting**. Plan for a networking meeting as thoroughly as you would for any other business meeting. Follow the agenda listed in step 6. **Remember: It is *your* meeting. You are the one running it.** Beforehand:

- Set goals for yourself (information and contacts).
- Jot down the questions you want answered.
- Find out all you can about the person, and the person's responsibilities, and areas of operations.
- Rehearse your Two-Minute Pitch and accomplishments.

   Develop good questions, tailoring them to get the information you need. Make sure what you ask is appropriate for the person with whom you are meeting. You wouldn't, for example, say to a senior vice president of marketing, "So, tell me how marketing works." That question is too general. Instead, do your research—both in the library and by talking with more junior people.

   Decide what information you want or

what contacts you want to build. Early on in your job search, networking with people at your own level helps you research the field you have targeted. At this point in your search, you are not trying to get hired. Later, meet with more senior people—the ones who are in a position to hire you someday.

Then when you meet the senior vice president, ask questions that are more appropriate for someone of that level. You may want to ask about the rewards of that particular business, the frustrations, the type of people who succeed there, the group values, the long-range plans for the business. Prepare 3 to 5 open-ended questions about the business or organization that the person will be able to answer.

If you find you are asking each person the same questions, think harder about the information you need or do more library research. The quality of your questions should change over time as you become more knowledgeable, more of an insider, and more desirable as a prospective employee. In addition, you should be giving information back. If you are truly an insider, you must have information to give.

If you think education is expensive, try ignorance.
Derek Bok

6. **Conduct the meeting**. If this is important to you, you will continually do better. Sometimes people network forever. They talk to people, but there is no flame inside them. Then one day something happens: They get angry or just fed up with all of this talking to people. They interview better because they have grown more serious. Their time seems more important to them. They stop going through the motions and get the information they need. They interview harder. They feel as though their future is at stake. They don't want to chat with people. They are hungrier. They truly want to work in that industry or

that organization. And the manager they are talking to can sense their seriousness and react accordingly.

Nothing great was ever achieved without enthusiasm.
Ralph Waldo Emerson, *Circles*

Business is a game, the greatest game in the world if you know how to play it.
Thomas J. Watson Jr., former CEO of IBM

Format of an Information-Gathering Meeting

Prepare for each meeting. The questions you want to ask and the way you want to pitch, or position, yourself, will vary from one meeting to another. Think it all through. **Review the "Format of a Networking Meeting" before *every* networking meeting**. If you use it, you will have a good meeting.

- **Exchange Pleasantries**—to settle down. This is a chance to size up the other person and allow the other person to size you up. It helps the person make a transition from whatever he or she was doing before you came in. One or two sentences of small talk: "Your offices are very handsome" or "Your receptionist was very professional" or "You must be thrilled about your promotion."
- **Why am I here?** The nature of your networking should change over time. In the beginning, you don't know much and are asking basic questions. But you can't keep asking the same questions. Presumably, you have learned something in your earlier meetings. As you move along, you should be asking different, higher-level questions—and you should also be in a position to give some information back to

people with whom you are meeting. That's what makes you an insider—someone who knows a lot about the field.

This is a basic example of *Why I am here*: "Thanks so much for agreeing to meet with me. David Madison thought you could give me the advice I need. I'm meeting with CEOs in the Chicago area because I want to relocate here." If the meeting is *in response to a targeted mailing*, you may say something like: "I'm so glad you agreed to meet with me. I've been following your organization's growth in the international area, and thought it would be mutually beneficial for us to meet." Remind the person of how you got his or her name and why you are there. He or she may have forgotten the contents of your letter or who referred you.

Here are additional suggestions on "Why I am here" (Notice how there is a progression going from early on to later in the search process):

- I'm trying to decide what my career path should be. I have these qualifications and I'm trying to decide how to use them. For example, I'm good at _____ and _____. I think they add up to_____. What do you think?
- I want to get into publishing, and I'm meeting people in the field. Dr. Cowitt, my dentist, knew you worked in this industry and thought you would be a good person for me to talk to.
- I've researched the publishing industry and think the operations area would be a good fit for me. I was especially interested in learning more about your organization's operations area and I was thrilled when Charles Conlin at the Publishing Association suggested I contact you.
- I have met with a number of people in the publishing industry and I think some meetings may turn into job offers. I'd like your insight about which organizations might be the best fit for me. I wrote to you because I will be in this industry soon and I know you are one of the most important players in it.

- I've worked in the publishing industry for 10 years and have also learned sophisticated computer programming at night. I am looking for a situation that would combine both areas because the growth opportunities are limited in my present firm. Vivian Belen thought I should speak with you, since your organization is so highly computerized.

- **Establish credibility with your Two-Minute Pitch**. (For more information about this important part of the meeting, see our book.) After you say why you are there, he or she is likely to say something like: "How can I help you?" You respond: "I wanted to ask you a few things, but first let me give you an idea of who I am." There are a number of reasons for doing this:
    1. The person will be in a better position to help you if he or she knows something about you.
    2. It's impolite to ask a lot of questions without telling the person who you are.
    3. You are trying to form a relationship with this person—to get to know each other a bit.

- **Ask questions appropriate for this person**. Really think through what you want to ask. Perhaps have your list of questions in front of you: You will look serious and keep on track.

- **As he or she answers your questions, talk more about yourself if *appropriate***. "That's interesting. The fact is I've had a lot of public relations experience in the jobs I've held." By the time you leave the meeting, you should know something about each other.

- **Ask for referrals if appropriate**. This is an opportunity to extend your network. "I've made a list of organizations I'm interested in. What do you think of them?" "Are there other organizations you would suggest?" "Whom do you think I should contact at each of the good organizations on this list?" "Could you tell me something about the person you suggested at that organization?" "May I use your name?"

As you probe, the person may respond that he or she does not know of any job openings. That's okay with you. You simply need to meet with more people in this industry, whether or not they have positions available: "I'm just trying to get as much information as possible."

Some job hunters get annoyed when they go away without contacts. They are thinking short-term and are not trying to build long-term relationships. But you were not entitled to a meeting with the manager. He or she was kind to meet with you at all.

If you get no contacts, be very grateful for what you do get. It may be that he or she has no names to give. On the other hand, because many people network incorrectly (aggressively and abrasively), managers are often reluctant to give out names until the job hunter has kept in touch for a number of months and proved his or her sincere interest. Many managers feel used by job hunters who simply want names and are not interested in *them*.

- **Gather more information about the referrals**. (For instance: "What is Harvey Kaplan like?")
- **Formal expression of gratitude**. Thank the person for the time he or she spent with you.
- **Offer to stay in touch**. Constantly making new contacts is not as effective as keeping in touch with old ones. "May I keep in touch with you to let you know how I'm doing?" You might call later for future contacts, information, etc.
- **Write a follow-up note, and be sure to follow up again later**. This is most important and a powerful tool. State how the meeting helped you or how you used the information. Be sincere. If appropri-

ate, offer to keep the manager informed of your progress.
- **Recontact your network every 2 to 3 months**. Even after you get a job, these people will be your contacts to help you in your new job—and maybe you can even help them! After all, you are building lifelong relationships, aren't you? See the chapter "Following Up When There Is No Immediate Job" in this book.

Remember:

- You are not there simply to get names. It may often happen that you will get excellent information but no names of others to contact. That's fine.
- Be grateful for whatever help people give you, and assume they are doing their best.
- Remember, too, that this is your meeting and you must try to get all you can out of it.

This is not a job interview. In a job interview, you are being interviewed. In a networking meeting, you are conducting the meeting.

Follow precisely the "Format of a Networking Meeting." If you use it, you will have a good meeting.

Many things are lost for want of asking.
GEORGE HERBERT, *Jacula Prudentum*

Other Meeting Pointers

- The heart of the meeting is relating your good points in the best way possible. Be concise and to the point. Don't be embarrassed about appearing competent. Be able to recite your Two-Minute Pitch and key accomplishments without hesitation.
- Keep control of the meeting. Don't let the person with whom you're meeting talk too much or too little. If he goes on about something inappropriate, jump in when you can and relate it to something

Format of a Networking Meeting

Prepare for each meeting. The questions you want to ask and the way you want to "pitch" or position yourself will vary from one meeting to another. Think it all through.

Be sure to read this chapter in detail for more information on the networking, or information-gathering, process.

The Format of the Meeting

- **Pleasantries**—this is a chance to size up the other person and allow the other person to size you up. It's a chance to settle down. Just two or three sentences of small talk are enough.
- **Why am I here?** For example: "Thanks so much for agreeing to meet with me. Ruth Rob-bins thought you could give me the advice I need. I'm trying to talk to CEOs in the Chicago area because I want to relocate here." Remind the person of how you got his or her name and why you are there.
- **Establish credibility with your Two-Minute Pitch**. After you tell the person why you are there, they are likely to say something like: "Well, how can I help you?" Then you can respond, for example: "I wanted to ask you a few things, but first let me give you an idea of who I am." There are a number of reasons for doing this:
  1. The person will be in a better position to help you if she knows something about you.
  2. It's impolite to ask a lot of questions without telling the person who you are.
  3. You are trying to form a relationship with this person—to get to know each other a bit.
- **Ask questions** that are appropriate for this person. Really think through what you want to ask. For example, you wouldn't say to the marketing manager: "So what's

it like to be in marketing?" You would ask that of a more junior person. Consider having your list of questions in front of you so you will look serious and keep on track.

- As the person is answering your questions, **tell him or her more about yourself if appropriate**. For example, you might say: "That's interesting. When I was at XYZ Company, we handled a similar problem in an unusual way. In fact, I headed up the project..."
- **Ask for referrals if appropriate**. For example: "I'm trying to get in to see people at the organizations on this list. Do you happen to know anyone at these organizations ?... May I use your name?"
- **Gather more information about the referrals** (such as: "What is Ellis Chase like?").
- **Formal expression of gratitude**. Thank the person for the time he or she spent with you.
- **Offer to stay in touch**. Remember that making a lot of new contacts is not as effective as making fewer contacts and then recontacting those people later (see Follow-Up).
- **Write a follow-up note and be sure to follow up again later**.

Remember:
- **You are *not* there simply to get names. You may get excellent information but no names of others to contact. That's fine.**
- **Be grateful for whatever help people give you and assume they are doing their best.**
- **Remember too that this is *your* meeting and you must try to get all you can out of it.**
- **This is not a job interview. In a job interview, you are being interviewed. In a networking meeting, *you* are conducting the meeting.**

you want to say. Remember, this is your meeting.

- Find out which of your achievements he is really impressed with. That's his hot button, so keep referring to those achievements.
- Be self-critical as you go along with this process. Don't become so enamored of the process that you become inflexible. Don't become a professional information gatherer or job hunter.
- Interview hard. *Probe.* Be prepared to answer hard questions in return.
- Take notes when you are getting what you want. This lets the manager know that the meeting is going well and encourages more of the same. The person to whom you are talking is just like everyone else who is being interviewed—everyone wants to do well.
- Show enthusiasm and interest. Lean forward in your chair when appropriate. Ask questions that sincerely interest you and sincerely try to get the answers.
- Don't be soppy and agree with everything. It's better to disagree mildly and then come to some agreement than to agree with everything 100 percent.
- Remember your goals. Don't go away from any meeting empty-handed. Get information or the names of other contacts.

Let your questions focus on the other person. Say, "What do you think?" rather than "Do you agree with me?"

BARRY FARBER, RADIO INTERVIEWER, *Making People Talk*

- Don't overstay your welcome. Fifteen minutes or half an hour may be all a busy person can give you. Never take more than one-and-a half to two hours.
- If you are meeting over lunch, go someplace simple so you are not constantly interrupted by waiters.
- If you are looking for a job, don't conceal it.

- **If the person you are meeting with suggests passing on your résumé to someone else, that is usually not helpful**— unless you know who the person is and can follow up yourself. Say, "I hate to put you to such trouble. Would you mind if I called her myself and used your name?" If the manager does not agree to this, then you must accept his or her wishes.
- **If the person you are meeting tells you of a job opening**, say, "I'd like to know more about that job possibility, but I also had a few questions I'd like to ask you." Continue to get your questions answered. If you follow up only on the job lead, you will probably wind up with no job and no information.
- It is important to remember that these are only suggestions. You must adopt your own style, your own techniques. You'll find that the more you meet with people, the better you'll get at it. Start out with friends or in low-risk situations. You do not want to meet with your most promising prospects until you are highly skilled at networking meetings. The more you practice, the better you will become.

Who Is a Good Contact?

A contact is any connection between you and the person with whom you are hoping to meet. Most often the contact is someone you've met in another information-gathering meeting, but think a little and you will find other, creative ways to establish links with people. (Also see the chapter "Targeted Mailings: Just Like Networking." Here are a few real-life examples:

Example one: A man's mother used to clean the office of the president of a good-sized corporation. One day the son wrote to the president, "My mother cleaned your office for 12 years." He was granted a meeting with the president and shown a good deal of courtesy. This may seem far-fetched, but it happened.

Example two: Clara wanted to leave an organization where she had worked for nine years. She thought about the person who had taught her data processing years earlier. Her teacher had left the organization to form his own business. She had never kept track of him, but he had impressed her as worldly and she thought he would be a good person to give her advice.

She wrote to him on personal stationery:

Dear Mr. Jones:

You taught me computer programming in 2003. I remember it well, since it was the start of my career, and I thought you would be a good person to give me the advice I need.

I'm interested in making a move during the next year or so, but I want it to be the right move.

I now have 10 years of computer programming experience, specializing in financial and personnel systems. I have used high-level languages and have designed complicated systems. You may be interested in some of the specific things I've done:

- Led a three-person team in developing a human resources system that linked salary administration, performance reviews, and employee benefits packages.
- Developed a sophisticated accounting system that allowed all of the computers in the organization to access certain information on the mainframe. All departments in the organization could see the same, updated information, but only the information they were approved to see.

I'll call you in a few days to set up a mutually convenient time to get together.

Of course, the man did not know Clara from Adam. She had been one of 28 students in the class he taught at a large university and was probably the most shy of the group. In fact, after she wrote to him, she became afraid and did not call for two weeks.

When she finally did call, she was told the business had been acquired by another firm and her former teacher had moved from Philadelphia to Chicago. She felt like a fool calling Chicago, but she finally got up the nerve.

When she identified herself to the administrative assistant, she heard, "Clara Horvath! We've been trying to reach you everywhere. Your note didn't contain a phone number!" The administrative assistant said Clara's former teacher was now a senior vice president in Chicago—and had sent the note to the head of the Philadelphia office.

When she called the Philadelphia office, the administrative assistant said, "Clara Horvath! We were hoping you would call. Your note didn't have your phone number."

The administrative assistant arranged for Clara to see the head of the Philadelphia office, who developed a job description for her. According to organizational policy, the job would have to be posted internally and the head of the Philadelphia office would have to interview qualified in-house candidates. After developing a job description to suit Clara, however, the chances were good that he would not find someone internally with her same qualifications.

Clara went to work at the company and it was many months before she finally met the man who was her former teacher. Neither one of them recognized each other, but that was fine!

Life is a series of collisions with the future; it is not a sum of what we have been but what we yearn to be.
José Ortega y Gasset

Other Sources of Contacts

Be sure to read the chapters on research for lots of ideas about associations, alumni groups, and so on. In addition, you can consider:

- Contacting acquaintances—even more than friends. Friends may be reluctant to act as contacts for you. You are more of a reflection on them than you would be for an acquaintance. And if things don't work out, they could lose your friendship—but acquaintances don't have as much to lose.

- Network every chance you get—on the bus, at parties. Don't be like those job hunters who don't tell anyone they are looking for a job. You never know who knows someone who can help you. Everyone you meet knows lots of people.
- Not contacting someone on the strength of Dun and Bradstreet, Poor's, or other directories. There is no true link between you and that person. Use your imagination to think of a better link, such as through LinkedIn.

Out-of-Town Search

The principles are the same wherever you are. If you have targeted another city, sometimes it is difficult to get face-to-face meetings with some of the people with whom you would like to talk. But plan ahead. If you are making business trips to or attending seminars or taking a vacation in that city, think about who you would like to contact there for your network. Telephone or write to him or her well in advance for an appointment. Keep your ears open about who might be coming through your area and try to get time with him or her if you can.

Summary

Networking is a powerful job-hunting tool—if it is used properly, which most often it is not. It is also a life skill that you can and should use throughout your career. Become expert at it and do not abuse people. Give them something back.

Keep away from people who belittle your ambitions. Small people always do that, but the really great make you feel that you, too, can become great.

MARK TWAIN

Our dignity is not in what we do but what we understand. The whole world is doing things.

GEORGE SANTAYANA, *Winds of Doctrine*

No matter what accomplishments you make, somebody helps you.

ALTHEA GIBSON, IN *Time*, AUGUST 26, 1957

It is better to die on one's feet than to live on one's knees, but some individuals appear actually to believe that it is better to crawl around on one's bare belly.

NATHAN HARE, IN *The Black Scholar*

God does not die on the day when we cease to believe in a personal deity, but we die on the day when our lives cease to be illuminated by the steady radiance, renewed daily, of a wonder, the source of which is beyond all reason.

DAG HAMMARSKJOLD, *Markings,* VINTAGE (2006)

Are You Conducting a Good Campaign?

The thing is to never deal yourself out... Opt for the best possible hand. Play with verve and sometimes with abandon, but at all times with calculation.

L. Douglas Wilder, in "Virginia's Lieutenant Governor: L. Douglas Wilder Is First Black to Win Office," *Ebony*, April 1986

The Quality of Your Campaign

Getting a job offer is not the way to test the quality of your campaign. A real test is when people say they'd want you—but not right now. When you are networking, do people say, "Boy, I wish I had an opening. I'd sure like to have someone like you here"? Then you know you are interviewing well with the right people. All you need now are luck and timing to help you contact or recontact the right people when they also have a need.

If people are not saying they want you, find out why. Are you inappropriate for this target? Or perhaps you seem like an outsider and outsiders are rarely given a break.

During the beginning of your search, you are gathering information to find out how things work.

Why should someone hire a person who does not already work in the field? Lots of competent people have the experience and can prove they will do a good job.

How You Know You Are in a Campaign

You feel as though you know a critical mass of people within that industry. When you go on "interviews," you contribute as much as you take away. You have gained a certain amount of information about the industry that puts you on par with the interviewer—and you are willing to share that information. You are a contributor. An insider.

You know what's going on. You feel some urgency and are more serious about this industry.

You are no longer simply "looking around"—playing it cool. You are more intense. You don't want anything to stand in your way because you know this is what you want. You become more aware of any little thing that can help you get in. Your judgment becomes more finely tuned. Things seem to fall into place.

You are working harder at this than you ever could have imagined. You read everything there is to read. You write proposals almost overnight and hand-deliver them.

Your campaign is taking on a life of its own.

At industry meetings, you seem to know everybody. They know you are one of them and are simply waiting for the right break.

When someone mentions a name, you have already met that person and are keeping in touch with him or her. The basic job-hunting "techniques" no longer apply.

You are in a different realm and you feel it. This is a real campaign.

There is a test to see if you are perceived as an insider. If you think you are in the right target, talking to people at the right level, and are not early on in your search, you need feedback. Ask people, "If you had an opening, would you consider hiring someone like me?"

Become an insider—a competent person who can prove he or she has somehow already done what the interviewer needs. Prove you can do the job and that the interviewer is not taking a chance by hiring you.

The Quantity of Your Campaign

You need to find a lot of people who would hire you if they could. You know by now that you should **have 6 to 10 things in the works at all times**. This is the only true measure of the effectiveness of your campaign to get meetings in your target area. If you have fewer than this, get more. You will be more attractive to the manager, will interview better, and will lower the chances of losing momentum if your best lead falls apart.

Use the worksheet "Current List of My Active Contacts by Target." At the beginning of your search, these will simply be networking contacts with whom you want to keep in touch. At this stage, your goal is to come up with 6 to 10 contacts you want to recontact later, perhaps every two months. In the middle of your search, the quality of your list will change. The names will be of the right people at the right level in the right organizations. Finally, the 6 to 10 names will represent prospective job possibilities you are trying to move along.

If you have 6 to 10 job possibilities in the works, a good number of them will fall away through no fault of your own (job freezes or hiring managers changing their minds about the kind of person they want). Then you'll need to get more possibilities in the works. With this critical mass of ongoing possible positions, you stand a chance of getting a number of offers and landing the kind of job you want.

There is a tide in the affairs of men, Which, taken at the flood, leads on to fortune;...On such a sea we are now afloat; And we must take the current when it serves, Or lose our ventures.

SHAKESPEARE, *Julius Caesar*

Developing Momentum in Your Search

A campaign builds to a pitch. The parts begin to help one another. You focus less on making a particular technique work and more on the situation you happen to be in. This chapter gives you a feel for a real campaign.

In your promotional campaign to get meetings, you see people who are in a position to hire you or recommend you. Keep in touch with them so they will...

- think of you when a job opens up,
- invite you to create a job for yourself,
- upgrade an opening to better suit you, and
- give you information to help you in your search.

When you are in the heat of a real campaign, a critical mass of activity builds, so you start:

- hearing the same names,
- seeing the same people,
- contributing as much as you are getting,
- writing proposals,
- getting back to people quickly,
- feeling a sense of urgency about this industry, and
- writing follow-up letters and making follow-up phone calls.

. . . the secret is to have the courage to live. If you have that, everything will sooner or later change.

JAMES SALTER, *Light Years*

… after the survival of a long and profound crisis, often after the painful shedding of one skin and the gradual growth of another, comes the realization that the world is essentially neutral. The world doesn't care, and is responsible neither for one's spiritual failures nor for one's successes. This discovery can come as a profound relief, because it is no longer necessary to spend so much energy shoring up the self, … the world emerges as a broader, more interesting, sweeter place through which to move. The fog lifts, as it were.

FRANK CONROY, *The New York Times Book Review*

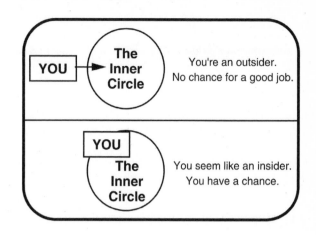

Networking Cover Letters

Asking for advice is appropriate early on in your search.

Gerry Cappelli
20 Trinity Place
New York, New York 10000
(222) 555-2231
GCappelli@earthlink.net

March 10, 201X

Mr. Max McCreery
Executive Vice President
Young & Rubicam
285 Madison Avenue
New York, New York 10017

Dear Mr. McCreery:

I am following up on the suggestion of Nancy Abramson, who refers to herself as a fan of yours, and am writing to ask for your counsel on my current career plans.

I have recently decided to leave my present company, McGraw-Hill Publishing, and continue my career elsewhere. Nancy thought you could give me the advice I need.

I have targeted the advertising industry as part of my search strategy because I believe that my skills in financial planning and problem solving, combined with my international experience, I could make an important contribution to good business management. In addition, I believe I would enjoy working in the dynamic and creative environment of most agencies.

Nancy suggested I ask for your response to my thoughts on how my experience in financial management in the publishing industry can be productively applied in advertising.

Briefly, my experience includes commercial banking (2007-2009) followed by financial analysis at CBS (2009-2011). The largest part of my career was with Time, Inc. (2011-2013), where I served in a variety of financial and administrative assignments, including tours as International Finance Manager, Financial Director of Time's fully independent Mexico subsidiary, and an assignment in the direct marketing group. Following Time, I became a principal in a small publishing company and since 2014 have been Vice President, Administration, at McGraw-Hill Book Clubs.

I look forward to speaking with you and will call in a few days to see when we can meet.

Sincerely,
Gerry Cappelli

May 19, 201X

Dear Mr. Dittbrenner,

Suzanne Howard suggested I contact you because she thought you could give me the information I need.

I'm interested in heading my career in a different direction. I've been with Rohm and Haas for nine years and I could stay here forever, but the growth possibilities in the areas that interest me are extremely limited. I want to make a move during the next year, but I want it to be the right move. Suzanne thought you could give me some ideas.

I'm interested in human resources. My nine years' experience in data processing included the design and implementation of Rohm and Haas' salary administration system as well as 3 years as Training and Development Director for the MIS Division. For the past two years, I have been in our Advertising Department and am now Advertising and Marketing Services Manager. What I'd like from you is some solid information on the job possibilities for someone like me.

I'd greatly appreciate half an hour of your time and insight. I'll call you in a few days to see when you can spare the time.

Sincerely,
Malka Weintraub

Mary Anne Walsh
February 2, 201X

Ms. Nancy Karas
Executive Vice President
Green Card International, Inc.
888 Sixth Avenue
New York, New York 10000

Dear Ms. Karas:

Tom Chuna suggested I get in touch with you.

I am a seasoned financial services marketer at SanguineBank with a strong package goods background and extensive experience in product development and merchandising, branch management, electronic banking, and innovative distribution planning.

- I created the SanguineBank Investment Portfolio, the bank's first complete presentation of its retail savings and investment products, and developed successful ways to sell the SanguineDip account in the retail setting.
- As an Area Director in the New York retail bank, I doubled branch balances in mid-Manhattan in only three years.
- Most recently, I have been developing a set of PC-based fund-transfer products for SanguineBank's Financial Institutions Group.
- Prior to SanguineBank, I rebuilt the baby shampoo division for Johnson & Johnson and managed all bar-soap marketing at Lever Brothers.

A résumé is enclosed for additional background.

I am seeking to move to a new assignment that would take full advantage of my consumer financial services marketing experience, and am extending my search outside of SanguineBank as well as inside. Rachel thought it would be worthwhile for us to meet briefly. I'll call in a few days to set up a mutually convenient time for us to meet.

I'm looking forward to meeting with you.

Sincerely,
Mary Anne Walsh

How to Contact Organizations Directly

I don't know anything about luck. I've never banked on it and I'm afraid of people who do. Luck to me is something else: hard work and realizing what is opportunity and what is not.

LUCILLE BALL

Beth conducted 5 direct-mail campaigns. She selected 5 clear targets and developed lists of names for each, ranging in size from 50 to 200 names. She emailed a cover letter and résumé to her first list. When she started to get calls for meetings, she emailed to her second list. At approximately 2-week intervals, Beth would send out another emailing. She received an excellent response (calls for meetings) from 3 of her 5 emailings.

To develop her interviewing skills and investigate each target area, Beth first had meetings at firms she did not care about. She treated these meetings as networking meetings. Beth probed, for example, to find out what the manager thought of other organizations on her list. If the comments were generally negative, she dropped those organizations. If the comments were positive, she asked if the manager might know someone in the organization whom she could contact. She got a lot of mileage out of her campaign because she combined direct mail with networking and worked the system with great energy.

The entire process took only one-and-a-half months. Beth had clear targets, followed the process, and prepared thoroughly for her meetings. She explored career possibilities in which she had been somewhat interested and refined her career direction. She turned down a number of job offers

before she accepted a high-level position that allowed her to combine her strongest skill area with something that was new to her and satisfied her long-range motivated skills. Beth took a two-week vacation before she started that job. She deserved it.

Jack's campaign strategy was very different. Jack is intelligent, articulate, research oriented—and also very shy. He targeted an industry that would result in a career change for him. He had read a lot about this industry and wanted to find out the job possibilities within it.

Jack meticulously researched organizations and selected 20 in which he was seriously interested. They were huge corporations, which made it relatively easy to get the names of people to contact. If he had simply emailed to that list, however, he might have gotten no response. As you will see later, 20 names is generally not enough for a direct-mail campaign. The effort would have been even more futile in Jack's case because he had, essentially, no hands-on experience in that field.

Jack did a targeted mailing—that is, he wrote letters to the 20 people and **followed up with phone calls** to all of them. His well-written and convincing letter proved his sincere interest in and knowledge of the field. He sent it without a résumé, because he was making a major career change, and told each of the 20 he would call him or her. He sent all the letters at once and called every person. It was quite an effort. Jack got in to see just about every person on his list and—as usually happens—some of them took a personal interest in his case. They gave him the names of others and told him how to break into the field.

Two of his contacts volunteered to sponsor him in their organization's training program.

The difference between direct mail and targeted mail:

- <u>Direct Mail</u>: *No follow up required*; You can contact 100 or more people with a slightly tailored cover letter.

- <u>Targeted Mail</u>: *Follow-up <u>is</u> required.* Because it takes an average of eight follow-up phone calls to get a meeting, most people can handle no more than 20—or possibly 30—targeted mailings.

"I'm sorry, but Mr. Taylor no longer engages in human interaction. He does check his e-mail once a week, though."

How It Works

Approximately 20 to 40 percent of all jobs are found through direct-mail campaigns. This technique is even more effective when you **combine it with networking**—as both Beth and Jack did.

You will do better in your direct-mail campaign when you:

- have clearly identified your target market,
- are familiar with the problems faced by organizations in that market, and
- know what you have to offer to solve its problems.

Know enough about your target market to compose an appropriate cover letter and to hold your own in a meeting. If you don't know enough, learn more through library research or networking. If you feel you may be caught off-guard in a meeting because of a lack of knowledge of your target market, do not use this technique until you have gained at least some knowledge.

These are not *job* interviews, but exploratory meetings that may lead to:

- more information,
- names of other people to contact, and/or
- a job interview.

Conduct the meeting using the same format as that of a networking meeting.

Don't let the interviewer know you blanketed the market. If an organization wants to see you, quickly do a little research on it. Tell the manager you wrote to him as a result of your research and name something specific about the organization of interest to you.

It doesn't matter if your meetings come from a direct contact or from networking. What matters is that you get in to see people who are in a position to hire you.

Benefits of This Technique

Direct mail blankets the market. In one fell swoop, you can find out the chances for someone like you in the market. You "market test" what you have to offer and also get your name out quickly to prospective employers. This technique is fast and as complete as you want it to be, as opposed to networking, which is slower and hits your target in a spotty manner.

What Is a Targeted Mailing?

A targeted mailing is direct contact followed by a phone call. Use it when you would like to see every person on your small list. Research so you can write customized letters (you may want to look up their annual reports, for example, or talk to people to get information about an organization). Follow the process for networking, paying special attention to the follow-up call, which requires a great deal of persistence. As with networking, you want to meet with people whether or not they have a job to offer.

Passion costs me too much to bestow it on every trifle.

THOMAS ADAMS

An Easy Way to Contact Lots of People

Typically, job hunters do not contact many people. Either the job hunter is unemployed and has the time to contact lots of people but may be suffering from low self-esteem—or is employed and simply does not have the time to contact people during the day. The direct-mail campaign allows a person to contact lots of potential employers despite reluctance or a lack of time.

Sometimes job hunters hit a slump and find networking overly stressful. Direct mail can help you get unstuck. You can hide away for a short while and grind out a mailing. You can sound more self-confident on paper than you actually feel and get your act together before you go out and talk to people. A direct-mail campaign can be a way out of a bind. But eventually you must talk to people. You cannot get a job through email or mail. Don't use this technique to avoid people forever. Remember, you are writing so you can get in to see them.

The man without purpose is like a ship without a rudder—a waif, a nothing, a no man. Have a purpose in life, and, having it, throw such strength of mind and muscle into your work as God has given you.

THOMAS CARLYLE

The Numbers You'll Need

In a small industry, your list will be smaller. In a larger industry, your list may be so large you'll want to hit only a portion of it as a test and then hit another portion later.

The "response rate" is measured by the number of meetings you get divided by the number of pieces you mailed. Meetings count as responses; rejection letters do not. Meetings count because there is the possibility of continuing your job search in that direction. Rejection letters, no matter how flattering, have ended your search in that particular direction.

In direct mailing, a 4 percent response rate is considered very good. The basic rule of thumb is this:

A mailing of 200 good names results in

- seven or eight meetings, which result in
- one job offer.

If your list is smaller, you may still do okay if you are well suited to that target and if there is a need for your services. If, however, your list has only 10 names, you must network in, or use a targeted mailing with a follow-up phone call.

Another factor that affects your response rate is the industry to which you are writing. Certain industries are very people oriented and are more likely to talk to you. Targeting industries that have a great demand for your service should result in a lot of responses.

Assuming that the job you are seeking is reasonable (i.e., you have the appropriate qualifications and there are positions of that type available in the geographic area you are targeting), persistent inquiries will eventually turn up some openings.

What makes men happy is liking what they have to do. This is a principle on which society is not founded.

CLAUDE ADRIEN HELVETIUS

Should You Enclose Your Résumé?

If your résumé helps your case, enclose it. Beth enclosed her résumé as a PDF; Jack did not. Direct-mail experts have proved that the more enclosures, the greater the response rate. You never know what may "grab" the reader and the reader is likely to glance at each enclosure. Your résumé, if it supports your case and is enticing, is another piece to capture the reader's attention. I have been called in for meetings because of what was on page three of my résumé.

If, however, your résumé hurts your case, change it or leave it out altogether. A résumé may hurt your case when you are attempting a dramatic career change, as Jack was. (Read the chapter "How to Change Careers" to get more ideas on how you can support your case.)

Cover Letters

The format you follow for your cover letter essentially can be the same whether you enclose your résumé or not. Your cover letter focuses your pitch more precisely than your résumé does and makes the reader see your résumé in that light. You can pitch to a very precise segment of the market by making only minor changes in the letter. The format for your cover letter is:

Paragraph 1—The grabber. Start with the point of greatest interest to your target market. This is the equivalent of a headline in an ad.

If your background is enough of a grabber for the target market to which you are writing, use it. For example, if you want a job in sales and have an excellent track record in that area, then open with a terrific sales accomplishment. Or if your expertise is in turnaround management, your cover letter might start like this:

As vice president of a $250 million organization, I directed the turnaround of an organization in serious financial difficulty. As a result, this year was more profitable than the previous 10 profitable years combined.

On the other hand, you can open your letter with a statement that shows you understand the problems faced by the industry to which you are selling your services. A successful letter to advertising agencies started like this:

Many ad agencies are coping with these difficult times by hiring the best creative and sales people available. While this may maintain a competitive edge, many agencies find their bottom line is slipping. The usual response is to send in the accountants. These agencies, and perhaps your own, need more than accounting help. As vice president of operations, I . . .

Here's a variation on the same theme aimed at organizations probably doing well financially:

I know this is a time of rapid growth and high activity for technology-based firms. I believe this is also a time when technology-based firms must be as effective as possible to maintain their competitive edge. If you are looking for new developers—either on an ad hoc or a permanent basis—consider a person like me.

If you work for a well-known organization in an area that would be of interest to your target market, you could start your letter like this:

I am at present with X Company in a position where I...

Perhaps your background itself would be your key selling point:

I started out in computers in 1986 and have been involved with them ever since. I am now at...

If you are targeting a small number of organizations, mention your specific interest in each one:

I have been interested in [your organization] for a number of years because of...

Paragraph 2—A summary of your background aimed at a target, perhaps taken from the summary statement on your résumé.

Paragraph 3—Your key accomplishments of interest to this target market. These can be written in a bulleted or paragraph format. Make them lively and interesting.

Paragraph 4 (optional)—Additional information. This could include references to your education or personality, or other relevant information, such as:

I am high in energy and integrity—persuasive, thorough, and self-confident—a highly motivated self-starter accustomed to working independently within the framework of an organization's policies and goals. I thrive on long hours of work, and enjoy an atmosphere where I am measured by my results, where compensation is directly related to my ability to produce, and where the job is what I make it.

Final paragraph—The close. Such as:

I would prefer working in an environment where my leadership and problem-solving abilities are needed and would be pleased to meet with you to discuss the contribution I could make to your organization.

Or use a statement like this one, which excludes those who may want to hire someone at a lower salary level:

Hiring me would be an investment in the mid-$70,000 range, but the return will be impressive. I would be pleased to meet with you to discuss the contribution I could make to the performance of your organization.

Or use this statement for a direct-mail campaign where you will not be making follow-up phone calls, especially to a list to which you have some relationship, such as that of an organization of which you are a member:

I can understand how busy you must be and therefore do not want to bother you with a follow-up phone call. However, I trust that you will give me a call if you come across information that would be helpful to me in my search.

You gain strength, courage and confidence by every experience in which you really stop to look fear in the face. You are able to say to yourself: "I lived through this horror. I can take the next thing that comes along." ...You must do the thing you think you cannot do.

ELEANOR ROOSEVELT, THE ELEANOR ROOSEVELT PAPERS PROJECT, A UNIVERSITY-CHARTERED RESEARCH CENTER ASSOCIATED WITH THE DEPARTMENT OF HISTORY OF THE GEORGE WASHINGTON UNIVERSITY

We African-American women have always worked outside of our homes, in slavery or in freedom—in the fields, in the kitchen, or in the nursery.

FREDERICA J. BALZANO, PH.D., *"And Ar'nt I a Woman?"* *The Five O'Clock News*, SEPTEMBER 1995

Happiness is not a matter of events; it depends upon the tides of the mind.

ALICE MEYNELL

Pain: an uncomfortable frame of mind that may have a physical basis in something that is being done to the body, or may be purely mental, caused by sthe good fortune of others.

AMBROSE BIERCE

Targeted Mailings: Just Like Networking

There's nothing to writing. All you do is sit down at a typewriter and open a vein.

WALTER ("RED") SMITH, IN *Reader's Digest*

Networking is not the only way to job hunt. Consider targeted mailings when:

- You want to see a particular person but have no formal contact. You must think of how you can create some tie-in to that person and contact him or her directly.
- You have selected 20 to 30 organizations in your target market that you really want to get in to see, and there are only a few jobs that would be appropriate for you in each company. For the 20 or 30 organizations you have chosen, research the appropriate person to contact in each one. Ask each for a meeting—whether or not they have a job for you. You want to get in to see them all because your target is very small.

There is no way of writing well and also of writing easily.

ANTHONY TROLLOPE, *Barchester Towers*

The Letter

- **Paragraph 1:** The opening paragraph for a targeted mailing would follow the format for a networking letter: State the reason you are writing and establish the contact you have with the reader.

Congratulations on your new position! I know you are extremely busy (I've heard about it from others). After you are settled in, I would be interested in meeting with you. I think it would be mutually beneficial for us to meet, although I have no fixed idea of what could come of it.

After you have found out something about the person or the organization, pretend you are sitting with that person right now. What would you say to him or her? Here's what one job hunter wrote to an executive:

I agree. Your position is truly enviable. With the merger of AT&T and United Telecom completed, AT&T is now positioned to become an even greater force in shaping telecommunications for the future, both domestically and internationally. However, with all the challenges comes the inevitable need for control, resolution of legal and regulatory issues, competitive threats, pricing issues, and reexamination of both the positioning and global packaging of AT&T. Clear, focused strategic and business plans become essential for success. I believe I can help you in these areas.

See the next chapter, "Targeted Mailing Cover Letter: A Case Study," for the rest of this letter. Here's another letter that reflects a great deal of thought:

As the banks look back on their risky involvement with groups like Campeau, it is clear that a better understanding of the retail business would have saved them from considerable losses. As a result, I'm sure many banks and lending institutions have gone to the opposite extreme. Another solution, however, would be to have an unbiased expert merchant involved in evaluating their retail plans.

Your opening should reflect whatever you know about the organization or the person:

Whenever people talk about organizations with excellent internal temporary services departments, Schaeffer's name always comes up. In fact, the people who run the Amalgamated Center, where I am now assigned, speak often of the quality of your work. I am interested in becoming a consultant in this field and I hope to meet with you.

- **Paragraph 2:**
  Give a **summary about yourself**.
- **Paragraph 3:**
  Note a few **key accomplishments that would be of interest to this target**.
- **Paragraph 4:**
  Ask for **half an hour** of his time, and say you will **call him in a few days**. For example:

  I am sure a brief meeting will be fruitful for us both. I will call your new administrative assistant in a week or so to see when I can get on your calendar.
  or
  I hope you will allow me half an hour of your time and insight to explore this area. I will call you in a few days to set up a mutually agreeable time.

If you plan to follow up with a phone call, say so. (But if you say so, do it—or you may get no response while they wait for your call.)

Life is like playing a violin solo in public and learning the instrument as one goes on.

SAMUEL BUTLER

Out-of-Town Search

For an *out-of-town search* (perhaps placed next to the last paragraph):

As a result of many years' travel to Seattle, I would prefer to live and work in that area. In fact, I am in Seattle frequently on business and can arrange to meet with you at your office.

Who has begun has half done. Have the courage to be wise. Begin!

HORACE, *Epistles*

Scannable Letters

As we have seen, other variations include the use of **underlining key points**, which can increase your response rate. This helps the busy reader scan the letter, be drawn in, and want to read the rest. Underlining makes certain key points pop out at the reader—anywhere in your text. Underline parts of sentences in no more than five places. Read the underlined parts to make sure they sound sensible when read together, have a flow, and make your point.

Even when I look at my own letters, I sometimes don't want to read them before I make them scannable. I rephrase my letters, underlining in a way that will make sense to the reader. People will read the salutation, then the first few words of your letter, and then the parts you have underlined. If they find these things compelling, they'll go back and read the rest of your letter.

Underlining should make sense. Don't underline the word "developed," for instance, which doesn't make sense. Underline what you developed, because that's probably the compelling part.

Take calculated risks. That is quite different from being rash.

GEN. GEORGE S. PATTON, LETTER TO HIS SON, JUNE 6, 1944

Do What Is Appropriate

Strange as it may seem, **sometimes it can be very effective to ignore all of this**. Do what works in your target area. Nat, who was interested in Japanese banks, wrote to 40 banks with a four-line cover letter along these lines: "Enclosed please find my résumé. I have had 20 years of banking experience, am mature,..."

Nat knew his market. He thought the Japanese would be put off by the typically aggressive American approach. He got an excellent response rate—and the kind of job he wanted.

Remember, it is sometimes better to follow your instincts rather than listen to the experts. You're smart. You know your market better than we do. Make up your own mind.

The Follow-Up Call (after a Targeted Mailing)

When you call, you will probably have to **start again from the beginning**. Do not expect them to remember anything in your letter. Do not even expect them to remember that you wrote to them. For example, when you phone:

- Say, "I sent you a letter recently. Did you receive it?"
- Remind them of the reason you wrote. You may again have to summarize your background and state some of your accomplishments.
- If they say they have no job openings at this time, that is okay with you—you were not necessarily looking for a job with them; you were looking for information or advice about the job possibilities for someone like you, or perhaps you wanted to know what is happening in the profession, organization, or industry.

Leave messages that you called, but do not ask to have them call you back. Chances are, they won't and you will feel rejected. However, be friendly with the administrative assistant and apologize for calling so often. If she would like to

have her boss call you back, tell her thanks, but you will be in and out and her boss will be unable to reach you: You will have to call again. After the first call, try not to leave your name again. **Expect to call seven or eight times**. Do not become discouraged. It is not personal.

The way to get good ideas is to get lots of ideas and throw the bad ones away.

LINUS PAULING, AMERICAN CHEMIST

The Meeting

When you go in for your meeting, **handle it as you would a networking meeting** (unless the manager turns it into a job interview):

- Exchange pleasantries.
- State the reason you are there and why you wanted to see this particular person.
- Give your Two-Minute Pitch.
- Tell the manager how he or she can help you. Get the information you want, as well as a few names of other people to whom you should be talking.
- As we have said, **be grateful for whatever help people give you**. They are helping you the best they can. If they do not give you the names of others to contact, perhaps they cannot because of a feeling of insecurity in their own jobs. Appreciate whatever they do give you.

For a more detailed description of how to handle the meeting, refer to the chapter "What to Do When Your Networking Isn't Working."

Form a Relationship

Take notes during your meeting. Your follow-up notes will be more appropriate and then you will feel free to contact this person later. Keep in touch with people on a regular basis. Those who know you well will be more likely to help you.

A targeted mailing is a very powerful technique for hitting *every* organization in a small target area. A direct-mail campaign hits every organization in a large target. Both can dramatically move your job hunt along. Try them!

Follow Up

Follow up with a customized note specifically acknowledging the help you received. These notes follow the same concept as follow-ups to networking meetings.

Final Thoughts

You will strike sparks with certain people you meet. They will develop a true interest in you and will surprise you with their help. I have had people invite me to luncheons to introduce me to important people, or call me when they heard news they thought would be of interest to me. I have even made new friends this way.

Of course, I have done my part too by keeping in touch to let them know how my campaign was going. If you are sincere about your search, you will find that the people you meet will also be sincere and will help. It can be a very heartwarming experience.

Without effort we cannot attain any of our goals in life, no matter what the advertisements may claim to the contrary. Anyone who fears effort, anyone who backs off from frustration and possibly even pain will never get anywhere....

ERICH FROMM, *For the Love of Life*

CASE STUDY *Ahmed*
Research and Focus

Ahmed had just moved to the United States from Turkey, so he had no contacts here. He had a background in international sales and trading.

He targeted nine major employers and did extensive research on each one. Then he wrote to the head of international sales at each of the nine companies. In his introductory paragraph, he said things like "I notice that your international sales have declined from 6 percent to 3 percent over the last year. I find that very disturbing. I was wondering why that is happening, given the state of the market now..."

Paragraph two was his summary. Paragraph three listed his bulleted accomplishments. Paragraph four was the close: "I would really appreciate meeting you..."

He called only two of them—because the other seven called him before he had a chance. This targeted mailing resulted in nine meetings and three job offers.

Direct Contact Requires Research and Excellent Writing Skills

Targeted mail works only if you've done your research and if you're a good writer. Furthermore, you must target the right person and have something interesting to say to each person you are contacting. That's why direct contact works best for job hunters who clearly understand their target markets and the important issues in them. And that's also why most people do not attempt direct contact until after they have done their research—through preliminary networking or the library.

Are You Sincere?

It's not enough to write to people and expect to get in to see them. They are probably busy with their own jobs and may be contacted by quite a few people.

Unless you sincerely want to see a person, you won't develop strategies to figure out how to get in to see him or her. You won't do your research. You won't do the follow-up phone calls required to prove your sincerity. You won't prevail when someone doesn't return your phone calls.

If you really want to see this person, you'll persevere. And you won't mind asking for an appointment one month from now if he or she is too busy to see you now. You may even say, "I know you're busy now. How about if we schedule something for a month from now and I'll call you in advance to confirm?"

To Enclose Your Résumé or Not?

A cover story in *Time* magazine was titled "Junk Mail." People said, "Why do junk-mail companies enclose so many things in these envelopes we get? They're wasting paper." In the Letters to the Editor, junk-mail companies said they had no choice because the response rate increased so dramatically with the number of additional enclosures carrying the same message. If they have fewer enclosures, their response rate decreases dramatically.

The same is true for the mailings and email-ings you are sending. Some people say, "If they see my résumé, they'll know I'm job hunting." But they'll probably know it anyway from your letter. People are very sophisticated today.

My rule of thumb is this: If it supports your case and it has a message that complements your cover letter, then enclose your résumé. You can say, "I've enclosed my résumé to let you know more about me." If you have a brilliant résumé, why not enclose it?

On the other hand, if you want to make a career change, you probably do not want to enclose your résumé because you can probably make a stronger case without it.

Do what is appropriate for you. Try it both ways and see which works better for you and your situation.

Unless you call out, who will open the door?

ＡFRICAN PROVERB

Stating Your Accomplishments in Your Cover Letter

Think of which of your accomplishments are of interest to your target market. You may want to list different accomplishments for the different industries to which you are writing.

Rank your bulleted accomplishments gener-ally in order of importance to the reader, as op-posed to chronologically or alphabetically. If some other order would be more appropriate in your case, then do that.

CASE STUDY *Rick*
Out-of-Town Search

A Five O'Clock Club job hunter was looking for a job in Denver. He conducted research by getting a listing of companies from the Denver Chamber of Commerce. He called each company and asked for the name of the department head for the area in which he was interested. He wrote to each one and followed up with a phone call.

He was employed at the time. Yet most of his effort did not take time away from his job. He did his research and wrote his letters evenings and weekends. Networking would have been an impossible way for him to start his search, espe-cially in another part of the country. But after he had made these initial contacts and had traveled to Denver, he could network around.

He wound up with 80 companies to contact— too many for follow-up phone calls. Even 20 is a lot. He followed up with 20 companies and sched-uled a three-day trip to Denver. Before he went, he had set up eight meetings for the first two days of his trip. When he met with those first eight, he networked into four additional companies and held those meetings on the third day of his trip.

He didn't have a lot of money, so he couldn't stay long in Denver. But this is also the best way to conduct an out-of-town search—a few days at a time.

When job hunters visit a city for two weeks and hope that something will happen, they usually come home empty-handed. It's better to do your research, contact all of the organizations ahead of time, and go there with meetings already set up. The meetings could be with search firms, in response to ads, or through networking or direct contact.

Go for three days. Tell the people you meet that you are planning to be in town again in a few weeks and would like to meet with other people in their organization or in other organizations. Go back home, do more work, return in another three or four weeks, and stay for another three days. This is how you develop momentum in your out-of-town campaign. A one-time visit rarely works.

Rick went back again six weeks later. It took a few more visits to land the job he wanted, but he did it all with direct and targeted mail as the basis for his campaign, supplemented by networking.

The following pages contain case studies of people who have been successful with targeted mailings. Rather than simply copying their letters, **think of *one* actual individual on your list to whom you are writing and the compelling things you should say to make that person want to meet with you.** Even if you write exactly that same kind of letter to 20 people, it will sound more sincere and have more life if you write that first letter with a particular person in mind.

Targeted Mailing Cover Letter: A Case Study

Faint heart never won fair lady.

CERVANTES, *Don Quixote*

Terry was very interested in AT&T. She researched the company and decided to write to the vice chairman of the board. This was an appropriate person for her to write to because he was head of strategic planning, her area of expertise.

She wrote a cover letter using our standard format. The cover letter started out by saying, "I agree with you completely..." Then she quoted from an article in which the vice chairman was mentioned. She was attempting to establish a business relationship with him.

Paragraph two was her summary paragraph. Paragraph three contained her bulleted accomplishments. Paragraph four was her close.

Before sending the letter, she called the company to find out the name of his administrative assistant. It was Kim. Then she called to say that she was writing a letter to Mr. Payan and would Kim please look out for it?

In the last paragraph of her letter, she said, "I would very much appreciate the opportunity to meet with you for half an hour to introduce myself... I'll call Kim next week to set up an appointment."

She wound up meeting with the vice chairman, and four other very senior people at AT&T. But the company had a hiring freeze and she ended up working elsewhere.

Was Terry's targeted mailing successful? The answer is yes! Did you forget? Mailings, networking, search firms, and ads are techniques for getting *meetings*. If she got a meeting, the technique was successful. Terry got the meeting she had wanted and more.

By the way, she enclosed her résumé. She was careful not to mention the business she had been in because it was very different from the one at AT&T. But she knew her skills were transferable because she had done so much research on AT&T and could prove it in her letter. She could talk about her background without emphasizing the exact product or service with which she had been involved.

Why Not Network Instead?

When Terry wrote to the vice chairman of the board, she really wanted to see him. If she had decided to network in, it would have taken her a very long time to meet someone who would be willing to introduce her to such an important person. Instead, she did her homework: extensive research and intensive follow-up. Be sure to include targeted mailing in *your* bag of tricks.

Note: Do not necessarily aim for a person at the top of the organization. See people who are appropriate for your level. As a rule of thumb, you want to see people who are two levels higher than you are.

Terry Iannaccone
Greenwich, CT 02555
212-555-1212 (day)
terryi@trusite.net
August 1, 201X

Mr. Ellis Payan, Vice Chairman
AT&T Corporation
Corporate Planning and Development
One Stamford Forum
Stamford, CT 06904

Dear Mr. Payan:

I agree. Your position *is* truly enviable.

With the merger of AT&T and United Telecom completed, AT&T is now in a position to become an even greater force in shaping telecommunications for the future both domestically and internationally. However, with all the challenges comes the inevitable need for control, resolution of legal and regulatory issues, competitive threats, pricing issues, and reexamination of both positioning and global packaging of AT&T. Clear, focused strategic and business plans become essential for success. I believe I can help you in these areas.

I offer 20 years' experience in management and marketing with more than half that time focused on international markets. In addition, having been primarily involved in start-up and turnaround ventures, I was directly responsible for developing both five- and 10-year strategic plans and one-year operating plans.

Other areas where my experience could assist your corporate planning and development area:

- Established and implemented a global marketing and sales strategy that ensured consistency of message and product delivery to customers.
- Developed an "insider" approach in the local markets for the products and services sold while adhering to corporate values.
- Instituted a global program aimed at ensuring zero defects for multinational clients. Given AT&T's product mix and its strategy for global expansion, superior-quality service is essential for success.
- Developed, installed, and managed a centralized core system for the business noted as the best in the industry.
- Hosted quarterly global sales and marketing conferences and training sessions to cement team spirit and ensure product, corporate and local communications were current and correct.
- Developed a global risk management program to control risk with "common sense" procedures to ensure compliance and support.
- Traveled globally at an 80% level. Focused on visiting/selling/cheerleading clients, prospects, industry leaders, and staff.
- Created and implemented a global promotion and advertising campaign to establish an image of a global yet local player.

I would very much appreciate the opportunity to meet with you for half an hour to introduce myself, discuss the AT&T environment, and identify any areas of your organization or the corporation that may need someone with my background and experience. I have the maturity and sophistication to deal with the wide variety of personalities, problems, and opportunities presented by the international markets plus the persistence to see things through to meet your goals.

I'll call Kim next week to set up an appointment. I look forward to meeting you.

Sincerely,

Terry Iannaccone

Targeted Mailing: My Own Case Study

Beginnings are always messy.

JOHN GALSWORTHY, ENGLISH NOVELIST

I enjoy research and writing. I sincerely want to meet with the people to whom I write and I therefore don't mind doing a lot of work to get in to see them. I use both targeted- and direct-mail campaigns.

Many years ago, IBM announced a new president of a company that had to do with employment. I thought I should get to know him because I was in the career-coaching field, although I couldn't find out exactly what the new company would be doing. I knew quite a few people who had tried to network in to see him with no success. The man was inundated with letters from people trying to see him using the name of somebody important at IBM. He turned them all down.

I wrote him a targeted mailing and enclosed a résumé. Before I wrote paragraph one, I tried to think about him as a person. That's what you need to do to make your letters more personal. "Gosh," I thought, "he must be so proud to be president of this company! He's probably never been the president of a company before."

When I am working with my clients, I want them to imagine the person to whom they are writing and write a letter aimed at that specific person—even in a direct-mail campaign, where they may write to 60 or 100 people. It is still better to write that first letter with someone specific in mind (even if you don't really know that person) rather than write to a mailing list.

What you want to say to that specific individual becomes the opening to the letter. In this case, I had to hedge my bets because I didn't know exactly what the company did, so I alluded to that fact. In paragraph two, I gave my summary statement. In paragraph three, I listed bulleted accomplishments.

Before I sent the letter, I called and found he had only a temporary administrative assistant. So, in paragraph four, I referred to this fact.

I said I thought it would be fruitful for both of us if we got together. And I enclosed my résumé.

As usual, I got cold feet after I sent the letter. What happens is that I start thinking, "Why would this person ever want to see me—especially when I know he has rejected so many?" Sometimes I get so scared I wait too long to follow up. Then I write again, usually saying there is some information I left out of my first letter. I send off the second letter and by that time, I can usually get up my nerve to follow up with a phone call.

In this case, the administrative assistant was expecting my call and the company president had asked her to reserve 45 minutes for me.

When I met with him, he told me he had received more than 800 letters, but met with only four people—including me. He said my letter was one of the most intelligent he had received and that I sounded sincere. In case you think the credentials you see in this letter are what got me in, I'd like to point out that I used this same technique even early on in my career when I had virtually no credentials. The four-paragraph approach increases anyone's chances of writing an intelligent letter.

A targeted mailing requires clear thinking, clear writing, and making a case for oneself. Most people realize this. On the other hand, when job hunters have a networking contact, they tend to cut short the hard work required to get in to see someone. And sometimes people resent getting networking letters and feeling as though they are being coerced.

Everyone is networking these days, and it certainly is an important technique, but it's not the only one. At least consider the other approaches to getting meetings in your target market.

I take a simple view of living.
It is: keep your eyes open and get on with it.

LAURENCE OLIVIER

Targeted Mailing Cover Letters

KATE WENDLETON
444 East Grenopple Street
New York, New York 10000

February 10, 1992

Mr. Rickey Allen
President, Employment Solutions, Inc.
c/o IBM Corporation
555 Black Horse Pike
Cherry Hill, NJ 07555

Dear Mr. Allen:

Congratulations on your new position! I know you are extremely busy (I've heard about it from others). After you are settled in, I would be interested in meeting with you. I think it would be mutually beneficial for us to meet, although I have no fixed idea of what could come of it.

I have started up, managed, and delivered a number of employment/counseling services. I also have a strong business background:

- I am Founder and Director of The Career Center at the New School for Social Research.
- I am Founder and Director of The Five O'Clock Club®, a career-coaching group that attracts 40 to 60 job hunters a week in Manhattan. We have seven coaches who help the job hunters through their searches.
- When I served as CFO of an outplacement firm with a professional staff of 100, that company was very successful and profitable.
- I coach senior executives at a major financial institution, a good prototype of an internal service, and the only one with a full-time staff serving clients (others rely on outside consultants).
- One of my books will be published in the fall by Random House under the title, *Through the Brick Wall: How to Job Hunt in a Tight Market*.

I know a lot of people in the field and perhaps have knowledge of some important developments in outplacement of which you may not be aware. I am sure our meeting will be fruitful for us both. I will call your new administrative assistant in a week or so to see when I can get on your calendar.

Yours truly,
Kate Wendleton

David Madison, III
140 West 81st Street
New York, New York 10000
dmadison678@landmine.net

July 17, 201X

Ms. Renee Rosenberg
Merrill Lynch
Liberty Place
165 Broadway
New York, New York 10000

Dear Renee:

I appreciate your offer to review and forward on my résumé. I think you'll see how I've used my skills of persuasion throughout the years. For example, while working on the "Friends of Bill Thomas" Mayoral Campaign, I was on the phone all day long convincing politicians across a broad spectrum to either publicly commit to my candidate or, as was the case at the outset when resistance was strong and reactions negative, to cooperate behind the scenes. The continual give-and-take involved a lot of listening, as people wanted to state their case, vent frustrations with personalities, and so on. I had to cajole and "massage" the local political types in an effort to have them deliver us an audience at events that we staged in their communities. These same techniques—reasoning with people, getting my message across, listening, wanting to please—all these would be assets in a job where rejection is the norm.

On the other hand, I find I enjoy analyzing business. For example, in my current job I monitor revenue and other statistics daily to determine trends and affect policy. While also working on systems problems (we are a computer-driven collections operation), the line management position I hold in day-to-day operations is responsible for a net revenue of $2 million plus per year. I supervise 22 city marshals who participate in the street impoundment program and also deal directly with 3 garage towing operations under contract to us. I've also been negotiating with realtors and prospective subcontractors to expand our operation.

I enjoy working in an atmosphere where there is a lot of activity, where I'm measured by my results, where compensation is directly related to my ability to produce, and where the job is what I make it. I want to be with interesting people, people who matter, people who can have an impact. I feel that the securities business and the opportunity to train and grow the best at Merrill would be a challenge and an education. In this situation, I feel the most severe limitations and constraints would be my own and I like that.

I would be pleased to meet with someone in your organization to further discuss how my qualifications may lead to a career with Merrill.

Sincerely,

PHILIP GITTINGS
10 West Fortieth Street
West Beach, New Jersey 08000
(222) 555-2231
Gittings483@aol.com

April 30, 201X

Name
Title
Company
Address
City, State, Zip

Dear _____:

I am writing to you because I am very interested in working for your company.

As biomedical research advances on international fronts, companies with global healthcare and pharmaceutical interests are facing intensified multinational competition. Dealing effectively with this kind of environment may require the resources of capable international planning analysts:

- to coordinate diverse, market-driven approaches to worldwide competition,
- to channel regionally developed strategic market plans in the direction of common organizational goals, and
- to establish and communicate that common vision to ensure worldwide leadership.

As an international market planning analyst with Exxon, I have dealt with these issues and would add important expertise to your planning and marketing activities. I have seven years' experience in market planning, operations, and financial analysis, gained through five diverse assignments with Exxon International Company. During this time, I have made some meaningful contributions to the organization's worldwide efficiency, competitiveness, and strength. I have:

- Developed an international market-planning approach for a $4 billion product line. It was acknowledged worldwide for substantially improving overall marketing potential and global communications.

- Analyzed the industry environments of several international product lines.

- Developed corporate outlooks and goals consistent with worldwide perspectives.

- Evaluated the reasonableness of regional market strategies (Europe, Far East, South America, Canada, U.S.A.). Worked with foreign marketing managers to assess competitive strengths and to define appropriate objectives and positioning.

My assignments with Exxon have taught me how to plan, market, and manage effectively the international product lines of a highly decentralized organization. The industry environment is one where widely varying economic conditions, regulatory requirements, and political practices are standard considerations. I would be immediately beneficial to your organization and in your industry because of this tested experience.

In addition to my market-planning responsibilities, I have also performed financial and cost/benefit analyses for efficient use of assets. I have implemented analytical applications on both mainframe and micro-computers. I have delivered oral and written presentations to top-level executives. My educational background includes an M.S. in Industrial Administration from Columbia and a B.S. in Mathematics and English.

Due to the restructuring of the oil industry and my assessment of the opportunities there, I am looking to match my skills with organizations that offer potential. Along with my credentials, I bring an intensely personal motivation to meet the challenges of contemporary health-care issues and to participate in the exciting developments promised the pharmaceutical industry by emerging technologies.

I am confident I can contribute importantly and meaningfully to your firm's international marketing and planning efforts. I look forward to an exploratory meeting with you where we can discuss in more detail my qualifications and how they can be of use to you.

I hope you are as interested in meeting as I am. I will call in a few days to see when a personal meeting can be arranged.

Sincerely,

Phil got in to see all of the people he wanted to see—because of his persistence in the follow-up phone calls. He was offered a number of options in the pharmaceutical industry, but he turned them down and accepted a position in a completely different field.

Helene customized the opening sentence of each letter. She also used a moderate amount of underlining and bolding to make it easier for the reader to scan the letter to see what she had done. This particular letter was aimed at companies involved in electronic commerce.

HELENE SEILER

2737 Flomenhaft Boulevard

Atlanta, GA 99997 212.555.5228 (Day)

Hseiler890@prodigy.net

GLOBAL STRATEGY AND MANAGEMENT CONSULTING

Mr. Richard Bayer
KPMG International
Three Chestnut Ridge Road
Montvale, NJ 07645

> Most Five O'Clock Club letters use exactly the same format:
> Paragraph 1: The opening.
> Paragraph 2: A summary about yourself.
> Paragraph 3: A few key accomplishments of interest to this target.
> Paragraph 4: Ask for a meeting; state who will call whom.

Dear Mr. Bayer:

What an exciting year this is for consulting firms and the explosive growth they enjoy. But clearly what attracts me the most to KPMG is its leadership in strategic marketing. This is why I am writing to you today.

I have been in **global strategic development** and **organizational communications strategies** for the past 20 years, injecting **operational effectiveness** to companies and increasing their revenues massively. During this time, I lived in Paris, London, New York, and Los Angeles (as a base for frequent and lengthy trips to Southeast Asia and Latin America).

By far, the most exciting venture I have been involved with was the strategic consulting and **implementation project** for a $6 billion company. This achievement resulted in moving that **company from #5 to #2** globally. Today that company is a prime target for takeover as its cash flow is one of the most attractive return-on-sale, all industries considered.

I truly help companies build their **global impact** and achieve **long-term profitability**.

You may be interested in some of the specific things I have done:

I implemented long-range business plans for major entertainment, media, and communications companies: **Time Warner, Sony/USA, and BMG North America**.

I drove the process forward, made the deals, and brokered trade-offs to ensure company executives saw the added value of **electronic commerce**.

My next goal is to join a top consulting firm and I would appreciate an informational conversation with you or one of your associates to find out more about your needs and to tell you more about myself. As I mentioned earlier, I see electronic commerce consulting as the next tremendous growth area and I have established my expertise in that area.

When I call your office in a few days I would appreciate your telling me who to contact in your Atlanta office to discuss this explosive industry and its challenges.

Sincerely,

Martin Byrne

mbyrne309@gmail.com

November 10, 201X

Ms. Vanessa Gathers
SVP & Controller
Bankers Trust
433 Market Street
San Francisco, CA 94000

Dear Ms. Gathers:

I am writing to you since I am seeking a senior financial and/or operations position in the San Francisco Bay area. Although I enjoy working for Chase Manhattan Bank, I'm afraid my 12 years in San Francisco has spoiled me forever, certainly compared to living in New York.

I am a senior financial manager with a strong background (Bank of America, Wells Fargo, Chase) in financial control and analysis, budgeting, forecasting, and data processing operations. I have strong management and administrative skills, have managed large groups of people, and have successfully turned around problem operations. I have an extensive knowledge of personal computers as well as database and spreadsheet applications.

I would very much appreciate the opportunity to meet with you for half an hour to introduce myself, discuss the current environment at Bankers Trust, and identify any areas of the bank which may, in the future, have a need for someone with my background and experience. I would also appreciate your ideas on other financial institutions in San Francisco that may offer future career opportunities.

I will be in the Bay area in early December (I still maintain my home in San Rafael) and will call you in advance to schedule a mutually convenient time. I appreciate your consideration and look forward to the possibility of meeting you.

Sincerely,

Direct-Mail Campaigns

Perfection of means and confusion of goals seem, in my opinion, to characterize our age.

ALBERT EINSTEIN

Does Direct Mail Work?

A technique "works" if it helps you get meetings in your target market. When you are mounting a full campaign, your goal is to have the organizations in your target market know about you as quickly as possible. You can supplement your networking by using search firms and answering ads, but you will still not have hit most of the organizations in your market. Regardless of how you get in, if you find you are being well received by some organizations in your target market, consider direct mail and/or targeted mail for the rest.

If you use direct mail, consider mounting campaigns to a number of targets. Out of four campaigns, for example, maybe two will be effective and result in meetings and two won't work at all. Part of it is selecting a target likely to be interested in you. Another part is being able to express yourself clearly and compellingly in writing. And a third part is a numbers game. If you get no response when you mail to a very small number, that mailing was not a good test.

Most job hunters expect every letter they write to result in a meeting, which is unreasonable. They don't expect every search-firm contact or every ad to result in a meeting. The same is true for direct contact.

CASE STUDY Diane
Getting More Job Possibilities in the Works

Last week, Diane accepted a job offer. She had uncovered two job possibilities through networking, but she wanted to have the requisite "6 to 10 things in the works." So she did an emailing of 250 letters, which resulted in four more job leads. Admittedly, that's a very small response rate from a mailing, but she wound up with four more job interviews than she would have had exclusively through networking.

Act As If This Company Is Important to You

One time I wrote a direct-mail letter to 200 companies. A manager at one company said to me, "How did you hear of us? No one ever writes to us." I said, "Oh, a number of people have mentioned your company." "Really. Who?" I said, "Pierre Charbonneau and Lillian Bisset-Farrell, to name two [making up the first two names that came to my mind]." The manager said, "I don't know them." "Well," I replied, "they've heard of you!"

If they take your letter personally, you cannot tell them you sent that same letter to 200 people.

For direct-mail campaigns using the Internet, see "Using Search Engines to Develop Your List" in the chapter, "Research: Developing Your List of Organizations to Contact."

Helen: Making It Sound Personal

Helen is an organizational-development person. She wrote a letter to 60 fellow members of the Organization Development Network, saying: "As a fellow member of the OD Network, I thought perhaps you might come across information to help me in my job search. I am interested in making a career move and I sure would appreciate hearing from you." Paragraph two was her summary. In paragraph three, she listed her accomplishments.

Paragraph four was very clever because she had no intention of calling these people, and she didn't want to make it sound like a mass mailing, so she said a variation of "I don't want to bother you with phone calls, but I trust you will give me a call if you come across information that would help me in my search."

She got six calls back about real job openings. She did another mailing to another 60 people in the same organization, got another six meetings, and eventually wound up with a job offer.

Which technique did she use? It was a direct-mail campaign.

If you have an association list, consider using it for a direct-mail campaign, and be sure to mention your membership in that association in your opening paragraph.

Results! Why, man, I have gotten a lot of results. I know several thousand things that won't work.

THOMAS A. EDISON

If you are not going to follow up your letter with a phone call, here's one way to end your letter (if this is appropriate in your situation):

"I don't want to bother you with a follow-up phone call. However, I am very interested in meeting with you. If you feel the same, I hope you will give me a call so we can set up a time to meet."

DOROTHY DOPPSTADT
2421 Maindays Boulevard
Columbus, Ohio 43700
231-555-1212
dd456@gmail.com

April 6, 201X

Name
Position
Company
Address
City, State, ZIP

Dear _____:

As a fellow member of the Organization Development Network, I am writing to explore with you potential opportunities in your organization.

Currently with Bell South as an internal corporate human resources consultant, I am seeking an opportunity in organization and management development. Perhaps it would facilitate this process if I share key highlights of my background:

- Management development specialist with more than **6 years of experience** developing and making presentations.
- At **Bell South**, I am responsible for designing and implementing projects to enhance the professionalism of more than 2,000 managers worldwide. This involves:
- — **Executive and high-potential development**—Assessing and identifying top performers to meet specific business talent needs, attend Executive University programs, and facilitate succession planning.
- — **Needs analysis**—Running focus groups throughout the United States and Europe for the purpose of creating and designing training programs.
- — **Organizational research**—Using statistical and research design (SPSSX) to conduct surveys, climate studies, and turnover studies.
- Experience in Asia as a process consultant to an American-based company. **Fluent in Japanese**.
- Hold **2 master's degrees from Columbia University** in organizational and counseling psychology.

What do you think? Are there any possibilities within your purview for someone with my skills and experience base? I realize you are busy and I don't want to be intrusive by phoning; however, if you are interested or would just like to discuss some ideas, please contact me at 231-555-1212. Attached is my résumé. I look forward to your input.

Thank you.

Sincerely,

Bruce: Before and after Direct-Mail Letters

Bruce Faulk (his real name) is a young actor who was working as a receptionist while waiting for his big break. Like most actors, he kept in touch with those who might advance his career. But like most job hunters, he left out the substance in his letters.

Because of The Five O'Clock Club approach, he became more methodical about everything he did in his search for his next acting job. Bruce's "after" letter is on the next page.

By the way, after appearing on Broadway as the youngest actor in *Hamlet*, Bruce toured the United States, and is currently touring Europe with *Hair*.

Bruce's letter proves that the approach works for anyone—regardless of their profession. At The Five O'Clock Club, we have worked with everyone from orchestra conductors to fine artists.

This just in from Bruce:

The "before" version of Bruce's direct-mail letter

Dear Martin Reed:

I am sending you my picture and résumé on the advice of Casey Childs, who has directed a number of *A Different World* episodes. I hope you will keep me in mind for any upcoming project for which I might be right. I will keep you apprised of my situation. Thank you.

Sincerely,

Bruce Faulk

Kate—

Europe is all I expected and more—so much so that I've extended my tour here a few more months. So far, most of the tour has been all over—and I do mean all over Germany; but there's still a lot of time for Zurich (where I am now), for the rest of Switzerland, for Austria, and a month and a half right outside Amsterdam. Next month, I'm off to Cannes, France, and a week in Sweden.

Not too shabby for a former receptionist?

Hope all is well with you. Please give everyone my love.

Always,
Bruce

BRUCE J. FAULK

286 North 50th Street—Apt. HL
New York, NY 10099
212-555-9809
bfaulk209@yahoo.com

March 18, 201X

Dear Mr. Reed:

Casey Childs, who has directed *A Different World*, suggested I contact you. He thought you and I might be able to work together.

I am a graduate of the High School of Performing Arts and Carnegie-Mellon University. I have performed repeatedly off-Broadway in New York. You may be interested in some of my specific experiences. For example:

- I am particularly proud of my work in The Island, a South African one-act by Athol Fugard. Many people said it was the best thing done that year at Carnegie. In fact, we were asked to repeat the show for Black History Month at the Pittsburgh Civic Center. (In addition, I was interviewed on TV as part of the show's promotion.) It was extremely well received and many people came up to me on the streets of Pittsburgh and said how much it meant to them; I have a video of the performance if you are interested in seeing it.

- Another example of my work is Broadway Cabaret. I played the part of the emcee, warming up the audience for about 10 minutes before opening the show and then singing and dancing throughout. We played to a packed house and a standing ovation every night of the run; it was the most popular show of the season and was extended. I was glad to develop a serious working relationship with the director/choreographer Billy Wilson.

I am a professional, I know how to put a part together and get a job done and I work very hard on whatever I take on. In addition, I am easy to work with and have a good sense of humor. I will keep you apprised of my situation so you may have a chance to see me in a piece. Casey thought you and I could work together. I hope we can.

Sincerely,

Bruce J. Faulk

Direct/Targeted Mailing Letters

If you have a target list of hundreds of organizations, divide them into separate markets. Tailor your letters to each target market, such as the "inorganic chemicals industry" in this example. Add the last line for those you plan to call directly, perhaps 20 out of every 100 mailed.

SYLVAN VON BERG

April 20, 201X

Name
President or CEO
Company
Address
City, State, Zip

Dear _____:

(In many companies) OR (In the inorganic chemicals industry), the use of **technology has not kept pace with the expansion of markets** and the need for more sophisticated information to service those sales opportunities. The need for logical, manageable information and its dissemination is paramount in today's world. I can help you with solutions to those issues.

I am a **senior information systems executive** with experience in **managing the information** needs for companies ranging from $250 million to more than $1 billion in annual sales. As a key member of the management team I can direct the implementation of technology to achieve the profit objectives of your organization. My experience has been both domestic and international and I have a unique ability to control major development projects to successful conclusions.

Here are some specific examples of my accomplishments:
- Developed a composite information database. Resulted in **higher market share** and greater penetration into existing market segments.
- Saved $1 million annually on a $5 million data-processing budget.
- Consolidated the technologies and systems of more than $1 billion in acquisitions, avoiding problems frequently associated with multiple acquisitions.

I am a strong hands-on strategic planner and leader and I would welcome the opportunity to discuss how my skills and experience could contribute to your company's objectives. I will call you in a few days to set up a mutually convenient time for us to meet.

Sincerely,
Sylvan Von Berg

Enclosure

> Tina sent this letter to 200 banks. It resulted in 8 job interviews and 2 offers.

TINA DAVIS
2 Bigelow Lane
Nashville, Tennessee 37333
(555) 555-2231 (day)
TinaDavis2231@aol.com

May 10, 201X

Name
President
Bank Name
Address
City, State, Zip

Dear _____:

Many companies' banking relationships are being disrupted because of new controls and regulations and the impact of mergers and acquisitions. In addition, frequent changes in account officers and terms of service are causing a loss of understanding between bank and customer.

Smooth-running banking relationships can make all the difference in the effective conduct of business. How can you, as President of XXX Bank, stay abreast of what is happening and even benefit from current developments?

I can help you with these issues. I offer 20 years' experience in banking, most recently as vice president with Mellon Bank's International Department. Furthermore, few have my connections in and knowledge of the industry.

Here are two specific areas where my experience could benefit you:

Banking Relationships: I know my way around the industry and know what a bank should be able to do for its customers. My experience would enable you to maximize the services available from your bank and enhance the degree of comfort the banks feel toward you, their customer.

Assessment of Credit Risk: Much of my career has been spent in the area of credit assessment and my broad experience could help you avoid many of the pitfalls inherent in doing business. I have the maturity and sophistication to be able to deal with a wide variety of personalities and problems and the persistence to see things through to a satisfactory conclusion.

I would welcome the opportunity to discuss with you how my skills and background could contribute to your company's goals.

Yours sincerely,

Tina Davis

Direct-Mail Campaign including Out-of-Town Search

Sent to 60 presidents of small/medium-sized advertising agencies or the appropriate people in large agencies. Resulted in 5 exploratory meetings that led to additional meetings and 3 job offers.

M. CATHERINE WENDLETON
410 Main Street Lancaster, PA
(555) 555-2231

May 10, 1983

Dear _____:

Many agencies are coping with these difficult times by hiring the best creative and sales people available. While this may maintain a competitive edge, many agencies find their bottom line is slipping. The usual response is to send in the accountants.

These agencies, and perhaps some of your own subsidiaries, need more than accounting help. As vice president of operations for a $10 million advertising agency, I directed the turnaround of a company that was in serious financial difficulty. As a result, 1982 was the most profitable year in company history and 1983 promises to be better yet.

This experience has taught me what can cause an agency to get into trouble. I know the danger signs and I can teach a company how to run itself with true efficiency and economy—not just with heavy-handed frugality. I have a record of success in making an agency run more smoothly and profitably. My accomplishments include:

- Trouble-shoot in all areas of agency operations (except Creative output).
- Improved employee productivity by 30%. Reduced the number of unprofitable accounts by 83%.
- Set up a management information system that gets to the core of the problems and encourages managers to act. Cleaned up a flawed computer system.
- Dramatically reduced the number of crisis situations in Creative and the number of over-budget situations.
- Instituted a comprehensive salary and performance review system. Developed hiring procedures to reduce turnover.
- As Chairman of the Executive Committee, instituted tight budgetary controls, improved responsibility accounting, and account margin and cost controls.

I have an M.B.A. as well as 12 years of progressive management responsibility in finance and strategic planning, data processing, personnel, and advertising and marketing.

As a result of many years' travel to New York, I would prefer to live and work in the New York area. In fact, I'm in New York frequently.

Hiring me would be an investment in the $xx,xxx range, but the return will be impressive. I would be pleased to meet with you to discuss the contribution I could make to the performance of your organization.

Yours truly,
Kate Wendleton

Direct-Mail Campaign From a Senior Executive

Nick sent this letter to 200 companies, in addition to his targeted mailings. Furthermore, he kept in close contact with search firms and key individuals he had met through the years.

NICHOLAS GAREFALOS
654 Kingston Road, Tampa, FL 99900
(555) 555-4431 nickg@bway.net

May 21, 201X

Mr. James Swann
Teleodymetric Corporation
460 Herndon Parkway
Battlesboro, MD 55170

Dear Mr. Swann:

Building market value is my expertise. Whether challenged to launch a start-up technology venture, orchestrate an aggressive business turnaround, or accelerate growth within a top-performing organization, I have consistently delivered strong and sustainable financial results:

- As Vice President & General Manager with full P&L responsibility for a new IBM business unit, achieved/surpassed all turnaround objectives and restored the organization to profitability with a 55% gain in gross market contribution.

- As General Manager of Paychex Information Consulting Services, orchestrated the start-up of a new strategic business unit and closed new contracts in product, technology, and service sales within an intensely competitive national market.

- As Vice President of Electronic Delivery Systems Development for JP Morgan Chase, led a team of 125 professionals in the development, market launch, and commercialization of advanced electronic and telecommunications technologies.

- Early management achievements include a series of increasingly responsible positions with revenue responsibility for up to $100 million in annual sales from markets throughout Europe, Africa, and the Middle East.

The strength of my performance lies in my ability to define corporate vision and strategy, translate into action, and deliver profitable results. Beginning my career with several major consumer products companies, I was able to transition the marketing, sales, leadership, and general management skills I developed into my more recent positions in emerging information, telecommunications, networking, interactive multimedia, and new media industries.

Currently, I am confidentially pursuing new executive opportunities either in the technology and/or services industries. Aware of the quality of your organization and your commitment to long-term, profitable growth, I would be delighted to have a chance to pursue such opportunities. I look forward to what I anticipate will be the first of many positive communications. Thank you.

Sincerely,

Nick Garefalos

Enclosure

Direct-Mail Campaign

This same letter could be used to contact search firms. Just change the next-to-the-last sentence to read: "If you have a search requiring these skills, I would like very much to get together."

MARJORIE HENDRICKSON
Mhendrickson88@netscape.com

February 2, 201x

Name
Title
Company
Address
City, State, Zip

Dear _____:

I am a seasoned financial services marketer with **10 years at Asarco Financial** and heavy package-goods experience at Lever Brothers, Johnson & Johnson, and Procter & Gamble.

My experience is in **developing and marketing financial products and services**, including electronic banking products, investment packages, and basic banking services to both consumer and corporate markets. I also have a strong track record in **building effective sales teams and turning around troubled businesses**. I am currently exploring opportunities to build a financial services business or to inject new life into an existing one.

A résumé is enclosed for additional background. If you would like to discuss the possibilities, I would like very much to get together.

I look forward to hearing from you.

Sincerely,

Marjorie Hendrickson

Enclosure

How to Answer Ads

Of all sad words
Of tongue and pen
The saddest are these:
"It Might Have Been."

Let's add this thought
unto this verse:
"It Might Have Been
A Good Deal Worse."

ANONYMOUS

Some people get excited when they see an ad anywhere — in the paper, or job boards, or elsewhere on the Internet. They *know* this is the job for them and their hopes soar.

But try to keep things in perspective. Don't be surprised if you answer 30, 50, 100 or more ads and *get no meetings*. Your résumé is one of perhaps hundreds or even thousands of responses. Major organizations get over a million résumés a year. What's more, your résumé is not being screened by the hiring manager.

Chances are, your cover letter and résumé will be screened by a computer or by a junior clerk. I once met a 20-year-old woman who reviewed résumés on behalf of blue-chip companies, screening thousands of professionals and managers in the $40,000 to $100,000 range. She decided who would get interviewed. This young woman was good at her job and often took a personal interest in the people whose résumés she saw—but she was only 20 years old. Writing a cover letter to intrigue or strike a responsive chord in her wouldn't have worked.

While writing creative cover letters will work for targeted- and direct-mail campaigns, stick to the basics in answering ads. If the ad asks for specific qualifications and experience, highlight those areas from your background. Respond point-by-point to each item mentioned. Show how you have everything they want. Keep your cover letter crystal clear. Remember, the reader of your letter may be 20 years old. If you don't fit exactly, you will probably be screened out.

Fewer than 10 percent of all jobs are found through ads, including both print and online ads. At The Five O'Clock Club, we say you should *consider all four techniques* for getting meetings in your target market—search firms, ads, networking, and direct contact—and then *notice* which techniques are working for you. "Working for you" means that a technique results in *meetings*. You don't measure the effectiveness of a technique by whether or not you got a *job*. You measure the effectiveness of a technique by whether or not it's resulting in *meetings* for you.

If an average ad in *The Wall Street Journal* or *The New York Times* gets a 1,000 responses, you have 999 competitors. Websites for large corporations can get one million résumés a year. Many people sit at their computers for hours on end, hitting that "send" button and wondering why no one is responding to them. Everyone else is doing the same thing. We frequently hear hiring managers say they don't even consider this accumulating database of résumés. It's a rare job hunter who even includes a cover letter in response to an Internet ad. Yet, the cover letter is the piece that can most significantly increase the chances you'll be called in.

"Actually, we're not hiring. We hold lots of interviews like this one, so our competition thinks we're busy."

The Cover Letter for Answering Ads

It's unlikely the hiring manager will be the one who does the screening. Instead, some junior-level person (or a computer) reviews the hundreds or thousands of responses. You can be sure the person wants to get through those résumés as quickly as possible. Their job is to get rid of all but 10 or 20 of them! So make it easy for them to screen you in. All you want is to be in the "*include*" pile.

You must **_personalize_ the cover letter when answering an ad**. Sometimes when we're looking for people to work in The Five O'Clock Club office, we may post jobs on the Internet and we are deluged with responses. Often we can't tell which job the person is applying for: an accounting job or a public relations job. People just unthinkingly hit the send button without a thoughtful cover letter.

So even when you respond to an Internet ad, be sure to use The Five O'Clock Club's four-paragraph approach. Make your cover letter very clear, very short, very readable. Show a strong match between you and the position they've posted. Then the résumé screener will at least know which pile to place you in. Here's our formula for the cover letter:

In paragraph one, be sure to mention the *position* for which you are applying, as well as the newspaper or Internet site where you saw the ad, and the date of the ad.

Paragraph two contains your summary about you as it *relates to this position*. Such as, "I have 10 years of international marketing experience in the chemical and pharmaceutical industries."

For paragraph three, if you *think* you're qualified for the job, use The Five O'Clock Club's two-column approach when mailing or emailing in the response. Your response will definitely stand out compared with all the other responses.

The first column says "You are looking for…" or "Your requirements," under which you list everything they've mentioned in the ad. In column two, you say "I have this to offer" or "My experience," and match up what you have to offer to what they're looking for. Of course, make sure what you have to offer seems better than what they're looking for.

List your points in the order in which they're listed in the ad. Most hiring managers will list first in an ad the requirements that are most important to them. So you want to list first those things that are most important to the hiring team. That way, the junior-level person who is screening all of these cover letters (even the ones the computer selected) will have an easier time including you rather than *excluding* you.

Use *their* terminology not yours. When answering an ad, make sure you use their terminology and not the terminology from your last position. If they say they're looking for a *trainer* and you've been a *teacher*, then just say you've had 12 years of *training* experience. Don't use a word that's inappropriate for their industry or their firm.

Use The Five O'Clock Club's two-column approach if you think you're a good match for the job. On the other hand, if you feel you're *not* a strong match and still want to answer the ad, don't use the two-column approach, which would highlight the fact that you're not a strong match. Instead, clearly state what you have to offer and say you think you're an ideal candidate and why.

In paragraph four, list any additional information about yourself that you think would be of interest to the hiring company.

Finally, as far as salary in concerned, *say nothing*. Many ads include the words, "Please tell us your salary requirements," yet savvy job hunters decline to mention salary because it increases the chances they'll be *excluded*.

What are the chances you're going to match whatever salary they have in mind? You'll name a number that's too high for them, too low—but rarely just right. The odds are against you. So it's a disadvantage for you to list your salary.

Therefore, job hunters generally say, "I'd be glad to discuss salary requirements upon mutual interest. I look forward to meeting with you to further discuss the position." That way, you're not ignoring their request for salary information.

Sometimes you'll see an ad stating, "You will absolutely not be considered for this job unless you provide your salary history." Those ads are usually placed by academic institutions or by the government. If an ad says you *must* name your salary history, the best approach is to provide *limited information*; don't disclose your *entire* salary history, because you reduce your chance of being called in *and* you reduce your chance of negotiating an appropriate salary. However, you can mention a broad range of what you're looking for. Be sure to think strategically. Research the industry you're targeting and its standard procedures and play it accordingly. No matter what the industry, don't disclose too much about yourself before you even get an interview.

By the way, these are the issues and details you should discuss with your small group. That's why we *have* a small group. You may face unusual situations, so be sure to use your group for guidance.

Surround the Hiring Manager

An ad for a job is as good as a flashing neon sign: The company is telling the world it has an opening! Your strategic thinking should go into high gear—if it's a company or a job that *really* interests you. Don't wait to get in by just responding to the ad. Network into the company or contact someone there directly, but not the person mentioned in the ad. "Surrounding the hiring manager" is a very effective technique. Get in to see someone—almost *anyone* other than the hiring manager. An insider can become an advocate for you and refer you in to the hiring manager. You'll have a better chance of standing out from your competitors—because you were referred in and will know more—and you'll do better in the meeting. You're no longer one more grubby job hunter who is simply responding to an ad— you're now someone who is sincerely interested in this company and knows how to go the extra mile. The hiring manager will get to know you in a different way from the other applicants and he or she may consider you even though you don't have all of the qualifications they listed. For more information on this technique, see the chapter "What to Do When You Know There's a Job Opening."

Bottom line: **If it's a good ad for you, answer the ad, then forget about the ad and try to get in some other way—without mentioning the ad.**

> If you meet all the requirements of the job, then make it very clear to the screener that you should *not* be screened out. Be sure to read "What to Do When You Know There's a Job Opening" in this book.

AUBREY OKPAKU
38 Cicily Place
West Hamstart, MO 59684
okpakua@worldwidenet.com

March 23, 201X

Mr. Richard Bayer
Employment Manager
National Data Labs
22 Parns Avenue
East Hamstart, MO 59684

Dear Mr. Bayer:

I believe I am a good fit for the Assistant Controller position advertised in the *Hamstart Times* on March 20, 201x.

Having been continually challenged and rapidly promoted at Toronto Dominion Bank, I have a proven track record in controllership functions. I've headed the controllership function in every major area of the company, including credit cards, travelers checks, and private banking. As you may be aware, Toronto Dominion has a rigorous budgeting, financial analysis, and cost-accounting process, similar to National Data Labs, and this has contributed to the success of the organization.
Here is a breakdown of my experience vs. your requirements:

Your Requirements

- 12+ years experience in private accounting/ management
- BBA, MBA a plus.
- Financial analysis/cost-accounting skills

My Experience

- 14+ years experience in financial management
- BBA in finance MBA in financial management
- Strong financial analysis skills—controller ship functions
- Strong cost-accounting skills—designed cost-accounting/unit-cost methodologies

I consider myself a sophisticated management professional with a significant number of business accomplishments, coupled with excellent ability to communicate both orally and in writing.
I would welcome an interview with you to review my experience in financial management.

Sincerely,

Aubrey Okpaku

Blind Ads

If you are considering a blind ad, be careful. Blind ads don't include the name of the organization seeking to hire someone. It could be placed by a search firm or by the company itself with just a box number. You don't know to whom you're sending your résumé. Be *especially* careful if you're currently employed. That ad could have been placed by your employer or by a search firm who works with your employer. Employed job hunters often respond with just a letter and no résumé. Their letter states why they're a match, but they don't mention their present place of employment. But even this can be risky. If you're employed, you may want to skip those blind ads.

If They Call You

If you do answer an ad, be prepared for a phone call, just in case. Someone may actually respond to your letter! So make sure your message machine doesn't have something silly on it, such as all three of your children saying, "Hi, this is Janet and this is Jim and this is Karen and we all live here." Your message should be professional or you may turn off prospective employers with a silly message or strange music. They may simply hang up and you won't even know they called. Job hunters need to be hypersensitive about *impressions*—and this includes the outgoing message on your answering machine.

If you *do* get a phone call, the first thing you may be asked is your salary range. And that's the *last* thing you want to talk about. So make sure you're ready to handle that. Read our book, *Mastering the Job Interview and Winning the Money Game*. You might say, "I think it's a little early to discuss salary. I'm sure salary is *not* going to be a problem." You want a *meeting*—in person—and you want to be prepared. It's certainly too early to discuss salary.

Remember, however: Most job seekers who respond to ads will never get a call. So don't expect to hear back and get on with your search.

Don't spend too much time trying to figure out how ads work. Figure out how *else* to get in.

Rejection Letters

If you get a rejection letter when you've answered an ad (which rarely happens these days), try not to give it a second thought. That letter is not personal. They don't even know you. They're just sending letters out routinely. So ignore the letter, but don't necessarily ignore the company! One Five O'Clock Club coach has on his office wall three framed rejection letters from the same company, which eventually hired him! He put these on public display so his clients could see that rejection letters *don't count*.

If there's a name on the rejection letter, you may want to respond to the letter—especially if you're interested in the company. Remember the person who "rejected" you may be the junior-level person who's going through all those résumés. So you may want to write to the *manager* saying you're disappointed and think you're a great match for the company—if not now, maybe in the future. Be sure to enclose your résumé: Remember that this person may never have even seen your résumé! We say at The Five O'Clock Club, "The ball is always in your court"—so a rejection letter may *still* be an opportunity!

Where to Find Ads

Where can you find ads? On company websites, in your local paper, in the national papers, in association journals having to do with your field or industry. If you have very well-defined targets, association journals, association websites, and other websites having to do with your field or industry can be a terrific place for ads.

> **If the ad gives a fax number, use the fax number to respond. But *also* respond through snail mail—and perhaps email— if possible. You never know which method may get their attention.**

Refining Your Response

Of course, ads point you toward current openings. But remember that ads—whether Internet or print—are great for *research*. Ads tell you who's hiring, what they're looking for, and the jargon they use. You may be able to spot trends by tracking the ads week after week. You can modify the approach to your entire search based on what you find out through this research. And ads give you the names of additional companies to target. Then you can try to get in to see people by contacting them directly or through networking.

Being Effective with Internet Postings

José was a Five O'Clock Clubber who had an e-commerce background. He'd been searching for *four* months before he came to the club, but with slim results—not even one interview. When the small group looked at José's résumé, they couldn't even *see* his e-commerce background. He was positioned incorrectly. So José's small group suggested changes for the top of his résumé. Instead of saying, "international marketing executive," the group suggested that he change it to say, "E-commerce executive with strong marketing background." They suggested he follow *that* headline with bulleted accomplishments related to his e-commerce background, followed by his international background.

José was comfortable with posting his résumé on the web because he was not employed at this time. He got a tremendous number of responses. However, most of them were inappropriate because the person (or machine) saw the words "E-commerce executive" and saw him as a technology person. So his small group suggested he refine his résumé one more time. They suggested he change it to "E-commerce *marketing* executive." *Now* José got called in just for e-commerce *marketing* positions.

José was with The Five O'Clock Club only six weeks. He got four offers. He accepted a job with a terrific firm and his group suggested he not close off conversations with the other companies until he had been in the new firm for about two weeks—just to try it out. But it was the repositioning that made the Internet work for him.

On the Internet, sometimes *people* are not looking at your résumé. *Computers* are looking at it. So the words you use, and *where* you use them are very important. Because José did not have the word "marketing" in the *first* line of his résumé, but had it in the *second* line, the results he got from the machine were completely different. So you owe it to yourself to think things through: The words on *your* résumé must be carefully chosen.

When you answer Internet ads or post your résumé on an organization's website, don't use esoteric words that were used only in your last firm. Use words that would be *generally* used, and especially use the words they use in the ad. If you're *employed, never post* your résumé on the Internet. Respond to ads posted by specific identified organizations. After all, you wouldn't post your résumé on the bulletin board in your local grocery store, would you? You don't want to put your résumé out there for *anybody* to see. Treat your résumé as a confidential document.

For an electronic résumé, put key words at the top. Depending on the software the hiring organization is using, you may need to repeat certain words. For example, certain software packages will rate a résumé higher if it has the word JAVA in it 13 times as opposed to one or two times. Ironically, somebody who may be more qualified but have the word JAVA in the résumé only once may be disqualified. So you might have to be very aware of these things until the software is upgraded. Pay attention to what is working in the market. However, the market is continually changing and you have to keep In mind that very few job hunters find jobs this way. Instead, when you see an ad, get in to see someone at that company some other way, such as through networking or direct contact.

Other chapters in this book cover more about writing an electronic résumé and using the Internet as a job-search tool. And don't forget the bibliography at the back of this book, and a more extensive one in the Members Only section of our website.

SHANA L. KINGSLEY

883 Ledger Lane, Minneapolis, MN 88888
(555) 555-2268 skingsley@msn.com
July 19, 201X

Mr. Theobold J. Yegerlehner
Vice President, Tax
United Telecom Corporation
United Telecom Building
Minneapolis, MN 88801

Dr. Mr. Yegerlehner,

Could United Telecom benefit from a hands-on tax director and counsel with international expertise and the ability to drive strategic initiatives?

I have designed and implemented tax strategies for businesses in the United States and more than 35 other countries.

I know how to work with operations, finance, and legal people to deliver tailored solutions that get results. I have managed cross-functional teams in North America, Europe, Latin America, and the Asia-Pacific region in complex projects, including:

- Executing a **$4 billion U.S. recapitalization**.
- Refinancing global operations to **extract cash from overseas** without crippling operations or paying significant taxes.
- Implementing a global trading company to streamline production, increase sales, and **reduce the global effective tax rate by 50%.**
- Reconfiguring a global sales organization to isolate and manage an estimated **$100 million foreign tax exposure.**

I am very interested in meeting with you. I believe you will find even a brief meeting beneficial. I will call your office in the next few days to see when I can get on your calendar.

Sincerely,

Although hers is a narrow field, when Shana wrote to 20 executives who had no advertised positions; 6 of them contacted *her* immediately for an exploratory meeting.

Getting Meetings From Job Fairs

by Paul Cecala, Certified Five O'Clock Club Career Coach

Will you find your next job at a job fair? It's a long shot—because your competitors are there by the hundreds. But these events can give your search a boost nonetheless. For example, you can learn more about the companies represented, which may (or may not) be hiring people with your expertise. You can gauge the status of the job market in your field, glean information about needed skills and experience, and identify the companies and industries that are growing. Job fairs are also a way to meet employees of targeted companies who might be able to introduce you to hiring managers.

The employer's goal is to meet as many people as possible who may be potential new hires. Company representatives expect to spend only one to two minutes speaking with each person he or she meets, so you should not go expecting to have long detailed conversations. This limited time means every moment and every word is precious to both parties. It is the job seeker's responsibility to make the first impression positive and productive.

But many job seekers do not understand how to make the best use of the limited time they spend with employer's representatives at job fairs.

Here are some tips to make your job fair experience as productive as possible:

1. **Dress for success**: wear the interview suit! Make the best possible impression. It is always amazing to me that people show up in jeans or shorts, rather than business attire.

2. **No eating or drinking** (other than water) while mixing and mingling. Juggling food and coffee while standing and holding a portfolio, wearing your business suit, is a scenario for disaster—and then there's the matter of bad breath or food in your teeth. Would you eat or drink during an interview?

3. **Research the attending companies**. If you can demonstrate knowledge of these companies while chatting with their representative, your chances of being remembered increase dramatically. Your research will also show if the organizations are likely to have positions appropriate for you.

4. **Be a consultant!** The Five O'Clock Club recommends approaching an employer in the same way a consultant does: try to identify their problems and explain how your skills and accomplishments may be appropriate. This automatically makes you more desirable than other candidates who are there "looking for a job." It's all about what you can do for them, not what they can do for you.

5. **Be concise and to the point**. Don't waste anyone's time. Have your Two-Minute Pitch rehearsed and ready. It will get critical information about you to the employer quickly, so that you both can assess the best next steps.

6. **Collect business cards!** Don't leave company representatives without information for following up. They meet hundreds of people and gather many résumés in a day. You will stand out from the pack if you contact them later in the week.

7. **Give out your business card**. Even if you're unemployed, you should prepare your own cards. You have handed out your résumé, but your card is another tool to help people connect with you later.

8. **Be courteous and polite to everyone**. You never know who may be your next boss, even the person standing in line behind you! Anyone you meet may become part of your network. The companies you are not interested in may be able to lead you to contacts in the companies that are on your target list.

9. **Bring at least one résumé for every company attending** and an extra 10 percent, just in case.

10. **Follow up with everyone you meet within 48 hours**. Let companies know you are interested. They need to hear from you, so send an influencing email or letter. Call to arrange a meeting or next contact. Keep the conversations going.

It is important to remain realistic about job fairs. The positions promoted at these events may be entry-level, sales or call-center related, and other high-turnover jobs. While these positions may not be of interest to you, the companies attending are, so it is still worth your time to work the fairs. You might run into people who can introduce you to the hiring managers in key departments. And you might be able to arrange for informational meetings in the weeks that follow the fair.

Take full advantage of these events to start, and then build, relationships. In the give-and-take of networking, the job seekers who find ways to be helpful and **give first** in the relationship do far better in creating lasting, productive connections. As the Five O'Clock Club says, "it's all about getting meetings with the right person at the right level in the right companies." If you take the right approach at job fairs (these Ten Tips!) you'll move forward in attaining this goal.

Discovering Spot Opportunities
to Advance Your Career

by Peter Hill, CMRW, Certified Five O'Clock Club Coach, Hawaii and Far East

In the contemporary realities of the 21st Century it pays to engage in non-traditional approaches to your career design or job search. One such approach is the practice of finding and taking advantage of "spot opportunities." Persistently capitalizing on spot opportunities can be an amazingly powerful interview-generating technique.

One consulting firm describes a spot opportunity as "any news event that indicates movement within a company." In other words, change is occurring. Spot opportunities make themselves known whenever something has transpired, will transpire, or might transpire within your chosen industry or field of interest. As a job seeker, you are challenged to discover or create employment opportunities by capitalizing on information of these events that are reported in the press or learned from other sources.

You will have to do a bit of legwork —some resourceful investigation—to pinpoint and make the most of spot opportunities, but you are likely to be rewarded handsomely for your efforts. Spot opportunities can benefit you in the following ways:

- You will have control over "being in the right place at the right time."
- You will be able to capitalize on the opportunity to address the pressing needs of an organization. By tailoring your letter to the firm's situation, you'll be viewed as genuinely interested in the target company.
- By steering clear of the competition, you

will amplify your marketability. Before your competition knows that a firm or industry is hiring, you will attract attention and create interviews.
- You can inherently avoid human resource departments. With most spot opportunities you will contact the hiring authority directly.
- You will be recognized as being creative and perceptive.

Like an effective résumé, correct use of spot opportunities can position you above other candidates—even those who may be more qualified than you. Your display of imagination, resourcefulness, and foresight can have a highly positive effect on employers.

There are scores of types of spot opportunities. Here are several examples:

- **News that a company will go public**. Part of the large influx of cash from the offering will likely go towards hiring talented personnel.
- **News of major financing**. This is a signal that the firm is planning major business initiatives or is struggling financially. Some of the new funds will, in many cases, be earmarked for recruiting additional employees.
- **News of construction or expansion of office space**. This real estate is costly and companies will work hard to populate it with additional personnel.

- **News that a company has just announced record profits**. Profitable firms are likely to be hiring.

Your window of opportunity is as much as six to eight months after fresh news that suggests that a company may be expanding its workforce. "Qualified employees who present themselves well are difficult to attract and retain," says Randy Stevens, President and CEO of R. L. Stevens. "Once the company has completed the initial hiring frenzy, they will discover that many of the new employees are simply 'not working out' or have moved on. This is yet another opportunity for the astute job seeker to contact the decision-maker and show value."

Spot opportunities are easy to find. They are within arm's reach on a daily basis. You'll discover them in national newspapers, such as the *Wall Street Journal* and *USA Today*. You'll find them in your local newspapers and business journals. They are everywhere in general news and business magazines like *Business Week, Time*, and *U.S. News & World Report*.

If you are focusing on a particular field, comb industry trade journals for spot opportunities. Journals, newsletters, and trade catalogs published by professional associations regularly contain valuable insights on industry trends. Membership directories will list names of key individuals. *The Encyclopedia of Associations* can provide you with all you need to know about professional associations relevant to your field.

Television and radio news, commentaries, and talk shows will tip you off on new business developments. And don't forget those commercials, which educate you on new products (and potential spot opportunities).

Finally, there is a saying that "90% of success is just showing up." Be present at networking events, seminars, trade shows, and conventions. Attendance at these affairs should be a natural part of your career development anyway. So "show up" and absorb as much first-hand information about products, industries, and key individuals as humanly possible.

Remember that spot opportunities uncover themselves with news of change within a company or industry. All change represents an opportunity, and you can help a company manage change.

There are fundamental differences between training and education. If you are trained you become the employee, if you are educated, you become the employer. If you are trained you have a J.O.B. (if you're "lucky"), if you are educated you have a career. If you are trained you have been taught to memorize, if you are educated you have been taught how to think.

JAWANZA KUNJUFU,
Countering the Conspiracyto Destroy Black Boys

It isn't possible to win high-level success without meeting opposition, hardship, and setback. But it is possible to use setback to propel you forward.

DR. DAVID SCHWARTZ, *The Magic of Thinking Big*

The
Five
O'Clock
Club®

Electronic Résumés, Online Company Applications, Answering Ads Online, and Having Your Own Website

For this chapter, we asked a group of Five O'Clock Club coaches to give us their opinions on this topic, and included coaches who have their own search firms, coaching businesses, or work in human resources. Their comments should give you a rounded perspective on the use of electronic résumés in your job search. The coaches are: Anita Attridge, Bill Belknap, Chip Conlin, Celia Currin, Rob Hellmann, Peter Hill, Laura Labovich, Mark Moyer, Bernadette Norz, and Damona Sain.

Perhaps you've heard the story about the Philadelphia-area human-resources executive who applied anonymously for a job in his own company as an experiment. He didn't make it through the screening process. Employers are starting to use ridiculous computer programs that screen applicants—and very few applicants can get through.

So what do job hunters do in response to this new software? They spend endless hours trying to get *around* those systems hoping their résumé can be selected. Give it up! Job hunters' time would be better spent trying to figure out the name of the person to contact and then contacting them directly. Contact *anyone* in that organization and get in to see them. We call it "surrounding the hiring manager." See our write-up on that topic in the chapter, "How to Answer Ads" just a few pages back.

If you are getting lots of meetings this way,

continue on that same path. But if you are not getting meetings, please change what you are doing.

Insanity: doing the same thing over and over again and expecting different results.

ALBERT EINSTEIN

Ten years ago, the prediction was that computer-scanned résumés would be the driving force in the selection process of the future. The career press talked of nothing else. As of this writing, however, electronic résumés have had little impact on the job searches of Five O'Clock Clubbers. Let's put electronic résumés in perspective. In this book, you will read that there are four basic ways to get interviews in your target market: through search firms, ads, networking, and direct contact. Five O'Clock Clubbers learn to consider all four techniques for getting interviews and then to assess which approach produces the most meetings for them. You should consider using search firms and ads in your job-search mix. In your particular field, they may be an important source of meetings. However, these approaches are passive: you have little control over the process. The search firm or the company that placed the ad must call you in. The use of electronic résumés is also a passive approach to job search. You must wait for someone to call you in.

On the other hand, networking and directly contacting companies are proactive approaches: you decide whom to contact and you contact them. While we encourage job hunters to consider every technique for getting interviews in their target markets, we want them to measure which techniques result in meetings with hiring managers. Those are the techniques you should use more. If electronic résumés result in meetings for you, then use them.

What is an electronic résumé?

In this chapter, we are no longer talking only about the résumés that get scanned into a company's database. Here we will cover everything from the way you attach your résumé to an email to the way you upload your résumé in company websites.

> **In spite of an online application, you are more likely to get the interview because of your résumé and your initiative in contacting the hiring manager.**

Courtesy of Jerry King, Cartoons, Inc.

"Sorry, Ralph, but I'm replacing you with Johnson here. I got him off eBay."

Making Your Résumé Scannable

Every time an online application asks you to cut and paste your résumé, a scannable version of your résumé is required. The guidelines that follow will help you to create a powerful scannable résumé.

If you have been using The Five O'Clock Club approach to developing your résumé, you are almost there. First of all, you have gotten rid of company jargon so the outside world can understand what you have done. You have also changed your job titles to reflect what you actually did, rather than using company-dictated titles that may not be as accurate. And you have made your résumé accomplishment- oriented (a good approach no matter what kind of résumé you have).

Electronic résumés are scanned into a database. They do not need to look pretty. In fact, you cannot have any hard tabs, underlining, bolding, bullets (use "*" or dashes instead of bullets), or other characters that may confuse the scanner: just use plain, straight text. In Word, save the résumé as plain text format, then edit it that way.

In addition to having a plain text format, your résumé must contain keywords that the hiring manager is most likely to search for regarding the kind of work you want to do. Therefore, at the top of your résumé, where you may have put Operations Manager, for example, add a string of words that would also be appropriate for you, such as:

operations manager, administrative manager, accounting manager, general manager, strategic planner, inventory control manager, materials manager, customer service manager, management consultant.

Important nouns should be included and repeated in various contexts. One recruiter whom we consulted uses only 34 keyword sorts; most use far more. She advises that an analysis of the ad will let the astute applicant know what the important keywords are for the résumé.

If you have prepared your résumé The Five O'Clock Club way, the body of your résumé should be fine. Again, choose words they are likely to look for. If you are adept at computers, list the hardware and software you know. Only list software that is generally available, not the company-specific systems you may have used. For example, you may list IBM, MAC, Lotus 123, or WordPerfect. But don't list ACS, your company's

Accounting Control System. That's a name that would not be recognized in the outside world.

The rest of your résumé would be the same as what you have already prepared, but without any highlighting.

But remember that only 3 to 6 percent of all jobs are found through recruiters, so please don't go crazy. One coach noted that all these bells and whistles don't mean that recruiters are more successful in getting the right person into the right job. In fact, they may be less successful because they are not figuring out the human element from the onset and are missing out on terrific candidates.

Some companies have equipment that scan thousands of résumés. A large company may get a million résumés a year! Theoretically, when someone in that company wants to hire a new employee, the manager asks to see only those résumés that fit the experience he or she is looking for. In real life, Five O'Clock Clubbers are getting jobs with companies that happen to use scanning equipment, but they are not getting many interviews through this technology. Instead, Five O'Clock Clubbers are getting in to see the hiring managers through networking, direct contact, search firms, or even answering ads. When you contact a company through its résumé-scanning technology, it is usually a dead end. If a company asks for a scannable résumé, provide one, but be proactive: find some other way in. That's what Five O'Clock Clubbers do. The interview is most likely to come from the "other way," not from an uploaded résumé.

> **Use the one-two punch: apply online, then contact the hiring manager or someone who works closely with that person. That's the Five O'Clock Club way.**

Online Company Applications

Companies commonly ask you to fill out an online application. However, as one coach warned, "Company applications are unforgiving. One online application disallowed any words in the 'salary required' box. So, my client could not write 'negotiable.' Of course, she researched her market value in her area and figured out a range. Then it wouldn't take a range, and only a 5-digit number!"

Another coach suggests that you avoid the questions involving references or income. If the application requires an income figure to proceed, try to select $1 or $100, etc. We're teaching you to play the odds here: you are more likely to be screened out when you state your actual salary than if you provide no salary number. On the application, keep referring back to your résumé so you don't need to be repetitive on the application. Leave references blank or "available upon strong mutual interest" (which is the Five O'Clock Club approach to references). The application is often a bureaucratic formality. You are more likely to get the interview because of your résumé and your initiative in contacting the hiring manager.

Another coach, who also works as a Human Resources executive, gave this example:

This whole trend toward electronic résumés and online applications reminds me of a few years ago when we first did a beta test on our new online application system at the company where I work. I pretended to be applying for an administrative assistant position and for each of the questions regarding my background experience and qualifications I doubled or tripled those required.

For example, when asked if I had a minimum two years college, I replied I had a graduate degree, and asked if I had a minimum five years related work experience, I replied I had 20 plus years.

However, one question asked in a multiple-choice fashion what would be the correct steps in sending out a merged mailing. Now, although I'm pretty good with computers, I had never performed a merged mailing, so I basically guessed at the answer.

Well, I guessed wrong on that one question and never made the first cut of having my application move forward for further review. The moral of the story is that no matter how qualified a person may be, and even if that person is the best possible fit for a job, answering applications online is all about acing the application, not the job.

A much more successful approach is what I call the one-two punch: a job hunter goes through the online application process because most companies will not even consider a person's candidacy unless they do so. But then network your way into the company. This is what The Five O'Clock Club suggests in general: answer the ad or fill out the application, then forget about it and find some other way in.

Some of our members are able to identify someone in their network (such as through their LinkedIn contacts) who then refers them to someone in the hiring department of the company with whom they had also applied online. In turn, hiring managers can quickly move their applications and résumés to the top of the pile, and generate an interview once they have more information on someone. Some will even go to the mat with HR if they want to see someone badly enough.

Remember that companies have specific ways that résumés need to be submitted (often as uploads onto their web portal for applications). As one coach notes, oftentimes an ad will state the preferred way of sending the résumé, so do what is required, but also network your way in or contact someone directly! And another coach notes: "It is quite clear that we coaches are all on the same page (after all, it's part of the methodology!) regarding the huge advantage an individual has by contacting the right person at the right level vs. online submission. All of our stats back that up."

Most coaches agree about the effectiveness of the one-two punch: apply online, then contact the hiring manager or someone who works closely with that person. That's the Five O'Clock Club way.

A majority of positions are filled without the outside world ever knowing about the opening. For example, the hiring manager could run into someone at the health club who talks about a neighbor's dog that bit a guy whose brother turned out to be a great candidate for that job.

Courtesy of Jerry King, Cartoons, Inc.

"Excuse me, Mr. Pomplin, but there's a gentleman here who says he's concerned because you haven't responded to not one of his 12,000 spams."

The Recruiter's Point-of-View

Executive search consultants prefer Word documents because they often do some light editing, perhaps tweaking the format to fit what their client companies expect and removing your contact information and adding their letterhead. But don't forget that the executive recruiter is a go-between.

One coach, who has been an executive recruiter for the past twenty+ years, says this:

I can safely attest to the ebb and flow over the years of how companies source their candidates, and yet the overriding truth remains that networking and direct contact get the job done far better and more efficiently for an individual job seeker than any other mode, including recruiters! Now that I have stated the obvious . . .

From my experience as an executive recruiter dealing directly with HR and internal recruiters, there are inefficiencies involved with the online application process, and these often restrict pulling in those candidates that would make the best fit for the role. As other coaches have noted, companies will ask specific multiple choice questions that are meant to pre-screen candidates before their résumés are seen. Data from the online application is assessed, and the search criteria are prioritized, which again may knock out qualified candidates who may match up quite well otherwise.

In their defense, most of my client companies insist that they eyeball many résumés of candidates who may not make it through the initial filter, or they simply read all of them, time permitting. Yes, you should attach a Word document or insert additional information in the space provided to help justify your candidacy if you lack the experience or skills for a specific job. However, do not rely on the online submission as the way into a company.

I agree 100% with the one-two punch recommendation, as I always suggest the same when coaching. A majority of positions are filled without the outside world ever being alerted about the opening. Typically, an unsolicited résumé arrives on the manager's desk and happens to be at the top of the pile, or the person who the hiring manager ran into at the health club talks about a neighbor's dog that bit a guy whose brother turned out to be a great candidate for that job.

Most of the HR professionals with whom I work often regard the online application process as a necessary evil, and they tell me to make sure my candidates apply online. But at the same time I email their résumés directly to the hiring manager and HR, as a failsafe to make sure they get in front of the right eyes.

Another coach noted that Applicant Tracking Systems (ATS) have moved from scanning to "parsing" content from a résumé into a standard format based on the employer's preferences. But he warns that this technology merely reinforces the "screen out" mentality, instead of creating any

kind of a meaningful platform to really find the best fit for any given position.

One of our coaches, who works with clients earning $200,000 and above, said:

> I have had only two or three clients in the last two years who have had to deal with requests for an electronic résumé and they just removed the bolding and changed the bullets to asterisks. In terms of applying online, most corporate sites either have their own format or just ask you to attach your Word Doc résumé. I have not had a single client who has ever had trouble answering an online ad.

In most cases, an online résumé is not worth it.

So, use your judgment about relying too heavily on electronic résumés. We all would like something magical to save us from the grueling work of searching for a job, but many of the ideas you may come across are not effective.

And a friendly reminder from yet another coach: "The downside of relying too much on company websites and online postings is that only 10 to 12% of jobs are found this way. Increasingly these postings are consuming more time to complete. Since 80% of jobs are found though networking and direct contact, job hunters will realize a far greater payoff if they spend 80% of their job search time on these activities. Most jobs are not posted. In fact, to avoid job postings, many companies are now offering monetary rewards to employees who refer a person who is selected for the job. Several clients have been told they would not have been hired if someone within the company had not recommended them."

Online and Multimedia Résumés for Creative and Technical Positions

Depending on your profession, you may want the hiring manager to see examples of your work.

Some job hunters create a multimedia résumé, with extensive background information; it may include video clips or samples of work, all packaged to be transmitted electronically. This method may be appropriate for creative and technical positions because it demonstrates use and understanding of the technology.

Then, there is the Web-Résumé, which is done in HTML formats and benefits a viewer who needs to see a broader, visually-oriented portfolio. Web pages can include photographs, links to other websites, design/layout graphics, streaming video, and other high-tech features. The benefit of having an HTML résumé is its presence on the Web 24/7, its universal compatibility, and its appealing appearance. At present, there is still a site called VisualCV that allows you to do a Web-type résumé. For a while it was the gold-standard for web portfolios, but technology changes so quickly, there may be a better site by the time this article is published!

VisualCV and other résumé websites help people to create their own résumé pages and video résumés. The issue with all of these is that résumés generally need to be positioned for a specific job target, so you need multiple versions—one for each target. This is a limitation with LinkedIn as well: you are allowed to have only one profile. In addition, Web-Résumés may be hard to update in some cases, particularly where video is involved. Remember, people are able to constantly make small revisions to their résumés, but changing a video requires real work. So **most coaches agree that the conventional résumé is not going away.**

One coach noted that posting using Box.net appears to be a useful tool since it integrates with LinkedIn: "VisualCV is fine for a static résumé, and has worked well as a simple static website for me. They have many samples to show you how it might look: www.visualcv.com. And if anyone is interested, here's mine: http://www.visualcv.com/phiconsulting."

The consensus of our coaches is that you should have an online résumé if you have only one job target or a consulting practice (and it therefore requires very little in the way of changes). Or, if you want to be a web developer and don't have any work yet to show online, developing your own website / résumé could showcase your work. Or, if you are in the visual arts or graphic design, having a website / résumé showing your designs is more powerful and can strongly complement, or even a substitute for, your résumé.

Other than those special cases, if you want to have an online résumé, consider using LinkedIn instead. As one coach said, "Sure your own personal résumé/website can be impressive—but is it worth the time—and the lack of flexibility in being able to have multiple résumés for each target? I would say in most cases an online résumé is not worth it."

"I'm sorry, Roberts, but as a traditionalist, I'm just not ready to buy into this 'computer' fad. However, I'm still considering your 'voicemail' suggestion."

Courtesy of Jerry King, Cartoons, Inc.

Your Positioning on LinkedIn

Be sure to read the article in the Members Only section of our website (www.fiveoclockclub.com), "Social Media: Using LinkedIn to Advance Your Career." Below is additional information from our coaches, specifically regarding how LinkedIn relates to your résumé.

In general, our coaches suggest that job hunters put their efforts into LinkedIn instead of other outlets for their résumé, making their LinkedIn profile top notch. As one said: "I am among the many coaches who believe that Linkedin is currently a 'must have' for anyone seriously job hunting at a professional or managerial level and above."

Another shares a similar opinion: "LinkedIn

is the number 1 professional networking site. The summary section, which is limited in the number of characters that can be used, needs to be compelling and should differentiate you from others in your field. After completing your résumé in The Five O'Clock Club style, it's time to update your LinkedIn profile."

One coach notes says that "'Profile' is a misleading word because on LinkedIn your profile should be your full-blown résumé. Both internal and external recruiters have told me they often ignore candidates when they see just a profile. They want to see the companies you have worked for, your results, and your key skills."

Another coach warns of the complexities: "On Linkedin, there are opposing views. But, to differentiate yourself from the now 100 million Linkedin users, you need to add some personality, humor, and stories to your profile, and give it a different feel than you give your résumé. The jury is still out on whether you should write your profile in 3rd or 1st person, but recently Linkedin (the company) gave celebrity blogger Guy Kawasaki's profile—an extreme makeover and put it in the 1st person. [www.linkedin.com/in/guykawasaki] You can see that Linkedin endorsed it. This fits his irreverent personality and it is highly readable and engaging."

One coach had these details to add:

LinkedIn is definitely the big gorilla in the room. I am of a school of thought that a LinkedIn profile should not be just a "cut-and-paste" of a résumé in its entirety. I see LinkedIn profiles as a bit of a teaser to hook an employer or recruiter with just enough information to contact the individual, who can then send the full résumé later. Attention spans online tend to be very, very limited, so I advocate the following strategy to my clients, which has been working quite well:

1. The SUMMARY section is written in the first person in conversational tone. This is by design as it personalizes this portion of the profile. I typically aim for one to three paragraphs, each containing one to three sentences.

2. The WORK EXPERIENCE & GOALS section is written in résumé language. Again, this is by design. A good formula here is one (maybe two) pithy sentences about responsibilities, and two or three very brief bulleted accomplishments for each entry. This gives the readers a snapshot of the most important things you want them to know about each experience. The further back you go in your employment chronology, the less information needs to be included.

Of course, keywords should be included for search engine optimization.

> **Since fewer people are using snail mail, it is more likely to get the hiring manager's attention, especially for more senior-level positions.**

Most coaches recommend that job hunters consider including a LinkedIn profile URL in the contact section of their résumé, and also on business cards they can hand out at networking events. You could include other links on your résumé as well, if it helps to sell yourself. These would include links to websites you designed, a video you created, and so on.

Just another reminder from yet another coach to bring us all back to real life: "Direct contact and networking still seem to be the best way to reach people, as stated in the current books. My clients reply to ads and never hear anything (and then they come to me for help!). But when reaching out directly to the hiring managers via networking or direct contact, everything changes, and they get meetings. This is what we've been saying in our books, and it's true."

This coach also notes that while LinkedIn profiles are essential, they are not a substitute for résumés in many (or most) cases, because:

- You can have only one profile, so that requires that you position yourself more generally than you would like if you have multiple targets.
- If you are currently employed, you have to be careful what you put on your profile

in terms of what you are going for. If it is very different from your current job, your boss might get suspicious.

- You might have to make your profile less accomplishment-oriented because it is so public. Actual numbers might work on a résumé that will be seen by a very targeted audience, but might not be appropriate for a LinkedIn profile. Be sure to discuss this with your coach or small group.

In sending your résumé via email, should you include your résumé in the body of the email or as an attachment?

The prevailing opinion seems to be that résumés should always be attached because formatting can really help in delivering your pitch/message. The cover letter, however, should always be in the body of the email, so it's more likely to be read. A good cover letter/email will stimulate enough interest so that the résumé will be opened.

Most coaches agree that the attached résumé should be in PDF format so that all recipients will see the same thing you see (different versions of Word, or Mac vs. PC, display résumés differently, such as inserting strange page breaks). You can even attach PDFs to online applications.

These days, most job hunters are contacting hiring managers via email. The reasons for using email are these:

- It works. Email is the language of business these days: everyone reads email.
- It's much easier on the job seeker to send an email—important from a time management perspective and psychologically.
- It's easy for the recipient to just hit reply.
- You may look outdated by sending a letter.

That said, you will need a compelling/relevant subject line to get people to open it, so it doesn't go into spam (e.g., "referred by ", "saw your article ", etc.). You also need an email address that has your name in it—it's a marketing opportunity and makes it less likely to go into spam. And you

generally need to follow up with a phone call—unless you really are spamming people.

Snail mail letters do have an advantage in that they can stand out (if they are read in a timely way, not always the case these days), show care and effort, and may appeal to "old school" hiring managers who don't consider this spam. What's more, since fewer people are doing it, it is more likely to get the hiring manager's attention, especially for more senior-level positions.

One person who coaches only the most senior executives said, "Whenever there is a chance that the firewall may knock the email into junk mail, my clients send it by both email and snail mail."

How much time should a job hunter spend on posting résumés online or answering ads?

This is a trick question in case you've missed our warnings throughout this chapter! As one coach said, "Very, very little time should be spent on this: less than 10 percent of a job hunter's time, for all the reasons we know as Five O'Clock Club coaches. This channel is more competitive, passive, and very time consuming. It is the 'passive' element that bothers me the most: I am a huge advocate of clients taking control of their searches—and maintaining control. **The big downside of relying too much on company websites and on-line postings is that opportunities will be lost if job hunters are not doing more productive things such as networking and direct contact**."

A final warning. We have written this chapter only because *job hunters* want to know about the subject *and* waste too much time posting their résumés online, developing their own websites (that no one will see), and filling out online company applications. Spend only ten percent of your job-search time that way. Become more pro-active in your search through networking and direct contact. However, be sure to read the chapter on *Using Social Media in Your Search (especially LinkedIn)*.

Good luck. Be wise. Follow the methodology. And thanks to all of our coaches who contributed to this chapter.

Using the Internet as a Job-Search Tool

The essence of the high-risk society is choice: the choice between embracing uncertainty and running from it.

MICHAEL MANDEL, *The High-Risk Society*

The Internet is a great research tool and may even help you connect with people. However, it does not provide the benefits of personal contact and valuable perspectives that one-on-one information-gathering meetings provide. Consider the Internet as simply another job-search tool to be added to your repertoire of Five O'Clock Club techniques. The following hints will help you make it an effective complement.

Develop an Internet Plan to Coincide with Your Job-Search Marketing Campaign

One of our biggest challenges at The Five O'Clock Club is to convince job hunters to spend less time on the Internet, primarily answering ads, or drifting off into irrelevant areas such as scrolling through databases, accessing career centers, looking at job postings, or chatting in newsgroups. Be very focused while you are online. The Internet can be interesting but it can also be somewhat addictive and can distract you from your real mission of targeted research, learning about an industry, field or person (such as through LinkedIn), and developing your target list of organizations and people to contact. It can also help you in your follow-up after a job interview. Or you can see job postings that tell you the correct words to use in your resume for the kind of position you're seeking. It may seem like productive time because a few hours online can generate a lot of information. However, the time may be better spent elsewhere. Be sure to balance the time you spend on the Internet (or in library research) with the time you spend talking to real people, writing letters and emails and following up after a job interview.

The best way to develop your Internet plan is to define specific tasks you will need to accomplish in your allotted Internet time. Include the Internet as part of the research component of your target list and then as a further source when obtaining information about specific companies. Consider online job postings as a great source of companies that are hiring, ones you can then contact directly in the departments or divisions that are appropriate for you.

The Internet has become another means of obtaining meetings to be added to the list: networking, direct mail, search firms, ads, and now the Internet. Also, keep in mind that there continues to be a lot of hype and media articles about the effectiveness of online campaigns as compared with other job-search methods. Be wary of those "research studies" that show the techniques hiring managers use to find job hunters, which can bear little resemblance to the techniques job hunters should use to get interviews. For example, at The Five O'Clock Club, we may post on Craig's List and use that as our primary source of back-office personnel. For one job opening, we will get 300 to 500 resumes within a couple of hours. That's good for us, but the odds are against all of those people who answered the ad. After all, we're going to hire only one person – not 500. Even those who are supposed to be helping job hunters, such as other outplacement firms, continually quote research on how employers find candidates. Remember that is a good market, only 6% of all jobs are found through job postings of all kinds and only 6% of all jobs are found through search firms. Therefore, spend only that percentage of your time on those techniques.

Choose the Websites Appropriate for Your Search

Finding the right websites to review online postings should be part of your initial campaign as you develop your target list. In the same way you'll find periodicals the movers and shakers in your industry read, you'll also find industry-specific websites. These websites often contain job postings or have links to affiliate job sites. More importantly, they will bring you up-to-date on what's happening in your field or industry so you do better in your meetings. During the course of your information meetings, ask about industry periodicals and industry websites, too. Check the website of industry organizations and associations as a source for leads through job postings, not to mention activities in your field for networking contacts. Be sure to visit LinkedIn to find out the background of every person with whom you will meet. Also Google those people to find out whether they have been quoted or mentioned in the business press.

Career sites often contain job postings for a company that are not listed on the firm's own corporate website. If it appears there are no open positions at a company, it may be because their jobs are listed elsewhere or not listed at all, so check through career sites for company-specific listings of your target firm. Keep in mind: Not all open positions are posted to websites and not all positions posted to websites are open.

Search firms often have sites allowing users to complete a profile then included in the candidate database. Complete the profile if you consider the firm reputable but make sure there's a notation about privacy so your résumé is sent out only with your permission. And, remember, you can spend hours on this, but your chances are slim.

Responding to Online Job Postings

Before responding to the online posting, verify whether the format you're using to send your cover letter and résumé is correct. Some companies want your résumé included in the body of the email with no attachments. Other firms want two attachments, the cover letter and your résumé. Some companies request responses in text format only, so sending a word-processed document is not appropriate. In that case, convert the word-processed document (.doc or .docx) into a text format (.txt) before sending. Some want .pdf only to avoid the risk of viruses. This may seem trivial but you don't want your response eliminated before it is even reviewed.

When sending your résumé as an attachment, include your last name as part of the document name. For instance, don't call the attachment "My Résumé." If the attachment gets separated from the email or if there is internal email correspondence about a number of candidates, you don't want your documents to be easily confused or misplaced. On the subject line of the email, try to include a notation that will address the topic but will also encourage the reader to open the email. For instance, instead of just "My Résumé" include a notation about your area of expertise (from the first line of your Two-Minute Pitch). Try to keep this line to a minimum as this field is not uniform across all Internet service providers.

Consider online job postings in the same way you would want ads in newspapers and trade periodicals Position your response by matching your background to their requirements. Your response may be scanned by a computer so be sure your résumé contains the appropriate buzzwords for your industry.

Before sending your email response to the company, send it to yourself first. Check the "From" box. **If you have a cutesy online name,**

change it to a more business-appropriate name, even if it means signing on to a new online service or expanding the existing membership with your current Internet service provider. Check your Subject line to see if all the characters you intended are included in this space. And refrain from using all lower-case, which will make you seem less serious.

There's often a tendency to be less formal when sending email than when sending written documents. Remember: This is still a job search so spell-check your email before it goes out. If your browser does not have a spell-check feature, cut and paste a word-processed document that you've verified off-line into the body of the email. Always add the email address as the last item so you don't accidentally send an incomplete letter while you're still working on it.

Posting Your Résumé Online

Many of the Internet career websites provide an area in which job hunters post their résumés for access by potential employers. However, access is not limited to just potential employers. Do you want your current boss looking at your résumé online? Who else has access to your personal information, credentials, and employment history? Would you tack up your résumé on a public bulletin board or hand it out to strangers just because

they asked for it? And how can you follow up effectively if you don't know who has viewed your credentials?

However, some job hunters have found posting their credentials helpful in their search and there are ways to minimize some of these concerns. For instance, you can post only a portion of your personal information so interested respondents can call you for further details, allowing you to screen them. Online posting is certainly an option but is not recommended and removing or replacing an online résumé is rarely as easy as posting it.

Remember, the Internet is another tool to supplement your Five O'Clock Club techniques. If you need a quick reminder of this methodology, simply check out our website at **www.fiveoclockclub.com.**

Jobholders do not see the organization as a shifting pattern of needs. The only "opportunities" they recognize are the jobs that are currently posted on bulletin boards down at Personnel. And they grumble about how damned few of those there are, failing to note all the while the expanding range of unmet needs all over the organization.

WILLIAM BRIDGES, *JobShift: How to Prosper in a Workplace Without Jobs*

The Five O'Clock Club®

Social Media: Using LinkedIn to Advance Your Career

We asked a group of Five O'Clock Club coaches to give us their opinions on Social Media in general and LinkedIn in particular. The coaches were: Damona Sain, Win Sheffield, Celia Currin, Mary Anne Walsh, Anita Attridge, Bill Belknap and Chip Conlin.

Technology changes, and you have to change with it, but the basic techniques and thought processes for career development don't change. As one of our coaches said, "I constantly give my clients this advice: even if you do not embrace social networking, you need to understand how business is using it because it will come up, sooner rather than later, in business conversations.

"So, please, for self-preservation, avail yourself of the data. By the way, www.mashable.com is one of the best sites for keeping pace with the business uses and business trends involving social media."

Yes, times have changed. In the 1960s and 1970s, if you left your house and the phone rang, you missed the call. People did not have home answering machines. Nowadays, people are connected to their cell phones everywhere they go.

Twenty years ago, the Internet did not exist. Today, it can dominate our lives. We think that the new Social Media are meant to extend our relationships, but there are perilous risks, as well as benefits.

We can all build lots of connections, but let's be smart about it. Facebook is the cause of many relationship break-ups. A 2009 study makes the claim that "increased Facebook use significantly predicts Facebook-related jealousy" in romantic relationships.

While Facebook tends to be more of a personal medium, LinkedIn is more for professional relationships. Used correctly, it can help you to improve your current career, find a new job, or build a consulting practice.

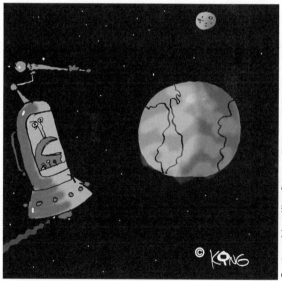

Courtesy of Jerry King, Cartoons, Inc.

"I've located the source of all that annoying spam we've been receiving...preparing to destroy."

Social Media in General

Keep up your contacts while working

Before Social Media came into being, we urged our clients who had landed jobs to make sure they had two networking meetings a week — no matter what — to keep up their contacts, keep up with what was happening in their fields and industries, and to already have developed contacts if they needed information to help them in their careers or wanted to search again.

Be smart about building your connections.

Social Media can help you to keep up your contacts, particularly given how busy everyone is these days, but our coaches caution that "nothing substitutes for face-to-face contact. Don't ever forget the value of a phone call over an email." Meeting people virtually does not replace meeting people directly — either in person or via telephone. One coach advised, "Make sure that 20 to 30 percent of your time — whether in your job or job hunting — is 'in the field' meeting and connecting with people face-to-face."

Social Media *are* a serious part of the resources and tools that help people in their jobs and in job search. The basics of managing your career, looking for a job, or building a consulting practice have not changed — just *the tools* that help people to connect have changed — ranging from email, online search, to LinkedIn, blogs and Twitter.

Use Social Media as _one_ tool to develop your career, build a consulting practice, or find a new job.

These tools help you to stay in contact with your network of people and companies, and to continue to build your network. You can use social networking tools to build your reputation as an industry or subject expert by blogging and tweeting — or every bit as important — responding and commenting on other people's blogs and tweets.

As one coach said: "Social networking should not be viewed as just a job-search tool. That's wrong and inefficient. This would be the equivalent of going to just one interview with the belief and expectation that it will produce a job offer. It's a resource for managing and navigating your career. Yes, you use social networking to conduct a dynamic job search, but it's so much more than that. Use it to expand your network, as a resource for information, and to build a community of like-minded people who will support you both on the job, as well as in job search."

Social Media Can Waste Your Time

Whether you are employed or not, we all know that anything on the Internet (or computer or handheld mobile devices, especially Smartphones) can suck up too much time. One coach advises that for one or two weeks, you should assess how much time per day you spend online. Track how often you click on interesting links and *surf to unrelated topics*. Then cut all your time in half for two weeks. Use that extra time to meet with people directly via phone and in person, rather than relying on virtual meetings alone.

As one coach put it: "Let's face it, it takes a lot of time and care to build Stage 1 and 2 contacts (getting to know people who know about your industry and field and then those who are more senior than you). It's easy to avoid the sometimes intimidating and anxiety-producing effects of reaching out to people in person. Social Media are also pretty much a '2-D' interaction. That can increase miscommunication possibilities."

Comparing Various Social Media

Facebook is generally for social purposes, rather than career development. Twitter can be very time-intensive and the tweets move so quickly that you can lose track of them easily if you stay away for a couple of days (even hours sometimes!).

Blogs are labor intensive, but can be effective if you like to write and *write well*. But check out the blogs you return to time and again, and figure out why they are appealing. Being too wordy with no graphics or other media (such as a short video) can be a recipe for a lack of traffic. Other media include verbal podcasts, but you need good recording equipment or no one will stay to listen. This coach notes: "I think well done video podcasts (NOT amateur YouTube versions!) on Twitter, Facebook, blogs, and whatever else there is, would likely appeal to more people—but ONLY if they are well done and if you are photogenic or a natural in front of a camera."

All of the above can take up so much of your time! Be sure to track the amount of time you are on the computer and what you are doing there. It is very easy to waste time digging through news-letters, blogs, junk mail, and it is important to keep the time invested *under control*.

What's more, Social Media can be a new way of "hiding out" instead of actually making contact with real people. The Internet in all of its forms is a great research tool. But as we used to say, if you are spending all of your time in the library (or on the Internet), get out more. If you are spending all of your time meeting with people, research more. You need both for a successful career today.

Finally, Social Media are used more heavily in certain industries and professions than others. Here's one coach's thoughts on the subject: "Social Media are a tool to support your career. Like any tool it's best used when the audience you're target-ing has embraced it and believes in it.

"Know whether your audience uses it" so you don't waste a lot of time using the wrong tools to advance your career or your search. If everyone in your desired target is heavily invested in social networking then you should be, too. For example, I have a client who just became the president of a digital ad agency. He's on Facebook and LinkedIn to keep his universe of contacts — both profes-sional and personal — apprised of his where-abouts and plans. He also uses and promotes other technologies to demonstrate his commitment to being 'wired.'"

LinkedIn

<u>Every professional needs to be on LinkedIn</u>. We have over 1,000 members in our Five O'Clock Club LinkedIn Group. LinkedIn has gotten rave reviews at The Five O'Clock Club. Wrote one Clubber to his group: "LinkedIn is a terrific tool that can help extend a person's network and sim-plify the process of identifying members of your network in target companies and industries. It's free to join so I've tried to recruit lots of other Five O'Clock Clubbers. As a quick anecdote, I received a cold call this morning from a distant contact in my LinkedIn network who is looking for help on a number of his projects. I was the perfect fit. A perfect lead! I wish you the same good luck, and pass it on. If you join, make sure you connect to me; the bigger your network the more effective it will be."

From one coach's point-of-view: "LinkedIn is being described as 'the best' online career-man-agement guide around; and rightly so. There is a huge WOW factor knowing that at least 45 million others are on LinkedIn.

"Remember more than 85% of recruiters are trying to find you daily. Just a few years ago we thought of career management as a ladder: Get that first job and hang on that rung until you or someone else decides it is time to go. The current thinking is to visualize your career as a ramp where you are consistently, conscientiously, and concisely moving forward up this ramp using all the tools available to you, especially the art of building and maintaining relationships on an on-going basis throughout your career. What better vehicle than LinkedIn to assist you in accomplish-ing this lifetime project of managing yourself?"

Another coach offers comfort to concerned employees: "Clients sometimes worry that their employer will see their activity on LinkedIn and assume they are looking for work. You can update your status on a quarterly basis, or at a minimum, when you complete each major project. You can even mention to your boss that you are tracking your accomplishments using LinkedIn."

Our coaches tend to agree that LinkedIn is simply a tool. As one said, "The key is to build relationships; to some extent LinkedIn can nurture or even extend a relationship. I think of LinkedIn as a fancy Rolodex and I rely on it as I would a Rolodex. It is not a substitute for developing the relationships. It is a *medium*, a sophisticated medium, but in the end, a medium."

> **Would you like to see a great LinkedIn profile? Look at Guy Kawasaki's. www.linkedin.com/in/guykawasaki**

Get the Professional Headline and Profile Right!

One coach represented many of our coaches when she said, "Mainly, I work with two categories of people — those high-potential clients who are on the cusp of promotion and are ripe for business coaching, and those individuals who are interested in transitioning into a new career. The most important first phase of coaching is assessment or identifying one's career distinction, which is a cornerstone piece to crafting a dynamic profile. I strongly suggest working with a Five O'Clock Club Coach at this assessment-stage to help you identify your professional reputation or positioning. Keep in mind that it is hard to do these alone and much more fun to do in concert with a professional coach."

Before writing your LinkedIn Heading and Profile, re-read the section of our *Interviewing* book on the Two-Minute Pitch. As we say at the Club, "if your pitch — the way you're positioning yourself — is wrong, everything is wrong." As one coach said, "Whether you are looking to advance your career, build a consulting practice, or are looking for a new job, it's extremely important that your profiles on LinkedIn and other social networking sites be consistent in how they position you professionally. It's amazing *how many disconnects* we see between a member's profile on LinkedIn, the Summary Statement on their résumé, and even they way they talk about themselves in their pitch."

The LinkedIn Professional Heading is a small field, but the most important. As one coach noted: "It is your positioning statement and is the reader's first impression of your perceived promise of value — and we all know how difficult it is to change a first impression! Remember your positioning lives in the hearts and minds of others for a long time." This same coach developed the following list for you to consider:

Coaching questions to ask yourself:

1. What is the impression I want to create in the Professional Headline?
2. What do others say about my Professional Headline?
3. Are these congruent thoughts?
4. What is the feeling you want it to evoke?
5. What is the feeling others get when they read your Professional Headline?
6. What does it say about your career distinction that you bring to an organization?

Compare the feeling you get when you read these two very real Professional Headlines — Joe: "In career transition" vs. Jill: "Big picture visionary who gets the job done using creative non-traditional tactics." Which person would you want to get to know?

Most people decide they want to reposition themselves depending on *where they want their career to go*. A Clubber who had worked for the big consulting firms her entire life wanted people to instead see her as a "Communications Executive with 10 years of international experience." How do *you* want to be seen?

Would you like to see a great LinkedIn profile? Look at Guy Kawasaki's: www.linkedin.com/in/guykawasaki

I know: Social Media are his job. The Internet is his life's work. But he is a good example of someone who has taken full advantage of what LinkedIn has to offer. Pay special attention to his summary statement. You can see that he's put a lot of thought into his. If you have been working closely with your coach, you may be able to simply insert your résumé summary statement onto your

LinkedIn page. Every Five O'Clock Club coach would tell you that you want to *consistently* communicate your pitch in all of your communications: résumé, cover letter, your verbal pitch about yourself, email messages, and all other Social Media.

Develop your LinkedIn heading and summary after you've completed your résumé. That way, they both position you the same way.

By the way, if you are proud of your LinkedIn profile, be sure to list your LinkedIn address (see Guy's address, above) in all of your email correspondence, at the top of your résumé, and so on. If you've done a good job on your LinkedIn profile, you want others to see it. And, rather than using the address that is assigned to you, you will want to change your LinkedIn address and use Guy's format (with his name as part of the url).

All of our coaches echo the same thought: Complete your LinkedIn profile *after* you have completed your résumé. The Headline, 120 character limit, should define who you are and what differentiates you from others. The summary, 2,000 characters, should position you strategically for your career development, consulting business or job search. Start with the summary section from your résumé. Use bulleted points or short paragraphs so that it can be read easily. LinkedIn doesn't give you the option for bulleted points, *but* you can get them by using a copy/paste of bulleted points from Microsoft Word into your profile, or simply use dashes or asterisks.

Another coach suggested: "I understand that people who have completed most of their LinkedIn profile *are more successful in attracting employers* through the LinkedIn service that finds people for employers."

Recommendations

We asked our coaches about the number and kinds of recommendations a person should have. Here's what *they* said:

- Have at least three or four. Be careful not to have too many "reciprocal" recommen-

dations (i.e., if you recommend me, I'll recommend you).

- People usually get a little suspicious about too many recommendations. (Even Guy Kawasaki has only six.) On this subject, when you ask people for a recommendation, it can be very helpful if you tell them quite specifically what you are hoping they will be comfortable in saying — to the point of writing a "draft" of a recommendation that they might want to use as a sample and change or adjust in any way that suits them. This takes the hassle out of the process for the recommender and helps you get the recommendation you really want.

- Recommendations should ideally be from previous managers or colleagues. As with references, if there are key points you would like them to include, let them know.

- Many of my clients have been contacted by both internal (company) recruiters, as well as external. Several were told they were being contacted because of the quality of their references. This is because I try (not always successfully!) to have my clients:

  1. Create a script for what they want said.
  2. Make sure the content from the reference is performance-based or behaviorally worded, NOT just a rave about the person. For example: "When Mary led the XYZ project team we met all of our committed delivery dates and came in under budget. I don't think we could have done this without her leadership."
  3. Choose the same people who are your job references; this makes the process much more efficient.

> **Too many recommendations make you look insecure.**

Why Update Your LinkedIn Page?

Some people — especially consultants — regularly update something on their LinkedIn page so that a notice will be sent to everyone in their network and keep them top-of-mind. Whether or not you are a consultant, you can let people know what projects you are working on. What our coaches say:

- Check your profile regularly to see if there's anything you can add that will keep your name and expertise showing up via status updates. Also, LinkedIn keeps adding features. Make sure that you take advantage of any that will showcase your skills.
- Like all updates (e.g., on Facebook), it can be overdone.
- People change their headline and summary as they become clearer about what is important to their target markets.

Using LinkedIn to Build a Consulting Practice

You can use LinkedIn to build a consulting practice by contacting companies or key people of interest to you.

Said one coach: "One financial client who wanted to work with small companies contacted all the smaller CPA firms on LinkedIn in his target market. He then met with them to let them know about his skills, since many small businesses contact the CPA firms to ask about recommendations for financial people." Excellent idea.

Another coach suggested using LinkedIn regularly to record your accomplishments and advertise your events.

Your LinkedIn Photo

I've seen some photos that were not professional looking. They were way too sexy. This is not a dating service. Our coaches say:

- Use a plain background, have a warm smile, use solid colors for background and clothing. Have your hair under control. Preview your photo and ask others for their input. If you have your own consulting business, it's best to have either a studio photo or one at high resolution so it can be reduced or enlarged for this and other purposes.
- The photo needs to be professional — ideally, professionally done. The photo is your business picture and should be as professional as your image and presentation would be at an interview.

> **Don't use a sexy photo. This is business, not a dating service.**

Should you put Personal Information on LinkedIn?

To repeat what we say at the Club, if it helps your search, put it in. If it doesn't help, leave it out. If you're interested in skiing, for example, a reader could have a positive or negative reaction to this information. Our coaches say:

- Be strategic about personal information.
- Don't think of LinkedIn as a place for any personal information. It seems out of place there — it's more appropriate on Facebook.
- The Club rule is right.

Joining Groups

Joining as many groups as possible increases your network base. Groups that can be most helpful are professional (industry and function), alumni groups, special interest groups and, of course, the Five O'Clock Club group. What else do our coaches have to say?

- Joining groups is a great idea, especially when you can participate in their discussions. Not only do they help you to showcase your knowledge and skills to a very targeted audience, but you can keep up-to-date in your field as you read others' posts. However, if you join too many groups, you can waste time with status updates; so prioritize the ones you think will be best for your purpose. Searching is all about finding the right keywords. I remember trying to help a client find groups related to accounting and the results were not what he was looking for. That might have been a keyword issue or simply that typical accountants don't set up these groups. (There were plenty of groups for CPAs, for example.)

- A footnote to the advice about not joining too many groups: If you are going to join a group try to be active in it and get to know the people in it. That's the point — not just having a laundry list of groups. As in all career development activities, you should be conscious of whether it is working for you. Are you seeing real results? Building a network? Study the metrics.
- Again, Club rules apply: if it works, do it, if not, stop.

> **Use LinkedIn the same as you would any other medium. Use it in a professional manner.**

How to Contact People through LinkedIn

I get requests all the time. The standard request that LinkedIn provides does not help me to figure out who this person is. Here's what our coaches have to say:

- Always customize your invitation to others you ask to join your connections list. The standardized invitation is very impersonal and shows you don't care enough to reach out personally.
- I absolutely agree that if you are building your network, you should personalize all correspondence — this is the chance to reach out and touch, and make it personal and leave an impression in someone's mind. Don't blow it to save two minutes.
- I am not offended if someone I know sends a standard request. Even so, I appreciate a custom note. If the custom note is from someone I don't know well, I feel it is a little pushy. In the end, I will only connect with those I know.
- Personalizing your LinkedIn request helps to make your request stand out from many other requests that the person may be receiving.

> **The standard request that LinkedIn provides does not help me to figure out who this person is.**

How to Build Your Network on LinkedIn

- Be sure you know the people you LinkedIn with — whether you are going to them or they are coming to you. Make sure that your network is full of people who actually know you and you know them.
- Check out the connections your connections have. If you find someone you'd like to reach out to, first check with your connection to find out how they know the other person, just as you would in a live networking situation. Then customize (always customize) your request appropriately.
- I stick to my contacts' contacts. I tried to go further and it fizzled out— no relationship, so no result.
- It's important to be selective in the invitations to accept. On most sites, as soon as you accept someone's invitation you become part of their network, and may get invitations from people who may really not fit within your network. If they cannot really help you, or you cannot be of help to them, why do it?

How to Contact Someone in a Targeted Organization

Should you simply contact that person directly (direct contact) or should you ask someone else for an introduction (networking)? Is contacting someone via LinkedIn any different from our typical advice?

- Most of our coaches agree: This is just like the Club's advice with other mediums: Contacting the person directly will provide you with the most control in connecting with someone. If you are trying to connect with a very senior person, you may want to contact a person you know before contacting the senior person. LinkedIn is the same as with any other medium.
- At The Five O'Clock Club, we advocate both ways to contact others. I'd look at the person's level. Unless you're a high-level executive, don't approach a CEO of a medium to large company directly. Remember our phrase, "contact people one to two levels higher than you are."
- Most job hunters I have observed are more successful when using LinkedIn and other sites to develop contacts and generate informational meetings. It's really about going after those Stage 2 contacts (people one or two levels higher than you are who are in a position to hire you or recommend that you be hired), then following up with a targeted mailing, and good old-fashioned phone calls.
- I have observed a trend among some job hunters using LinkedIn to identify the hiring manager, or someone of influence within the company for which they have applied online for a position. It's what I call the "one-two punch" — the same as if you were answering an ad, but also get your résumé bumped up because of your effective use of direct contact or networking.

Some General LinkedIn Suggestions

- I think it is important to regularly spend some time on LinkedIn and to be thoughtful about extending your network before you might really need to. LinkedIn makes networking quite easy and it lets you reach out and touch lots of contacts before you need the favor — and when you might be able to put some money in the favor bank.
- As for the time you might spend on LinkedIn, review it as you would ads, maybe look at it after the workday, once a day or look at it once a week.
- LinkedIn should be used as any other resource on an as-needed basis and with a purpose. It's important to build your LinkedIn network by including groups. With a rich LinkedIn network, you can then use it to source candidates and companies. Like any of the social networking tools, it should be used with a purpose in mind.
- Check your privacy settings. Look at your progress bar and try to have it at least 75% complete. Look for groups pertaining to your industry/profession and join them. Follow discussions and contribute whenever possible.

Getting a Job Interview Through LinkedIn

We asked our coaches whether any of their job hunters have ever gotten a job interview through LinkedIn ads. Here are some of their answers:

- One group member did and was surprised to be hired for a position overseas.
- None of mine, but I have heard of people getting interviews through it.
- I have clients who have gotten interviews through recruiters. As many have noted, recruiters regularly troll LinkedIn for candidates.
- One client today said a recruiter called her about a position that he had posted,

since her skills fit the profile. It appears that recruiters — both independent and for companies — are more aggressively using LinkedIn to identify candidates.

> **If you're not using Google Alerts, you're not a player in your organization, industry or profession.**

Some Cool Advice

One coach suggested this very powerful LinkedIn technique:

"Use the counterintuitive approach of typing in your target company's name in the People box. If you type in Medco, as an example, the search engine brings up the names of all the people 1, 2 and 3 degrees of separation from you who work [or used to work] at Medco. Very powerful.

"**You can also do this on Twitter and Facebook**. For those who are social-network challenged or cynical (believe it or not many of my clients are...but not for long!), this will quickly tell you if some of your targets are social-network savvy. For example, Medco and WebMD (and hundreds of Fortune 500 companies) pay for Twitter ads. Currently, many of the world's largest companies and consulting firms use Twitter as part of their recruiting strategy.

If you do the above on Facebook (e.g., type Medco in the people search box), it will give you a list of people who work or have worked at Medco and are on Facebook. It also give a hotlink so you can make Direct Contact! How cool is that?

Keeping Plugged into Your Industry and Profession

One problem is that we tend to focus on the next hot thing, but spending your time wisely matters! Whether you are employed or not, you need to conduct research to stay up with what's happening in your industry or field. Don't forget the basics that we teach at The Five O'Clock Club. If your only source of research is LinkedIn, that's not good. Consider the following basics for starters:

- Many members **use Google for industry, company or people information**, even if they're going after esoteric industries such as social service agencies, ethics, education policy, think tanks and nanotechnology. Key any industry name into Google and see what comes up. You may have to look through a few pages of information, but there will probably be a site that is a key one for your industry or field. Key in the people you are trying to research. Chances are, you'll find them.

- Make sure you use **Google alerts** for the organization you work for and your main competitors. If you're not doing that, you're not a player. Just go to Google, key in the word "alerts" and it will take you to the Google alert page. Key in the words you would like an alert for, see a preview of the kind of results you would get, modify the word if you don't like the results, and note how often you would like to get alerts on these keywords. You've probably already Googled *yourself* to see what the world would see. If not, *you really ought to.*

- **Go to the Google Blog page** and see what comes up. You might get some really good (but not necessarily trustworthy) information about a person or organization.

- Take a look at our **Research Resources** in this book and in the Members Only section of our website: www.fiveoclockclub.com.

- **Subscribe to online journals about your field or industry**. You'll get their newsletters with the hot topics of the day.

- And, one of our tried and true favorites: **Join professional or trade associations**. You really do need to get out there and see real people.

The Five O'Clock Club®

How to Work with Search Firms

Once-in-a-lifetime opportunities come along all the time—just about every week or so.

GARRISON KEILLOR, *A Prairie Home Companion*

If you've been learning the Five O'Clock Club approach, you know by now that there are four ways to get meetings in your target market. You can get meetings through search firms, ads, networking and by contacting companies directly. A technique is working for you if it results in meetings.

Of these techniques for getting meetings in your target market, search firms and ads are the most passive because you have to *wait* for something to happen rather than *making* something happen. If you contact a search firm, you have to wait. If you answer an ad, you have to wait.

In addition, when you rely on search firms and ads, you automatically have competition. These job openings were *posted!* Other people are applying for the same job. On the other hand, if you contact a company through networking or through direct contact, you have no competition and you can be proactive: you can *do* something to get in to see someone at this company.

It's also good for you to know that in good times only ten percent of all jobs are found through ads. And only ten percent of all jobs are found through search firms. **In bad times, the number drops to about six percent for both methods combined.**

So most people get meetings and jobs through the other techniques: direct contact and networking. At the Five O'Clock Club, we say that you should consider all four techniques for getting

interviews in your target market, and then notice which techniques are working for you.

> **A good recruiter in a search firm usually places only one or two people a month. This is the most important statistic for you to know about search firms.**

"A gentleman left his resume. Apparently, he wanted to ensure it didn't get lost with the others."

"Working for you" means that a technique results in meetings for you. **"Meetings" are the only way to measure the effectiveness of a technique.** You don't measure the effectiveness of a technique by whether or not you got a job. You measure the effectiveness of a technique by whether or not it's resulting in *meetings* for you.

So, *if* search firms (and ads) are basically passive techniques, and *if* only a total of six percent of all jobs today are found through search firms and ads *combined*, how can you better understand how search firms work?

How Search Firms Work

Who naught suspects is easily deceived.
PETRARCH, 1304-1374, ITALIAN POET, *Sonnets*

There are *good* search firms and there are *bad* search firms. There are good recruiters and there are bad recruiters. We're going to tell you mostly about the *bad* search firms and the *bad* recruiters because if we only told you about the good ones, that's not going to be helpful. You don't need to be warned about the *good* ones. You need to be protected against the *bad* ones.

There are two kinds of search firms in general, although the line has blurred in recent years. First, there are *contingency* search firms. These search firms are paid by the employer when they *actually make a placement*. An employer might give the job opening to four, five, six contingency firms and they're all fighting to find people and put them in for interviews. When someone is hired, the firm that did the placement gets the fee, and the others get nothing.

Retainer search firms are also paid by the employer that has a job opening to fill. But the retainer search firm has an *exclusive* ⌧ no other firm gets the assignment — and the retainer search firm gets paid whether they fill the job themselves or not. Employers use retainer firms usually when they need to fill more-senior positions or very difficult-to-fill positions. The retainer search firm gets the fee regardless of who gets hired or *how* that person got hired. Even if the company finds the person themselves, they pay the fee to the retainer search firm.

A good recruiter in a search firm usually places only one or two people a month. This is the most important statistic for you to know about search firms. This information will affect your entire *thought* process about search firms. Again —a good search person places only one or two people a month. Recruiters need to place one person a month to pay their mortgage! Recruiters who deal with junior-level people need to place two people a month to pay their mortgages. **Recruiters who deal with the very highest-level people may place only *six people a year!*** And yet, some coaches who are not trained in The Five O'Clock Club techniques might tell their job-hunting clients, "at your senior level all jobs are filled through search firms," when the opposite is true. **Don't go on until you're sure that you have fully absorbed this important point.**

So search firms are not handling as many jobs as you think and your whole life does not depend on this search person. It's actually very *unlikely* that a search firm and a specific recruiter will be able to place you. Should you talk to search firms? Sure you should talk to search firms. Should you be afraid of them or count on them? Not a chance. There's no reason to be afraid of search firms. They actually have very little power. And, for goodness sake, don't *count* on them because they have very few actual jobs that they're trying to fill.

So this should put it in perspective for you. Now here are a few more pieces of information. Try to absorb them all. For a recruiter in a search firm, it's harder to find positions to fill, that is, job orders from employers, than it is to find people to fill them. The search firm is paid by the company, not by you. **They don't represent you; they represent the employer.** The employer is the one they want to please. And, yes, there are nice recruiters who really truly want to help people, but that's just because they're nice people. The people they really have to please are the employers.

Now. Let's go even deeper. **Why might a search firm *not* put you in for a job even though you are the *perfect* person for that job?** This happens a lot.

161

Here's an example. Jim, a Five O'Clock Club member, was the best networker in the club. I had never seen anybody before or since who could network into so many companies. Jim was a marketing guy, so he was a great marketer. During the course of his search, he uncovered fifty-two job openings. *Fifty-two job openings.* Of those, forty-eight were being handled by retainer search firms. During the course of his networking, he had already contacted every search firm that was appropriate. Yet those search firms didn't tell him about the openings. However, when he networked into or directly contacted the hiring companies themselves, and got in to see the right person in each of those companies, the *hiring* managers said, "We really like you and we have a job that's out for search right now. Here's the name of the search firm. Call them and use my name."

These were search firms Jim had *already* contacted, and they told him *nothing* about those openings. So, Jim contacted the search firms again saying that the hiring manager sent him to discuss a certain opening. I had to convince Jim to be nice to the search firms when he finally met with them. Jim calmed down. The search firms interviewed him for the jobs. Jim ended up with at least five offers.

This has happened to lots of Five O'Clock Clubbers who have met with search firms, and were told they were absolutely inappropriate for the job or that there were no jobs for them. Then The Five O'Clock Clubber contacted the company directly and got in. Many Five O'Clock Clubbers got jobs *after* they had been rejected by a search firm.

Life will give you what you ask of her if only you ask long enough and plainly enough.

E. NESBITT

Why might a retainer search firm not put you in for a job even though you may be the perfect person for the job? Remember that search firms are hired by the organization to go out and "search." That's why they're called "headhunters." They're hunting for "heads." They're hunting for the right people for the job. So say that a retainer search firm has already *put in* three candidates.

They say to their client organization, "I've done a thorough search and these are the three best candidates — or the *five* best candidates — for the job." They normally sequence them so the first person they put in is *not* the best and the second one's not the best; maybe the third one *is* the best. So they try to engineer the interview sequence. And then *you* come along. They're not going to say to the employer, "Oops, by the way, Mr. hiring manager, I've found another person for you." That won't make them look good.

Or it may also happen that in a larger search firm there's a recruiter, only one recruiter, who is handling that search. When you contact that search firm, you contact a *different* recruiter in the firm. Perhaps the one you're talking to doesn't refer you over to the recruiter who is handling that particular search. It's just too much trouble. So they tell you that they don't have any openings right now that are appropriate for you.

There are a lot of reasons why a recruiter might not submit your name for a position, such as it might make them look bad or they are too far along in the process.

Why might a search firm tell you that a company is not interested in you when they haven't even *told* the company about you? It happens all the time.

A retainer search firm says to you, "I've shown your paperwork to the organization, but the organization said they're not interested in you." When you contact the organization directly—because the search firm has already rejected you—you find that the organization has never even heard about you!

That's because the search firm was pushing somebody else. They don't want to show your résumé to the organization. They have it lined up just nicely without you. They just don't want to tell you that they're not putting you in for the job.

Feel free to ask them where you stand, but take the answer with a grain of salt.

<u>Therefore, if the search firm says that an organization is not interested in you, and that you will not even be considered for the job, you now have license to contact the organization on your own.</u> Once a search firm has rejected you, *contact the employer yourself.* However, don't mention that you heard about them from a search firm. Instead, read in detail our chapter titled, "What To Do When You Know There's a Job Opening" in this book.

Search-Firm Cover Letter

Dear Ms. Bruno:

In the course of your search assignments, you may have a requirement for a technically knowledgeable IBM Power Systems professional.

I have been both a "planner" and a "doer" of the steps of the System Development Life Cycle at companies such as General Motors and Proctor & Gamble, where I have spent most of my career. My accomplishments span the gamut, including the following:

- Evaluation of application and system software and hardware,
- Installation/setup of a new computer site,
- Conversion of IBM AS400-System 38, RPG and Web development programs,
- Requirements for and design of applications,
- Development and programming,
- Quality assurance and testing, and
- Optimization of performance for applications and systems.

At this juncture, after many years of commuting to Manhattan, I'm interested in seeking permanent employment in New Jersey, where I live.

The enclosed résumé briefly outlines my experience over the past 15 years. My base is now in the $90,000 range plus the usual fringes.

If it appears my qualifications meet the needs of one of your clients, I would be happy to further discuss my background in a meeting with you.

Yours truly,

Enclosure

Why might a search firm say that you're a strong candidate for the job when they really see you as weak? Because they don't want you to drop out of the picture. If you drop out of the picture, they have to dig up somebody else.

Here's another point. Once you have met with the hiring team at the employer's organization, follow up directly with the *hiring* organization, not with the search firm. When we talk about following up after a job interview, we mean **the follow-up you do with the organization itself, not follow-up with the search firm.**

Some search firms get nervous when Five O'Clock Clubbers say, "I'm writing a proposal for the employer." Recruiters may be afraid you're going to mess it up. But Five O'Clock Clubbers are actually better at this process than most recruiters are. So **don't *worry* the recruiter about the follow-up you're doing. Ask your small group for advice on this.**

Recruiters are paid between 25 to 33 percent of your first year's salary to place you. *Theoretically,* the more money you make, the more money they make.

So why might a recruiter not always be interested in getting you the highest salary possible? Remember: recruiters make one or two placements per month. They'd rather have one placement at a *lower* salary and get a *lower* fee than make no placements that month. It's like a real estate agent who just wants to move that house. Better to sell it at a lower price and get a lower commission, than get no commission at all.

What's more, they can brag to the employer what a great job they did: "Did I find a bargain for you!" Remember, they work for the *hiring* organization, not for you!

I've told you a lot of negative things. Yet, some of my best friends are recruiters. Many recruiters are lovely people who went into that field because they wanted to help people. Still, remember that **being a recruiter is basically a sales position.** And it's my job to warn you about the bad guys, not to tell you how lovely some of the good guys are — and they *are.* My job is to remind you that recruiting is basically a sales position. Recruiters

are trying to match people up. It is like a real estate agent who is trying to sell a house or is trying to get the seller and buyer together. The realtor is trying to get them to come together on price and **the realtor wants to stay in the middle.** In both fields, possibilities are sometimes presented as "once-in-a-lifetime" opportunities. And often, the actual matches are just as rare!

If you're trying to change careers, chances are a search firm cannot help you. It's not their job to reposition you and market you to the right people. That's your job.

Now, how you can find good headhunters? One of the best ways is through networking:

- When you're networking, just ask people, "Are there any search firms you've used or that you think I should talk to?"
- **Be suspicious of ads**. Some contingency firms will place ads even when they have no openings because they need to get in a fresh batch of résumés. The people they have on file have already gotten jobs. So you call about an ad you've seen and they say, "That job is filled; let me talk to you about *other* jobs that may be right for you." You can't trust that every ad you see represents a real job.

  Think about that the next time you see an ad and you think *that job's too good to be true.* It probably *isn't* true. They placed a great, generalized ad to pull in a lot of résumés.
- On the other hand, ads do list search firms that handle the kinds of jobs you're looking for. So *contact* those search firms, but not necessarily for the job they have listed.
- Another resource to locate search firms is Kennedy Information (www.kennedycareerservices.com), which has online and print tools for finding and connecting with recruiters.

Five O'Clock Club Clubbers have an exclusive resource for finding an extensive variety of recruiters, as well as other job-search resources (in print and online) in our *Career and Job Search Bibliography*, online at our website (for members only) and also in this book.

"One of those corporate head-hunters called about you today. But it's not what you think. They have offered to pay us to keep you here."

Courtesy of Jerry King, Cartoons, Inc.

However, as you'll hear later, we don't think you should contact contingency search firms blindly because bad things could happen. Instead, have a targeted list of search firms to contact, rather than giving your résumé to everybody.

- **If you're leaving a company because of a downsizing, ask your human resources department which search firms they use.** If you're staying in the same field, contact the search firm that your prior employer used. That will give you some *clout* because you can say that, "Jane Doe in Human Resources at ABC, Inc. suggested I call you." Since ABC pays the search firm for placements, their search firm is likely to try to help you.

Remember that **we are reluctant to encourage you to do a mass mailing to contingency search firms because there are good and bad search firms. Search firms can help you, but some can actually harm you.** For example, a firm — even one that's normally a retainer search firm — could say to you: "Oh, don't worry about your search. I'll take care of it for you." Then they blanket the market with your résumé — or contact companies *you* would have contacted on your own anyway. Now the hiring company *cannot* consider *ever* hiring *you* unless they want to pay a fee. When you contact the company, they say that

they already *have* your résumé from a search firm, and, "We don't want to pay a fee." Therefore, the search firm becomes your competitor. They got into the company before you did.

Contact companies on your own. If the search firm offers to market you, it sounds like a gift. Don't do it. Market *yourself*. If employers don't want to pay a fee, they will not even touch you.

- Make sure to tell the search firm, "Don't send out my résumé without calling me first." Keep control of where your résumé is going. Don't let them mass-mail your résumé. They may even send it to your present employer by accident! They have a list and they give it to the *assistant* to send it out.

- One of our coaches, who used to be in human resources, tells about the time she received résumés from *four* different search firms on the *same* day for the *same* person. The résumé looked great, but she wouldn't meet with the applicant because then she'd be in the middle of a fight over who should get the fee if she ever hired this person. Find out what a search firm plans to do with *your* résumé.

Recruiters may be on your side or may *not* be on your side. They *may* be trying to promote *another* candidate and get information from you so they can use it *against* you. Be careful. Tell the search person enough to be put in for the interview. Then *you* deal with the hiring organization. Be savvy. Don't be such an innocent.

The wise man avoids evil by anticipating it.
PUBLILIUS SYRUS, C. 42 B.C., ROMAN WRITER, *Maxims*

Some job hunters are afraid that if they turn down a job offer they got through a search firm, they'll never be considered for another job again from that search firm. *Will* the search firm refuse to work for you?

No. You've proven yourself to be marketable. You're a person who can land jobs. Recruiters have a hard time finding people who can actually *get* offers so if you got *one* offer, you can probably get another one. However, if you turn down *too* many offers, then you're not worth their time.

Why might an unethical contingency recruiter call you after you have six months on the job, and try to move you to another company? Why might a recruiter call you after you've been in the job just *one* month, find out you're unhappy, and urge you to give it a try — "just for six months. If you're still unhappy, I'll try to help you find another position."

That's because the fee agreements often state that you need to be in the job for six months. If the recruiter moves you after that, they can get another fee.

A contingency recruiter asks you where else you've interviewed and who you have talked to there. They say, "I really need to know the kind of positions you're looking for. And who did you talk to there? I want to know where you're seeing people so I don't send your résumé to the same places." *Why* do they want to know where you're interviewing?

Because recruiters need to find *job openings*. As soon as you leave their office, an unethical recruiter could be on the phone to that hiring manager telling her that they have the *ideal* candidate for the job—and it won't be you! They'll put one of their other clients in for the job so *they* can get the fee.

Retainer firms work differently and you're not as much at risk by answering this question. However, **if a retainer firm fills jobs for your present employer, they cannot help you to leave your present employer!** In fact, some major organizations will actually put a search firm *on* retainer just so that the search firm *cannot* recruit from them.

Be suspicious of recruiters who ask for names of references the first time they meet with you. They may be looking for other people to put in for jobs. Hey, they're supposed to know *your* industry inside out. They should be able to

pick up the phone and ask *anyone* about you. They shouldn't need references right away.

Try to meet directly with the recruiter. Make sure this recruiter is someone you want to represent you. Any recruiter who doesn't want *you* to be part of the follow-up process or the salary negotiation process is doing you a disservice.

Don't be scared to use search firms. Just be on your guard against those firms that may use tactics that are not in your best interests. When times are good, search firms may be less likely to resort to these tactics. But when times get tough and business is more difficult to come by, firms are more likely to do things that you need to guard against. **Should you use search firms? Absolutely! Should you rely on them? Absolutely not!**

Now that you're ready to use search firms, **here's how to contact them.** Let the search firm know how marketable you are—in your cover letter:

Paragraph 1 might say: "In the course of your search assignments, you may need a " List a few job titles, industries and geographic areas. They *need* to know your targets, so tell them up front. They also need to know your level, so you have to give them a salary range, a very broad one. If you were referred in by someone, be sure to use that person's name up front.

When you write a great cover letter, which has bulleted accomplishments, the recruiter can then pick up the phone and use your cover letter to *sell* you to a company. The recruiter could say, "Gee, Joe, I've got right here a person who has increased sales 40% at his last firm, and trained a sales force of 20 people, and a bunch of other accomplishments I think you're looking for." Help the recruiter to help you.

Paragraph 2: Your summary.

Paragraph 3: Your bulleted accomplishments.

Paragraph 4: the close.

If the recruiter wants you to redo your résumé, do it if you're very interested in the job they're talking to you about. But some recruiters become very idiosyncratic and narrow. They want the résumé done a certain way, but they forget

167

that **you got in to see *them* with your present résumé**. It worked for *them*, but they think it won't work for anyone else. They also forget that ***their résumé technique "works" not because of their résumé approach but because they actually get on the phone with someone and *talk* about you***. Just change your résumé for them, but in general, don't change your résumé for the rest of your search *just* because of what a recruiter wanted. Because you're insecure, you may be willing to listen to any "experts" who today are dealing with only a small percentage of the job market. Instead, listen to your small group at the Club.

Don't bother a recruiter with follow-up phone calls. They get *thousands* of résumés. If, however, you can help them because you know lots of people, then you can follow up with a call because you have something to offer *them*. Generally, the time to develop a relationship with a search firm is *not* when you're job hunting, but helping them when you're employed.

Be courteous to all, but intimate with few; and let those few be well tried before you give them your confidence.

GEORGE WASHINGTON, 1721-1799,
Letter to Bushrod Washington

Finally — *do* use search firms. But be sensible. Remember that search firms do *not* hold your future in their hands. Use them, but do your *own* search and you'll feel more powerful and be more in control of your own destiny. And now you know a lot more about search firms and ads than you did before.

Pain: an uncomfortable frame of mind that may have a physical basis in something that is being done to the body, or may be purely mental, caused by the good fortune of others.

AMBROSE BIERCE

Note: This chapter is an excerpt from one of our audio lectures (40 minutes each), meant to provide you with the inside scoop and research on every portion of the job search.

What to Do When you Know There's a Job Opening

To paraphrase Peter Drucker, effective people are not problem-minded; they're opportunity-minded. They feed opportunities and starve problems.

STEPHEN R. COVEY,
The Seven Habits of Highly Effective People

You've heard about a job opening from someone, or you've seen an ad in the paper. Answer that ad. But to increase your chances of getting a meeting, find an additional way in besides the ad (through networking or through directly contacting the organization).

When using networking or direct contact, most job hunters aim for the hiring manager. After all, he or she is the one with the job, so why would you contact anyone else?

But consider contacting someone other than the hiring manager. He or she is being inundated with requests for meetings by people who have heard about the job. To the hiring manager, those who network in may seem just like those who responded to the ad: another job hunter who knows there is a job opening.

But you are different. You're not a grubby job hunter. You're sincerely interested in this organization, aren't you? You want to meet with someone regardless of whether or not he or she has an opening, don't you? In fact, you are so interested in this organization you would be glad to speak with other people there, not just the hiring manager.

If you first meet with others, you will learn a lot about the hiring manager, the organization, its needs, and the kinds of people who work there.

They can refer you in to the hiring manager—with their recommendations. You will be much better prepared than those who got in through the ad. After the formal job interview, you will have advocates in the organization who can coach you and speak to the hiring manager on your behalf.

Some job hunters worry that the job may be filled before they get to the hiring manager. That's possible, but unlikely. Most jobs take a long time to fill. Résumés may sit for weeks before anyone even looks at them. In most cases, you will have time to meet with other people first.

To gather basic information, it's okay to meet with people junior to you or at your level to gather information. But it is sometimes difficult for those lower in the organization to refer you up to the boss. Those at your boss's level, or perhaps higher, are in a better position to refer you up, so make sure you aim to meet with them.

CASE STUDY Madge
I've Followed Your Organization

Jean, a participant at The Five O'Clock Club, met with five people at Conference Associates and received an offer. It was an interesting place, but she decided the job was too low-level and took another job.

When Jean announced at The Five O'Clock Club that she had turned down an offer from Con-

169

ference Associates, Madge became very interested in the position.

Jean and Madge spoke later so Madge could learn more about the organization, the job, and the people with whom Jean met. Madge also did Internet and library research on the organization. Since she knew exactly who all the players were, she could easily have contacted the hiring manager. In fact, she could have networked in through Jean. But that's not what she did.

In this case, we decided Madge should write directly to the president, who was three-up in the chain of command (the person who would be her boss's boss's boss). In her letter, she said she had long been interested in Conference Associates and she referred to issues Jean had told her were important. **She did not refer to the fact that she knew there was a job opening.**

The cover letter Madge wrote (with a résumé enclosed) is on the next page. The president suggested Madge meet with human resources, the hiring manager, and others. By the way, **this is _not_ networking. This is a targeted mailing.**

Through this technique, Madge got the meeting she wanted. Through her follow-up, she got the job. Read about follow-up in our book _Mastering the Job Interview and Winning the Money Game._

Let your own discretion be your tutor:
Suit the action to the word,
The word to the action.

WILLIAM SHAKESPEARE, _Hamlet_

This is the cover letter Madge sent. She also enclosed her résumé.

MADGE WRIGLEY
345 East Ball Park Avenue, Scottsdale, AZ 44555
(555) 555-0121
mwrigley555@aol.com

July 3, 201X

Ms. Nancy Deering, President
Conference Associates
5637 Columbus Avenue
Phoenix, AZ 44555

Dear Ms. Deering:

These days, the last thing an executive looking to improve profitability probably wants to hear is, "Go to a conference." But that is precisely what he or she may need to find ideas to solve problems back home. I am writing because Conference Associates' goal of encouraging interaction and furthering the exchange of knowledge is one I would like to promote.

I'm currently a manager at AT&T marketing directly to credit-card customers. I manage about $32 million in revenue annually. I've been successful in building a market for expensive products, some, such as life insurance, with negative connotations to overcome.

The key has been twofold: (1) setting clear-cut goals and guiding both the creative and managerial processes to see them realized and (2) carefully researching and identifying a target market, then developing compelling communications to reach them. Now, though, I would like to put my 10 years of business development and marketing experience to work for Conference Associates, specifically in order to take a broader, and global view, of business.

Several aspects of Conference Associates' activities are particularly aligned with my interests and skills:

• The customer orientation: I would like to make companies my customer, evaluating their needs and delivering the services to meet them.

• The Associates' stated goals for expansion in Europe: I firmly believe my international experience could prove beneficial. I'm fluent in French and Spanish, and have worked in France and Sweden.

• I'm an educator at heart: I enjoy managing and developing staff and making connections among people and ideas.

In sum, I believe I could offer a trained and critical eye to understand the need and persuasive marketing programs to communicate the service.

At your convenience, I would be most interested in having a chance to speak with you. I'll call your office shortly to see if that may be possible.

Sincerely,

Madge Wrigley

MADGE WRIGLEY
345 East Ball Park Avenue
Scottsdale, AZ 44555
mwrigley555@aol.com

August 17, 201X

Mr. Charles Conlin
Director, Personnel
Conference Associates
5637 Columbus Avenue
Phoenix, AZ 44555

Dear Chip:

First of all, it was a pleasure to meet you last Wednesday. I enjoyed hearing your assessment of the potential that exists for C.A., and seeing your commitment and enthusiasm for the organization.

You spoke of the unique position of C.A. as a nonprofit service organization run more and more like any business in a competitive environment. The role of a new marketing director, then, would be to develop a strategy for the business to position C.A. for the next level of growth. It's fortunate that C.A. has a solid base to grow from, including a reputation for quality and service. The challenge would be to enhance that reputation while building new markets and customers.

One of the things we spoke about was the need for the marketing director to work closely and productively with other departments. Rob Hellmann and I spoke about that as well. I feel particularly motivated by that type of challenge and have been successful in working with diverse groups. For example, recently at AT&T a major new segmentation strategy and methodology for my product line required tying in systems, finance, and new products, in addition to marketing. It wasn't easy, but the reward is a successful expansion of our business and a precedent set for productive cross-departmental projects.

Getting a business built depends a lot on people who don't report to you and buying them into the goals and the process is the only way of getting the job done well. It requires using a balance of sensitivity and toughness and relating to colleagues with flexibility and creativity. If C.A.'s marketing department is going to become a vital and integral part of the operation, it has to establish itself as responsive, knowledgeable, and resourceful.

I truly believe this position is a solid match with my experience and interests, both for the specific skill base required and the opportunity to build a comprehensive marketing program. I've developed marketing plans for organizations ranging from small nonprofits to AT&T and achieved positive results with the implementation.

The common thread in that success has been what you called "ownership." In both my professional experience and my community volunteer work, I tend to approach the task at hand with energy and commitment. After all, the most effective marketer is the one who can combine strategic development and proven skills with genuine product enthusiasm. I would be most interested in putting that same experience and enthusiasm to work for C.A.

Looking forward to speaking with you again soon.

Best,

Madge Wrigley

MADGE WRIGLEY
345 East Ball Park Avenue
Scottsdale, AZ 44555
mwrigley555@aol.com

August 18, 201X

Mr. Rob Hellmann
Senior Vice President, Development
Conference Associates
5637 Columbus Avenue
Phoenix, AZ 44555

Dear Rob:

It was good meeting with you last Wednesday. I got a clear picture of the requirements of the marketing director position and the kind of challenges to be met.

First and foremost, you expressed a need going forward for someone who can develop a comprehensive, integrated marketing strategy and can communicate that plan effectively and appropriately in all facets of its implementation.

That requires the skills of listener, evaluator and diagnostician, coupled with an ability to generate and harness ideas and turn them into positive results. The goal would be to establish C.A. as a leading source of business intelligence and creativity for corporations and their executives.

I've had a chance to think about some of the ways we discussed to accomplish that goal. It seems that both the stated mission of C.A. and its profitability center on building and enhancing its relationship with members, working to have members' resources and activities become a more familiar and integral part of corporate life. One of the priorities you outlined was devising ways to package existing products and services, maximizing both internal marketing efficiency and external perception of value. That would include targeting different people within the same organization with relevant services, as well as determining the right level of pricing.

You also mentioned C.A.'s global objective, trying to serve both U.S. companies competing internationally and many of their foreign competitors. Although I understand the Paris affiliate handles much of the activity in Europe, one of the components of an integrated marketing plan would be defining the optimum balance between a U.S. and global emphasis.

I firmly believe my experience and personality fit the job at hand and that the skills required play to my strengths. I have demonstrated success in strategic and creative planning, researching, and identifying target markets, then developing compelling and appropriate communications to reach them. At both AT&T and previously at RCA, I have developed new businesses and products, including pricing, positioning, and packaging existing services. Efforts I've directed include advertising that increased response from 58% to 93%, and market expansion of 30% with new targeting programs.

I've found ways to run marketing activities more efficiently, saving on both fixed overhead and variable production costs. Finally, as I mentioned, I'm in charge of all writing for the business unit, working closely with each area to communicate group and corporate monthly results as well as the five-year and annual strategic plans.

From my conversations with you and Deborah, the goals for the position, the products of C.A., and its environment seem to represent a strong match with my background and interests. I look forward to speaking with you again soon and having a chance to discuss the position further.

Sincerely,

Madge Wrigley

MADGE WRIGLEY
345 East Ball Park Avenue
Scottsdale, AZ 44555
mwrigley555@aol.com

October 18, 201X

Ms. Nancy Deering
President and CEO
Conference Associates
5637 Columbus Avenue
Phoenix, AZ 44555

Dear Nancy:

While everything is now official and I'll be starting Thursday, October 24th, I wanted to let you know what a pleasure it was to finally meet with you and how delighted I am to be joining C.A..

When we met, you spoke of approaching the task of marketing C.A. with an eye to challenges and opportunities, building on a strong foundation to find better ways to position ourselves in an increasingly competitive market. That includes keeping the focus on senior-level executives. Your outline of the process you've undertaken to evaluate C.A.'s activities was extremely helpful, as well as your expectations for staff to initiate and persuade, even without direct-line responsibility. I particularly appreciated your straightforward review of the financial position.

You also spoke specifically of the need for someone to bring to the position not only marketing expertise but also an enjoyment of your intellectual, knowledge-based product. I firmly believe in that genuine product combination. I'm looking forward to working with that combination and with colleagues who are clearly committed to the organization.

One of them is certainly Melanie. We had a terrific meeting, reviewing everything from general history to specific programs. Particular attention was paid to the strategic plan and development of C.A. over the past few years and the challenge of communicating that strategy both internally and to our customer base. I'm very much looking forward to working with her on integrating a marketing strategy into the overall planning process and new product development, and incorporating that strategy into marketing the programs. I'll also be able to meet with Aaron before I start.

Over the past few weeks, I've had a chance both to think about my conversations with you and others with whom I've met and to review some of C.A.'s materials (50th anniversary history, last year's annual report, etc.). I believe there is enormous potential to spread the word—and the work—of C.A. to a wider audience and to enhance the value of the organization to its current customers. A major component of the task is communication—defining those characteristics that differentiate us in the marketplace and translating them into language that sells. Your commitment to testing new approaches is welcome, understanding the need for moving thoughtfully and with careful planning.

I look forward to the 24th and to a wonderful association at my new home.

Very best,

Madge Wrigley

Following Up When there Is No Immediate Job

Contrary to the cliche, genuinely nice guys most often finish first, or very near it.

MALCOLM FORBES

During each meeting, you have taken up the time of someone who sincerely tried to help you. Writing a note is the only polite thing to do. Since the person has gone to some effort for you, go to some effort in return. A phone call to thank a person can be an intrusion and shows little effort on your part.

In addition to being polite, there are good business reasons for writing notes and otherwise keeping in touch with people who have helped you. For one thing, few people keep in touch so you will stand out. Second, it gives you a chance to sell yourself again and to overcome any misunderstandings that may have occurred. Third, this is a promotional campaign and any good promoter knows that a message reinforced soon after a first message results in added recall.

If you meet someone through a networking meeting, for example, he or she will almost certainly forget about you the minute you leave and just go back to business. Sorry, but you were an interruption.

If you write to people almost immediately after your meeting, this will dramatically increase the chance they will remember you. If you wait two weeks before writing, they may remember meeting someone but not remember you specifically. If you wait longer than two weeks, they probably won't remember meeting anyone—let alone you.

So promptly follow the meeting with a note. It is important to remind those to whom you write who you are and when they talked to you. Give some highlight of the meeting. Contact them again within a month or two. It is just like an advertising campaign. Advertisers will often place their ads at least every four weeks in the same publication. If they advertised less often, few people would remember the ad.

"I'm sorry, but Mr. Konklin is extremely busy today. Can I take a message and have him get back to you?"

175

What Michael Did

This is a classic—and it worked on me many years ago! I wanted to hire one junior accountant for a very important project and had the search narrowed down to two people. I asked my boss for his input. We made up a list of what we were seeking and we each rated the candidates on 20 criteria. The final scores came in very close, but I hired Judy instead of Michael.

In response to my rejection, Michael wrote me a note telling me how much he still wanted to work for our organization and how he hoped I would keep him in mind if something else should come up. He turned the rejection into a positive contact. Notes are so unusual and this one was so personable, that I showed it to my boss.

A few months later, Michael wrote again saying he had taken a position with another firm. He was still very much interested in us and he hoped to work for us someday. He promised to keep in touch, which he did. Each time he wrote, I showed the note to my boss. Each time, we were sorry we couldn't hire him.

After about seven months, I needed another helping hand. Whom do you think I called? Do you think I interviewed other people? Do you think I had to sell Michael to my boss? Michael came to work for us and we never regretted it. Persistence pays off.

We make a living by what we get,
but we make a life by what we give.

WINSTON CHURCHILL

What to Say in Your Follow-Up Note

Depending on the content of your note, you may type or write it. Generally use standard business-size stationery, but sometimes Monarch or other note-size stationery, ivory or white, will do. A job interview follow-up should almost always be typed on standard business-size ivory or white stationery.

After an information-gathering meeting, play back some of the advice you received, any you intend to follow, and so on. Simply be sincere. What did you appreciate about the time the person spent with you? Did you get good advice that you intend to follow? Say so. Were you inspired? Encouraged? Awakened? Say so.

If you think there were sparks between you and the person with whom you met, be sure to say you will keep in touch. Then do it. Follow-up letters don't have to be long, but they do have to be personal. Make sure the letters you write could not be sent to someone else on your list.

Sample Follow-Up to a Networking Meeting

PETER SCHAEFER

To: Laura Labovich

Thanks again for contacting Brendan for me and for providing all those excellent contact names.

There's such a wealth of good ideas in that list that it will take me a while to follow up on all of them, but I'm working hard at it and will let you know what develops.

Again, thanks for your extraordinary effort. (By the way, should you ever want to "review your career options," I would be delighted to share a few names, or more than a few, with you.)

Stay tuned!

Peter

To keep in touch, simply let interviewers/network contacts know how you are doing. Tell them whom you are seeing and what your plans are. Some people, seeing your sincerity, will keep sending you leads or other information.

It's never too late to follow up. For example: "I met you a year ago and am still impressed by... Since then I have... and would be interested in getting together with you again to discuss these new developments." Make new contacts. Recontact old ones by writing a "status report" every two months telling them how well you are doing in your search. **Keeping up with old networking contacts is as important as making new ones.**

Some job hunters use this as an opportunity to write a proposal. During the meeting, you may have learned something about the organization's problems. Writing a proposal to solve them may create a job for you. Patricia had a networking meeting with a small company where she learned that it wanted to expand the business from $5 million to $50 million. She came up with lots of ideas about how that could be done—with her help, of course—and called to set up a meeting to review her ideas. She went over the proposal with them and they created a position for her.

However, you are not trying to turn every networking meeting into a job possibility. You are trying to form lifelong relationships with people. Experts say most successful employees form solid relationships with lots of people and keep in touch regularly throughout their careers. These people will keep you up-to-date in a changing economy, tell you about changes or openings in your field, and generally be your long-term ally. And you will do the same for them.

Has a man gained anything who has received a hundred favors and rendered none? He is great who confers the most benefits.

RALPH WALDO EMERSON, *"Essay on Compensation"*

177

The Five O'Clock Club

Following Up after a Networking/ Direct-Contact Meeting

Opportunities are usually disguised as hard work, so most people don't recognize them.

ANN LANDERS, SYNDICATED ADVICE COLUMNIST

The follow-up after a networking meeting— or a meeting resulting from having directly contacted an organization (through a direct-mail campaign or a targeted mailing)—is very different from the way you follow up after a job interview.

Analyze the meeting. In your letter, thank the interviewer. State the *specific* advice and leads you were given. Be personable. Say you will keep in touch. Do keep in touch.

Follow up every few months with a "status report" on how your search is going, an article, or news of interest to the manager.

Make sure people are thinking about you. You may contact the manager just as he or she has heard of something of importance to you.

Recontact those you met earlier in your search. Otherwise, you're like a salesman who works to get new leads while ignoring his old relationships. Get new leads but also keep in touch with people you've already met.

It's never too late to follow up. For example: "I met you three years ago and am still impressed by_____. Since then I have_____and would be interested in getting together with you again to discuss these new developments." Make new contacts. Recontact old ones. It's never too late.

If you know anything that will make a brother's heart glad, run quick and tell it; and if it is something that will only cause a sigh, bottle it up, bottle it up.

Old Farmer's Almanac, 1854

If (a man) is brusque in his manner, others will not cooperate. If he is agitated in his words, they will awaken no echo in others. If he asks for something without having first established a (proper) relationship, it will not be given to him.

I CHING: BOOK OF CHANGES, CHINA, c. 600 B.C.

> **Trouble getting started? What would you say to the person if he or she were sitting across from you right now? Consider that as the opening of your follow-up letter.**

In differentiation, not in uniformity, lies the path of progress.

LOUIS BRANDEIS, U.S. SUPREME COURT JUSTICE, *Business—A Profession*

> **Job hunters make a mistake when they fail to *recontact* people with whom they have formed relationships earlier in their search. Keep in touch on a regular basis so you increase your chances of contacting them just at a time when they have heard of something that may interest you—or may have a new need themselves.**

Follow up with a customized note specifically acknowledging the help you received.

JOHN WEITING
163 York Avenue—12B
New York, New York 10000
(212) 555-2231 (day)
(212) 555-1674 (message)
jweiting@attnet.net

June 25, 201X

Ms. Patty Bradley
Director of Outplacement
Time-Warner Communications
8 Pine Street
New York, NY 10001

Dear Ms. Bradley:

Thanks so much for seeing me. Your center is very impressive and seems very well run. But of course, I had heard that before I met you.

As you suggested, I sent for information on ASTD and was pleasantly surprised to see your name in there! It sounds like a great organization and I can't wait until they start to have meetings again in the fall.

I will definitely follow up with both Win Sheffield and Maritza Diaz, and appreciate your giving me their names. I've called them each a few times, but they and I are very busy people.

After I left your place, I wished I had asked you more about your own career. Only at the very end did you bring up the interesting way you got your job. I had wrongly assumed you came up through the ranks at Time-Warner Communications. Perhaps some other time I can hear the rest of the story. You certainly seem to know your stuff.

I've enclosed The Five O'Clock Club calendar for June, July, and August. In addition, I'll be speaking at The New School in a few weeks and have a lot planned for myself for the fall. I will keep you posted regarding my activities and perhaps I'll even run into you at ASTD meetings.

Thanks again for your time and insight. Till we meet again.

Cordially,

John Weiting

EUGENE NOKES

August 24, 201x

Dear Mary Ann:

Just a quick note to thank you for taking the time to meet with me yesterday. Even though it seems I've located most of the places that could use my skill set, it's always nice to revalidate that opinion.

I was interested to learn of your new position in national product engineering. Although I understand your current situation, I'm always excited to discover new possibilities for becoming involved in Big Red's national campaign. I've long believed this effort is paramount to Big Red's continued dominance in the industry. In fact I expressed just such an opinion to Sharon Small on Tuesday. Sharon is involved in Big Red's advertising program to develop a national brand image and I commented to her how much I liked the concept.

I am very flattered, too, that you would consider involving me in your developing organization. As I mentioned to you, I am quite good at "start-up" positions requiring a great amount of vision to allow for working in an indeterminate environment. Clearly my marketing liaison and consulting activities would be a natural for your charter as well. If I can help you in any way as you define your area, I would be happy to offer you my assistance.

I would like very much to contact you again in a few weeks to learn more about your progress. In the meantime I am going to try to contact Bill Belknap and others involved in the National Marketing effort to keep abreast of this exciting new area.

Thanks again for your time—hope to see you again soon.

Sincerely,

Eugene

SYLVAN VON BERG

To: Judy Acord

I enjoyed our conversation, which I found most helpful.

I will meet with Betsy Austin when she returns from overseas, and will talk to Jim about seeing Susan Geisenheimer. I'll also contact Bob Potvin and Clive Murray, per your suggestion.

Again, thanks for your help. I'll let you know how things develop.

Sylvan

CARL ARMBRUSTER

To: Nancy Abramson

Thanks again for contacting Brendan for me and for providing all those excellent contact names.

There's such a wealth of good ideas in the list it will take me a while to follow up with all of them, but I'm working hard at it and will let you know what develops.

Again, thanks for your extraordinary effort. (By the way, should you ever want to "review your career options," I would be delighted to share a few names, or more than a few, with you.)

Stay tuned!

Carl

Mr. Miguel Villarin
President
Commerce and Industry Association
Street Address
City, State

Dear Miguel:

Thank you for the time from your busy schedule. I enjoyed our discussion and appreciated your suggestions about marketing myself in the northern part of the state. Your idea on using the Big 8 firms as pivot points in networking is an excellent one. As you requested, I have enclosed copies of my résumé. I plan to call you next week, Miguel, so that I can obtain the names of the firms to which you sent my résumé.

I have been thinking about using Robert Dobbs (Dobbs & Firth) in my networking efforts. Since he is a past president of Commerce and Industry, I would be foolish not to tap such a source. Thanks again, Miguel.

Sincerely,

Janet Vitalis

Enclosures

How to Handle Rejection Personally and Professionally

In nature, there are neither rewards nor punishments—there are consequences.

ROBERT GREEN INGERSOLL

First, the pragmatics:

Rejection in Response to a Networking Contact You Tried to Make

The person did not understand you were seeking information. If many people respond to you this way, reassess your approach to networking.

Rejection Following a Job Interview

This is a true rejection. It used to be it took seven job interviews to get one offer, but the figure may now be higher. If you are still interested in the organization, don't give up. (Read what Michael did in the chapter "Following Up When There Is No Immediate Job."

Lessons to Learn

When you get rejected after a job interview, think about it. How interested are you in that firm? Did you hit it off with the interviewer? If you think there was some mutual interest, see if there might be other jobs with the organization later— perhaps in another department. Or perhaps the person hired instead of you might not work out. Keep in touch. Job hunters rarely do, but employers like to hire people who truly want to work for them and show it by keeping in touch.

CASE STUDY *Stan*
Turning a Rejection into an Offer

Stan was told an offer was being made to another candidate. He was crushed, but he immediately dashed off a letter to the hiring manager and hand-delivered it. The brief letter said in part:

> I was disappointed to hear you have offered the position to someone else. I truly believe I am right for the position and wish you would keep me in mind anyway. You never know— something could happen to the new person, and you may need a replacement. Please consider me no matter when this may occur, because I believe I belong at your institution.

The next day, Stan received a call with an offer. Some people may think the offer to the other candidate fell through. However, I believe Stan's letter influenced the hiring manager. When he saw the letter, he thought to himself, We're offering the position to the wrong person! and he allowed the negotiation with the other candidate to lapse.

And now, handling your emotions.

Cut down on stress and you'll increase your chances of finding a new job. If you've been out of work a while, you're really feeing it. Money woes. A sense of rejection. Questions and pressure from family and friends. If you've lost your job, you know this dismal laundry list all too well.

It's all too easy to convince yourself that you will never find another job, a mindset that can turn into a self-fulfilling prophecy. Here are a few suggestions that will help you push through your job-hunt stress:

- **It is OK to be "between jobs."** When you don't have a job, "So what do you do?" becomes a dreaded question. We resort to a euphemism, "I'm between jobs."

  You must learn to ignore the inner voice that in your darkest moments says, "I'll never get a good job again." Even if you have just been turned down for three jobs, remind yourself that you got three interviews and you can get three more.

- **Stay in touch with colleagues and friends from your former workplace.** When you are unemployed, the daily camaraderie of the office is gone. One of the most painful aspects of not going to work every day is missing people who were fun to be around. In addition, they will be able to remind you of your past achievements.

- **Treat your job search like a job.** The lack of a job-day routine can be disorienting. You can feel that you have been cut loose.

  The best way to overcome the loss of your daily routine is to create a new one. Treat your job search as your new job. Providing yourself with the day-to-day structure you are familiar with will help you keep your sanity and get you going in your job search more quickly.

- **Exercise regularly and keep a healthy lifestyle.** Regular physical exercise and a healthy diet help to reduce tension and stress. If your former routine involved going to the gym and you can still afford it,

keep going. If you can't, a half-hour walk every day will do the trick.

Keep an eye on what you're eating as well. Healthy foods give you energy.

- **Take time to enjoy the change of pace.** Being freed from the 9-to-5 grind means you finally have time to take stock of what you really want to achieve in your life. Think about your life and plot course corrections. Some questions to consider as you plan your job search:

  1. What matters to me the most?
  2. What do I want to do differently?
  3. What hasn't worked for me in the past?
  4. What was my own role in my job loss? What can I do better the next time?
  5. How am I taking care of myself?

- **Stay away from negative news and nay-sayers.** Even in good economic times, you don't have to go far to find negative news about the world situation. During a recession, it's in your face 24/7, and it's something you should stay away from if you can. Similarly, stay away from naysayers. Their negativity will only get you down.

- **If you need to vent, vent!** Getting it all out does have healing power, and there is nothing especially heroic or brave about trying to go it alone. Find support groups at churches and synagogues, libraries and community centers. You will find people who will listen and whose stories will help you to feel less isolated.

- **Your unemployment is a business problem.** When you had bad days at work, you analyzed whatever problem was plaguing you, marshaled resources and people, and came up with solutions. In the same way, set your objective: To find a satisfying job that pays the bills. And develop your business strategy for achieving it.

- **Celebrate short-term successes.** When you get up in the morning, set up some achievable goals for the day so that you can end it with a sense of accomplishment. Write five more targeted letters.

Identify 10 more companies to contact. Make 10 follow-up phone calls. Set up one or two meetings to network. Just being able to cross these goals off your list at the end of the day is a good feeling. And, of course, they often lead to something even better.

- **Keep on top of your game**. Not going into the office is no excuse to let your skills and knowledge slip. There's no better time than a job search to make sure you stay current and sharp. Catch up on reading journals and attending meetings of your professional associations. You might consider taking a course, one that you could never find the time for when you were employed.

- **Have fun**. In the same way that you get burned out on your job after working nonstop for a month or two, you can get burned out on your job search. You need to stay fresh.

If you stay positive and make, "I will persevere!" your motto, you will land a great job, sooner or later.

The
Five
O'Clock
Club®

PART FOUR

Managing Your Campaign

ARE YOU CONDUCTING A GOOD SEARCH?

How to Handle the Phone: A Life Skill

The greatest mistake you can make in life is to be continually fearing you will make one.

ELBERT HUBBARD

I wrote to Betty, a senior human resources executive whom I have known for years, asking her to be on a panel addressing about 100 other executives. A few days later, I called her office. Her assistant, Jeb, said he could see someone in her doorway talking to her and he would ask her to call me. Betty didn't call: She's a very busy lady and I never expected a return call. When I called again that afternoon, I joked with Jeb, asking him if there was someone still standing in Betty's doorway. I asked him not to interrupt his boss because I understood how busy she was, but he said he would buzz her anyway and I then spoke to her.

This is the way it works in everyday life. When you're making routine work-related phone calls or calling your friends, if they don't return your call, you assume they're busy. And you think nothing of calling them again if you really want to talk to them. But when you're job hunting, you assume they don't call back because they don't *want* to talk to you. You become fearful of rejection. Unfortunately, you cannot get a job unless you actually meet with people—usually lots of people. And it's difficult to get those meetings without using the telephone.

I had no trouble calling Betty. But when I have to recruit speakers I have never met, I dread making those calls even though prospective speakers are usually flattered.

> **What should you say first? What if they don't answer? What if they do answer? And, yes, in this day of voice mail, things are certainly more complicated.**

Making follow-up phone calls is the part of the job-search process people tend to dislike the most. Yet, the calls must be made:

- as a follow-up to a letter asking for a meeting—the most common reason for making a call,
- as a follow-up after an interview, and
- as part of your research to find out the name of the right person to contact.

In this chapter, we'll cover how to ask for a meeting.

The Set-Up: Usually by Letter (Email or Snail-mail)

A mailed (rather than emailed) letter has more impact because people rarely get them. If your emails are not working out for you, try a mailed letter.

Any letter followed by a phone call is effective because most executives do not like to be caught off guard. They want to know what your phone call is about. If you have been following The Five O'Clock Club process, you have been contacting people with networking letters or targeted mailings. *Networking* means you are using the name of someone else to help you get the meeting: "John Doe suggested I contact you because he thought you could give me the advice I need."

187

A targeted mailing differs from networking because you are *not* using someone else's name. Instead, *you* create a tie-in to that person. You may write, for example, "I have been following your organization for some time and noticed your international sales have been dropping. I'd like to talk to you about that" or "Congratulations on your new position!"

Whether you are writing a letter using someone else's name or establishing your own connection with that person, the last paragraph of your letter says: "I will call you in a few days."

> **Most people find it difficult to make those follow-up phone calls after having written to someone.**

Learning the Art of Calling

To get the meeting you want, you will have to pick up the phone.

What should you say first? What if they don't answer? What if they *do* answer? And, yes, in this day of voice mail, things can certainly be more complicated.

You'll have to practice to become good at your follow-up phone calls. This means tracking results. Observe what is working and what is not. Modify your script to suit yourself and the situation at hand. You will soon learn to think on your feet and get that meeting or a referral to someone else—without annoying people. But this comes with repetition and practice.

Getting Started

I am a great believer, if you have a meeting, in knowing where you want to come out before you start the meeting. Excuse me if that doesn't sound very democratic.

Nelson Rockefeller

Before you make that call—even before you write that letter—be sure you know the purpose of your call and what you want to get out of it. If you have unclear goals, you are less likely to accomplish anything worthwhile.

You may be calling to get:

- an in-office meeting with the person, unless the person is in a distant city,
- a phone meeting if that is the only reasonable option, or
- the name of an appropriate person with whom you should talk—if the person you're calling is at too high a level or in a different area.

> **"May I have Mr. Jones call you back?"**
>
> **"No, thanks, I'll be in and out a lot myself. I'll call him back later. When would be a good time for me to call?"**
>
> **Keep control of this process. If you say to your group, "I've left four messages and they haven't called me back," your group will say, "Stop leaving messages." Instead it's *your* responsibility to put in the effort to make the connection happen eventually.**

Become Friends with the Assistant

A long time ago, I wanted to meet with the person in charge of outplacement coaching at a Fortune 10 company. Even with research, I could not uncover the name of that person. So I wrote to Kevin Altria, the head of human resources, *knowing* he was inappropriate because he was too senior. I didn't need to get in to see Kevin or even speak to him. I just wanted him to refer me on. Then, when I contacted the appropriate person, I would be able to use Kevin's name.

So, before I finished the letter, I called Kevin's assistant to get her name (Jane) so I could include it in the letter and tell her to watch for it.

I followed The Five O'Clock Club format for cover letters. In the opening paragraph to Kevin, I wrote, "I know you're not the right person for me to contact, but I assume you know who's in charge of outplacement coaching at your firm. I'd like to tell that person something about myself and find out more about your company's outplacement department."

Paragraph two was my summary about myself. Paragraph three, the bulleted accomplishments. In the closing paragraph, I said, "I will call *Jane* in a few days to find out who you suggest I contact."

But there's more. On my letter, I put a sticky note saying, "Jane, this is the letter I told you about." When Jane opened her boss's mail, she saw my note with her name on it. She took the letter in to her boss and got the information I needed. Then I called Jane back (by now, we're friends) and I said, "Hi Jane, this is Kate Wendleton again. I'm following up about the letter I sent your boss." And she said, "We sent your letter on to Sylvia Norwood, who is in charge of outplacement here." I never had to bother Jane's boss.

At this point, I could have simply *called* Sylvia. But I didn't want anything to go wrong, so I *wrote* to Sylvia and said, "Kevin Altria suggested I contact you." This was my standard letter. And again, I followed the routine of finding out Sylvia's assistant's name (Jason) and using the sticky note. So, when I called back, I talked directly to Jason again and asked him to help me set up a meeting with Sylvia.

Notice I don't use the assistant as a messenger, asking him simply to tell Sylvia that I called. Instead, I want the assistant to be my ally. I tell Jason a little about my background, why I want to meet with Sylvia, and ask Jason to pass that information on to her. Sometimes, it may take five or six talks with the assistant to set something up. Eventually, Jason said, "Sylvia's very busy and she manages her own calendar, but I'll get her to talk to you."

This is a slow but fairly sure approach for getting in to see appropriate senior-level people. I had a two-hour meeting with Sylvia and was referred on to excellent people in the field.

Very senior people tend to have very smart assistants on whom they rely. So I can "pitch" to an assistant and ask him to make sure the boss sees my letter. And I don't try to meet with people who are inappropriate for me to see, irritating them and wasting their time.

- Have goals for your phone calls.
- Develop an outline of what you want to say.
- Practice to become smooth and natural.

What Are Your Back-Up Plans?

Sometimes you will not get what you want. Perhaps the person is in the middle of a major project right now or sees herself as an inappropriate person for you to talk to. You can still get something out of the conversation. You can at least try the following tactics.

- Determine when the person may have more time to schedule a meeting with you. The manager may have said to you: "We're in the midst of a crisis" "The next month is murder for me" or "We're reorganizing. I don't even know what's going to happen. The dust isn't going to settle for three months."
- Try to book something. "How about if we schedule something for a month from now? I'll call you ahead of time to confirm." Or—in the worst case—"May I call you back in [a month] to see if the situation has changed?"
- Get other names. For example, the manager may have said, "I'm leaving the organization in a few weeks" "This department doesn't concentrate on that" or "We don't use financial people in this department."

  You can say, "Can you direct me to others in your organization you think it would be appropriate for me to talk with?"

For most people, getting in to see a specific, appropriate person is not easy and requires a high degree of motivation. It must be important to you or you will not think of the right things to say

189

and you will give up too quickly. Do you want a meeting with this person or not? If not, go back to *Targeting a Great Career* and rethink what you want to do with your life.

> **Why should a person meet with you now just because you wrote to them? You're sitting by the phone, but they're busy.**

It's a Self-Selection Process

You wrote a letter. Why should a person meet with you—and meet with you now—just because you wrote them a letter now? Not only are they busy with their jobs, but personal things come up: There's been a death in the family; he's suffering from the flu; she's on vacation; she is out of the country 90 percent of the time.

You're sitting by the phone, but they're busy.

Part of getting meetings is a self-selection process: You decide how important this meeting is to you and you put in effort *to the extent you want it to happen*. Five O'Clock Club research shows that it takes an average of eight follow-up phone calls to land a meeting. The research also shows the more senior the person, the more calls you will have to make. Senior-level people travel a lot or are in meetings; they are difficult to track down and returning your call is not the most important thing on their "to do" list. If you really want to see them, prove it by your effort. You can show your interest without irritating them, such as when you acknowledge, "I'm sure you must be very busy..."

> **It's a self-selection process. If meeting with this person is important to you, put in the effort.**

One Five O'Clock Clubber—a senior-level marketing executive—sent targeted mailings to 20 important, high-profile people. He got in to see

people like Craig McCaw of McCaw Cellular and John Kluge, one of the richest men in America. On average, this process required *15 follow-up phone calls*—15 conversations with assistants. He met with approximately half the people on his list. He ended up spending four hours with Craig McCaw at Newark Airport—the only mutually convenient place they could arrange. His search was very successful, but he also understood he needed to prove to these in-demand people that it was important that they meet. By the way, he spent four days preparing for his meeting with Craig McCaw.

Busy and important people must have their calls screened or they would never get their work done. On the other hand, part of their job is to look at new talent, make sure they don't miss someone, and keep up with what is happening in the industry.

> **It takes an average of eight follow-up phone calls to get a meeting. The more senior the person, the more calls it takes. But leave a message only once.**

How can an important person decide with whom he should meet? Part of that person's decision is how important the meeting is to you. Have you done your homework? Do you know how to talk to his assistant? Do you make a good pitch to the assistant? Do you call back frequently, but without becoming a burden? You have to break through the clutter of all the other people vying for a place on his calendar.

When I was in my early 30s, living in Philadelphia, I had my day job but loved artwork and art museums. I was at the Philadelphia Museum of Art every single Sunday, did a lot of volunteer work there, and knew a lot about that museum. It was announced that Jean Boggs, who was at Harvard, was going to come in as the new head of the museum. *I wanted to see Jean Boggs* because I had so many ideas for that museum.

Would I be able to network in to see her? Not a chance. *No one* in Philadelphia would have introduced "Kate who?" to Jean Boggs. Instead, I wrote to Jean Boggs at Harvard *six months* before she was scheduled to come to Philadelphia. I said essentially, "You and I should meet. I have a lot of interest in the museum and a lot of ideas."

Then a month before Jean was to arrive at the museum, I wrote to her *again*, saying, "Do you remember me? I know you're coming to Philadelphia in a month and when you get here I think you and I should meet." A little arrogant of me!

When she got to Philadelphia, I wrote her a *third* time and I said, in so many words, "Hi, it's me again. I know you've arrived and I still want to see you."

When she got to Philadelphia, I was so persistent in making those follow-up phone calls— and not leaving messages for her to call me—that poor Jean Boggs eventually agreed to meet with me. I was passionate about the museum, so these calls were easy despite my shyness.

When I met with Jean, I was enthusiastic and had plenty of ideas. She graciously granted me 15 minutes and then took me down the hall to meet Noble Smith, who actually ran the museum on a day-to-day basis. I had a great meeting with Noble and he came up with a project for me. I worked with about 20 people who were on staff and shared my ideas and we implemented a lot of them. I actually got paid a small amount so I could say I was a paid consultant.

Although I have always been shy, I've managed to meet with anyone I've ever targeted. Who was I to get in to see Jean Boggs? I was just a lowly volunteer with no connections. I didn't have great credentials in the art area. I simply wanted to see someone for what I thought was a good reason, I wrote a letter using no one else's name, and I followed up—a lot. Being successful in a targeted mailing has to do with being sincerely interested, doing a fair amount of research, contacting the right person, and not being put off when you make those follow-up phone calls.

> **If I'm afraid of making 20 follow-up phone calls, the good news is that only two people will actually be there!**

The Follow-Up Call

You *must* make those follow-up phone calls. Don't leave a message saying you called and hope they'll call you back. Instead, say to the assistant, "I don't want to leave a message for Ms. Boggs to call me. I'm going to be in and out a lot myself, so I'll call her back."

Do Not Leave Your Phone Number

If you leave two or three messages asking them to call you back and they don't call, you are stuck. Instead, stay in control. Leave one message saying you called, and then keep calling until you reach them.

The first time you call, you can leave a message saying, "Hi, this is Jane Doe. I wrote you a note and I'd like to meet with you." And repeat some of the pitch you made in your note. Have your note in front of you. You can even say, "I'll call you back, but my phone number—just so you have it—is 222-555-3456."

But after that, don't leave messages for them to call you. *You* must call them back. Don't complain to your group, "I've left three messages but they haven't called me back." You shouldn't expect it or complain about it. Hiring managers have their "9 to 5" obligations and plenty of people who want to get in to see them. They don't have time to drop everything and call you back. You screen yourself in by doing your research, by doing those follow-up phone calls, and by becoming friends with the manager's assistant.

CASE STUDY *Philip*
His 28 Follow-Up Phone Calls

Philip, a Five O'Clock Clubber in his 60s, landed three offers from Fortune 500 companies. But this might not have happened. When he had made his 27th call to one of the companies, he said to himself, "My ego can't take this anymore."

But Philip made a "research" call to the purchasing department where he thought there was an opening and asked for the purchasing manager, the job he was hoping to get. The person who answered the phone said, "I'm sorry, we don't have a purchasing manager right now. Maybe I could help you." So he knew the job was still open. He called the hiring manager for the 28th time and the hiring manager said, "Thank you so much for being persistent." That's normally what happens. As long as you don't leave messages for them to call you back, they're usually apologetic when you finally get to talk to them.

If it takes an average of eight follow-up phone calls, some job hunters have to call some people 20 or 30 times to get a meeting. You can call lots of times—as long as you don't leave messages or ask to be called back. You know how it is: You get voice mail. Just hang up and call later.

It's a Mental Game

Very few job hunters enjoy doing follow-up phone calls. I've always disliked doing them. But my attitude was this: My anxiety level gets extremely high for even one follow-up call and when I finally make that call, the person isn't there anyway. So I've wasted all that anxiety on one phone call. Making 20 follow-up phone calls takes the same amount of anxiety. And, chances are, *most* of the people I call won't be there anyway! I'll probably reach only 2 people out of 20. So I was able to force myself to make those calls when I was job-hunting because I expected to reach *no one*. If I got someone on the phone, it was almost a surprise.

When I have my list of calls to make, I call a friend first. Or you could call a job-search buddy, and say, "Hi Jim, this is Bob. I've got to make some follow-up phone calls. The minute I hang up this phone, I'm going to dial that first number without even thinking so I can get on that phone and start talking to people." And then your friend Jim may say, "I'm going to talk to you in an hour, Bob, to make sure you *made* those calls." Sometimes you need that kind of help. You might as well call 20 people because you're going to reach almost no one. Make a clump of phone calls at once and

don't waste all that anxiety on one call!

It's your responsibility to find some way to get in to see the people on your target list and then keep in touch. I used to get *so* anxious, I would postpone and postpone making those calls. Then I was forced to write to the people again and say, "I wrote to you some time ago, but got off track. I'm contacting you once again because I think it's important we meet." By that time, I was humiliated, but I would *finally* make my follow-up phone calls.

Remember, you are calling people because they really *should* meet with you.

> **Through a targeted mailing—and 15 follow-up phone calls—one client got to spend four hours with Craig McCaw of McCaw Cellular.**

You Do Not Want to Be Interviewed on the Phone

Unless you live far away, there is no substitute for an in-person meeting: You can pick up nonverbal information, there will be fewer distractions (the person is unlikely to be sorting mail while you are in the room), and you will be better able to establish rapport and, hopefully, a relationship.

In addition, the person is more likely to give you more and better information, and may even shuffle through his Rolodex® to give you names or pick up the phone and make a call on your behalf.

Very senior-level job hunters want to meet others in person even though this may require travel. They may conduct a screening call, but then it may be worth using their frequent-flier miles. "I can be in Chicago early next week so we can meet in person. Which day would be best for you?"

> **Important people must have their calls screened or they would never get any work done. But part of their job is to look at new talent.**

Your Answering Machine

If someone calls you in response to a mailing, be prepared. Have an appropriate, businesslike message on your answering machine—no kids' voices, blaring music, or flip comments ("Hi, this is Jake. You know what to do."). Have your script handy; know your Two-Minute Pitch *cold*. For direct-mail campaigns, you can figure on a *4 percent response rate*, meaning 4 percent of the people to whom you write may call you in for a meeting. So if you mail to 100 people, four are likely to call you for a meeting.

Before Making the Call

- Call into your own phone answering machine, practice your pitch, and listen to your voice. You will probably need to polish your presentation.

- Practice with other people and get feedback. If you don't do this, you may sound canned or unnatural.
- Warm up by calling a friend.
- Don't make just one call at a time. Bunch your calls together so you can get on a roll.
- Sit up straight and smile. The listener will hear the energy in your voice. Some Five O'Clock Clubbers prefer to stand up as they talk so their total presence is focused on the call.

Your Basic Script

If you followed the basic Five O'Clock Club "four-paragraph formula" for your cover letter, use that as the starting point for your script. But people don't talk the way they write, so don't repeat the opening paragraph of your letter verbatim, even though it will be the basis for your introduction on the call.

The quickest way to success is to build a relationship with the person you are calling. Using the key points in your opening paragraph in your greeting, establish potential mutual interests.

"Hi. This is Peter Song. I wrote to you a few days ago because I've researched your organization and I am so impressed with your bold move into the European market. (Pause.) I have 15 years of international marketing experience with companies such as ___ and ___ and I was hoping to meet you at some point to find out more about your organization and tell you something about myself."

The first 15 or 20 seconds establishes the tone of the call. You have to practice so your call will sound *conversational*. An actor doesn't read a script the first time and go on stage; he reads it dozens of times to sound natural.

Prompt the person you are talking with when it's time for a response. In other words, be quiet! If you do all the talking, it's not a conversation. You should also ask open-ended questions: "I'm so impressed with what you are doing...I'd love to hear more about that."

If you don't practice your pitch, you'll stumble or sound canned or unnatural.

You want a brief conversation—if only a minute—that covers something of interest to the person you've reached. This helps you form a relationship with the person and increases the odds of your achieving your objectives—in most cases, getting a meeting.

Your cover letter outlined the most important points you want to make in your phone call: the points of mutual interest, why you want to see the person, your background, and your key accomplishments.

Some people find it easier to list their "talking points" and goals on a card. With this kind of miniscript handy when they make the calls, they can cover the bases and become more conversational. Some examples follow.

"I'm sorry, Sir, but God is in a meeting at the moment, would you like to leave a message? God's office, please hold... God's office, please hold..."

If the Assistant Answers

The assistant may be a great help. Talk as if you were conducting normal business: You wrote a letter to Mr. Jones and you're following up.

For the first call, leave a message saying you called. After that, do not leave a message. Instead, keep calling back. Keep the ball in your court.

You: Hi. Mr. Jones, please.

Assistant: I'm sorry, he's not in right now. May I take a message and have him call you back?

You: This is Kevin Walters. Who am I speaking with, please?

Assistant: My name is Dorothy Black.

You: Hi, Ms. Black. I had written a letter to Mr. Jones asking for a brief meeting. I'll be in and out a lot so I'll have to call him back later. When would be a good time for me to call?

Assistant: I don't know. He'll be in and out of meetings also.

(Become friendly with her. However, it's always preferable to use "Mr." or "Ms." in your first contact. Later it may be appropriate to use first names.)

You: Dorothy, I'll call back later. Maybe I'll be lucky and find him in.

Call frequently. If you wait too long, they won't remember who you are and will sense no urgency on your part.

Later

You: Dorothy, hi, this is Kevin Walters. We spoke earlier. Is Mr. Jones available now by any chance?

Dorothy: He's in a meeting right now. May I have him call you?

You: No, he can't call me back, so I'll have to call him later. You must have your hands full managing his schedule, but I know we will link up soon.

Sometimes you can try early in the morning or in the evening when senior executives may answer their own phones. Voicemail systems, however, have made this more difficult. Call frequently. If you wait too long, they will not remember your letter. You'll get no momentum going.

If you are calling voice mail—but not leaving messages—you may even call back three times in one day. It's not a bother because the person doesn't know you called. [Note: Remember, your target may have Caller ID, a feature sold by the phone company that identifies your phone number to the person you are calling. Simply call your local phone company and ask them to block your identification. To cancel out caller I.D. for that one call only, use *67 and then the number.]

Sometimes you may be able to get the assistant to set up a meeting for you or a time to connect:

You: I really wanted a few minutes of his time. (Here's the reason why.) I was wondering if you could facilitate the process. Do you happen to handle his calendar? If not, I'll just keep trying.

Eventually

You: Hi, Dorothy, this is Kevin again. You're probably starting to recognize my voice. I hope I'm not bothering you. Is Mr. Jones in?

Assistant: It's terrible that he is always so busy. You've tried so often. I'll try to get him to talk to you. He's in a meeting right now, but I'll ask him to take your call.

To Get Your Paperwork to the Boss

You: Dorothy, do you know if Mr. Jones read my letter?

Dorothy: No, I don't know. He receives so much mail.

You: Well, I'll fax you a copy. You can put it in his "to read" pile so he'll know why I'm calling.

If They Did Not Receive Your Letter

You: I sent him a note a few days ago. Has he seen it?

Assistant: I don't remember it.

You: Well, let me fax (or email) it to you now. What is your fax number?

[Note: Fax your résumé to yourself and see what it looks like. If the type is too small, it may be unreadable by fax. If possible, fax from your computer to lessen degradation. Also, be mindful of the "message" your fax may be automatically printing at the top of transmissions!]

If the Boss Answers

First, establish a connection. For example, "Hello. In my letter to you, I pointed out my interest in your new European campaign." Then, go through your script or checklist.

Handling Objections

In addition to your basic script (which should relate to your cover letter), it is valuable to put together an "objections card." Then you will have a ready response when an objection is thrown at you.

You are most likely to handle objections smoothly if you develop your skills of active and reflective listening. This will help you understand the situation of the person you're calling. Listed below are a few basic objections from bosses and some possible answers. Believe it or not, objections can be an *opportunity*. You want to uncover the real concerns of the person, even if the objections seem like a closed-end statement. Paul Miller, a Five O'Clock Club member and marketing executive, suggested some of the following responses to objections:

a. **There are no jobs here now.**
   I didn't expect there would be. I'm contacting you because of your knowledge of the industry. I'm very interested in your organization and your industry. I have 20 years' experience in direct marketing and a lot of it has been with an industry directly competing with yours. I thought it would be good for us to meet.

   I have read that you are being challenged by Monmouth Company. Is that one of your chief concerns right now?

b. **I'm busy.**
   I can understand with so much going on. May we set up a time a month from now? I will call to confirm to make sure it's still a good time for you.
   [Note: If you show consideration of their time, they will sometimes suggest that you "come in tomorrow."]

c. **I didn't get your résumé.**
   I'll fax (or email) it to you right now and then I'll give you a call back. What's your fax number?

d. **We don't need people with your skills now.**
   See (a) above. Try to ascertain their one or two greatest issues/problems. You may have experience that is a match.

e. **How did you get my name?**
   You *can't* say you did a mailing to 200 people. You *can* say you found the names of several key players through research or you can say what I have sometimes said:

"A few people mentioned I should contact you."

"Really, who?"

"Sharon Nuskey and Deirdre Cavanagh (two of my friends)."

"I don't know them."

"Maybe not, but they know you!"

> **Prepare an "objections card." Then you will have ready responses for objections they throw at you.**

Here are some basic objections from assistants and possible answers:

a. **He's very busy.**
   I'll bet. You must have your hands full with his schedule. What would be a good time to call?

b. **I sent your résumé to human resources.**
   Thank you. However, I really wasn't calling about a human resources matter. I thought Mr. Jones would be interested in discussing a project I've done that relates to what he is doing at United Widget.

c. **We have no openings now.**
   I didn't expect you had openings. See (a) under bosses' objections.

What to Do If You Get Voice Mail

First, you can try the company operator to see if you can get the name and number of Mr. Jones' assistant or the name and number of someone who sits near him. Talk to that person and say you've been trying to reach Mr. Jones, but you only get voice mail. Has he been in? How would they suggest you reach him? Does he have an assistant?

Otherwise, use voice mail as an introduction to begin getting your message across.

Early on: "Hi. This is Kevin Shaw and I'm calling to follow up on my letter." You want them to hear your name and that you sent something. Say that you will call them back.

Here's a danger: If you leave your phone num-ber, you may get a blow-off message on your voice mail that would make it very awkward for you to call again. You don't want people to call you back if you have not had a chance to explain yourself.

> **Always try to understand the situation of your listener. "I understand how busy you are with so much going on..."**

How to Handle Rejection

If you aim to talk to 10, 20, or 50 people, you can never expect 100 percent success. There are no perfect scores in this game. But learn to *use* rejection. Hearing *why* you have been rejected is a way to modify your pitch. A "no" requires you to probe.

If you are perceptive, you can pick up on the negatives. One good rule is: Don't ask a question that can be answered "yes" or "no." You want to keep the conversation going and "no" can kill the conversation.

Be polite and direct, but *probe*!

You: I have been trying to break into United Widget (or the Widget category). I'm sure that's a fine place to work. I'd really like your opinion of how I can further my candidacy at United Widget.... Thanks. Is there someone else you suggest I speak with?

> **Rejection is a way to modify your pitch. A "no" requires you to probe.**

They Don't Teach You This in School

Improved telephone techniques are both job-search and *life* skills. With the help of your small group, you can get through this part of the job-search process.

Can we talk?

JOAN RIVERS

CASE STUDY *My Brother*
Call When You Think They Have Your Letter

My brother, Robert, is a scientist and marketer in a very narrow industry with very few companies in his specialty field. He wrote a very detailed, intelligent letter to the president of one of them, a small company in a remote geographic area. This was a targeted mailing—there were no job openings he knew of.

Because his letter was so intelligent and on target, he thought the president would pick up the phone and call him right away. Well, Robert waited a week and the president didn't call him. So instead of calling him, Robert wrote *another* detailed, very intelligent, analytical letter. Again, no call. Finally, I said to Robert, "Just pick up the phone and call the guy." I come from a *family* of shy people and we're all reluctant to call strangers. So my brother finally found his courage, picked up the phone, called the president, and said, "Listen, this is who I am. I've written to you twice and this is what I said."

The president didn't remember having seen either of the letters. "But," he said, "I'm interested in what you're telling me and I'd be delighted to meet with you." My brother was absolutely dumbstruck that the man had not read his letters! The president dug them up later. In fact, hiring managers will often ask you to send letters again because they can't find them. Those follow-up phone calls are critical.

But don't wait two weeks to call, wasting too much valuable time. Among other things, you need to know if the letter arrived. If you figure it takes four days for your letter to arrive, call on day four. If they haven't received it yet, that doesn't matter. You can say, "Hi, this is so-and-so. I sent you a note recently." In response to, "I don't think I've gotten it yet," you can say, "Well, let me tell you what it said." Have your note in front of you:

That's your script. So, you see, there's no downside to calling a little bit prematurely—before the letter arrives. If you wait two weeks to call, you may be too late.

> **Time your call so they get your note and your follow-up call at the same time.**

It's now 4-1/2 minutes before 8:00—just in case the time means anything to you.

HEARD ON A RADIO SHOW IN JAMAICA

Someone Offers to Make a Call on Your Behalf

What if Martin, a networking contact, says he'll call a few people on your behalf and ask them to see you? If you don't know who Martin is contacting, you're helpless. Say two weeks pass, and you haven't received any calls from Martin's referrals. Then you call Martin again and ask him if he had a chance to contact any of the people he promised he would. Pretty soon, Martin sees you as a pain. Martin was enthusiastic when he met with you, but now he's back doing his work. He meant to make those phone calls, but life keeps interrupting him. To him, it doesn't feel like so much time had passed, but to you the time is dragging.

What is wrong with this scenario? The ball will never be in your court if you're waiting for someone else to make calls for you. If *you* had asked Martin to give you the names of the people he was planning to contact, then you could have immediately written to each person saying, "By now you've probably heard about me from Martin Radice," or, " By now, you may have received my résumé from Martin Radice." And the rest of your cover letter would follow the standard Five O'Clock Club format. You could enclose your résumé and do a follow-up phone call later. You've got to ask for the list because if Martin doesn't actually call the people while you're sitting there, chances are good that it won't happen—ever.

So, the next time someone volunteers to make a call or two on your behalf, ask who it is they're planning to call and help them to help you.

Keeping Up Your Contacts after Landing That New Job

We tell our job hunters that *after* they land their next job they should make *at least* one networking contact a week, which isn't that much. That's one phone call, or one lunch date, or one getting together for a cup of coffee after work. People who have a solid network in their field have quicker and easier job searches than those who are careless about staying connected. Those with no networking contacts have to start from scratch to build up their contacts, which takes time. So write your long-term career plan and build your networking contacts *now* for the targets you plan to have in the future. That's what successful people do.

Is this the party to whom I am speaking?

LILY TOMLIN

When Networking with Fellow Five O'Clock Clubbers

Club members and alumni are important contacts. The Club attracts people who are intelligent, proactive, and helpful. They know how to get along in a group. These are not your average everyday people. Club members expect you to know the process. So be prepared before you contact other members. Wait until your fourth

group session before you start networking with other members. Then you'll know your Two-Minute Pitch and you'll know what you want out of meetings with them. You'll also know how to network by then. Five O'Clock Clubbers will bend over backwards to help you, as you will with other members who contact you. So don't abuse or waste these contacts.

Write a letter or email if appropriate. And do your follow-up phone calls. Don't ask for a job— ask for information and guidance! Email a thank-you note after a networking meeting. And if a fellow Five O'Clock Clubber opens the door for you to someone else, make sure you go *through* that door, and follow up with the contacts they've set up for you.

The moment you feel foolish, you look foolish. Concentrate, block it out, and relax. Of course, that's not always easy.

MICHAEL CAINE, *Acting in Film*

In all human affairs, the odds are always six to five against.

DAMON RUNYON

Take calculated risks. That is quite different from being rash.

GEORGE S. PATTON

How to Control Your Campaign

*Do not fear death so much, but rather
the inadequate life.*

BERTOLT BRECHT

Your overall campaign can be managed with just a few important worksheets:

- Use the **Interview Record** for every meeting— both networking and job. (See our book *Mastering the Job Interview and Winning the Money Game*.)

- The most important worksheet for controlling your search is the **Current List of My Active Contacts by Target**. At the beginning of your search, these will simply be networking contacts with whom you want to keep in touch. At that stage, your goal is to come up with 6 to 10 contacts you want to recontact later.

Later, the quality of your list will change. Then the names will be prospective job possibilities that you are trying to move along.

If you have 6 to 10 job possibilities "in the works," five of them will fall away through no fault of your own (because of job freezes or the hiring manager changing his or her mind about the kind of person wanted). Then you'll need to get more things in the works. With this critical mass of ongoing possible positions, you stand a chance of landing the kind of job you want.

Other Worksheets

The worksheets mentioned above are critical to the management of your search. Other work-

sheets guide specific parts of your search. You can find these worksheets in our books and/or in the Members Only section of our website.

- In the beginning, **the Seven Stories Exercise** and **Your Fifteen- / Forty-Year Vision** will help you select job targets appropriate for you (see our book *Targeting a Great Career*).

- **Measuring Your Targets** will assure that you have targets of a size that have a reasonable chance of working.

- The **Summary of What I Have/Want to Offer** will help you "position" yourself appropriately to each of your targets.

- **People to Contact in Each Target Area** is a way to get your search off to a quick start through networking or targeted mailings.

- The **Format of a Networking Meeting** is your guide to properly managing the networking-type meetings you get through networking, targeted or direct mailings, or cold calls.

- The **Summary of Search Progress** and **How to Assess Your Campaign** help you clearly assess how you are doing with regard to each of your targets.

- **The Follow-Up Checklist: Turning Job Interviews into Offers** (in our book Mastering the Job Interview and Winning the Money Game) will help you assess the interview and decide what to do next. Your goal, after all, is to move the process along and see if you can create a job for yourself.

- Assessing whether you are at **Stage 1, 2, or 3** of your search will help you see where you really stand, rather than you hoping for a job offer too soon.

Four-Step Salary Negotiation (from our book *Mastering the Job Interview and Winning the Money Game*):

- Are you keeping all four steps in mind?
  – Negotiate the job
  – Outshine and outlast your competition
  – Get the offer
  – Negotiate the compensation package

- Are you **negotiating the job** to make it appropriate for you and for the hiring manager?
- Are you **paying attention to your competition**, what they have to offer, and what you must do to outshine and outlast them? Are you aware that your competitors may not be real people, but may be in the mind of the hiring manager?
- Are you trying to postpone discussion of salary until after you **get the offer**?

Current List of My Active Contacts by Target

Make copies of this page for each target and keep track of your active contacts in each target area. To see how well you are penetrating each target market, compare the total number of appropriate contacts in your market with the number you have actually contacted. Keep adding names to your list. Certain people will become inappropriate. Cross their names off. You should probably have some contact once every month or two with the people who remain on your list.

After your search is up and running, keep track of your contacts by the stage you are in for each one. This will tell you how well you are doing in your search and will give you some idea of how likely it is for you to get an offer.

For Target _____:
    Geographic area: _____
    Industry or company size: _____
    Position/function: _____

Name of Contact	Company	Position	Date of Last Contact	Targeted Date of Next Contact
1.				
2.				
3.				
4.				
5.				
6.				
7.				
8.				
9.				
10.				
11.				
12.				
13.				
14.				
15.				
16.				
17.				
18.				
19.				
20.				

Current List of Active Stage-1 Contacts
Networking Contacts With Whom You Want To Keep in Touch

The Beginning of a Search

__Measure the effectiveness of your search__ by listing the number of people with whom you are currently in contact on an ongoing basis, either by phone or mail, who are in a position to hire you or recommend that you be hired. The rule of thumb: If you are seriously job hunting, __you should have 6 to 10 active contacts going at one time. At the beginning of your search, these will simply be networking contacts with whom you want to keep in touch__. You are unlikely to get an offer at this stage. You are gathering information to find out how things work—getting your feet wet. You look like an outsider and outsiders are rarely given a break. Keep adding names to your list because certain people will become inappropriate. Cross their names off. You should probably have some contact once a month with the people who remain on your list.

Because you have already developed targets for your search, please note below the target area for each contact or note it is serendipitous and does not fit in with any of your organized targets. This will help you see the progress you are making in each target area.

Name of Contact	Company	Position	Date of Last Contact	Targeted Date of Next Contact	Target Area
1.					
2.					
3.					
4.					
5.					
6.					
7.					
8.					
9.					
10.					
11.					
12.					
13.					
14.					
15.					
16.					
17.					
18.					
19.					
20.					

Current List of Active Stage-2 Contacts

The Right People at the Right Levels in the Right Organization

The Middle of a Search

The nature of your "6 to 10 things in the works" changes over time. Instead of simply finding networking contacts to get your search started, you meet people who are closer to what you want.

Getting a job offer is not the way to test the quality of your campaign. A real test is when people say they'd want you—but not now. Do some people say: <u>**"Boy, I wish I had an opening. I'd sure like to have someone like you here"**</u>? Then you are interviewing well with the right people. All you need now are luck and timing to help you contact (and recontact) the right people when they also have a need.

If people are not saying they want you, find out why not. If you think you are in the right targets talking to people at the right level and are not early on in your search, you need feedback. Ask: "If you had an opening, would you consider hiring someone like me?" Find out what is wrong.

Become an insider—a competent person who can prove he or she has somehow already done what the interviewer needs. *Prove* you can do the job and that the interviewer is *not* taking a chance on you.

You still need 6 to 10 contacts at this level whom you will recontact later. Keep adding names to your list because certain people will become inappropriate. Cross their names off. You should probably have some contact once a month with the people who remain on your list.

Name of Contact	Company	Position	Date of Last Contact	Targeted Date of Next Contact	Target Area
1.					
2.					
3.					
4.					
5.					
6.					
7.					
8.					
9.					
10.					
11.					
12.					
13.					
14.					
15.					
16.					
17.					
18.					
19.					
20.					

Current List of Active Stage-3 Contacts

Moving Along Actual Jobs or the Possibility of Creating a Job

The Final Stages of a Search

In this stage, you **uncover 6 to 10 actual jobs (or the possibility of creating a job) to move along**. These job possibilities could come from any of your target areas or from serendipitous leads. Find a lot of people who would hire you if they could. If you have only one lead that could turn into an offer, you are likely to try to close too soon. Get more leads. You will be more attractive to the manager, will interview better, and will not lose momentum if your best lead falls apart. A good number of your job possibilities will fall away through no fault of your own (such as job freezes or major changes in the job requirements).

To get more leads, notice which targets are working and which are not. Make additional contacts in the targets that seem to be working or develop new targets. **Recontact just about everyone you met earlier in your search**. You want to develop more offers.

Aim for three concurrent offers: This is the stage of your search when you want them. When an offer comes during Stage 1 or Stage 2, you probably have not had a chance to develop momentum so you can get a number of offers. When choosing among offers, **select the job that positions you best for the long term**.

Name of Contact	Company	Position	Date of Last Contact	Targeted Date of Next Contact	Target Area
1.					
2.					
3.					
4.					
5.					
6.					
7.					
8.					
9.					
10.					
11.					
12.					
13.					
14.					
15.					
16.					
17.					
18.					
19.					
20.					

The Five O'Clock Club®

The Stages of Your Job Search

Most job hunters say, "I'll know my job search was good if I get a job." That's not a very good way to measure your search. You need to be able to tell **as you go along** if you have a good search. This is the test: Do you have six to ten things in the works? That is, are you talking on an ongoing basis to six to ten people who are in a position to hire you or recommend that you be hired? Which stage are *you* in? Start at the bottom of this page.

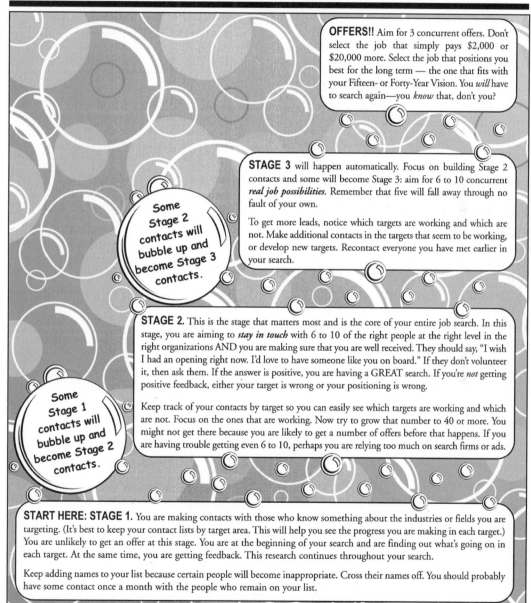

OFFERS!! Aim for 3 concurrent offers. Don't select the job that simply pays $2,000 or $20,000 more. Select the job that positions you best for the long term — the one that fits with your Fifteen- or Forty-Year Vision. You *will* have to search again—you *know* that, don't you?

STAGE 3 will happen automatically. Focus on building Stage 2 contacts and some will become Stage 3: aim for 6 to 10 concurrent *real job possibilities*. Remember that five will fall away through no fault of your own.

To get more leads, notice which targets are working and which are not. Make additional contacts in the targets that seem to be working, or develop new targets. Recontact everyone you have met earlier in your search.

Some Stage 2 contacts will bubble up and become Stage 3 contacts.

STAGE 2. This is the stage that matters most and is the core of your entire job search. In this stage, you are aiming to *stay in touch* with 6 to 10 of the right people at the right level in the right organizations AND you are making sure that you are well received. They should say, "I wish I had an opening right now. I'd love to have someone like you on board." If they don't volunteer it, then ask them. If the answer is positive, you are having a GREAT search. If you're *not* getting positive feedback, either your target is wrong or your positioning is wrong.

Keep track of your contacts by target so you can easily see which targets are working and which are not. Focus on the ones that are working. Now try to grow that number to 40 or more. You might not get there because you are likely to get a number of offers before that happens. If you are having trouble getting even 6 to 10, perhaps you are relying too much on search firms or ads.

Some Stage 1 contacts will bubble up and become Stage 2 contacts.

START HERE: STAGE 1. You are making contacts with those who know something about the industries or fields you are targeting. (It's best to keep your contact lists by target area. This will help you see the progress you are making in each target.) You are unlikely to get an offer at this stage. You are at the beginning of your search and are finding out what's going on in each target. At the same time, you are getting feedback. This research continues throughout your search.

Keep adding names to your list because certain people will become inappropriate. Cross their names off. You should probably have some contact once a month with the people who remain on your list.

How to Assess Your Campaign

Based on Marketing Plan for John Smith
Target Functions: Publishing Sales/Sales Management

Stage 1	Stage 2	Stage 3	Current Offers
Target #1: Consumer Publishing	**Target #1: Consumer Publishing**	**Target #1: Consumer Publishing**	**Target #1: Consumer Publishing**
Time Warner Condé Nast Hearst Hachette Meredith KIII Holdings Gannett Times-Mirror Bertelsmann/G&J Reader's Digest McGraw-Hill Outdoor Services Parade NY Times Corp. Tribune Corp. Contact Perf Arts Network	Time Pathfinder *Inc.* magazine Time Relationship Mktg. *Boston Globe* *Washington Post* Fancy Publications Thirteen-WNET	*USA Today* —Baseball Weekly met w/4 execs Media Vehicles —GE Capital met w/3 execs MAMM and POZ met w/2 execs	Tradewell The Sales Associates —Offered VP, Sales and Head of Internet Sales *Inc.* magazine
Target #2: Trade Publishing	**Target #2: Trade Publishing**	**Target #2: Trade Publishing**	**Target #2: Trade Publishing**
Fairchild Pub. Reed Travel Progressive Grocer James G. Elliot Co.	McFadden M. Shanken Wine and Food BPI Cahners	Supermarket Business Final 2 out of 465 for NE Sales Mgr.	
Target #3: Internet/Computer	**Target #3: Internet/Computer**	**Target #3: Internet/Computer**	**Target #3: Internet/Computer**
CMP Intl Data Mgmt. Ria Group	Preview Travel i33 Communications IDG-Games Mpath-Mplayer	Planet Direct/CMG 2 meetings	Interactive Advertising Net. —1 of 10 selected

Stuck in Your Job Search?
What to Do Next

Drive thy business, or it will drive thee.
BENJAMIN FRANKLIN

How to Measure the Effectiveness of Your Search

Most job hunters say, "I'll know my search was good when I get a job." That's not a very good way to measure your search. You need to be able to tell as you go along whether you are heading in the right direction. There are a number of hints you can pick up along the way.

What Stage Are You In?

As you go along, the basic measurement tool to use in your search is this: Do you have 6 to 10 things in the works? That is, are you talking to 6 to 10 people on an ongoing basis who are in a position to hire you or recommend that you be hired?

The quality of your contacts varies with where you are in your search.

- In the beginning of your search, you will speak to as many people as pos-

sible in your target market—regardless of the organization for which they work. At this stage, you simply want market information. If you plan to stay in touch with them on an ongoing basis, they are Stage-1 contacts. To have any momentum going in the beginning of your search, keep in touch with 6 to 10 people on an ongoing basis (every few months).

Over time, you will talk to more and more people who are Stage-1 contacts—perhaps 60 to 100 people during the course of your search. Some of those contacts will bubble up and become Stage-2 contacts.

- Stage-2 contacts are people who are the right people at the right level in the right jobs in the right organizations in your targeted areas. They are senior to you, perhaps future hiring managers. Your goal is to have contact with 6 to 10 of the right people on an ongoing basis. Then you have a full Stage-2 search going: You are in the middle of your search.

However, you will rarely get a good job offer at Stage 2. You aren't even talking to these people about real jobs at this point. You just want the right people to know you and remember you. And if one later happens to have a job opening, you still need to go after 6 to 10 other job possibilities, because 5 will fall away through no fault of your own. If you do get an offer at Stage 2, you won't have many others with which to compare it. Keep in touch with your current Stage-1 contacts (using *networking* follow-ups), and develop additional Stage-1 contacts so more will bubble up to Stage 2. Some of those will bubble up to Stage 3 (real job possibilities)—and then you're really cooking.

- You are in a full Stage-3 search when you are talking to 6 to 10 people on an ongoing basis who actually have a job opening or who have the possibility of creating a job for you. Then you have a number of opportunities that you can move along (using job follow-ups), and are in the best possible position to get the right job for you: the one that positions you best for the long term and the one that pays you what you are worth.

If you have 6 to 10 possibilities in Stage 3, you have the chance of getting 3 offers. Remember, these do not have to be ideal jobs—some may even be disgusting. But an offer is an offer and makes you more desirable in the market. You don't have to want to work at each of these places, but at least you will have a fallback position and can honestly say, if appropriate, "I have a number of job offers, but there's no place I'd rather work than yours." With a number of offers in hand, you are less likely to be taken advantage of by a prospective employer who thinks you are desperate.

Life moves on, whether we act as cowards or heroes. Life has no other discipline to impose, if we would but realize it, than to accept life unquestioningly. Everything we shut our eyes to, everything we run away from, everything we deny, denigrate or despise, serves to defeat us in the end. What seems nasty, painful, evil, can become a source of beauty, joy and strength, if faced with an open mind. Every moment is a golden one for him who has the vision to recognize it as such.

HENRY MILLER, *THE HENRY MILLER READER*

How's Your Search Going?

When I ask you how your search is going, I don't want to hear that a prospective employer really likes you. That's not a good measure of how well your search is going, because one prospect could easily fall away: They may decide to hire no one or they may decide they want an accounting person instead of a marketing person. A lot can happen that is beyond your control.

Instead I expect you to tell me how many things you have in the works. You would say, for example, "My search is going great. I have five Stage-1 contacts in the works. I'm just getting started."

Or you might say, "I have nine Stage-2 contacts and three contacts in Stage 3." If you are expert at this, you may even add: "I want more Stage-3 contacts, so my goal is to get 30 more in Stage 2. Right now, I'm digging up lots of new contacts and keeping the other ones going. With my Stage-2 contacts, I'm generally doing networking follow-ups and with my Stage-3 contacts, I'm generally doing job follow-ups."

That kind of talk is music to my ears.

It usually takes very little effort to get a few more things "in the works." Simply recontact your network, network into someone you haven't met with yet, directly contact someone, talk to a search firm, answer an ad. You will soon have more activity in your search.

I know God will not give me anything I can't handle. I just wish He didn't trust me so much.

MOTHER TERESA

What Job Hunters Do Wrong

In addition to looking at the *stage* of your overall search, it is also helpful to look at what can go wrong in each *step* of your campaigns. Some job hunters err in their overall search approach or attitude. Then things can go wrong in the assessment step or in the other parts of your campaigns (the planning, interviewing, or follow-up steps).

We'll examine each of these to determine what you may be doing wrong, if anything.

The Overall Search: What Can Go Wrong?

Here are some problems that are general to the entire search:

- **Not spending enough time** on your search. If you are unemployed, you should be spending 35 hours a week on your search. If you are employed, spend 15 hours a week to get some momentum going. If you spend only two or three hours a week on your job search, you may complain that you have been searching forever, when actually you have not even begun. If you are employed, you can do most of your work in the evenings and on weekends—researching, writing cover letters and follow-up letters. You can even schedule your meetings in the evenings or early mornings.
- **Not having enough fun.** Some job hunters— especially those who are unemployed—say they will start having fun after they get a job. But your search may take many months and you are more likely to come across as desperate if you are not allowing yourself to have some fun. Having fun will make you seem like a more normal person in your meetings and you'll feel better about yourself. The Five O'Clock Club formula is that you must have at least three hours of fun a week.
- **Not having 6 to 10 things in the works.** See the beginning of this chapter about Stages 1, 2, and 3 of your search.
- **Talking to people who are at the wrong level.** At the beginning of your search, talk to peers just to gather information to decide whether a prospective target is worth a full campaign. When you have selected a few good targets, talk to those who are at a higher level.

- **Trying to bypass the system.** Some job hunters feel they don't have time for this and simply want to go on job interviews (usually through search firms or answering ads). Others want to skip the assessment process (see our book Targeting a Great Career) or don't even do the Seven Stories Exercise. Their campaigns are weaker because they have no foundation.

  At least touch on every step in the process. You will have a quicker and more productive search.
- **Lowering your salary expectations just because you have been unemployed a while.** Even those who have been unemployed a year or two land jobs at market rates. They get what they are worth in the market because they have followed the system. At The Five O'Clock Club, half the people who attend are employed; half are unemployed. Many of those who are unemployed have been out of work for a year or two. Usually, they have been doing something wrong in their searches, and the coach and their group can help them figure out what it is. When they get a job (which they almost certainly will if they stick with the system), they usually wind up getting something appropriate at an appropriate salary level.

  Sometimes, if people really need money, we suggest they take something inappropriate to earn some money and continue to search while they are working.

The world is moving so fast these days that the man who says it can't be done is generally interrupted by someone doing it.

Harry Emerson Fosdick

- **Getting discouraged**. Half the battle is controlling your emotions. Jack had been unemployed one-and-a-half years when he joined us. He seemed very agitated—almost angry— which happens when a person has been working at a job search for so long. I told him I was afraid he might come across that way during meetings. He assured me (with irritation in his voice) that he was completely pleasant during meetings but was simply letting his hair down in the group.

In career coaching, we have nothing to go on but the way the person acts in the group: The way you are in the group probably bears some resemblance to the way you are in the interview. We would recognize you as being the same person. Anyway, it's all we have to go on, so we have to point out to you what we see.

The next week, Jack still seemed angry. I asked the group what they thought and of course they could see it too. It was easier for him to hear it from his peers, and, because he was a mature person, Jack listened to them.

The third week, Jack laughingly announced that he had had a lobotomy and was a completely different person. He said he had changed his attitude and that his meetings reflected this change.

The fourth week he announced that he had had another lobotomy because he felt he still had room for improvement. He was a noticeably different person and did not seem at all like someone who had been out of work a long time. Every day Jack read the books we use at The Five O'Clock Club and provided very good insights to the other job hunters in our small group.

By the fifth week, Jack was almost acting like a co-coach in the group. He had made great strides in his own search (with three Stage-3 contacts and lots of contacts in Stage 2) and was able to astutely analyze the problems others were having. He was a wonderful contributor.

By the seventh week, Jack was close to a number of offers and in the eighth week, Jack proudly addressed the large group and reported on his successful search. We were sorry to see him go.

By the way, Jack did not have to take a pay cut or a job that was beneath him. His prolonged search did not affect his salary negotiation.

Do what you need to do to keep your spirits up. Don't ask yourself if you feel like searching. Of course you don't. Just do it anyway. And act as if you enjoy it.

- **Not having support.** Looking for a job is a lonely business. You may want to "buddy" with another job hunter. You can call each other every morning to talk about what you are each going to do that day and to review what you each accomplished the day before. You could also join free emotional-support groups at places of worship. You may find you need such help in addition to the job-search strategy you get at The Five O'Clock Club. Or you may find you would like to see a coach privately to help you with specifics having to do with your search, such as your résumé, a review of your search, salary negotiation, or the follow-up to a very important job interview. Get the help you need.

- **Inflating in your own mind the time you have actually been searching.** You may feel as though you've been searching forever. But if you are searching only three hours a week, you have not yet begun. If at the end of a year, you finally start to put in the required 15 to 35 hours a week, you have just really started to search. Then when people ask how long you have been searching, the correct answer is "a few weeks." It's good to be honest with yourself about how long you have actually been searching.

Procrastination is the fear of success. People procrastinate because they are afraid of the success that they know will result if they move ahead now. Because success is heavy, carries a responsibility with it, it is much easier to procrastinate and live on the "someday I'll" philosophy.

DENIS WAITLEY

During the Assessment Step: What Can Go Wrong?

In the assessment step you use our book, *Targeting a Great Career*, to go through the exercises (Seven Stories, Values, Forty-Year Vision, and so on) and select job targets (industries or organizations of a certain size and the position you would like in each target and geographic area).

If you are not sure what you should do with your life, assessment is a time to explore—perhaps with the help of a career coach. What can go wrong in this step?

- **Selecting 1 or 2 targets too quickly.** Rather than exploring, a job hunter may pick a target, go after it, find out it doesn't work, and then not know what to do next. Instead, brainstorm as many targets as you can at the beginning of your search, rank them, and go after them in a methodical way.
- **Not being specific in selecting a target.** Some job hunters say, "I just want a job. I don't care what it is." You may not care, but the hiring team wants someone who cares about their specific industry and organization. In the beginning of your search, you want to explore and stay calm while you are doing your research to find out what the likely targets are for you. If you don't have targets defined (such as "being a Web developer in a medium-sized organization in the Albuquerque area"), then you are still exploring and

that's okay. But it is not an organized search. And even when your search is organized and targeted, you will still have plenty of room for serendipitous leads.
- **Not doing the right research.** Read the chapter on research, including the bibliography at the back of this book. Research is critical throughout your search and separates those who follow The Five O'Clock Club method from other job hunters. Instead of just doing research, why not learn to enjoy it and make it part of your life?

  The better your research, the richer your targets will become—well defined rather than superficial—and the more knowledgeable you will sound to prospective employers. In addition, you will save a lot of time as you discover where the markets are and which ones are the best fit for you.
- **Not ranking your targets.** Some job hunters go after everything at once. For a more organized search, overlap your targets, but still conduct a condensed search focusing on each target and keeping them separate in your mind.

  Take a look at the chart below, which shows a campaign aimed at each target (Target 1, Target 2, and Target 3). Yet the targets overlap to speed up the search.

Next, let's look at what can go wrong in the various steps of the campaign aimed at each target.

Quit now, you'll never make it. If you disregard this advice, you'll be halfway there.

DAVID ZUCKER

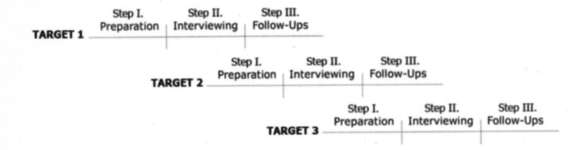

During the Preparation Step: What Can Go Wrong?

- **Relying on only one technique for getting meetings**. Consider using all four techniques for getting meetings: networking, direct contact, search firms, and ads (in print and online). Even in fields where people like to talk to people, such as sales or human resources, though networking is easier, it is not thorough. It is a scattered approach.

   Make a list of all the organizations in your target area—say, 120.
   — Perhaps network into 20 of them;
   — Do a targeted mailing into 20—it's just like networking: use a letter with a follow-up phone call. Remember that you want to see this person whether or not he or she has a job opening;
   — Talk to search firms (if appropriate); and
   — Answer ads.
   — Do a direct-mail campaign (no follow-up phone call) to the remaining 80 organizations—just to be thorough so all the organizations in your target area know that you exist and are looking.
- **Contacting the wrong person**. The human resources person is the wrong one unless you want a job in human resources. The right person is one or two levels higher

than you are in the department or division in which you want to work. If you are very senior and want to work for the president, the right person for you to contact is the president or perhaps someone on the board. If you want to be the president, the right person is someone on the board, or whoever may influence the selection of the president.

- **Being positioned improperly**. If you are not positioned properly, you will not be able to get meetings. Write out your Two-Minute Pitch. In your small group, be sure to practice your pitch. Try role-playing. Tell the group who they are pretending to be, and ask them to critique you. You want to make sure you have your pitch down pat. Write it out.
- **Using skimpy cover letters**. We use a four-paragraph approach that is thorough. Most job hunters write paragraphs one and four and skip the meat.
- **Having a weak or inappropriate résumé**. If your résumé doesn't speak for you in your absence and tell them exactly who you are, your level, and what you bring to the party, develop one that helps you. We have a whole book on this topic—along with case studies of real live people.
- **Skipping the research step to develop a good list of target organizations**. If you have a good list, you will get more out of every one of your networking contacts. Show your list of prospective organiza-

tions to your contacts, ask them what they think of the organizations on the list, who they suggest you should contact at the good organizations, and ask, "May I use your name?"

The thing always happens that you believe in; and the belief in a thing makes it happen.

FRANK LLOYD WRIGHT

If you want a quality, act as if you already had it. Try the "as if" technique.

WILLIAM JAMES

During the Interviewing Step: What Can Go Wrong?

(See our book *Mastering the Job Interview and Winning the Money Game* for a more detailed description of each area listed below.)

Trying to close too soon.

- Being seen as an outsider.
- Not using the worksheets.
- Not thinking like a consultant.
- Not looking or acting like the level for which you are searching.
- Not seeing the meeting as only the beginning of the process.
- Not getting information/giving information to move it along.
- Not preparing for the meeting by having a 3X5 card or finding out with whom you will be meeting. The 3X5 card contains your summary statement about yourself as well as three to five accomplishments you want to make sure you cover with the hiring team.
- Not being in sync with their timing (trying to close too soon or not moving quickly enough).
- Not listening to what is really going on.

"Mr. Billings realizes you traveled a long way to meet with him. However, he decided to change the meeting to next week."

Courtesy of Jerry King, Cartoons, Inc.

During the Follow-Up Step: What Can Go Wrong?

(See our book *Mastering the Job Interview and Winning the Money Game* for a more detailed description of each area listed below.)

In addition to targeting, follow-up is the most important reason Five O'Clock Clubbers land jobs quickly. This is the brainiest part of the process. Notice that the earlier diagram showed the three parts as equal: Preparation, Interviewing, and Follow-Ups. Spend an equal amount of time on each.

Study those parts of this book thoroughly. Some of the obvious things that go wrong include:

- Taking the first offer.
- Not recontacting your contacts.
- Not studying the books.
- Stating your salary requirements too soon.
- Not reassessing where you stand in your search.

Now that we've taken a break from your search to assess how you are doing, it's time to get back to work. Use the work sheets that follow to note the organizations/people you have contacted for each stage of your search.

To laugh often and much; to win the respect and the affection of children; to earn the appreciation of honest critics and endure the betrayal of false friends; to appreciate beauty; to find the best in others; to leave the world a bit better—whether by a healthy child, a garden patch or a redeemed social condition; to know even one life has breathed easier because you have lived. This is to have succeeded.

RALPH WALDO EMERSON

If you are distressed by anything external, the pain is not due to the thing itself, but to your estimate of it; and this you have the power to revoke at any moment.

MARCUS AURELIUS

How We Respond to Life's Difficulties: The Most Important Factor in Success in Life

Books (and their electronic equivalent) have not lost their influence. Members read and re-read those that have affected them, and so do I. Beyond Shakespeare and the Bible, which both taught me a lot about human nature, the most important book in my life has been George Vaillant's *Adaptation to Life*, the forty-year study of 268 male Harvard graduates. The study analyzed who succeeded, who didn't, and why. Because of the homogeneity of the group, the study proved that "the relatively broad socioeconomic differences among the subjects upon college entrance had no correlation" with later success. Participants born to economic privilege did not do better than those from relatively poor backgrounds, such as those on need-based scholarships.

What a hopeful thought that the luck of the draw in how we were born is not so relevant to our future success. Everyone has a chance.

> **How we were born is not so relevant to our future success.**

Vaillant concluded that family circumstances is not the major determinant of future success. The study showed that **everyone has major setbacks, but** how we respond to life's difficulties **is the most important factor in success in life**. A broken love affair may lead one man to write great poetry and another to commit suicide.

We can choose how we react and those choices affect our success—in love and in work. Vaillant ranks 15 coping mechanisms by their relationship to successful results.

The study also observed that maturation continued over the span of a person's life. **We stop growing when our human losses are no longer replaced**. The study proved that it is "sustained relationships with people, not traumatic events, that mold character." **Without love, it is hard to grow**.

So I know that there is hope for each of us depending on our responses and our attitudes. Even a good book can offer hope.

You must find some way to hope in your future. Here's a quote I've saved for many years:

"Hope has proven a powerful predictor of outcome in every study we've done so far," said Dr. Charles R. Snyder, a psychologist at the University of Kansas. Daniel Goleman, the famous author, says: "Having hope means believing you have both the will and the way to accomplish your goals, whatever they may be . . . It's not enough to just have the wish for something. You need the means, too. On the other hand, all the skills to solve a problem won't help if you don't have the willpower to do it."

So think long-term about your situation. Do whatever you can right now to keep your body and soul together, and build for the future—regardless of how bleak things may seem for you right now.

Sample Summary of Search Progress

	# of companies in this target	# contacted	# met with	Quality/Status of Contacts
For Target 1:				
Geog. area:	Chicago metro	10	3	Stage 3: 1 job lead
Ind. or org. size:	Consumer goods companies			Stage 2: 2
Pos./function:	Director of direct mail	Note: Not a great target. Keep in touch with same 5 people.		Stage 1: 2
For Target 2:				
Geog. area:	Chicago metro	70	30	Stage 3: 3, 1 close to offer
Ind. or org. size:	Direct marketing service cos.			Stage 2: 9
Pos./function:	Director of direct mail	Note: I'll aim to get 80 Stage-1 contacts; 30 Stage-2 contacts.		Stage 1: 16
For Target 3:				
Geog. area:	Chicago metro	11	4	Stage 3: 0
Ind. or org. size:	Direct marketing—based co.			Stage 2: 0
Pos./function:	Vice pres., marketing	Note: I need to do a lot more work in this target.		Stage 1: 4
For Target 4:				
Geog. area:	Chicago metro	15	4	Stage 3: 0
Ind. or org. size:	Advertising agencies			Stage 2: 0
Pos./function:	Director of direct mail	Note: This is the field I'm in now, but I want to get out of it.		Stage 1: 2

Note: In the far right column, **note those contacts you are keeping in touch with on an ongoing basis**:

Stage 1 contacts: People with whom I want to keep in touch—regardless of level or ability to hire.

Stage 2 contacts: The right people at the right levels in the right organizations. (Potential hiring managers with whom I am keeping in touch. They may be telling me: I wish I had an opening. If I did, I'd like to hire someone like you.)

Stage 3 contacts: Moving along actual jobs or the possibility of creating a job.

Summary of Search Progress

# of companies in this target	# contacted	# met with	Quality/Status of Contacts
For Target 1: Geog. area: _____ Ind. or org. size: _____ Pos./function: _____			Stage 3: Stage 2: Stage 1:
For Target 2: Geog. area: _____ Ind. or org. size: _____ Pos./function: _____			Stage 3: Stage 2: Stage 1:
For Target 3: Geog. area: _____ Ind. or org. size: _____ Pos./function: _____			Stage 3: Stage 2: Stage 1:
For Target 4: Geog. area: _____ Ind. or org. size: _____ Pos./function: _____			Stage 3: Stage 2: Stage 1:

Note: In the far right column, **note those contacts you are keeping in touch with on an ongoing basis**:

Stage 1 contacts: People with whom I want to keep in touch—regardless of level or ability to hire.

Stage 2 contacts: The right people at the right levels in the right organizations. (Potential hiring managers with whom I am keeping in touch. They may be telling me: I wish I had an opening. If I did, I'd like to hire someone like you.)

Stage 3 contacts: Moving along actual jobs or the possibility of creating a job. (I aim to have a total of 6 to 10 when I am in Stage 3 of my search.)

The
Five
O'Clock
Club®

PART FIVE

Career and Job-Search Bibliography

COMPILED BY RICHARD GREENE

Career and Job-Search Bibliography

What's New? Just about everything.

This Revised Edition has been updated to cover the lightning changes in how we do business and manage our lives and our careers.

- We start out with books on cutting-edge careers in **Section I**: 150 Best Jobs for a Secure Future, 2012, and Best Jobs for the 21st Century, Laurence Shatkin, 6th ed., 2011.
- Then **Section II** takes a close look at how culture and technology are reshaping jobs.

    Every listing in Sections II and III, and those in Section I as well, has been updated to include the way the world functions now. With few exceptions, there is nothing here that was published before 2010.

Today, those who haven't had their fingers on a computer keyboard or a smart phone or a tablet often lacks the skills needed to keep pace with trends and function in a wide number of professions and industries. Throughout this whole guide, there is a focus on how cyberspace is changing our careers.

And there are parts of industries that are growing so fast that they suddenly outstrip all the other sectors in the industry, showing staggering profits and growth—and opening up new and exciting careers. For example, *Satellites* (a new category) is the largest and fastest growing sector of communications and technology. So to keep up with our changing world, we've also made the following changes:

- *Banking* has new information in iBanking.
- Freelance/self-employed work—According to the Freelancers Union, nearly one in three working Americans is an independent worker. So we've made significant changes here: in *eMedia* (a new category), there are resources to understand what the new media are, plus how to start your own blogging, social media or other business. *Franchising* and *Freelancing* have been updated to include more opportunities to be on your own.
- *Journalism*, a new category, along with *Publishing,* which now includes *Writing, including Freelancing,* offer more information on expanding ways of freelancing, as well as getting your own work into print or on the Internet. The market for freelance writers, researchers, journalists and reporters, and editors and proofreaders keeps growing.

We have incorporated the growing trends in work and how we live.

- *Architecture*, a new category, includes *Green Design*, and *Construction and Building*, and has been widened to include *Green Building.* The green revolution is also reflected in a greater focus on *Environmental,* which has added *Green Careers*, which includes a separate listing for environment-related careers.

- *Health Care* and *Nursing* now delve deeper into newer trends with greater coverage overall, and there is now a new listing: *Pharmaceutical and Medical Sales*, reflecting the boom in these areas.

The role of **eMedia** is apparent throughout this guide, and category titles have **changed for two professions: Public Relations**, which is now *Public Relations and Integrated Marketing Communications* and **_Library Science_** is now *Library and Information Science.*

As Boomers are approaching what used to be retirement age, and as those 40 and over feel that they are facing a battle to stay in the job market, we have changed the previous *Aging Workers* category to **_Seniors and Those 40 and Up_**. According to the U.S. Census Bureau, by 2030, 19.7% of the population, or about 71.5 million Americans, will be 65 or older, compared with just 12.4% in 2000. This will affect society, from health care to financial markets, and has implications for the U.S. labor market. Here is an up-to-date and expanded guide for those in their 40s and up for staying in the job market, moving up, starting a career, or having their own business. What skills and abilities are needed to help you stay employed, get promoted, or go off on your own?

Now that more military have come home, **_Veterans_** has been updated to include more information and opportunities for our returning heroes.

Volunteering has become almost a prerequisite for many college grads to get a full-time job, and a smart choice for many seniors, and we have responded to these trends in **_Volunteering_**. And the topic **_Vocational Training/No Four-Year College Degree_** is now a hot topic. According to author Thomas Snyder, vocational training is a way to get a practical education without massive debt, and enter a field that's actually hiring. Millions of great jobs will be opening up in growth areas like advanced manufacturing, biotechnology, health care and more. These jobs can pay as well as, or more than, the jobs that the average four-year college graduate lands. Snyder offers insights on how to save money over a lifetime by getting an *affordable* college education that leads to high-paying jobs.

The last section is now **_Section III: International Careers and Cross-Cultural Business, including Wholesaling and Distributing/Importing and Exporting_**. This includes information on the way international business has been adapting to working with people and organizations that speak a different language, and do business in differently than we do. There are new guides that help you to conduct your affairs when going international. Plus now there are guides to the diplomatic service.

How to Use this Section (Properly!)

These resources for creating your target list of organizations are arranged in three sections:

Section I: General References of company and industry information, directories, plus compendiums of associations, regional resources, selected job boards, and more. This is a good way to start making up your list of job targets while finding out more about potential employers and the industries and professions that interest you. The trend is from print to databases, but many are still offered in print, or both. **A word of caution: Job boards, especially the biggies, are tempting places to hang out. However, only about 6 percent of all jobs get filled via these sites. The Five O'Clock Club approach is not to hang out on job boards, but rather to develop lists of persons to contact for targeted and direct mailings, as well as for networking.** Don't spend more than 6 percent of your time on job boards (6 percent of 35 hours amounts to a little more than 2 hours maximum per week).

Section II: Professions, Industries, Interests alphabetically lists some of the most common professions and industries, along with some of the fast-growing segments, such as biotechnology and satellite communications. Also included are listings for minorities, senior citizens, veterans, and more.

For each Profession/Industry/Interest, career guides are listed first. These provide overviews, with tips and other information to get started and further your career. Such guides can be helpful to those already in a profession or industry.

Following these, there are resources that contain directories and websites (many of which are job boards). Some job boards have resources and links to other sites. Resources in these sites may include news of the profession or industry, books and other publications, e-newsletters, career advice, user discussion rooms, blogs, and much more.

Some online databases offer trial periods. Subscription services are geared for businesses and can be costly. Check with your local or main library to see if it subscribes.

Information and job listings can be found in the following categories:

Academic and Education
Accounting
Advertising, Including Graphic Art and
    Design
Architecture, including Green Design
Apparel, Textiles, Fashion, and Beauty
Art and Design
Automotive
Aviation and Aerospace
Banking, Finance, Investing, Securities, Trad-
    ing, Credit, and Other
Biotechnology
Business
College/Liberal Arts/Recent Graduates
Construction and Building, including Green
    Building
Consulting
Disabled
Diversity and Minorities
eMedia, including Blogs, Social Media,
    Streaming Video, Web Design and IT
Electronics and Digital Systems, including
    Games
Energy, Alternative Energy and Utilities
Engineering
Entertainment, including Media
Environmental and Green Careers

Ex-Inmates
Film, Video and Photography
Food and Beverages
Franchising
Freelancing
Government
Green Careers
Health Care and Medicine
Human Resources
Information Technology/High Tech, including
    eCommerce
Insurance
Journalism
Law and Paralegal
Law
Paralegal
Library and Information Science
Manufacturing
Nonprofit
Nursing
Pharmaceutical and Medical Sales
        Pharmaceutical Sales
        Medical Sales
Public Relations and Integrated Marketing
    Communications
Publishing and Writing, including Freelancing
Real Estate
Retailing
Sales and Marketing
Satellites
Seniors and Those 40 and Up
Small Businesses
Summer Jobs and Internships
Telecommunications
Transportation (Shipping, Marine, Freight,
    Express Delivery, Supply Chain)
Travel, Leisure and Hospitality (Including
    Hotels, Food Service, Travel Agents, Res-
    taurants, Airlines)
Veterans
Vocational Training/No Four-Year College
    Degree
Volunteering
Wholesaling and Distributing/Importing and
    Exporting

Section III: International Careers and Cross-Cultural Business, including Wholesaling and Distributing/Importing and Exporting contains print and online resources to tap the worldwide market. Three important things to remember: (1) many of the print and online materials in Sections I and II contain global listings; (2) many of the international listings in this section include the U.S. as well; and (3) there is an incredible amount of information on international jobs and careers—too much to include here. So, you can scour the Internet and come up with a long list for your own interests. However, the resources included here are comprehensive and among the best available. Note: This section has been expanded to include listings for guides on how to do business with persons in other cultures (Cross-Cultural Business), because of the rapidly growing global scope of business today,

What If I Don't Find Resources That Cover My Job Interests?

If, for example, you want to look for a position as a "Whatever Manager" and need more specific sources, follow these steps:

1. Consult the Associations section. Almost every kind of job, profession, "Whatever" has it own association (or associations). Look at the association's website, consider joining, and even be so brazen as to call its office and ask for help.
2. Search the Internet. Type in Whatever and pair it with Job, or Career, or Directory, or Association, or just by itself. The last option will generate millions of hits: Look at the first few for keywords to use with Whatever in another search. You don't have to look through pages and pages of Internet sites. If it isn't on the first or second page, refine your search.

Be careful of directories that are more than a year or so old, since companies and employees change. Does this research method work? It certainly does. That's how this entire listing was put together, albeit with an initial list of resources from the New York Public Library.

Section I: General Reference

Note: For the North American Industry Classification System (NAICS), the official U.S. Census Bureau listing of all NAICS, see www.census.gov/epcd/naics02/.

The Best Places to Live, About.com
moving.about.com/lr/best_places_to_live/1555085/2/
Links to a great variety sites that cover various aspects of relocating.

money.cnn.com
Compare the cost of living among cities and creates "best places" list using a screening tool.

Directories in Print, Gale annual
www.gale.cengage.com
Provides users with instant, convenient access to profiles of more than 17,000 directories, guides, and other print or non-print address listings in the United States and around the world. Users find an unparalleled depth of well-organized information in this user-friendly, award-winning directory, including local and regional directories as well as national and international listings.

Associations

AssociationExecs.com
Lists over 51,000+ decision-making executive contacts at 17,000 of the nation's largest associations, as well as 400 association management firms. Tracker feature allows you to flag, take notes on, and schedule follow-up reminders with any executive in the database. Site is updated daily and profiles all major executives including executive directors, meeting planners, CFOs and membership directors.

Associations Yellow Book
Leadership Directories
www.leadershipdirectories.com
Stay current with semiannual editions of the Associations Yellow Book—it gives you invaluable contact and biographical information for over 32,000 officers, executives, staff, and board members at more than 1,000 associations.

All mailing addresses, titles, direct-dial telephone and fax numbers, biographical data, and emails are verified by our in-house editorial staff. Full range of association contacts: association executives, board members, committees and chairs, government affairs representatives, foundations, subsidiaries, and PAC directors

Encyclopedia of Associations, Gale
www.gale.cengage.com

There are several versions of this series (see following). Current versions are in print; previous editions are eBooks. See also **Associations Unlimited, the online database,** listed further in this section. This compendium combines data from the entire **Encyclopedia of Associations** series, plus some additional material.

Note: Current versions of the following encyclopedias are available in print; previous editions are online.

Encyclopedia of Associations, National

Comprehensive source for detailed information on nonprofit American membership organizations of national scope. Entries with a wealth of data, typically including the organization's complete name, address and phone number together with the primary official's name and title; fax number, when available; and more. There are two companion volumes: **Volume 2**, Geographic and Executive Indexes; and **Volume 3**, Supplement.

Encyclopedia of Associations: Regional, State and Local Organizations

Contains interstate, state, intrastate, city or local, with scope and interests; trade and professional associations; social welfare and public affairs organizations; health and medical organizations; educational organizations; and more. This information is not duplicated in the *Encyclopedia of Associations National Organizations in the U.S.*

Encyclopedia of Associations: International Organizations

Covers multinational and national membership organizations from Afghanistan to Zimbabwe —including U.S.-based organizations with a bi-national or multinational membership. Entries provide information on executive officers and others, with contact information; the group's history, governance, staff, membership, budget and affiliations; and much more.

Associations Unlimited, online database

Combines data from the entire Encyclopedia of Associations series and includes additional IRS information on nonprofit organizations, for a total of more than 456,000 organizations.

American Society of Association Executives
www.asaecenter.org/career/careerhq.cfm

The **Directories & Guides** page has links to: Societies of Association Executives, Global Forum of SAEs, Great Ideas from Industry Partners, Guide to Association Management Companies, Guide to Consulting Services, Guide to Insurance & Financial Services, and much more.

Associations on the Net (ipl2)
www.ipl.org

Search homepage for "associations"; then search again for a specific field, e.g., engineering associations. Links to hundreds of associations. A collection of Internet sites to a variety of professional and trade associations, cultural and art organizations, political parties and advocacy groups, labor unions, academic societies, and research institutions. Lists more than 500 associations. Site has links to resources, tools, publications and more.

Leadership Directories, Inc., print and online
www.leadershipdirectories.com/

Leadership Nonprofits Premium, database

Online contact directory of key U.S. leaders at nonprofit organizations. Access to associations, foundations, colleges and universities, charities, museums, and much more.

Nonprofit Sector Yellow Book, print

Covers foundations, universities, museums, libraries, charities and more. Find nonprofit emails, phone numbers and career information for over 27,000 executives and 22,000 board members.

The Leadership Library Online

This online directory allows connection to thousands of people across nonprofits, as well as in governments and corporations. Many entries contain emails that go beyond "info@," direct-dial phone numbers, addresses, career history, education backgrounds, and more for over 40,000 organizations. *See also listing below for Leadership Directories.*

National Council of Nonprofits
www.councilofnonprofits.org

Nonprofit network with more than 25,000+ member organizations in 36 states. Search national-state-local network that operates through the 36 state associations across the country.

WEDDLE's Association Directory
www.weddles.com/associations/index.cfm

Free information resource for: HR practitioners, corporate and staffing firm recruiters, and job seekers and career activists. Professional associations and societies often operate websites featuring job boards, resume banks or other employment-related services (these can include job agents, banner advertising and discussion forums for networking). Lists several thousand associations from around the world by their primary professional/occupational focus and/ or industry of interest and provides a link to the website they operate. For the most current listings of associations and a summary of the employment resources offered at the sites (e.g., job board, resume bank, online networking capability), see **WEDDLE's Guide to Association Web Sites** in (www.weddles. com/catalog.htm).

Yahoo
www.yahoo.com

Google
Google.com

To find a specific association, type in "accountant," and "association", for example. For accounting, Google's first result is AICPA, the American Institute of CPAs. Also, by typing "accountant" and "job" Yahoo and Google will lead you to sites and publications on a wide variety of job, career, and company information. Generally, the job boards appear on the first page of the search. The type of job and "association" will generate a list of associations for that type of job, many with links.

National Directories of Companies and Industries

The Business Journals
www.bizjournals.com

Media solutions platform for companies strategically targeting business decision-makers, with a total audience of over 10 million people via 42 websites, 61 publications and over 700 annual industry-leading events. Products provide comprehensive coverage of business news from a local, regional and national perspective. **TBJ Online** features business news from around the nation, updated throughout the day. **bizjournals** is the online media division of **American City Business Journals**, the nation's largest publisher of metropolitan business newspapers. **The Business Journals Online** is comprised of 41 market-specific sites serving local business decision makers from coast-to-coast. The **Book of Lists** has information on the leading buyers, businesses and employers in over 60 of the U.S.'s most dynamic markets.

The Corporate Yellow Book, Leadership Directories, Inc.
www.leadershipdirectories.com

National directory of the people who manage and direct the largest and fastest-growing public and private companies in the United States. See listing below under **Leadership Directories, Inc.**

Dun & Bradstreet's
www.dnb.com

Global source of commercial information and insight on businesses. D&B's global commercial database contains more than 205 million business records. D&B has: D-U-N-S Number, the *Data Universal Numbering System*, a means of identifying business entities on a location-specific basis. Other products: Worldwide Network—-an alliance of commercial information providers covering more than 190 countries, creating comprehensive source of local and global business information (link to WWN page); Global Database—the largest single source of local and global business information and actionable insight.

Leadership Directories, Inc.
www.leadershipdirectories.com/

Leadership Directories, Inc. (LDI) provides high-quality contact information for the leaders of major U.S. government, business, professional, and nonprofit organizations. Leadership Directories publishes 14 **Yellow Books,** each a specialized directory of a particular area of organizational activity.

As a whole, the collection is known as **The Leadership Library Online,** a database of hundreds of thousands leaders at over 40,000 organizations.

Available in print, online, on-demand, and as lists or datafeeds. Updated daily.

There are **print** directories for: *Government, Media,* Legal and *Non-Profit.*

Leadership Online Directories—Several **online** directories for each of these sectors: *Government, Business, Media, Legal, and Non-Profit.* See **www.leadershipdirectories.com/** for a listing of all of these directories, with details on each.

Other online resources: For the above sectors, there are multiple products for each sector: Leadership Lists and Datafeeds and Leadership Profiles on Demand.

Plunkett Research Ltd.
www.plunkettresearch.com

Plunkett's **online subscriptions** and **almanacs** provide complete **data and market research** for the industry(s) of your choice: market research; industry trends analysis; statistical tables; technologies analysis; business intelligence and "hard-to-find" facts; corporate executive contracts; key industry associations (with contact information); industry glossary; and data export tools.

At press time, **the industries/topics covered are**: Advertising & Branding Market Research; Airlines, Hotels, Travel & Tourism Market Research; Alternative Energy Market Research; American Employers Market Research; Apparel & Textiles Market Research; Asian Companies; Automobile Market Research; Banking, Mortgages & Credit Market Research; Biotech Market Research; Chemicals, Coatings & Plastics Market Research; Consulting Market Research; E-Commerce & Internet Business Market Research; Energy Market Research; Engineering Market Research; Entertainment & Media Market Research; Food Market Research; Games, Apps & Social Media; Green Technology; Health Care Market Research; Infotech Industry Market Research; Insurance Market Research| International Companies Market Research; Investment Market Research; Manufacturing Market Research; Mid-Size Employers; Middle Market Research; Nanotechnology Market Research; Outsourcing & Offshoring Market Research; Private Companies Market Research; Real Estate & Construction Market Research; Retail Market Research; Sports Market Research; Telecommunications Market Research; Transportation Market Research; Wireless, Cellular, Wi-Fi & RFID Market Research; The Next Boom.

Major Market Share Companies: Americas
(See International Directories)

Business Rankings Annual, Gale
www.gale.cengage.com

Business Rankings Annual—Working from a bibliographic file we have built up over the years, we have culled thousands of items from periodicals, newspapers, financial services, directories, statistical annuals and other printed material. The *top 10* from each of these rankings appears in this volume, grouped under standard subject headings for easy browsing.

Readers can quickly locate all rankings in which a given company, person or product appears by consulting the comprehensive index. In addition, a complete listing of sources used to compile Business Rankings Annual is provided in the bibliography. Each edition includes a cumulative index, published separately.

Encyclopedia of Business Information Sources, print, Gale   **www.gale.cengage.com**

A bibliographic guide to citations covering over 1,100 subjects of interest to business personnel. Includes abstracts and indexes, almanacs and yearbooks, bibliographies, online databases, research centers and institutes and much more.

SAIBooks, Schonfeld & Associates, Inc.
www.saibooks.com/

Develops and markets business information products. SAI has thousands of customers on six continents in a wide range of industries, from food and financial services, to publishing and telecommunications, and including major national and international companies, state and federal governmental agencies, advertising agencies, accounting firms, corporate libraries, universities and others. Customers include major national and international companies, state and federal government agencies, major advertising agencies, accounting firms, libraries, universities and others. **Business Research Reports** offer up-to-the-minute data for managers seeking a competitive advantage.

Small Business Sourcebook, 2012, print, Gale
www.gale.cengage.com

Covers over 340 specific small business profiles and 99 general small business topics; small business programs and assistance programs in the U.S., its territories, and Canadian provinces; and U.S. federal government agencies and offices specializing in small business issues, programs, and assistance.

Ward's Business Directory of U.S. Private and Public Companies, 2013, Gale
www.gale.cengage.com
Ward's now lists more than 112,000 companies, 90% of which are private. Volumes 1, 2 and 3 provide current company information in a single A-Z arrangement. Volume 4 is a geographic company listing, offering at-a-glance evaluations of industry activity through rankings and analysis. Consult Volume 5 for national rankings by sales within SIC codes at the 4-digit level; Volume 8 presents these rankings by NAICS codes. Volumes 6 and 7 rank companies in each state by sales within 4-digit SIC codes and provide brief evaluations of industry activity of leading companies for each state. Print, CD-ROM and on GDL. Now available digitally in the **Gale Directory Library**.

Hoover's *is now Dun & Bradstreet. See* **www.dnb.com.**

Standard & Poor's
www.standardandpoors.com
With offices in 23 countries and a history that dates back 150 years, Standard & Poor's is known to investors worldwide as a leader of financial-market intelligence.

S&P provides investors to make better-informed investment decisions with market intelligence in the form of credit ratings, indices, investment research and risk evaluations and solutions. **S&P Indices** maintains a wide variety of investable and benchmark indices to meet an array of investor needs. Over $1.25 trillion is directly indexed to Standard & Poor's family of indices, which includes the **S&P 500.** The **S&P Capital IQ** (McGraw-Hill Companies (NYSE:MHP)), provides of multi-asset class data, research and analytics to institutional investors, investment advisors and wealth managers around the world.

Industry Profiles and Information

Bureau of Labor Statistics, United States Department Of Labor
www.bls.gov/bls/infohome.htm
The Bureau of Labor Statistics of the U.S. Depart-

ment of Labor is the principal Federal agency responsible for measuring labor market activity, working conditions, and price changes in the economy. It collects, analyzes, and disseminates essential economic information to support public and private decision-making. As an independent statistical agency, BLS provides products and services that are objective, timely, accurate, and relevant. All information is kept current, with free online access; paper versions of some products are available for a nominal fee. Editions mentioned below are often updated; the years mentioned change with new editions.

Occupational Outlook Handbook (OOH)
www.bls.gov/ooh/
Profiles cover hundreds of occupations and describe What They Do, Work Environment, How to Become One, Pay, and more. Each profile also includes BLS employment projections for the 2010–20 decade. There is an A-Z index.

These sections contain additional information about the **2010-20 projections** and the **2012-13 Occupational Outlook Handbook**: overview of the projections, data for occupations not covered in detail, occupational information included in the *OOH*, teachers guide to the *OOH*, sources of career information, technical documentation, the O*NET-SOC to *Occupational Outlook Handbook* crosswalk, and acknowledgements and important note. The Occupational Outlook Handbook is a nationally recognized source of career information, designed to provide valuable assistance to individuals making decisions about their future work lives. The Handbook is revised every two years. Includes job-search tips, plus a wealth of information of dozens of occupations from management, to professional to construction to the armed forces. The **Handbook** contains these sections: **Overview, Population, Labor Force, Employment, Total Job Openings, Education, and Training Classification System.**

The OOH includes the **Employment Projections (EP)** program which develops information about the labor market for the Nation as a whole for 10 years in the future.

The U.S. Occupational Outlook Employment Projections from the Bureau of Labor Statistics (BLS)
www.bls.gov/emp
The Office of Occupational Statistics and Employment Projections develops information about the labor market for the nation as a whole for 10 years

into the future. Includes such topics as the occupations with the largest job growth, showing the number of jobs for the start and end of a 12-year period, with changes in the number of positions and the growth rate. Employment projections are available for most industries, which are broken down by occupations.

Gale
www.gale.cengage.com/

Gale, part of Cengage Learning, is a leader in e-research and educational publishing for libraries, schools and businesses. The company creates and maintains more than 600 databases that are published online, in print, as eBooks and in microform. **Gale Directory Library** —accesses all of the company's directories.

Directories and **Encyclopedias**—In addition to those already mentioned in this section, Gale and its various imprints publish a large number of Directories on industries, professions, markets (including global), and other topics. Some are listed in Sections II and III. Doing a quick search at the website above often leads to information essential to your career. *See listing following for Graham and Whiteside.*

Graham & Whiteside
gale.cengage.co.uk/graham—whiteside.aspx

Graham and Whiteside (G&W) is a provides of global business and professional information, in **print** and as **databases**. Traditionally, G&W information is worldwide, excluding North America. However, many current products have listings for USA and Canada. G&W's information is available as: **regular e-feeds**; **customised data feeds**; and **international business directories**. These directories are published annually. The **Gale Directory Library platform** unlocks data contained in Graham & Whiteside's "**World Major Companies**" Series and **Industry Sector print series.**

Major Companies Series: Arab World; Europe (7 volumes); Asia and Australasia; Central and Eastern Europe & the Commonwealth of Independent States; Latin American and Caribbean; and Sub-Sharan Africa. **Major Industry Sector Directories of The World**: Petrochemical and Chemical; Energy: Telecommunications; Pharmaceutical & Biotechnology; Financial Institutions; Food and Drink Companies; and Information Technology.

OneSource
www.onesource.com/

Business information solutions; delivering company, executive, and industry intelligence. A comprehensive source for **global information** on companies, industries and executives. **OneSource iSell** is a personalized prospecting engine delivering the hottest prospects with contact and company information, and more, for **U.S./North America and U.K. OneSource Business Browser** offers unlimited access to world-class business information in four regional editions: **North America, the U. K., Europe, and Asia Pacific.**

OneSource Industry Solutions—The industries covered are: technology, computer software, business services, consulting, financial services, recruitment, accounting, banking, and insurance.

OneSource Solutions by Function Covers: sales, marketing, research, procurement, m&a/finance, legal, commercial banking, recruitment, and consulting.

Salary Information
(Also see individual listings in Section II.)

JobStar
jobstar.org

Connect to over 300 free online salary surveys, from accounting to warehousing. Contains Career Guides, job boards, market information, and more.

Salary.com
www.salary.com

Salary.com enables salary calculations and salary-related advice. Also provides advice on making life's decisions.

Cutting-Edge Careers and Top Employers Directories

150 Best Jobs for a Secure Future, 2012, Laurence Shatkin, Jist Works

Uncovers the 150 most secure, well-paying jobs in good and bad times. Approximately 175 best jobs lists rank secure occupations by pay, growth, and openings, plus by education level, personality type, age, self-employment, and more. Bonus lists reveal jobs highly sensitive to economic downturns and jobs highly vulnerable to offshoring. Detailed job descriptions include useful facts on pay, growth, openings, skills needed, education and training, and more.

Best Jobs for the 21st Century, Laurence Shatkin, 6th ed., 2011, Jist Works

Features the 500 jobs with the best pay, fastest growth, and most openings, and presents more than 65 best-jobs lists. Turns the government's occupational data into a helpful reference for job seekers, students, career changers, and others. Gives information on each career cluster and pathway, plus the top three industries for its growth and employment; and more.

Occupational Outlook Handbook
www.bls.gov/emp
(See listing above)

Business Information Websites

First Research
www.firstresearch.com/
Provider of market analysis for sales and marketing teams. **First Research Industry Profiles**— cover over 900 industry segments. Updated monthly and contain critical analysis, statistics and forecasts. **First Research State and Province Profiles**—deliver industry and economic insight, employment and real estate trends, and links for each state, including and 10 Canadian Provinces. **Subscriptions**—Each report consists of key statistics and analysis on market and competitive landscape characteristics, operating conditions, business challenges, industry trends, current and historical industry growth, and more. Many reports also include a global industry analysis.

Kennedy Information
www.kennedyinformation.com
Kennedy Consulting Research & Advisory—provides buyers and sellers of consulting services with research and advice on management and IT consulting professions. **G2 Intelligence** offers coverage of the **diagnostic laboratory industry**. **Green Markets** offers fertilizer news, pricing, regulations and supply chain.

Shibui Markets
www.shibuimarkets.com
Shibui Markets is a leading Global Financial Portal that goes beyond simple facts and figures and into understanding financial information. It offers hard-to-find fundamental financial information about companies from all over the world as well as quotes for foreign currencies, emerging market bonds and selected international equities.

Wetfeet.com
www.wetfeet.com
WetFeet Insider Guides Products for job seekers include: Over 65 **Insider Guides** that cut down on the time doing job research. Guides for **Careers and Industries**—We survey publicly available information and conduct in-depth interviews of rank-and-file employees. Currently, there are about 25 books in these areas; see the website. There are books on job hunting, career development, and three **25 Top** books that cover **Consulting Firms, Financial Service Firms,** and **Global Leaders**. The **Advice** section has articles on career advice for a variety of topics: from job interviews to accepting a job offer, and more. **Blog** gives up-to-date information and insight.

Business.com
www.business.com
Online destination for businesses of all sizes to research, find, and compare the products and services they need to run their businesses. Decision-makers use Business.com's 50,000+ how-to guides, price comparison tools, expansive library of white papers, and leading **online B2B directory.** Its **Guides & Articles** cover industries including, video surveillance, medical supplies, care facilities, office coffee, office furniture, and more. Searching under "business directory" pulls up links to directories to 20+ industries.

Hoover's
www.hoovers.com
See D&B listing.

Manta
www.manta.com
Manta helps small businesses profit, connect and grow through the largest online community dedicated entirely to small business. Millions use Manta each day to buy from, partner with and connect to companies via the Internet.

Regional and Local Directories

Encyclopedia of Associations: Regional, State, and Local Organizations
See previous listing.

Craig's List
www.craigslist.org
This site has a local job board, by city. The list of cities keeps growing.

Career Fairs, Trade Shows, and Multi-Industry/Profession Job Boards

Career Fairs
www.careerfairs.com
A resource for career fair organizers, colleges, employers, professionals, and college students. Offers a zip code search feature to help locate an event within a 25 mile radius of your desired location.

EventsEye
www.eventseye.com
Today, our consistently growing database features nearly 9,000 trade shows, exhibitions and conferences coming from over 2,300 fairs organizers, with a total of over 16,000 events dates, spanning about two years from the current month. New trade shows and exhibitions are added in every month. Featuring a classification of activity topics, covers major Trade Exhibitions worldwide. We also focus on brand new events, especially in emergent market regions. Our directory contains 1,400 trade show venues from over 800 Cities, among 128 Countries. We provide links to as many as 13,650 websites and over 9,000 emails.

Expo Central International
www.expocentral.com
Local, national or global information about trade shows, festivals, exhibitions, trade fairs, conventions, conferences, seminars and other events. With over 8,000 events, ExpoCentral.com is one of the most popular Directories on the Web providing the most comprehensive information about international and local business and public events, companies, products and services.

National Career Fairs
www.nationalcareerfairs.com
Over 300 career fairs in 76 cities, listed by city.

6Figure Jobs
www.6figurejobs.com
A premiere executive career community & job board that offers relevant online job search resources and content for $100K+ job seekers and recruiters.xs

CareerOneStop
www.acinet.org/acinet
Source for employment information and inspiration. The place to manage your career. Sponsored by the U.S. Department of Labor, has tools to help job seekers, students, businesses and career professionals. CareerOneStop products include: **America's Service Locator** connects individuals to employment and training opportunities available at local One-Stop Career Centers. The Web site provides contact information for a range of local work-related services, including unemployment benefits, career development, and educational opportunities. **America's Career InfoNet** helps individuals explore career opportunities to make informed employment and education choices, featuring occupation and industry information, salary data, career videos, and other resources relevant to the global marketplace. **mySkills myFuture** helps laid-off workers and other career changers find new occupations to explore. Users can identify occupations that require skills and knowledge similar to their current or previous job, learn more about these suggested matches, locate local training programs, and/or apply for jobs. Other topics are **Competency Model Clearinghouse, Worker ReEmployment, and Key to Career Success.**

job-hunt
www.job-hunt.org
Free job search information, expert advice, and links to 18,375 employers & job search resources.

GlassDoor
www.glassdoor.com
A jobs and career community that offers an inside look at jobs and companies. Employee-generated content contains—anonymous salaries, company reviews, interview questions, and more—all posted by employees, job seekers, and sometimes the companies themselves.

The Riley Guide
www.rileyguide.com
Although a job board, it contains a directory of job, career, and education information sources.

Job Hunter's Sourcebook: Where to Find Employment Leads and Other Job Search Gale Resources, 12th ed., 2012

A comprehensive guide to sources of information on employment leads and other job search resources. It streamlines the job-seeking process by identifying and organizing the wide array of publications, organizations, audio-visual and electronic resources, and other job-hunting tools.

New York Public Library, Science, Industry and Business Library (SIBL)   www.nypl.org/
Located at 188 Madison Avenue @ 34th Street, New York, (917) 275-6975
Job Search Central @ SIBL

A one-stop-shop for job seekers. Containing books; accessible premium, online databases; links to career websites; job search events; Drop-In Job Club for college graduates in their twenties; New York State Job Bank' Indeed.com's Industry Employment Trends; advice and consulting for small businesses available free; onsite advisory service from SCORE to help you plan to start your own business. Borrow books on jobs, careers, and résumés. Try out NYPL e-books and borrow the latest e-books on résumés, careers, jobs, interview tips, and more without a trip to the Library. Use your NYPL library card and see what's available.

    SIBL has a staff trained in job search. One-on-one appointments can be scheduled. Free Career coaching services by appointment. Sign up for a career coaching session online. **Use:** Any person who lives, works, attends school or pays property taxes in New York State is eligible to receive a New York Public Library card free of charge. **Note:** If you are ineligible, contact your local library.

Jist Publishing
http://jist.emcpublishingllc.com/
Jist's products help millions plan their education and career, find jobs, and succeed in the world of work. Materials cover the essential topics people need guidance. Topics include: job search, career exploration, occupational information, job retention, college preparation, life skills, and character education. Product lines include assessments, workbooks, reference books, trade books, textbooks, DVDs, software, posters, games, and online workshops. Its website details an extensive listing of products on career topics.

WEDDLE's 2011/12 Guide to Employment Sites on the Internet, Peter Weddle, June 2011
www.weddles.com
Published every other year,, this volume is a guide to the 100,000+ recruitment services and job-search support sites on the Web. It covers: social media sites, professional networking sites, career portals, job boards and more. The Guide's information is organized into two sections: **The Top 100**, our pick of the 100 best employment sites on the Internet. Each site is described with a full-page profile of its features, services and fees. **The Best and the Rest**, a directory of over 10,000 sites organized by the career field, industry and geographic location in which they specialize.

Section II: Professions/Industries/Interests

General

Infobase Publishing
www.infobasepublishing.com
A leading provider of supplemental educational materials to the school and library markets. Products include books, eBooks, online databases, eLearning Modules, videos, and digital products under such names as Facts On File, Films for the Humanities & Sciences, Cambridge Educational, Chelsea House, Bloom's Literary Criticism, and Ferguson Publishing. With thousands of titles, Infobase provides students, librarians, and educators with authoritative, reliable resources supporting the curriculum across a wide variety of subject areas, from history, science, and literature to careers, health, and social issues.
Guides to Finding a New Career, **20 volumes,** each by profession/industry are aimed at those looking to take their career in a new direction. Each book explores a career field and provides readers with the necessary tools to transition to a new job.

Leadership Directories
See listing under Section I

JIST Publishing
jist.emcpublishingllc.com/
JIST helps millions to plan their education and career, find jobs, and succeed in the world of work.

Materials cover the topics people need guidance on to achieve a rewarding life and career. These include: job search, career exploration, occupational information, job retention, college preparation, life skills, and character education. Our product lines include assessments, workbooks, reference books, trade books, textbooks, DVDs, software, posters, games, and online workshops. We also offer train-the-trainer workshops for career development professionals who need techniques for helping their clients succeed.

Plunkett Research, Ltd.
www.plunkettresearch.com
See listing in Section I

Vault Career Intelligence
www.vault.com
Vault is a provider of information and solutions for professionals and students who are pursuing and managing high-potential careers.

Online: comprehensive information, including: **Employer profiles and rankings**, which combine the inside perspective of anonymous employee reviews with context from Vault's editors. **Industry blogs** and news stories that help professionals stay on top of the issues affecting their careers. **Message boards**, where users freely discuss issues, ask questions and get advice. **Vault's job board**, and **education information**.

Print: Vault publishes more than 120 print and digital career guidebooks, including annual guides, such as the **Vault Guide to the Top 50 Banking Employers, the Vault Guide to the Top 100 Law Firms and the Vault Guide to the Top 40 Accounting Firms**; and best-selling guides to résumés, cover letters and interviews. Note: Some of the Vault Guides are listed in Section II. However, check Vault's website to find those that are appropriate for you, as it is not possible to list all of them here.

www.wetfeet.com
See listing above.

Science, Industry and Business Library (SIBL), New York Public Library
www.nypl.org/locations/sibl
See the listing under Section I.

www.tradepub.com
Free trade magazine subscriptions & technical docu-

ment downloads. Extensive list of free business, computer, engineering and trade magazines, white papers, downloads and eBooks; topics include management, marketing, operations, sales, and technology. Simply complete the application form and submit it. All are absolutely free to professionals who qualify.

Academic and Education

Best Careers for Teachers: Making the Most of your Teaching Degree, Editors of LearningExpress LLC, 2010, LearningExpress, LLC
This book is designed to guide current, former and aspiring teachers towards ways to leverage their teaching education and experiences to find more-rewarding careers. For both who are planning to change careers, and for those who want to explore opportunities in addition to teaching full time. Relevant for primary, secondary and post-secondary educators.

How to Be Successful in Your First Year of Teaching Elementary School: Everything You Need to Know That They Don't Teach You in School, Tena Green, 2010, Atlantic Publishing Group Inc.
Learn how to: ask principals and administrators for help; memorize names quickly; create seating charts; write lesson plans; help struggling readers; gain respect; get a mentor; and much more. Compiled by those who have been there.

I Want a Teaching Job: Guide to Getting the Teaching Job of Your Dreams, Tim Wei, 2010, CreateSpace Independent Publishing Platform
Real-world advice on landing your job. A complete guide to getting the teacher job of your dreams, even in today's ultra-competitive market. Includes the best way to answer the 50 most common teacher interview questions, insider tips to make your resume and cover letter stand out, and more.

Inspired College Teaching: A Career-Long Resource for Professional Growth, Maryellen Weimer, 2010, Jossey-Bass
Provides goals best positioned for beginning, mid-career, and senior faculty, as well as activities faculty can use to ignite intellectual curiosity from both students and themselves. This book presents a way for faculty to obtain and sustain teaching excellence throughout their career.

Surviving Your Academic Job Hunt: Advice for Humanities PhDs, Kathryn Hume, 2nd ed., 2010, Palgrave Macmillan

Gives essential advice for academic job hunters and gives them the skills and knowledge to land a job in the humanities. Fully revised and updated, this book offers a comprehensive look at the do's and don'ts of the application and interview process and provides indispensable tips and a variety of practical tools.

Teacher Preparation in Career Pathways: The Future of America's Teacher Pipeline, Karen Embry-Jenlink (ed.), 2012, R&L Education

Offers a critical and timely discussion of what teacher preparation should look like in the 21st century and why. Embry-Jenlink speaks directly of the decreasing quality in America's teacher work-force and the dismal recruitment of teachers from historically underrepresented and underserved populations. The voices of deans, faculty, school administrators, and directors of non-profit agencies resound with an emerging workforce solution.

Thinking About Teaching High School? What You Need to Know Before You Sign the Contract by Faye Allen, 2010, Kindle ed., Faye Allen

A great outline of what someone needs to know their first year of teaching. It would even be useful for someone with years of experience. Even experienced teachers need to be reminded of this stuff from time to time.

What Teachers Make: In Praise of the Greatest Job in the World, Taylor Mali, 2012, G. P. Putnam's Sons

The right book at the right time: an impassioned defense of teachers and why our society needs them now more than ever.

Chronicle of Higher Education Career Network chronicle.com

The Chronicle of Higher Education is the source of news, information, and jobs. Based in Washington, The Chronicle has a domestic staff and foreign correspondents. Online, **The Chronicle** contains news, advice, and jobs. The Chronicle's **website** has the latest issue; daily news and advice columns; current job listings; and more. In **print**, The Chronicle contains news and jobs. Subscribers receive **The Almanac of Higher Education** and special reports.

Europa World of Learning, Routledge Reference, Taylor & Francis Group, U.K., 2013, print (annual) and online
www.worldoflearning.com

Over 30,000 universities, colleges, schools of art and music, libraries, learned societies, research institutes, museums and art galleries worldwide are listed, and information on more than 200,000 staff and officials. Plus information on more than 550 international cultural, scientific and educational organizations. Online version is revised and updated throughout the year. The online version provides a full range of sophisticated search and browse functions, and regular updates of content.

Accounting

Accounting, Business, and Finance (Field Guides to Finding a New Career), Candace S. Gulko, 2010, Ferguson,Infobase Publishing

Aimed at readers looking to take their career in a new direction, this book provides advice and essential tips for career changers. Has self-assessment questions, further resources, and advice on ways to reach career goals.

Careers in Accounting; Wetfeet Insider Guide, 2011
www.wetfeet.com

Among the topics covered are: how industry scandals have affected the big four and their employees; alternatives to the big four for those seeking a mid-sized firm; a typical day in the life of a staff audit accountant, senior audit accountant; descriptions of career paths for accounting professionals currently working in the industry.

The Inside Track to Careers in Accounting, Stan Ross and James Carberry, 2010, American Institute of Certified Public Accountants

For new accounting professionals and students who want to expand their understanding of what CPAs do and navigate the available opportunities. It focuses on careers in public, corporate, government, and nonprofit accounting; plus academia and starting your own business.

Vault Guide to the Top 50 Accounting Firms, 2012 Edition, Derek Loosvelt, 2011, Vault, Inc.

Rates approximately 75 firms with significant accounting operations in North America.

Accounting.com
www.acounting.com

In addition to listing jobs, this site covers education, software, an accounting dictionary, and more resources.

AICPA: American Institute for Certified Public Accountants
www.aicpa.org

AICPA's career information includes career paths, jobs, mentoring, and more. The Institute also covers all aspects of the profession.

Careers-in-Accounting.com
www.careers-in-accounting.com

Site covers various aspects of the profession, such as skills and talents needed, salaries, facts and trends, links and resources. It features books, videos, blogs; as well as other resources about the profession and a job board broken down by function.

Advertising, Including Graphic Arts and Design

Becoming a Graphic Designer: A Guide to Careers in Design, Steven Heller and Teresa Fernandes, 2010, Wiley

This guide provides a comprehensive survey of the graphic design market, including print and electronic media, and the digital design disciplines. This visual guide has hundreds of illustrations and features the latest material on interactive design, information design, motion, and more.

How to Put Your Book Together and Get a Job in Advertising, Maxine Paetro and Giff Crosby, 2010

The industry standard that all aspiring creatives turn to for honest—and often droll—career advice, updated to reflect what most impresses today's top firms.

Pick Me: Breaking Into Advertising and Staying There, Nancy Vonk and Janet Kestin, 2008, Adweek

Breaking into this field; money, awards, on-the-job advice. A comprehensive guide about working in advertising, with useful tips, and gurus writing on their collective wisdom.

Starting Your Career as a Freelance Web Designer (Starting Your Career), Neil Tortorella, 2011, Allworth Press

This book guides web designers step-by-step down the path to success and helps them avoid common pitfalls.

Careers in Advertising and Public Relations, 2011, WetFeet
www.wetfeet.com

How to select the ad or PR agencies where you should apply. The forces and trends— from TiVo to Twitter—that are shaping these industries. How new ad and PR campaigns are conceived and developed. The top ad and PR agencies. What real people working in these fields like and dislike about their jobs. How much you're likely to earn, more.

2012 Artist's & Graphic Designer's Market, Mary Burzlaff Bostic, 37th ed., 2011, North Light Books

Reference guide for emerging artists, who want to establish a successful career in fine art, illustration, cartooning or graphic design. Includes a free one-year subscription to *ArtistsMarketOnline.com*.

Advertising Red Books
www.redbooks.com

Identify agency clients and find the critical information about them; the right contacts at those clients; pinpoint a company by the brand it owns and more. There are three formats—web, raw data and print. Contains over 15,000 U.S. and international agency profiles and 21,000 global advertiser profiles. The Web version is updated twice weekly and the print version is published twice a year with supplements.

Advertising Ratios & Budgets, SAIBooks, Schonfeld & Associates
www.saibooks.com

Covers over 4,500 companies and 300 industries with historical 2011 advertising budgets, 2012 ad-to-sales ratios and ad-to-gross margin ratios, as well as 2012 and 2013 budget forecasts and growth rates. Used by major advertising agencies, media companies, advertisers, and libraries. Kept current.

U.S. Sourcebook of Advertisers

A directory of publicly owned corporations that advertise.

Corporate name, address, telephone number and website are provided, along with the names and titles of three senior executives, ad budgets, sales, fiscal year closing, and more. **Advertising Growth Trends** gives information on publicly owned corporations that spend on advertising. Organized by SIC and alphabetically by company name within each SIC. Each company's historical information includes: advertising spending for each of the last five calendar years in constant 1990 dollars, percent of advertising in relation to total spending by all companies within the same SIC, and more.

Adbrands.net
www.adbrands.net

Information about the global advertising industry. Some job postings are here, but this site is best for company profiles and account assignments. **Adbrands Company Profiles** assess more than 1,000 leading advertisers, brands and agencies, with each company's business record, geographic strength and comparative performance within its chosen sector, including strengths, weaknesses, history, up-to-date news and top-line financial information.

Adbrands Account Assignments online database tracks account management for the world's leading brands and companies; which advertising agency handles which accounts in which countries. The database contains almost 25,000 worldwide account assignments for just under 6,000 leading brands and more than 1,700 advertising and marketing agencies.

AIGA|Aquent annual
www.aiga.org/salary-survey/

Survey of Design Salaries—Each year, AIGA and Aquent join forces to conduct an extensive compensation survey for the communication design profession—the largest of its kind. The 2012 survey includes resources from more than 8,000 design professionals nationwide and features an interactive overview of compensation, insights from respondents and a comparison calculator. **AIGA|Aquent Survey of Design Salaries 2011**—in 2011, AIGA and Aquent expanded the list of positions and descriptions to include a broader cross section of the design industry. Responses were collected from more than 7,000 design professionals and a new interactive format was launched online to help hiring managers, designers and students evaluate compensation trends across the profession and throughout the country.

GraphicDesign.com

GraphicDesign.com is a leading source of news and information devoted entirely to the graphic design industry. Employers, students, and freelancers come to GraphicDesign.com to read and discuss current news, information, and events in the graphic design industry.

Media Bistro
mediabistro.com

Site is for anyone who creates or works with content, or who is a non-creative professional working in a content/creative industry. That includes editors, writers, producers, graphic designers, book publishers, and others in industries including magazines, television, film, radio, newspapers, book publishing, online media, advertising, PR, and design. Our mission is to provide opportunities to meet, share resources, become informed of job opportunities and interesting projects and news, improve career skills, and showcase your work.

Architecture, including Green Design

(*see also,* Building and Construction, including Green)

The Architect in Practice, David Chappell and Andrew Willis, 10th ed., 2011, Wiley-Blackwell

A fully updated version of 1952 classic. The message and philosophy remains the same as the original: to provide the student of architecture and the young practitioner with a readable guide to the profession, outlining an architect's duties to client and contractor, the key aspects of running a building contract, and the essentials of management, finance and drawing office procedure.

The Architecture Career Guide, Harrison Barnes and Architecture Crossing, 2011, Kindle ed., Amazon Digital Services

Articles by professionals. This e-book explores areas of importance to both practicing architects and those seeking a career in the industry. Information on professional degrees, courses, training standards, and examinations.

Becoming an Architect: A Guide to Careers in Design, Lee W. Waldrep, 2nd ed., 2011, Kindle ed., Wiley

This visual guide to preparing for and succeeding in the profession is based upon interviews with professionals. Starting with the requirements needed, the book shows how a career can go.

Ethics for Architects: 50 Dilemmas of Professional Practice, Thomas Fisher, 2010, Princeton Architectural Press

Features newly relevant interpretations adapted to the pervasive demands of globalization, sustainability, and developments in information technology.

How to Architect, Doug Patt, 2012, The MIT Press

For those just starting that journey or thinking about becoming an architect. If you are already an architect and want to remind yourself of what drew you to the profession, it is a book of affirmation. And if you are just curious about what goes into the design and construction of buildings, this book tells you how architects think. With letters from professionals.

Towards a New Architect: The guide for architecture students, Yasmin Shariff and Jane Tankard, 2010, Taylor & Francis

Helps grads to make the right moves when starting out. How to research the opportunities available, prepare your CV, make sure that it gets you noticed for the right reasons, and deliver a successful interview.

Zoom Factor for the Enterprise Architect: How to Focus and Accelerate Your Career, Sharon C. Evans, 2012, Firefly Media

A career guide for aspiring or current Enterprise Architects or leading EA teams, or someone considering this role as a career change. This book will help you understand what is in store for you.

AIA Architect Finder
architectfinder.aia.org
Locates architecture firms by area. You can search by city and state; or U.S. Zip Code and radius; or by firm name. To locate international firms, different countries are listed using their three-character ISO Country Code.

The Architects Directory
architects.buildingpros.com

Paid listings for architects throughout the U.S. and Canada.

Architects USA
www.architectsusa.com
Over 20,000 firms listed.

Architecture Week—Professional Directory of Firms
www.architectureweek.com/directory/firms_i.html
The Architecture Week professional directory includes thousands of architects and firms, large and small, local and global, from the U.S. and internationally..

Directory of Commercial Architects (BoogarLists), Steve Boogar, 2011, Kindle ed., BoogarLists

Leading commercial architecture firms located in major U.S. metro markets. Contains company name, street address, telephone/fax & URL where available, and a one-paragraph organization description (source: the company's web site or press materials).

Info.com
www.info.com
Type in "architect" and a directory of numerous links will come up—-firms, associations, publications, design, and much more.

Apparel, Textiles, Fashion, and Beauty

A Career as a Skin Care Specialist (Careers Ebooks), Institute For Career Research, 201

Covers education, skills needed, the tasks performed by skincare specialists, and where to find work.

Careers in Cosmetology—Beautician (Careers Ebooks), Institute For Career Research, 2012, Kindle ed., Amazon Digital Services

For hairdressers, stylists, makeup artists, nail and skin care professionals.

Fashion: The Industry and Its Careers, Michele M. Granger, 2nd ed, 2012, Fairchild Pubs

A thorough exploration of fashion careers across the board, including designer, textile manufacturer, retailer, wholesaler, illustrator, model, product developer, journalist, publicist, trend forecaster and much more.

The Fashion Careers Guidebook: A Guide to Every Career in the Fashion Industry and How to Get It, Julia Yates and Donna Gustavsen, 2011, Barron's Educational Series

This practical book will guide you through fashion's different career paths, explain the industry's jargon, and help you stand out from the crowd.

In Fashion: From Runway to Retail, Everything You Need to Know to Break Into the Fashion Industry, Annemarie Iverson, 2010, Clarkson Potter

Everything you need to know to get an "in" into fashion.

Fashion & Textiles: The Essential Careers Guide, Carol Brown, 2010, Laurence King Publishers

An in-depth review of the wide-ranging career options in the fashion and textile industry, profiling over 50 careers that span the creative, technical, retail and media fields.

How To Get The Best Beauty Therapy Jobs (Beauty Recruitment), Nicole Beecher, 2010, Beauty Recruitment Publishing

Explains to both students and qualified beauty therapists how to get the best out of agencies, job boards and applying for jobs directly to salons.

Real-Resumes for Retailing, Modeling, Fashion & Beauty Jobs, Anne McKinney, 2012, CreateSpace Independent Publishing Platform

Resumes and cover letters in this book actually worked in real job hunts. Covers retail buyer, merchandise manager, customer service manager, district supervisor, assistant sales manager, beauty consultant, model, store manager, buyer, and many other disciplines.

2012 Davison's Textile Blue Book, annual, Davison Publishing
www.textilebluebook.net
Directory of textile mills, dyers, and finishers in the U.S., Canada, Mexico and Central America—from fiber, through finished fabric.

Fashiondex
www.fashiondex.com
Apparel Industry Sourcebook 2012—Directory for apparel manufacturers, designers, merchandisers, trim buyers, fabric buyers and production departments in the men's, women's, children's and accessory markets. **Directory of Brand Name Apparel**

Manufacturers and Importers 2012—Directory listing brand-name labels and manufacturers in the women's, men's, children's and accessory markets.

The Fashion Designer's Directory of Shape and Style: Simon Travers-Spencer and Zarida Zaman, 2012, Kindle ed., Barron's

More than 1,200 detailed illustrations provide the building blocks for designing imaginative and original clothing.

Apparel Search—Fashion Industry Guide
www.apparelsearch.com/
The website is a fashion industry directory that provides members of the international fashion community with educational information regarding virtually every aspect of the apparel and textile market. Covers various elements of fashion, textiles, clothing, and related products & services.

The National Register
www.thenationalregister.com
Publishers of apparel directories: apparel manufacturers, apparel sales reps, fashion accessories, and apparel wholesalers. See website for complete listing. Typical directories include: **Apparel Marketplace: Wholesalers, Importers, Exporters, Men & Boy's Manufacturers Apparel Directory, and Women & Children's Manufacturers Apparel Directory.**

Cosmetics & Toiletries

www.cosmeticsandtoiletries.com
Site for this publication has networking (events) news and industry news, and more.

Fashion Net
www.fashion.net
Fashion Net provides millions of savvy fashion followers direct and comprehensive access to the very sources that inform the world of fashion.

Fashion Career Center.com
www.fashioncareercenter.com
Articles, news, fashion schools and career advice.

The Fashion Center, Business Improvement District, New York City
www.fashioncenter.com
The Center promotes the Fashion District as a strategic midtown business location and ensuring New York's position as the fashion capital of the world.

Art and Design

I'd Rather Be in the Studio: The Artist's No-Excuse Guide to Self-Promotion, Alyson B. Stanfield, 2nd ed., 2011, Pentas Press

Practical and innovative approaches that help get your art out of the studio and in front of buyers and collectors.

Making It in the Art World: New Approaches to Galleries, Shows, and Raising Money, Brainard Carey, 2011, Allworth Press

How to be a professional artist and what are the new methods that define what success means, and how to realize it. Ways of advancing your plans on any level.

New Markets for Artists: How to Sell, Fund Projects, and Exhibit Using Social Media, DIY Pop-Ups, eBay, Kickstarter, and Much More, Brainard Carey, 2012, Allworth Press

Whitney Biennial–featured artist and career coach Carey reveals the opportunities that you didn't know existed. This book works as a course (downloadable syllabus available) and as a companion volume to Carey's recent book, **Making It in the Art World.**

The Successful Artist's Career Guide: Finding Your Way in the Business of Art, Margaret Peot, 2012, North Light Books

Peot offers real-world advice on everything from bidding on jobs and promoting yourself, to filing taxes and getting health insurance.

Art & Design Online
www.artanddesignonline.com/

Resource tool for the art and design community. Members can upload their images or text onto their pages whenever they want, without relying solely on costly programmers. **The Guide,** a database, has information on thousands of artists, designers, design centers, showrooms, art reps, and much more.

New York Foundation for the Arts (NYFA)
www.nyfa.org

NYFA empowers artists at critical stages in their creative lives. The **NYFA Classifieds** is a career-development tool, and is the largest national online resource for jobs and internships, opportunities and services, event listings and studio spaces for artists, arts administrators and museum professionals. **NYFA Source** is a national directory of awards, services, and publications for artists.

WWAR: World Wide Arts Resources
www.wwar.com

Site for contemporary art, art news, art history, contemporary artist's and gallery's portfolios. Site now has Art Blogs—information on: contemporary artists and masters, museums, galleries, fine art, art history, art education, antiques, dance, theater, and more.

Automotive

Auto Sales: How to Excel in the Career of Selling Cars, JB Zegalia, Kindle ed., 2012, Llumina Press

Learn how to set up your business, build rapport, gain credibility, and acquire other traits for making the sale.

Real-Resumes for Auto Industry Jobs, Anne McKinney, 2012, CreateSpace Independent Publishing Platform

Whether you want to stay in the auto industry or transition into another field, this book will help. It shows samples of resumes and cover letters that worked for real people, who found technical, management, and sales positions.

Retail Auto Sales, Making It To The Top!: Making $100,000 A Year, Michael Thanem, Kindle ed., 2012, Amazon Digital Services, Inc.

A comprehensive text for beginning sales consultants in the auto industry.

Automotive Dictionary, John Barach, Kindle ed., 2012, Amazon Digital Services, Inc.

Contains over 22,000 entries and over 700 images. Has a menu index and hyperlinks.

Dictionary of Automotive Engineering, Ingo Stuben, 2010, Expert Verlag

For experts (engineers or mechanics), students and others.

Business Monitor International
www.businessmonitor.com

Search for "auto" on this site **The BMO Automotive Service** A data and intelligence tool for industry analysis, forecasts, and an assessment of company activity and sector trends worldwide.

WardsAuto
wardsauto.com
Data Center—Browse by region: North America, Asia Pacific, Europe, World, and others.

WardsAuto Supplier Directory—information on parts and services; detailed capabilities and contact information for many of the world's top automotive suppliers. **WARD'S Automotive Yearbook**— puts the entire automotive year in review. Data now available on CD-ROM.

Aviation and Aerospace

Ace The Technical Pilot Interview 2/E, Gary Bristow, 2nd ed., 2012, McGraw-Hill Professional
This second edition has over 1,000 questions and answers, many of them all-new.

Airline Pilot Interview Questions and Answers (Testing Series), Lee Woolaston, Kindle ed., 2012, How2Become/Amazon Digital Services
This workbook provides candidates with approximately 500 sample interview questions, non-technical test questions and insider information on how to score high during the airline pilot selection process.

Cleared for Takeoff: Have You Got What It Takes to Be an Airline Pilot?, Lisa Thompson, 2009, Compass Point Books/Capstone Press
What skills are needed, what's in a day's work, and where piloting can take you. Learn about airplane controls and equipment, famous pilots, and various types of aircraft.

Career in Aerospace Science (Careers Ebooks), Institute For Career Research, 2010, Kindle Ed., Institute For Career Research/Amazon Digital Services
Contains unbiased information about aerospace science careers.

Careers in Focus: Aviation (Ferguson's Careers in Focus), 2nd ed., 2010, Ferguson Publishing Co.
Job profiles include: aeronautical and aerospace technicians, aerospace engineers, aircraft mechanics, airport security personnel, and more. Presents opportunities, the education necessary, personal qualifications required, earnings, and descriptions of different job specialties.

How to Land a Top-Paying Aerospace Engineer, Aerospace Product and Parts Manufacturing Services Job: Your Complete Guide to Opportunities, Resumes and ... What to Expect From Recruiters and More!, Brad Andrews, 2010, tebbo
Compiles information candidates need to apply for the first aerospace engineer, aerospace product and parts manufacturing services job, or to apply for a better job. Has worksheets with outlines that make it easier to write about a work experience and ensure that resumes are well-structured and include all important history.

Flyr: Network for Pilots
www.flyronline.com
Social network for pilots, with a magazine, website, mobile apps, and FlyrTV.

25th edition of the European Space Directory, 2010, Eurospace Publications
eurospace.pagesperso-orange.fr/esd.html
Available from ESD Partners's Paris office. Gives information on the Space Industry in Europe. Companies from ESA countries form the core of the Directory. Major features: profiles of EC-funded space research projects; company profiles; who's who; and a buyer's guide.

Jane's IHS
www.janes.com
IHS Jane's Defense Equipment and Technology Solutions deliver insight into defense and aerospace equipment and technology, accessing information in land, sea, air & space, weapons, and more. Other titles: **IHS Jane's All the World's Aircraft: Development & Production, IHS Jane's All the World's Aircraft: In Service, IHS Jane's All the World's Aircraft: Unmanned, IHS Jane's Space Systems & Industry, IHS Jane's Flight Avionics**, and **IHS Jane's Aero Engines.**

Banking, Finance, Investing, Securities, Trading, Credit, and Other

An Introduction to Investment Banks, Hedge Funds, and Private Equity, Kindle ed., David Stowell, 2010, Academic Press, Amazon Digital Services, Inc.
This description of the symbiotic relationships among investment banks, hedge funds, and private

equity firms shows how firms simultaneously compete and cooperate, giving the ways these firms are reinventing themselves in the post-crash regulatory environment and, through ten extensive cases, the ways in which they are increasing their power and influence.

The Best Book On Investment Banking Careers, Donna Khalife, updated and expanded, Kindle ed., 2011, Hyperink Investment Banking Jobs

Knowing the ins and outs of the industry can help you make your big break.

The Best Book On Getting An iBanking Internship (By An Investment Banking Intern At JP Morgan, UBS, & FT Partners), Erin Parker, 2011, Hyperink Investment Banking Internships

Parker guides you stepwise process from interview preparation to conquering the 90-hour work-week.

But I Never Made a Loan: My Career in Banking—he Early Years, Carter H. Golembe, 2009, iUniverse

The author writes on his involvement in banking since the end of World War II.

Career Guidebook for IT in Investment Banking, Essvale, 2010, Essvale Corporation Limited

A complete handbook that provides a guideline to careers in Investment Banking IT.

Career Opportunities in Banking, Finance, and Insurance, 2010, Facts on File, part of Gale. CENGAGE.com

This Second Edition profiles 86 jobs, including eight new to this edition.

Careers in Investment Banking (Careers Ebooks) by Institute For Career Research, 2012, Institute For Career Research

Discusses what it takes to be an iBanker: good analytical, interpersonal, and technical skills.

How to Land a Job on Wall Street: 25 Tips to Get an Awesome Job in Finance, Zack Miller, 2012, Kindle ed., Tradestreaming Media LLC/Amazon Digital Services

Based on his own experience and hundreds of interviews with thought-leaders in investing about finding jobs, Miller offers the best tips for landing a job on Wall Street.

Investment Banking Jobs 101: Know Your Product Groups, Kindle ed., Brian DeChesare, 2012, Hyperink, Amazon Digital Services, Inc.

Covers the industry vs. product-group debate. The notion that industry groups are 100% marketing and product groups are 100% execution, is wrong.

American Banking Assoc.
www.aba.com

ABA Financial Institutions Directory—Acuity—This print directory about U.S.-based financial institutions, has financial information, as well as contact information on key personnel. ABA offers other directories and financial information. See the website.

A.M. Best Company
www.ambest.com

The company is a full-service credit rating organization dedicated to serving the **insurance industry**. A worldwide insurance-rating and information agency. A.M. Best issues in-depth reports and financial strength ratings about insurance organizations. Its flagship publication and database, **Best's Insurance Reports,** offers coverage of insurers and reinsurers in the U.S., Canada, and worldwide. The firm publishes **books**, **directories**, **CD-ROM** products and **Internet-based** services. See the website for listings.

BAI
www.bai.org

Products and services include research and performance metrics, professional learning and development programs, and in-depth editorial coverage through **BAI Banking Strategies.**

Graham & Whiteside
gale.cengage.co.uk/graham—whiteside.aspx

Global business and professional information, supplying company data, in **print** and as **databases**. Traditionally, G&W information was worldwide, excluding North America. However, many current products now have listings for U.S. and Canada. It publishes **Major Financial Institutions of the World.** For more on G&W, see the listings online.

Financial Planning.com
www.financial-planning.com

Financial Planning, part of SourceMedia, delivers information that independent advisors need to make informed decisions about their business and the clients they serve. We are the only website dedicated to the needs of the independent financial planner. We also produce podcasts, conferences, custom publications and eNewsletters.

Financial Yellow Book, semiannual
Leadership Directories
www.leadershipdirectories.com

Lists board members and PR representatives at the most important financial organizations in the U.S. Find contact information and career records for over 26,000 executives and 535 public and private financial companies across the U.S.

Lipper Marketplace
www.lippermarketplace.com/

Lipper supplies mutual fund information, analytical tools, and commentary. Lipper's fund data, fund awards designations and ratings information provide insight to advisors, media and individual investors. The **Marketplace data** include: **Investment Managers and their Products** and **Pension Fund Consultants**.

Pratt's Guide to Private Equity & Venture Capital Sources, online and print, Thomson Reuters
thomsonreuters.com

Reference source to the actively investing private-equity and venture-capital firms operating around the world, with a complete list of company information including website, type of firm, management roster, capital under management, recent investment activity, and industry, location and stage investment preferences.

Standard & Poor's
www.standardandpoors.com

Standard & Poor's is known to investors worldwide as a leader of financial-market intelligence. For more information see listing in Section I.

Thomson One Banker
banker.thomsonib.com/

Investment Banking provides bankers, private equity & venture capital professionals, lawyers, consultants and academics with market news and quotes, plus comprehensive reference data to monitor changing market conditions and to gain important insight into a company, industry or event.

Biotechnology

Careers In Biotechnology, Linley Erin Hall, 2012, ReadHowYouWant

Explores some of the many careers and discusses the education and training needed, plus ethics and future biotech careers.

Careers in Biotechnology (Careers Ebooks), Institute For Career Research, Kindle ed., 2012, Institute For Career Research

Overview of the major fields in biotech.

Introduction to Biotechnology, William J. Thieman and Michael A. Palladino, 3rd ed., 2012, Benjamin Cummings

With coverage of basic cell and molecular biology, fundamental techniques, historical accounts, new advances and hands-on applications, the Third Edition emphasizes the future of biotechnology and your role in that future.

Glossary of Biotechnology Terms, Kimball Nill, online
biotechterms.org/

This free, online glossary is kept current by the author.

ArgosBiotech
www.argosbiotech.de/

A worldwide information source on all aspects and areas of biotechnology and related fields. Its **Internet Directories (biodirectory.com)** focuses on different aspects of the industry, such as cloning, molecular biology, jobs, and the biotech industry in general.

BioPlan Associates
www.bioplanassociates.com

Scientific information through industry-leading surveys, reports, publications, and databases, headed by some of the top players in biotech.

Publications and databases include: The 7th Annual Report and Survey of Biopharmaceutical Manufacturing Capacity and Production, 2010, and Biopharmaceutical Products in the U.S. and European Markets, Online Database Edition. The company covers the industry, both here and abroad, with a great variety of products.

Biopharma, Biopharmaceutical Products in the U.S. and European Markets, Biotechnology Information Institute
www.biopharma.com

Database concerning biopharmaceutical products. Includes monographs on products' biotechnology and commercial aspects. Includes all biopharmaceuticals, and information about the players involved.

Agriculture Network Information Center
www.agnic.org

Guide to agricultural information on the Internet.

Biofind
www.biofind.com

Home of the biotechnology discussion online, providing a variety of services; the Rumor Mill tracks the news and gossip from around the industry.

BiolinkDirect
www.biolinkdirect.com

BiolinkDirect is a life sciences portal, with links to worldwide company websites, searchable by geographical region or by name. Links to companies, biotechnology associations, and venture capital organizations, worldwide.

BioSpace
www.biospace.com

A job board, but it also runs career fairs across the U.S. Has newsletters, events, news, career resources.

life sciences world
www.lifesciencesworld.com

An online resource for biotechnology, pharmaceutical, medical devices and life sciences industries, with news, jobs, events, articles and a directory of organizations. Resources include links to medical biotechnology websites.

U.S. Food and Drug Administration
www.fda.gov

FDA announcements, regulations, and recommendations regarding biotechnology. Search the website under "biotechnology."

Business

See individual listings for general information and those for individual entries in this section (Professions/Industries). Also consult Section I for industry and company

information. Note: For more sources on business careers and the profession, see the individual listings in this section.

Contemporary Business: 2012 Update (Coursesmart), Louis E. Boone and David L. Kurtz, Wiley

This 14th edition is the most current and comprehensive introduction to business that builds on the wide array of new concepts from all aspects of the business world, including marketing, management, accounting, finance, and economics.

The Career Journey: A book on career management, Ram Iyer, 2012, CreateSpace Independent Publishing Platform

Specific guidelines for the corporate professional. Considers matters such as: What is the best profession for me? Should I take or reject that job offer? Should I consider pursuing a master's degree or not?

The MBA Student's Job Seeking Bible: Everything You Need to Know to Land a Great Job by Graduation, Elizabeth Freedman, 2011, eBookIt.com

Practical tips, do's and don'ts, and and's; examples, exercises and strategies geared to help the MBA job seeker get hired.

Small Business Management: Entrepreneurship and Beyond, Timothy S. Hatten, 5th ed., 2011, South-Western College Pub

Provides a balanced introduction to both entrepreneurship and small business management with a focus on achieving and maintaining a sustainable competitive advantage. Current issues include global opportunities, service, quality and technology.

College/Liberal Arts/Recent Graduates

Occupational Outlook Handbook, Bureau of Labor Statistics
www.bls.gov/oco/home.htm, Print and online
See listing in Section I.

College Majors Handbook with Real Career Paths and Payoffs, 3rd ed., Neeta P Fogg, Paul E. Harrington, and Thomas F. Harrington, 2012, JIST Publishing

Provides information on the actual jobs and earnings of college graduates in 50 majors, based on an updated U.S. Census Bureau data. Information for choosing college a major or what to do with a degree already earned.

NOTE: JIST offers numerous products on education and career, finding jobs, and succeeding in at work. Topics include: job search, career exploration, occupational information, job retention, college preparation, life skills, and character education. JIST has a wide range of materials and resources on job search, job success, occupations, and more. See the website for the extensive listing. *See JIST's website for a great variety of materials about college and beyond.*

Getting from College to Career: 90 Things to Do Before You Join the Real World, Lindsey Pollak, 2012, HarperBusiness

How do you get a job without experience and get experience without a job? Pollak offers a guide to building the experience, skills, and confidence you need before starting your first major job search, with 90 action-oriented tips.

Grad to Great: Discover the Secrets to Success in Your First Career, Anne Brown and Beth Zefo, 2010, Dalidaze Press

A no-nonsense, no-fluff guide to career success for recent graduates.

Life After College: The Complete Guide to Getting What You Want, Jenny Blake, 2011, Running Press

For graduating students and young professionals. It features practical, actionable advice that helps to focus on the BIG picture of your life, not just the details.

The Money Book for the Young, Fabulous & Broke, Suze Orman, 2007, Riverhead Trade

Money expert Suze Orman answers a generation's cry for help—and gives advice on matters such as credit card debt, student loans, credit scores, and the first real job.

Construction and Building, including Green Building

(See also listings under Architecture *in this section)*

Becoming a Construction Manager, John J. McKeon, 2012, Wiley

Covers all that is needed to become a construction

manager—from formal education to getting the first job.

Becoming a Green Building Professional: A Guide to Careers in Sustainable Architecture, Design, Engineering, Development, and Operations (Wiley Series in Sustainable Design), Holley Henderson, 2012, Wiley

For those considering a new career or a career change focused on green and sustainable building and design, this guide offers practical information on educational requirements, career options, guidance and tips, and first-hand interviews with green building professionals.

Construction Management JumpStart: The Best First Step Toward a Career in Construction Management, Barbara J. Jackson, 2nd ed., 2010, Print and Online, Sybex

Walks readers through each stage of construction management. Written from the constructor's perspective, it shows how Building Information Modeling (BIM) is impacting the profession.

Green Careers in Building and Landscaping (Green Careers in Building & Landscaping), 2010, Peterson's

ARRA has authorized $4.5 billion alone for greening federal buildings. Here is a resource for entry into the burgeoning green building sector.

Sustainable Construction: Green Building Design and Delivery, Charles J. Kibert, 3rd ed., 2012, Wiley

Reflects the latest developments of the U.S. Green Building Council's LEED rating system, plus other tools.

B4UBUILD.COM
www.b4ubuild.com

Offers residential construction and custom-home building information. Has links to products, architecture, gardening, loans and more.

www.bidclerk.com

From owners and architects to contractors and suppliers, BidClerk allows contractors to find construction projects.**The Blue Book and Building Construction Network, Print and Online**

www.thebluebook.com

Targeted information in the construction industry. In addition to **thebluebook.com**, the largest construction search engine, the company publishes 28 regional Blue Book directories. Its **AEC Solutions** simplifies workflow.

www.constructionstate.com

A resource site for construction, home improvement and the real estate industry, this site is for both the homeowner and contractor.**Construction WebLinks**

www.constructionweblinks.com

A comprehensive guide to construction, engineering, infrastructure and architecture resources on the Internet.

McGraw-Hill Construction
construction.com

Connects people, projects and products across the design and construction industry, serving owners, architects, engineers, general contractors, subcontractors, building product manufacturers, suppliers, dealers, distributors, and adjacent markets.

Reed Construction Data
www.reedconstructiondata.com

Portfolio of products and services that includes national, regional and local construction data, building product information, construction cost data, market analytics and more for the U.S. and Canada; data resource for the architectural, engineering and construction industries.

Sweets and SNAP (McGraw-Hill)
products.construction.com

Sweets is a premier source for building product information, where A/E/C professionals find content from manufacturers. **SNAP**, in **print** and **digital** formats, keeps you current on new products and related information-—a quarterly building product publication.

TenLinks
www.tenlinks.com

A network of websites and newsletters that together form the largest community of CAD, CAM and CAE users on the Internet. Has a job board.

Consulting

CONSULTING 101: 101 Tips for Success in Consulting, Lew Sauder, 2010, Booklocker.com, Inc.
Skills other than business knowledge are needed to

succeed as a consultant. Here are 101 tips to optimize your professional performance and jump-start your consulting career.

The Consulting Bible: Everything You Need to Know to Create and Expand a Seven-Figure Consulting Practice, Alan Weiss, 2011, Kindle ed., Amazon Digital

For veteran consultants or newbies, entrepreneurs or principals of a small firm, Weiss covers everything needed to create and expand a seven-figure independent or boutique consulting practice.

The Everything Start Your Own Consulting Business Book: Expert, step-by-step advice for a successful and profitable career (Everything Series), Dan Ramsey, 2009, Adams Media

This guide features tips and tricks to help beat the competition, including how to: set and keep personal and financial goals; price and market-specific services; and minimize risks.

Getting Started in Consulting, Alan Weiss, 3rd. ed., 2009, Kindle ed., Wiley/Amazon Digital
Practical guidance on beginning a consulting business. How low overhead and a high degree of organization can translate into a six-figure income, often by working at home. Topics include: financing a consulting practice; writing proposals that sell; fee setting, and more.

An Insider's Guide to Building a Successful Consulting Practice, Bruce L. Katcher, 2010, Kindle ed. AMACOM/Amazon Digital

Featuring real stories from consultants in diverse industries, this book offers ways to: identify a market and narrow your focus; transition from employee to independent consultant; develop a marketing strategy; and much more.

Launch Your Consulting Career, Patrick Mallory, 2012, Kindle ed., Amazon Digital Services

How to break into management consulting? What is needed to be successful early in your career? A stepwise guide to identifying the right consulting firm for you, and more.

The Secrets of Consulting: A Guide to Giving and Getting Advice Successfully (Consulting Secrets), Gerald Weinberg, 2011, Kindle ed.

Explains why consulting seems so irrational, and

gives practical steps to make it more rational. Topics include: gaining control of change; marketing and pricing your services; what to do when they resist your ideas, and more. Also available is Weinberg's **More Secrets of Consulting: The Consultant's Tool Kit.**

Consultant Directory
www.consultant-directory.com/
Links to websites in over 35 industries, from advertising to transportation.

Consultants & Consulting Organizations Directory, 37th ed., 2012, Print, previous editions are eBooks, Gale CENGAGE Learning
www.gale.cengage.com
More than 26,000 firms and individuals are arranged in sections under 14 general fields of consulting, ranging from agriculture to marketing. More than 400 specialties are represented. Data include contact information.

Disabled

Asperger's on the Job: Must-have Advice for People with Asperger's or High Functioning Autism, and their Employers, Educators, and Advocates, Rudy Simone and Temple, Grandin, 2010
Future Horizons
Detailed lists of "what the employee can do" and "to employers and advocates" provide balanced guidelines for success, while Simone's "Interview Tips" and "Personal Job Map" tools will help Aspergians, young or old, find their employment niche.

Career Success of Disabled High-Flyers, Sonali Shah, 2005, Jessica Kingsley Publishers
This book assumes that disabled employees are not all alike, and poses questions, such as: What is disability? How do people with physical impairments define success? Based on interviews with successful people, it is often society, rather than impairment that hinders professional progression. Offers role models and insights for young career-minded disabled people.

Disabilities Job Search Package with Envision Your Career, with DVD
Disabilities Job Search Package with Picture Interest Career Survey (PICS), with DVD

jist.emcpublishingllc.com/page-jist/
These two packages have DVDs and Workbooks.
JIST also offers:

Interviewing Skills for Job Seekers with Physical Disabilities, DVD—job seekers learn how to help interviewers focus on their abilities—not their disabilities.

Job Search Handbook for People with Disabilities, Daniel J. Ryan, 3rd ed.,2011, Print and eBook
This extensive handbook shows how to overcome obstacles when searching for employment.

Quick Job Search for People with Disabilities, (Workbook) 2007
Covers the same job search steps as the popular **Quick Job Search.** However, it also addresses the unique issues that people with disabilities face, such as: assessing challenges, as well as skills; determining the pros and cons of disclosing a disability in a cover letter or resume; and more.

Job Success for Persons With Developmental Disabilities, David B. Wiegan, 2009, Jessica Kingsley Pub
A comprehensive approach to developing a successful jobs program for persons with developmental disabilities; helpful for families of persons with developmental disabilities, as well as for professionals in this field.

Self-Employment Work for People with Disabilities, Cary Griffin and David Hammis, 2003
Paul H. Brookes Pub. Co.
With an emphasis on the involvement of community programs and school transition staff, this book shows how to identify and use the business supports necessary for developing self-employment opportunities for people with disabilities.

Adult Career and Continuing Education Services-Vocational Rehabilitation (ACCES-VR)—New York State agency
www.acces.nysed.gov/vr
ACCES-VR offers access to a full range of employment and independent living services that may be needed by persons with disabilities through their lives. It's job programs pre-screen job-ready applicants for potential employers. The agency averages 13,000 workers employed per year from entry level to professional and managerial.

Disability.gov
www.disability.gov
This is the federal government's site for information on disability programs and services in communities nationwide, with links to more than 14,000 resources from federal, state and local government agencies; academic institutions; and nonprofit organizations. **Disability Employment** has information on: both national & state levels; state only; and national resources, as well as links to learning about job accommodations, job training & career counseling, getting help in finding a job, and more.

U.S. Department of Labor Disability Resources
www.dol.gov
Disability Resources
The Department of Labor has several agencies that can help to find meaningful work and launch successful careers, help employers hire people with disabilities, and help federal contractors stay within the law when hiring. See the website for what's available.

Diversity and Minorities

Advice from the Top: What Minority Women Say about Their Career Success, Valencia Campbell, 2009, Praeger
Campbell reviewed research on career success, then interviewed 14 extraordinary minority women, each who shared stories about the path to the top, reporting on what constitutes success and the factors important to their success, plus the obstacles they overcame. The result: action steps to help readers vault the hurdles encountered by the women profiled.

The Complete Success Guide for the Immigrant Life: How to Survive, How to Thrive, How to Be Fully Alive, Monette Adeva Maglaya, 2004, PDI Books
Among the topics covered are the employment route; desperately looking for employer sponsorship; finding an immigration lawyer; using employment agencies and headhunters; working under the table and in the shadows; employers from hell, oppressive working conditions and basic human rights; and the labor market.

Finding A Way To The Top: Career Moves For The Minority Manager, Randolph Cameron, 2004, AuthorHouse

This step-by-step guide tells what's needed to not only survive, but to thrive in the job market. Cameron served such clients as Columbia Pictures and Mobile Oil.

Good Is Not Enough: And Other Unwritten Rules for Minority Professionals, Keith R. Wyche, 2009, Penguin Group
A division president at a Fortune 500 company offers this no-nonsense guide for minorities in business who want to make it to senior management.

The Human Rights Campaign
www.hrc.org
The Human Rights Campaign represents more than one million members and supporters nationwide — all committed to making HRC's vision a reality. HRC advocates on behalf of LGBT Americans, mobilizes grassroots actions in diverse communities, invests strategically to elect fair-minded individuals to office and educates the public about LGBT issues. HRC has a lot of resources on its site. The categories include a blog; and issues, such as coming out and transgender; and resources, such as the two listed here.

The 2012 Corporate Equality Index chronicles a decade of progress in workplace equality. 2012 marks the first year of new more-stringent criteria regarding transgender health benefits. About 190 participants earned the top rating of 100 percent, evidence the CEI has helped transform the American workplace for the better over the past ten years.

Buyer's Guide—Whether you are buying a cup of coffee or renovating your home, by supporting businesses that support workplace equality you send a powerful message that LGBT inclusion is good for the bottom line. Use this guide as one component when determining if a business's social practices make it worthy of your dollars.

Life in the USA: An Immigrant's Guide to Understanding Americans, Planaria J. Price and Euphronia Awakuni, 2009, University of Michigan Press/ELT
Among the nine broad topics covered is the workplace. This guide uses a question-and-answer format in form of letters from immigrant students to their teacher, as a means of offering help and advice.

Managing Diversity in Today's Workplace [4 volumes]: Strategies for Employees and Employers

(Women and Careers in Management), Michele A. Paludi, 2012, Praeger

These books cover succession planning, formal mentoring programs, discrimination in religious organizations, transgender female workers, flexible work schedules, generational cohorts, and paid leave policy.

Workplace Diversity: Does Not Mean Equal Opportunity, Equal Growth, and Equal Advancement, Richard Brown, author & publisher, 2011, Kindle ed.

Despite laws and knowledge, there are those who still stifle minorities. This book identifies steps a person can take when they are suffering abuse.

The Minority Handbook of Office Survival, 2011, Kindle ed., Team Anonymous, Amazon Digital Services

This book discusses topics such as empowerment and dressing for the job.

National Minority and Women-Owned Business Directory 2012

    Diversity Information Resources Inc.

The only print directory listing certified minority and women-owned businesses.

    The **Supplier Diversity Information Resource Guide 2012**—provides detailed information on processes and resources (including legislation).

    2012 Purchasing People in Major Corporations—lists over 800 procurement contacts and supplier diversity professionals. The **Supplier Diversity Data Management Portal** is available under different levels of subscription.

National Directory of Minority Owned Business Firms, 15th ed., 2012, Business Research Services/ Gale

This edition adds fax numbers and previous government contracting experience; detailed entries include contact information, minority type, and more. SIC and geographic indexes facilitate research.

eMedia, including Blogs, Social Media, Streaming Video, Web Design and IT

Blogging by Million, Earn By Millions: How the Young Savvies Earn Millions by Blogging, Totally Committed to Their Current Job, Yet Still Progress in Their Career, Laura Maya, 2010, Kindle ed.,

Outskirts Press/Amazon Digital

The know-how provided in this book is meant to help you succeed online and earn your big pot of gold. This book shows the latest tips and a guide map to Internet marketing and blogging, with support through social network marketing.

Careers in GIS: an Unfiltered Guide to Finding a GIS Job, Todd J. Schuble, 2012, Kindle ed., Amazon Digital

A job-hunting strategy guide for people entering or already in the geographic information systems (GIS) industry.

Find an IT Job: Information Technology Careers From Bioinformatics to Web Design, Paul E. Love, 2012, CreateSpace Independent Publishing Platform

Examines IT careers, what each job involves and its requirements, the job market, and positions that may match your interests and qualifications.

Get Bold: Using Social Media to Create a New Type of Social Business, Sandy Carter, 2011, IBM Press

Carter demonstrates how leveraging powerful collaborative tools will transform your business into a vibrant social business.

Getting Started in the Information Technology Field: With or Without a Technical Degree, Gale R Stafford, 2012, BookBaby

Learn about the career options available, and where you fit in. Find out the most direct way to secure great paying and satisfying IT work, that which makes the best use of your strengths.

How to be a Web Designer, Brent Laminack, 2012, Kindle ed., Amazon Digital

This is a guide to the career path that web designers go down. Is web design a good fit for you? What training and tools will you need? How do you break into the business?

How To Build A Profitable Niche Blog, Dee Ankary, 2012, Kindle ed., Moonpreneur/Amazon Digital

The secret to a building a profitable niche website is: the right keywords, great content and some judicious promotion.

How To Make Money Blogging: How I Replaced My Day-Job With My Blog, Bob Lotich, 2010, Kindle ed., Amazon Digital

Covers four steps to start blogging in 10 minutes; the blogging basics; how to publish and sell your articles on Kindles; tips for short documents.

How to Start a Home-Based Web Design Business (Home-Based Business Series), Jim Smith, 4th ed., 2010, Globe Pequot

Everything you need to know to run a profitable Web design business from your home.

Information Technology Jobs in America: Corporate & Government Career Guide, 2012 Edition by Partnerships for Community, Info Tech Employment

Covers jobs in the IT services sector and in U.S. federal and state and municipal government agencies and departments.

Information Technology, 2010, eBook, Facts on File/Gale

Provides the tools necessary to take your career in a new direction. Features tips and advice for career changers interested in IT.

IT Career JumpStart: An Introduction to PC Hardware, Software, and Networking (Jumpstart (Sybex)), Naomi J. Alpern, et al., 2012, Sybex

Aimed at aspiring IT professionals, this book discusses this topic in a clear and concise manner so that IT beginners can understand the fundamental IT concepts.

Likeable Social Media: How to Delight Your Customers, Create an Irresistible Brand, and Be Generally Amazing on Facebook (And Other Social Networks), Dave Kerpen, 2011, McGraw-Hill

Helps you harness the power of word-of-mouth marketing to transform your business.

Media Career Guide: Preparing for Jobs in the 21st Century, James Seguin and Sherri Hope Culver, 8th ed., 2011, Bedford/St. Martin's

Guides readers through the process of researching, interviewing for, and landing that perfect media job. Offers career advice from professionals and emphasizes the importance of creating and maintaining a professional online presence for the workplace. Has information on how to start your own business.

The New Rules of Marketing & PR: How to Use Social Media, Online Video, Mobile Applications, Blogs, News Releases, and Viral Marketing to Reach Buyers Directly, David Meerman Scott, 2011, Wiley

Offers a step-by-step action plan for harnessing the power of the Internet to communicate with buyers directly, raise online visibility, and increase sales.

Social Networking for Career Success: Using Online Tools to Create a Personal Brand, Miriam Salpeter, 2011, LearningExpress

How you can create an effective, compelling online presence; advice from successful professionals; the ins and outs of social networking sites, and more.

The Social Media Bible: Tactics, Tools, and Strategies for Business Success, Lon Safko, 3rd ed., 2012, Wiley

A 700+ page social media resource that will teach corporate, small business, and non-profit marketers strategies to use social media effectively.

Starting Your Career as a Freelance Web Designer (Starting Your Career), Neil Tortorella, 2011, Allworth Press

This book guides web designers stepwise to success and helps to avoid common pitfalls.

The Web Designer Job Description Handbook and Career Guide: The Complete Knowledge Guide you need to Start or Advance your career as Web Designer, Practical Manual for Job-Hunters and Career-Changers, Andrew Klipp, 2009, Emereo Publishing

A guide to finding, keeping and succeeding in web design roles and environments.

Working the Crowd: Social Media Marketing for Business, Eileen Brown, 2010, British Informatics Society Ltd

Facebook, YouTube, and Twitter; Blogs, microblogs, social networking and social news sites are new tools for effective marketing and sales. Here is a resource for anyone planning a social media strategy or individual campaign.

AV Marketplace 2012, Information Today

Fully revised and updated, this guide has more than 6,500 companies that create, apply, or distribute AV equipment and services for business, education, science, and government.

Encyclopedia of Computer Science and Technology, 2010, Facts on File

This updated version has a more than 600 updated entries. Helpful appendixes include a chronology of significant events in computing, and more.

Streaming Media Industry Sourcebook 2012 Edition, annual, Eric Schumacher-Rasmussen, ed., Information Today

Geared for technology managers and executive decision makers who are implementing rich media within their organizations.

Electronics and Digital Systems, including Games

Breaking Into Video Game Design—A Beginner's Guide, Charlie Czerkawski, author, and Catherine Czerkawska, ed., 2011, Kindle ed.

Aimed primarily at students without any work experience, this book offers practical advice on the role of a game designer from different angles.

How To Start a Career in Game Design (Lazy Designer Game Design), Brent Knowles, 2011, Kindle ed., Amazon Digital

Practical advice on starting a career in the video game industry and improving your design skills. It discusses how to obtain a design position, such as a writer, level designer, or game system designer.

www.electronics-manufacturers.com
Searchable by products and manufacturers.

Electronics and Electrical Web Directory
www.elecdir.com
Searchable by products or country—U.S., U.K., Canada, China, India, Taiwan, Australia and Germany.

Energy, Alternative Energy and Utilities

(see also Biotechnology and Green Careers)

Energy (Green Careers), Pamela Fehl, 2010, Kindle ed., Ferguson Publishing Company/Amazon Digital
Provides professionals with what's needed to take their careers to the next level.

Green Careers in Energy (Green Careers in Energy: Your Guide to Jobs in Renewable Energy), 2010, Kindle ed., Peterson's
Pinpoints the best opportunities in renewable energy—solar, wind, geothermal, and more—with data on the various jobs, organizations, and training/retraining.

Also available: **Green Careers in Energy: Energy-Related Jobs in Construction and Building**

Operations, 2010, Kindle ed. *There are more titles in this series; see* **www.petersons.com/.**

Renewable Energy—Facts and Fantasies, Craig Shields, 2011, Kindle ed., Amazon Digital
Shields interviewed specialists covering the technology, economics, and politics of renewables to come up with a book that separates the truth from talk.

2012 Global Cleantech Directory: 100 Cleantech Lists That Matter (Volume 1), Shawn Lesser, CreateSpace Independent Publishing Platform
A resource guide on recent clean technology developments, initiatives, and influencers around the world, that covers technology ranging from solar to wind.

EnergyPlanet—Renewable Energy Directory
www.energyplanet.info
A visual and interactive web directory of information resources about renewable energy technology.

Energy Resource Directory
www.energydir.com
Index of energy sciences information and business resources. List all types of energy resources, such as energy conferences, science and energy education, organizations, science and energy publications, and much more.

Environmental Resource Handbook, 2011/12 Edition, Print and Database, Grey House Publishing
www.greyhouse.com/enviro.html
Print—An up-to-date source for environmental resources and statistics. **Section I: Resources**—provides detailed contact information for thousands of resources. **Section II: Statistics**—provides statistics and rankings on hundreds of important topics.

Online—**Environmental Resource Handbook: Online Database**—key contacts, sales data, employee sizes and more, on thousands of organizations. It encompasses over 7,000 associations, organizations & government agencies, and much more.

The Global Oil & Gas Industry: Management, Strategy and Finance, Andrew Inkpen and Michael H. Moffett, 2011, PennWell Corp.
A nontechnical book for those with technical backgrounds to understand the business of oil and gas.

International Petroleum Encyclopedia 2010,
Joseph Hilyard, ed., Pennwell Books
www.pennwellbooks.com/20inpeen1.html
The Encyclopedia contains maps, statistics, survey charts, country reports, and more. Available in print and on Windows or Mac format CD-ROM.

Major Energy Companies of the World, Christine Oddy, David J Smith & Chris Tapster, eds., 16th ed., 2012, Graham & Whiteside
www.gale.CENGAGE.com
Covers more than 4,850 companies in coal mining and coal products; electricity supply; fuel distribution; natural gas supply; nuclear engineering; oil and gas exploration and production; oil and gas services and equipment; and oil refining worldwide. Entries typically provide contact information.

Nontechnical Guide to Petroleum Geology, Exploration, Drilling & Production, Norman J. Hyne, 3rd ed., 2012, PennWell Corp.
From upstream operations— how oil and gas are formed; how to find commercial quantities; how to drill, evaluate, and complete a well—to production and improved oil recovery.

Unconventional Fuels, Part I: Shale Gas Potential, U.S. House of Representatives, Subcommittee on Energy and Mineral Resources of the Committee on Natural Resources), 2012, CreateSpace Independent Publishing Platform
House hearing on unconventional fuels.

Under the Surface: Fracking, Fortunes, and the Fate of the Marcellus Shale, Tom Wilber, 2012, Cornell University Press
First book-length journalistic overview of shale gas development and the controversies surrounding it.

www.oilandgassuppliers.com
Oil and Gas Suppliers is a directory focused on manufacturers and suppliers of materials, products & services for the oil and gas industries.

2010 Renewable Energy Databook, pdf, U.S. Department of Energy
Free, downloadable, 136 pp., lists key findings, and data on alternative energies.

Renewable Energy Directory, Energy Planet
www.energyplanet.info
A visual and interactive web directory of information resources about renewable energy technology.

Solar Energy Directory
solarenergydirectory.com
Links to applications, associations, companies, employment, news, products, professional services, more.

Engineering

The Career Guide Book for Engineers, John A. Hoschette, 2010, Wiley
The complete, one-stop career resource guide for engineers, engineering managers, and human resources personnel. Step-by-step guidance in handling a multitude of career issues.

Careers In Nanotechnology, Corona Brezina, 2012, ReadHowYouWant
Career guide presents a comprehensive view of the nanotech revolution and offers students a leg up in preparing for future nanotech careers.

Gateway to Nanotechnology: An Introduction to Nanotechnology for Beginner Students and Professionals, Paul Sanghera, 2009, BookSurge Publishing
For students and professionals, including executives and managers. Covers a spectrum of topics: including the science behind it; nanomaterial characterization; nanofabrication; nanooptics; as well as environmental, health, and safety implications of nanotechnology.

The Green Engineer: Engineering Careers to Save the Earth, Celeste Baine, 2012, Engineering Education Service Center
The opportunities to combine engineering with sustainability and environmental stewardship in a green collar career are skyrocketing. Covers opportunities in six green disciplines.

How to Land a Top-Paying Biomaterials Engineers Job: Your Complete Guide to Opportunities, Resumes and Cover Letters, Interviews, Salaries, Promotions, What to Expect From Recruiters and More, Joseph Gomez, 2012, tebbo
Has helpful worksheets and cheat sheets for presenting all information need to apply for a position as a biomaterials engineer. Successfully challenges conventional job search wisdom to offer radical, but inspired suggestions for success.

Is There An Engineer Inside You?: A Comprehensive Guide to Career Decisions in Engineering, Celeste Baine, 3rd ed., 2011, Professional Publications, Inc.

Turn yourself into a top-notch engineering student and be a successful engineer with the ideas and information in this one-of-a-kind resource.

Ready for Takeoff! A Winning Process for Launching Your Engineering Career, Dean C. Millar, 2010, Prentice Hall

Millar offers examples and insights from experts to explain the steps you need to identify, and then go after the engineering job that's right for you.

Workplace Skills: Science, Technology, Engineering, and Math, 2011, McGraw-Hill

This volume of the **Workforce's Career Companion** series explores career pathways and jobs, education and training requirements, work environments, and current industry trends.

ChemIndustry.com
www.chemindustry.com

Comprehensive directory and search engine for chemical and related industry professionals. Our databases of Web sites include more than 75,000 related sites and contain the full text of millions of pages.

EngNet
www.engnetglobal.com

This online **Directory/Search Engine/Buyers Guide Service** is for engineers, technicians, tradesmen, etc., to find suppliers in the engineering industry. All types of engineering professions are covered.

Vocational Information Center
www.khake.com

Explore careers in engineering, science and math with links to job descriptions, which include information such as daily activities, skill requirements, salary and training required. Links to a very large number of topics and disciplines. A comprehensive look at many topics with extensive links that provide a wealth of information.

Entertainment, including Media

(*See* Film and Photography *below for additional information on these industries*)

Beginner Guide to Sport and Entertainment Venue Management, Bradley Acker, 2011, Kindle ed., Amazon Digital

Find out the inside secrets to beginning a career in venue management. Perfect for sport management or sport and entertainment management majors.

Careers in Radio Broadcasting (Careers Ebooks), Institute For Career Research, 2012

The radio business is evolving rapidly. Satellite radio is slowly crowding out local broadcast radio. Here is information on starting in radio broadcasting, from the education needed to how much you are likely to earn.

Entertainment Power Players: The Premier Fashion, Film, Music, Sports & TV Directory, Dackeyia Q. Sterling, 4th ed. 2010, Key Quest Publishing

This mainstream directory contains contacts, information & inspiration; featuring 5,000+ contacts in more than 75 categories, exclusive interviews, the hottest ads, products & services from industry leaders, it is a "how-to" entertainment career advice & more.

Hollywood Game Plan: How to Land a Job in Film, TV and Digital Entertainment, Carole M. Kirschner, 2012, Michael Wiese Productions

An in-depth, how-to guide for aspiring Hollywood hopefuls that provides a step-by-step strategy to land a job in the entertainment industry.

Hollywood Screenwriting Directory Fall 2012: A Specialized Resource for Discovering Where & How to Sell Your Screenplay, Jesse Douma (Sep 30, 2012), F+W Media

What's valuable to an aspiring screenwriter are the details you can only get through years of experience. This directory is the product of more than three decades of working directly with the people behind the world's favorite films.

The VIP Book: A Deluxe Compilation of Entertainment Industry Awards Shows, Conferences, Events & More (Entertainment Power Players "How To" Series), Dackeyia Q. Sterling, 2012, Kindle ed., Key Quest Publishing/Amazon Digital

Fill your calendar with the entertainment industry events listed in The VIP Book. Featured events include awards shows, conferences, conventions, expos, festivals, seminars, summits and more—in fashion, film, media, music, sports, TV and video gaming.

You're Funny: Turn Your Sense of Humor Into a Lucrative New Career, D. B. Gilles, 2011, Michael Wiese Productions

This is the next best thing to being in a comedy writing class. It covers the different ways to earn a living as a comedy writer, including writing sitcoms, jokes for late night talk shows, parody, stand up, and screenwriting.

Writing the TV Drama Series: How to Succeed as a Professional Writer in TV, Pamela Douglas, 3rd ed., 2011, Michael Wiese Productions

This edition builds on the book's reputation by bringing in the very latest information, insights, and advice from major writers and producers; for anyone who wants to write and produce for a television drama series or create an original series.

Gale Directory of Publications & Broadcast Media, 149th ed., 2013, annual, Print, previous editions are in Print or as eBooks, Gale
www.gale.cengage.com

This directory contains thousands of listings for radio and television stations and cable companies. **Print media** entries provide address, and contact information; key personnel, including feature editors; and much more. **Broadcast media** entries provide contact information; key personnel; owner information; hours of operation; networks carried, and more.

AV Market Place 2009: The Complete Business Directory of Products and Services for the A/V Industry, Information Today, Inc.
infotoday.stores.yahoo.net/avmarplac20.html

Details more than 6,500 companies that create, apply, or distribute AV equipment and services for business, education, science, and government. An index of more than 1,250 AV products and services. Information on key personnel for each company listed.

Television & Cable Factbook, Warren Communications News, annual, Print and Online
www.warren-news.com

More than 930,000 detailed records in four sections: telco/IPTV, cable systems, TV stations, and a combined search. The new Television and Cable Factbook and the Advanced TV Factbook Online contain accurate and reliable business information for the TV, cable and related industries.

Environmental and Green Careers

(See also Energy, and Biotechnology)

Best Green Careers: Explore Opportunities in the Rapidly Growing Field (Best Green Careers: Finding a Job in Today's Economy), LearningExpress, 2010, LearningExpress

For from recent college graduates to anyone looking to make a career switch into green and green-collar jobs. Maps out a strategy for new graduates to forge a long-lasting career in the green sector while helping experienced workers understand how they can translate skills they have already learned into positions within this field.

Environment & Natural Resources (Green Careers (Ferguson)), Pamela Fehl, 2010, Ferguson Publishing Company

A guide to the career options.

Environmental Consulting Fundamentals: Investigation and Remediation, Benjamin Alter, 2012, CRC Press

Introduces the basic building blocks of environmental consulting. Rather than formulas and equations, it emphasizes the thought processes that go into designing an environmental study, interpreting the data, and selecting the next step—be it further investigation or remediation. Covers regulations, science and more.

Green Careers For Dummies, Carol L. McClelland, 2010, For Dummies

Learn how to navigate the world of green careers and get the inside scoop on the green economy. Details a variety of job titles in over 50 industries that make up the green economy.

Green Careers in Energy (Green Careers in Energy: Your Guide to Jobs in Renewable Energy), Peterson's, 2010

Pinpoints the best opportunities in the fast-growing and most promising renewable energy fields.

Green Collar Jobs: Environmental Careers for the 21st Century, Scott M. Deitche, 2010, Kindle ed., Praeger

All aspects of green careers, beginning with an overview of green jobs from environmental, economic, and political perspectives. Chapters describe specific types of green jobs and career paths.

Re-Greening the Environment: Careers in Cleanup, Remediation, and Restoration (Green-Collar Careers), Suzy Gazlay, 2011, Crabtree Publishing Company

Overview of this sector of green-collar jobs.

The Environment Encyclopedia and Directory, Routledge, Taylor & Francis (UK); 5th ed., 2010
www.taylorandfrancis.com

This volume includes detailed maps, an extensive bibliography and a Who's Who section.

2012 Global Cleantech Directory: 100 Cleantech Lists That Matter, Shawn Lesser, 2012, CreateSpace Independent Publishing Platform

A quick resource guide to recent clean technology developments, initiatives, and influencers around the world. This book spotlights these achievements and offers an easy way to stay informed about the exciting things happening in cleantech today. Clean technology is one of the fastest growing sectors in the global economy. Has contacts, meetings and events, recent developments, initiatives, and influencers worldwide, and more.

The Directory Of Environmental Web Sites, Online Abridged Edition 2012, Print and htm Fle Download
www.earthdirectory.net

Lists over 3,000 websites; directory of the Environmental Movement on the Internet.

The Only Green Directory
theonlygreendirectory.com

The Only Green Directory is the Internet's first and truly comprehensive reference guide to all businesses and blogs promoting green living and eco-friendly

issues. A one-stop shop for all things environmental. Recycling centers, eco-travel and green tours for vacationers, green apparel and gifts, yoga instructors, Green MBA Programs. Links to other green resources: education, news, organizations, and more.

Environment Complete (EBSCO)
www.ebscohost.com/public/environment-complete

Offers deep coverage in applicable areas of agriculture, ecosystem ecology, energy, renewable energy sources, natural resources, marine & freshwater science, geography, pollution & waste management, environmental technology, environmental law, public policy, social impacts, urban planning, and more. Contains more than 2.5 million records from more than 1,350 active core titles.

Who's Who in Environmental Engineering, 2012, American Academy of Environmental Engineering
www.aaee.net

Provides an alphabetical listing of each BCEE and BCEEM together with a biographic profile. Cross-referenced geographically and by specialty.

Ex-Inmates

Best Jobs for Ex-Offenders: 101 Opportunities to Jump-Start Your New Life, Ron Krannich, 2008, Impact Publications

Profiles 101 opportunities (job outlook, nature of work, qualifications, earnings, contacts) that are open to ex-offenders. It also identifies various jobs closed to ex-offenders.

Beyond Bars: Rejoining Society After Prison, Jeffrey Ian Ross and Stephen C. Richards, 2009, Alpha

Guide for ex-convicts and their families about managing a successful re-entry into the community and includes: tips on how to prepare for release while still in prison; ways to deal with family members, especially spouses and children, how to find a job. Free resources to rely on for support—-and more.

The Ex-Offender's Job Hunting Guide: 10 Steps to a New Life in the Work World, Ron Krannich, 2005, Impact Publications

Provides answers to many re-entry questions facing ex-offenders, beginning with an examination of 20 myths/realities and 22 principles for success, these leading employment experts reveal 10 steps to job and career success.

The Ex-Offender's Job Interview Guide: Turn Your Red Flags Into Green Lights, Caryl Krannich and Ron Krannich, 2008, Impact Publications

How to deal with job market challenges. Focuses on the critical job interview, it emphasizes turning obvious red flags into green lights by developing effective communication skills.

How to Do Good After Prison: A Handbook for Successful Reentry (w/ Employment Information Handbook), Michael B. Jackson, 4th ed., 2008, Joint FX Press

Two barriers to an ex-con's successful re-entry into society; those created by public policy and public attitude; and those that are self-created by such things as lacking a plan, not having the right attitude. This guide offers advice, insight, and motivation to help succeed after prison.

Playing the Job-finding Game: A Rule Book for Ex-offenders, Terry Pile, Marci Hobbs, ed., 2012, Kindle ed., Career Advisors/Amazon Digital

A strategic approach to obtaining employment, regardless of past transgressions, based on advice from a veteran career counselor.

The Fortune Society
www.fortunesociety.org

The Society offers counseling, referrals to vocational training, job placement, tutoring in preparation for the GED, Basic Adult Literacy and English as a Second Language classes, and substance abuse treatment.

The Osborne Association
www.osborneny.org

Offers opportunities to those who have been in conflict with the law to transform their lives through innovative, effective, and replicable programs that serve the community by reducing crime and its human and economic costs.

Film, Video and Photography

The Complete Film Production Handbook, Eve Light Honthaner, 4th ed., 2010, Focal Press
For working film/TV professionals and students

alike. For those who want to break into in film production, you'll know what to expect, you'll be prepared, and you'll be ten steps ahead of everyone else just starting out.

Digital Stock Photography: How to Shoot and Sell, Michal Heron, 2010, Kindle ed., Allworth Press/Amazon Digital

Everything you need to know to create digital stock photos that sell. From organizing a shoot, to raking in the profits as the pictures sell and sell and sell again.

The Hollywood Assistants Handbook: 86 Rules for Aspiring Power Players, Hillary Stamm and Peter Nowalk, 2008, Workman Publishing Company

This book contains 86 lessons that explain the unwritten rules of how to get a foot in the door and make all the right moves as you climb to the top.

Movie Speak: How to Talk Like You Belong on a Movie Set, Tony Bill, 2009, Workman Publishing Company

Covers the jargon used on a movie set, plus what it's really like to be a director or a producer or an actor or a crew member.

The Production Assistant's Pocket Handbook, Caleb Clark, 2011, Lulu.com

For new PAs: how to get your first job, the basics of lock-downs, radio communication, running talent, what to bring to a set, and driving.

SELLPHOTOS.COM: Your Guide to Establishing a Successful Stock Photography Business on the Internet, Robin Engh, 2011, Writers Digest Books

Even if you're new to the world of cyberspace, this guide makes it simple. It begins with the basics of the Internet and how it can work for you. You'll learn how to create your own webpage, promote your site, and transact business and much more.

What I Really Want to Do On Set in Hollywood: A Guide to Real Jobs in the Film Industry, Brian Dzyak, 2010, Kindle ed., Lone Eagle

A complete, insightful look at the biggest jobs on the movie set for anyone who wants to work in film. Offers a detailed look at the industry. Explores more than 35 jobs from around the film industry.

2012 Hollywood Screenwriting Directory, The Writers Store

This Directory is a resource for discovering where and how to sell your screenplay, with over 1,500 listings for industry insiders, such as studios, production companies, and independent financiers. NOTE: *See www.writersstore.com for other products for writers and others in entertainment.*

Film Land
www.filmland.com

Links for industry news, crew calls, and services, a bulletin board, festivals, a dictionary, more.

Food and Beverages

Career Opportunities in the Food and Beverage Industry, Kathleen Hill, 2010, Kindle ed., Checkmark Books

Covering titles from bakery manager to sommelier—this is a guide to top culinary careers, that includes key information on more than 80 jobs in this industry, with position descriptions, salary ranges, employment outlook, tips for entry, and more.

Careers in Food Science: From Undergraduate to Professional, Richard W. Hartel and Christina P. Klawitter, 2008, Springer

Has guidelines for students and new employees to ensure a successful start to their career, explained in a stepwise manner. Career advice and tips on such matters as, which classes to take in college, to internships, and finally how to land, and keep, the first job.

Culinary Careers: How to Get Your Dream Job in Food with Advice from Top Culinary Professionals, Rick Smilow and Anne E. McBride, 2010, Clarkson Potter

Instead of giving glossed-over, general descriptions of various jobs, *Culinary Careers* features exclusive interviews with both food-world luminaries and those on their way up, to help you discover what a day in the life is really like.

Food Jobs: 150 Great Jobs for Culinary Students, Career Changers and Food Lovers, Irena Chalmers, 2008, Beaufort Books, Inc.

Experts tell what it's really like to work in the food and related industries.

Running a Restaurant For Dummies (For Dummies (Business & Personal Finance)), Michael Garvey, Andrew G. Dismore and Heather H. Dismore, 2011, Kindle ed., For Dummies/Amazon Digital

The easy way to successfully run a profitable restaurant.

Will Write for Food: The Complete Guide to Writing Cookbooks, Blogs, Reviews, Memoir, and More (Will Write for Food: The Complete Guide to Writing Blogs), Dianne Jacob, 2nd. ed, 2010, Da Capo Lifelong Books

Food writing is everywhere and it's constantly adapting to evolving palates, publishing trends, and technologies. Jacob covers the most popular genres of food writing including: cookbooks, recipes, memoir, fiction, culinary travel, restaurant reviews, and a large new chapter on food blogging.

Beverage Marketing Directory, 2012, Beverage Marketing Corp., Print, online, CD-ROM, pdf, Web, and multi-user license.
www.beveragemarketing.com

Contact information, brand affiliation, production capacity, sales volume, and fleet data for virtually every U.S. and Canadian beverage producer and distributor, plus the industry's largest personnel database, featuring nearly 2,4500 beverage executives.

Also available: **The Beverage Marketing Reports** and **The Beverage Marketing State Books.**

Food Industry eBook Directory of Venture Capital and Private Equity Firms (Job Hunting? Get Your Resume in the Right Hands), Jane Lockshin, 2012, Kindle ed., Custom Databanks, Inc./Amazon Digital

This directory is drawn from our database of more than 2,500 venture capital and private equity firms. We chose U.S. and Canadian venture capital/PE firms that invest in the food industry.

Food411
food411.com

An editorial food resource directory for everything on the Web related to gourmet food finds, online food shopping, ingredients, recipes, regional specialties, food blogs, unique food gifts, and meals delivered.

www.fooddirectories.com
FoodDirectories.COM is a website that focuses on the business-to-business marketplace only for the

food industry. We own the fastest growing food industry database with tens of thousands of members from more than 220 countries. Free to join.

Major Food and Drink Companies of the World, 16th ed., 2012, Print, Gale
www.gale.cengage.com

Covers more than 9,200 of the leading food, alcoholic, and nonalcoholic drink companies worldwide. Entries typically provide company name; address; phone, telex, and fax numbers; names of senior management, including more than 45,000 senior executives; description of business activities; brand names and trademarks; subsidiaries and associates; financial information for the previous two years; and more.

Food and Beverage Market Place, 2013, Print, Database, Grey House Publishing
www.greyhouse.com/food.htm

Available in a three-volume printed directory, a subscription-based Online Database, as well as mailing list and database formats. Completely updated for 2013, the 2013 Edition contains more information than ever before, including thousands of new entries, and enhancements to many existing entries. With over 40,000 companies, and 80,000+ key executive contacts.

2012 Fact Book, The Beverage Information Group
www.bevinfostore.com

Rules and regulations pertaining to the distribution and sale of beverage alcohol by state. A Web subscription provides access to the continuously updated database and allows the user to search all fields. Includes what's sold where, direct shipping, promotions, merchandising, and product tastings. *Note: Other directories are available. See the website.*

World Drinks Marketing Directory, 2010, Euromonitor International
www.euromonitor.com/
world-drinks-marketing-directory/book

Provides information on the leading companies in the international drinks industry. This reference book presents detailed profiles of 1,000 major manufacturers operating internationally and nationally. *Note: Other directories are available. See the website.*

Food Info Net
www.foodinfonet.com

Internet portal devoted exclusively to the food industry with 180,000 visitors per month. We offer various options for marketers looking to reach a targeted food business audience. We also provide viewers with a single-access port to a broad range of information on market research, food ingredients, equipment, services, trade shows, jobs, books, etc.

Franchising

Become a Franchise Owner!: The Start-Up Guide to Lowering Risk, Making Money, and Owning What you Do, Joel Libava, 2011, Wiley

This book will arm you with the insights you need as you search for a franchise opportunity that's right for you. Explains the joys and perils of the franchise model, offering straightforward, step-by-step tips and advice on how to properly (and carefully) research and select a franchise business.

The Economics of Franchising, Roger D. Blair and Francine Lafontaine, 2010, Cambridge University Press

This book describes in much detail both how and why franchising works. It also analyses the economic tensions between the franchisor-franchisee relationship; plus presents a great deal of empirical evidence on franchising, its importance in segments of the economy, and much more.

The Educated Franchisee: The How-To Book for Choosing a Winning Franchise, Rick Bisio, 2nd ed., 2011, Bascom Hill Publishing Group

Among the topics covered are: how to find a franchise that is right for you; how owning a franchise can create wealth; where to find quality franchisors; what qualities franchisors look for, and others.

Entrepreneur 2012 Franchise 500
www.entrepreneur.com/franchise500/index.html

Our 33rd Annual Franchise 500 ranking reveals popular industries and the trends making an impact on their future. This is a reference guide with everything you need to know about buying a franchise. Culled from *Entrepreneur* magazine's 30 years of research and reporting on the world of franchises, this book gives practical, how-to advice. Site also has

The Top 10 Franchises for 2012, plus other information on the market and how-to guides.

Franchising & Licensing: Two Powerful Ways to Grow Your Business in Any Economy, Andrew J. Sherman, 4th ed., 2011, AMACOM

Filled with illuminating examples, stories from the field, and dozens of forms for drafting franchising agreements and licensing programs, the fourth edition covers all the strategic, legal, financial, and operational aspects of these complex, but highly profitable business strategies.

Franchising For Dummies, Michael Seid and Dave Thomas, 2nd ed., 2010, For Dummies

All the inside insight and smart advice to make sure you pick the right investment opportunity and make the most of it.

Grow to Greatness: How to Build a World-Class Franchise System Faster, Steven Olson, 2012, CreateSpace Independent Publishing Platform

A best-seller, this book, is a must-read guide on how to build a world-class franchise system—faster. It delivers advice and proven, step-by-step systems and processes for emerging and established franchisors, as well as for anyone considering franchising their business.

Grow Smart, Risk Less: A Low-Capital Path to Multiplying Your Business Through Franchising, Shelly Sun, 2011, Greenleaf Book Group Press

Experienced franchisor Sun shares practical advice and her own experiences to help you discover the power of and avoid the pitfalls of franchising your business. From deciding whether you have a concept worthy of franchising and how to adjust your concept if you don't, to assuming new challenges of leading a larger, more diverse organization, this book covers a wide range of topics.

How Much Can I Make?, Robert E. Bond, ed., 12th ed., 2012, Source Book Publishers

The most important task for a prospective franchisee (or small businessperson) is to prepare a realistic cash flow statement that reflects the economic potential of a franchise (or small business). Here is a guide that provides historical sales, expense and/ or profit data on actual franchise operations, so as to establish a solid basis upon which to make these critical financial projections.

Street Smart Franchising: A Must Read Before You Buy a Franchise!, Joe Mathews, Don DeBolt and Deb Percival, 2011, Entrepreneur Press

Franchise experts Mathews and DeBolt and Percival deliver an insider's view of how franchising works, imparting real-world tactics and strategies, and empowering you to decide if franchising is for you.

What No One Ever Tells You About Franchising: Real-Life Franchising Advice from 101 Successful Franchisors and Franchisees (What No One Ever Tells You About...), Jan Norman, 2006, Kaplan Business

Jan Norman, journalist and expert in entrepreneurship, gives readers a look at franchising from the trenches.

www.franchising.com

A source of franchise information on the web. It provides resources for franchise buyers, multi-unit franchisees and franchisors.

Source Book Publications—Print and Online **www.sourcebookpublications.com**

The Franchise Bookstore offers over 50 recent books, proprietary in-depth reports and databases on franchising. As new publications and reports become available, they will be added to the Bookstore, including many by Bond's, such as Bond's Franchise Guide and Bond's Top 100 Franchises 2012 Edition, as well as books on various topics covering franchising. *See the website for an extensive listing.*

www.franchise.com

The place for people beginning their business opportunity search and the journey of franchise ownership, as well as for those already involved in the world of franchising. Serves as a unique search tool for finding the right business for sale and a franchise industry resource that offers website visitors franchise information, the latest franchise industry news, and high-demand resources.

www.franchisegator.com

Franchise opportunities and business directory for entrepreneurs, with resources; blogs, directories, lists of top franchises, and more.

www.franchiseopportunities.com

Source for on franchises and small businesses for sale. It identifies, creates and distributes information regarding franchising and small business opportunities.

Freelancing

Be a Successful Online Freelancer—Your Online Freelancing Guide to Making Money at Home in the Lousy Economy, by Angie T. Lee, 2012, Amazon
The guide begins with insights into how you can discover, develop, and market the skills you can sell online. It brings you up-to-date on the Internet's hottest freelance sites and other potential work sources.

Breaking Into Freelance Illustration: A Guide for Artists, Designers and Illustrators, Holly DeWolf, 2012, Kindle ed., How/Amazon Digital
Provides a step-by-step roadmap for promoting yourself and running your own creative business. Offers up-to-date advice about the best business practices, ideas for new promotional tools, answers to common questions, and words of wisdom and inspiration from top illustrators.

Creative, Inc.: The Ultimate Guide to Running a Successful Freelance Business, Joy Deangdeelert Cho and Meg Mateo Ilasco, 2010, Kindle ed. and Print, Chronicle Books/Amazon Digital
For all types of creatives, illustrators, photographers, graphic designers, animators, and more, this how-to book has everything from creating a standout portfolio to navigating the legal issues of startup business.

Freelancing for Dummies, Susan M. Drake, 2011, Kindle ed., For Dummies/Amazon Digital
A total guide to starting and running a freelance business, for anyone thinking about striking out on their own, or who's already decided to make the move into self-employment.

Freelancing Expertise: Contract Professionals in the New Economy (Collection on Technology and Work), Debra Osnowitz, 2010, ILR Press
A qualitative study of decision making, work practices, and occupational processes among writers and editors who work in print and web communications, and programmers and engineers who work in software and systems development, culled from nearly 80 interviews with experts.

Getting Started As Freelance Writer, Robert W. Bly, 2008, Sentient Publications

This expanded edition goes beyond advice as a business writer to include the more creative forms of writing, such as poems, short stories, novels, and essays, plus a section on cartooning.

Getting Started as an Online Freelance Writer 2011, Kathy Gleason, 2011, Kindle ed., Amazon Digital
Becoming an online freelance writer is easier than it seems. In this short guide, find out how to get started and tips for success.

Getting Started on the Web for Writers, Kandie Delley, 2011, Kindle ed., 3rd Koast Publishing/Amazon Digital
This is for newbies who want to establish a digital brand, but who are bogged down by the business side of freelancing. Using this book can expedite the process.

Guide To Successful Online Freelancing—Establish Yourself As A Professional Freelancer And Earn Massive Lines Of Clients! AAA+++, Manuel Ortiz Braschi, 2009 Kindle ed., Unique Enterprises/Amazon Digital
This guide is a fun and easy to follow, detailing how you—or anyone—can kick-start and grow your profitable career online as an expert freelancer while working from home.

Starting Your Career as a Freelance Editor: A Guide to Working with Authors, Books, Newsletters, Magazines, Websites, and More, Mary Embree, 2012, Allworth Press
A clear, concise, and stepwise guide to making a living as a freelance editor. Covers topics such as: requirements in various fields; how to get started; promoting yourself; and more.

Starting Your Career as a Freelance Illustrator or Graphic Designer, Michael Fleishman, 2012, Kindle ed., Allworth Press/Amazon Digital
Digital illustration and design, online portfolio sites, and more have radically changed how illustrators and graphic designers work. Fleishman details every business aspect of commercial art and how to succeed in a digital world.

The Wealthy Freelancer: 12 Secrets to a Great Income and an Enviable Lifestyle, Steve Slaunwhite, et al., 2010, ALPHA
Whether you call yourself a freelancer, consultant,

independent contractor or solo professional of any kind, here are steps to having a great income and an enviable lifestyle.

Freelancers Union
www.freelancersunion.org

Nearly one in three working Americans is an independent worker. Freelancers Union believes all workers should have the freedom to build meaningful, connected, and independent lives—backed by a system of mutual and public support. Freelancers Insurance Company, a nonprofit part of the Freelancers Union, covers over 23,000 New York freelancers and their families for about a third less than other options, and has members throughout the country. The site has other resources for freelancers.

Government

150 Best Federal Jobs, Laurence Shatkin, Ph.D., 2012, JIST Works

Helps readers target their federal job searches toward the most promising occupations in just two steps—(1) study the 55 "best federal jobs" lists, organized by pay, growth, openings, etc.; and (2) explore 150 job descriptions to see which the occupations are of greatest interest. See why the federal process is unique and discover how to search for and apply for jobs in the fed.

The Book of U.S. Government Jobs: Where They Are, What's Available and How to Get One, Dennis V. Damp, 2011, Kindle ed., Bookhaven Press/ Amazon Digital

This new edition offers job seekers all of the tools necessary to land a high paying civil service job. Discover where the jobs are, how to apply, and, most importantly, where to find them.

Careers in Focus, Government, 2nd ed., 2010, **Facts on File**

Covers 20 jobs in the government.

The Complete Idiot's Guide to Getting Government Jobs, The Partnership for Public Service, 2010, Print and Kindle ed., The Partnership for Public Service

Readers will learn how to navigate the government application process to find stable employment at county municipalities, as well as state and federal

agencies. Includes advice on drafting resumes suited to the specific requirements of the hiring agency.

Federal Resume Guidebook, Fifth Edition: Strategies for Writing a Winning Federal Resume, Kathryn Kraemer Troutman, 2011, JIST Works

Candidates must understand how federal resumes are different from those for other employers. Recently, the Hiring Reform Initiative changed the federal hiring process. Troutman explains these new processes and procedures and teaches people how to write winning federal resumes.

Government Jobs in America: [2012] Jobs in U.S. States & Cities and U.S. Federal Agencies with Job Titles, Salaries & Pension Estimates—Why You Want One, What Jobs Are Available, How to Get One by Government, 2011, Partnerships for Community

This book covers all aspects of getting high-paying government employment. It covers getting work in state, city, and federal government agencies and departments. Shows job titles in these areas, including salaries, 5-year salary projections, and pension estimates, in chart form.

How to Land a Top-Paying Federal Job—Your Complete Guide to Opportunities, Internships, Resumes and Cover Letters, Networking, Interviews, Salaries, Promotions, and More! Lily Madeleine Whiteman, 2012, AMACOM

Guide to securing a government job, internship, or fellowship, which is based upon over 100 interviews with federal hiring managers.

Encyclopedia of Governmental Advisory Organizations, 27th ed., 2012, Print
www.gale.cengage.com

Contains entries describing activities and personnel of groups and committees that function to advise the President and various departments and bureaus of the federal government, as well as detailed information about historically significant committees. Complete contact information is provided.

Green Careers

(See also Biotechnology, and; Energy, Alternative Energy and Utilities *NOTE: Guides about green jobs, are also listed under* Energy, *so be sure to check those listings.*)

183 Green Business Opportunities for 2012, Robert Wingate Jr., 2011, CreateSpace Independent Publishing Platform

Green business opportunities—franchises, distributorships, affiliations, vending, network marketing, retail, mutual funds and individual stocks. With descriptions and contact information.

Green Careers: Choosing Work for a Sustainable Future, Jim Cassio and Alice Rush, 2009, New Society Publishers

This career guide, based on labor market research, covers green jobs representing almost every area of career interest. The book answers such questions as: What green careers are available? What education do I need? What is the demand for this profession? How do I change to a green career?

Green Careers For Dummies, Carol L. McClelland, 2010, For Dummies

This book explores the green frontier of careers and shows you how to find a field that is best-suited to your primary interests, skills, and goals; and then translating that into the sustainable job sphere.

Green Careers in Energy, 2010, Peterson's

Pinpoints the best opportunities in the fast-growing and most-promising renewable energy fields—solar, wind, geothermal, hydroelectric and marine, biofuels, and hydrogen, with data on colleges, organizations, and institutions that offer courses, degrees, certification, and training/retraining.

Green Collar Jobs: Environmental Careers for the 21st Century, Scott M. Deitch, 2010, Praeger

An easy-to-reference guide that will help students, recent graduates, job seekers, and career changers at all levels find the latest information and job resources in this burgeoning field. Examines all aspects, with an overview discussing green jobs, from environmental, economic and political perspectives.

www.1sky.org

A collaborative campaign aimed at bringing hundreds of diverse organizations together to support a unified platform for transformational change. 1Sky works to combine 643 allied organizations, 203,500 climate advocates, 4,256 volunteer leaders in 50 states, and our own team to effect change in the nation's capitol.

2012 Global Cleantech Directory: 100 Cleantech Lists That Matter, Shawn Lesser, 2012, CreateSpace Independent Publishing Platform

A quick resource guide on recent clean technology developments, initiatives, and influencers around the world. This book spotlights achievements in cleantech and offers an easy way to stay informed about the most exciting things happening in cleantech today. Clean technology is one of the fastest growing sectors in the global economy. The directory has contacts, meetings and events, recent developments, initiatives, influencers worldwide, and more.

The Only Green Directory
theonlygreendirectory.com

A comprehensive Internet reference guide to all businesses and blogs promoting green living and eco-friendly issues. Includes recycling centers, eco-travel and green tours for vacationers, green apparel and gifts, yoga instructors, green MBA Programs, as well as links to other green resources, educational opportunities, news, green organizations, and more.

GreenBiz.com
www.greenbiz.com

GreenBiz Group provides clear, concise, accurate and balanced information, resources, and learning opportunities to help companies of all sizes and sectors integrate environmental responsibility into their operations in a manner that supports profitable business practices.

Green Corps
www.greencorps.org

Green Corps trains organizers, provides field support for critical environmental campaigns, and graduates activists who possess the skills, temperament and commitment to fight and win tomorrow's environmental battles. The Corps has a one-year, full-time, paid Field School for Environmental Organizing program that intersperses classroom instruction with multiple campaign efforts. Trainees gain hands-on experience running field campaigns to win environmental protections and public health initiatives.

Health Care and Medicine

Basic Training For Careers In Health Care, Vanessa O'Sullivan, 2010, Kindle ed., Amazon Digital

Many of these jobs require no more than a high school diploma or less. O'Sullivan reports from the trenches, detailing the information you need.

Covers HIPPA, different health insurances (such as commercial and governmental insurance), lab tests, prescriptions, medical terms, medical terminology, and more.

Career Launcher: Health Care Management, 2011, Ferguson Publishing Company

Gives the information to understand the current health care system and shows how to launch a successful career. Key information on health care management, along with case studies of common industry problems and their resolution, ethical dilemmas, tips for effective communications and networking.

Career Opportunities in Health Care, 3rd ed., 2010, Facts on File

Profiles of more than 80 specific jobs in 18 key branches of this field. Each profile reflects the latest trends in training, job duties, salaries, advancement prospects, and more. Has a glossary, plus appendixes listing schools, associations, organizations, publications, and periodicals.

The Everything Guide To Careers In Health Care: Find the Job That's Right for You, Kathy Quan, 2012, Kindle ed., Amazon Digital

Explore the employment possibilities, and how to chose the right career, from nursing and psychology to pharmacy technology and art therapy—and many more. Also covers self-assessment, working conditions and lifestyles, and more.

Health Careers Today, Judith A. Gerdin, 5th ed., 2011, Mosby

Describes more than 45 health careers, and offers a practical overview to help you make an informed decision in choosing a profession. Discusses the roles and responsibilities of various occupations, plus the skills needed for all health careers. A companion Evolve website includes skills videos, animations, quizzes, and flashcards. Author Gerdin also has a companion workbook: **Workbook for Health Careers Today.**

Hot Health Care Careers: More Than 25 Cutting-Edge Occupations With the Fastest Growth and Most New Positions, Andrew Morkes, 2011, College & Career Press

Hottest careers for any educational background, from high school to MDs. Also lists books, websites, and other information.

Introduction to Health Care & Careers, Roxann DeLaet, 2011, Lippincott Williams & Wilkins

Provides student beginners with the fundamentals needed to develop personal and professional skills, understand their chosen profession, and succeed in the world of health care.

Ferguson Career Coach: Managing Your Career in the Health Care Industry, 2010, Facts on File

This career book is loaded with tips for success, and covers careers from patient care to health care administration. Acting as a personal coach, this guidebook features practical insight to help readers achieve career success in any area of health care. Practical advice is given on making contacts, self-marketing, interviewing, career strategies, and more.

Professionalism in Health Care: A Primer for Career Success, Sherry Makely, 4th ed., 2012, Prentice Hall

Makely offers an understanding of professional standards that all healthcare workers need to provide excellent care and service; with complete coverage of these and other crucial "soft skills"; work ethics, character, relationships, teamwork, communication and etiquette, honesty, and more.

The Recruiter's Hiring Secrets for Getting a Job in the Healthcare Field, Kelly Smith and Ashley Krulikowski, 2008, Excellent Enterprises, LLC

Learn from actual resumes, cover letters, emails and comments from hiring authorities on how to obtain employment in the growing healthcare field.

Top 100 Health-Care Careers (Top 100 Health-Care Careers: Your Complete Guidebook to Training And Jobs In Allied Health, Nursing, Medicine, And More), Saul Wischnitzer and Edith Wischnitzer, 2010, Jist Works

Career guidance, including choosing the health-care career that is best for you, how to get the education, and how to relate to patients. Contains details on 100 jobs, including scope, activities, educational requirements, salary range, advancement, certification, outlook, and more. There is a directory of education/training programs, plus a self-assessment for choosing the right career in the field, with job search tips, more.

Encyclopedia of Medical Organizations and Agencies, 24th ed., 2012, Gale

Access to public and private agencies concerned with

medical information, funding, research, education, planning, advocacy, advice and service. Sixty-nine chapters represent an entire range of contemporary medical fields: allergy and immunology, alternative medicine, biomedicine, chiropractic, gastroenterology, hypnosis, neurology, osteopathic medicine, reproduction and family planning, substance abuse and more. Entries provide contact and descriptive information.

Health Care Careers Directory, Online links to pdfs, American Medical Association
www.ama-assn.org

Provides information—history, career description, employment characteristics, salary, outlook, and education/certification—on the types of jobs in the following areas: allied health; complementary and alternative medicine and therapies; communication sciences; counseling; dietetics; dentistry and related fields; expressive/creative arts therapies; health information and communication; laboratory science; medical imaging; nursing; pharmacy; physician; physician assistant; podiatry; psychology; therapy and rehabilitation; veterinary medicine; and vision-related professions.

Healthcare Lists and Databases, SK&A
www.skainfo.com

Up-to-date information on the industry, including supplemental information, such as ownership, organization size, practice specialty, affiliations and more. Our diverse mix of industry information comes from sources such as: company and corporate directories; websites, state licensing information; professional associations, and more. Databases include: physicians; hospitals; pharmacies; nurses; group practices, and more.

Health Resources Online
www.healthresourcesonline.com

This is a web source for finding top management and professional resources for healthcare industry executives, from hospices, to managed care, to wellness. Participating publishers include: **Health Resources Publishing (www.healthrespubs.com)**—newsletters, books and special advisory services; **The Managed Care Information Center (www.themcic. com)**—a clearinghouse for healthcare executives' managed care information needs, offering newsletters, advisories, guides, manuals, special reports and

books; and **Wellness Junction (www.wellnessjunction.com)**, the online resource for professionals and consumers interested in health and wellness issues. This site offers a variety of health care directories and resources. Directories include: **The National Directory of Managed Care Organizations; National Directory of Physician Organizations; The National Directory of Health Systems, Hospitals, and Their Affiliates;** and **The National Directory of Medical Directors Database.**

Management Resources for Healthcare & Medical Professionals, Pam Pohly
www.pohly.com/

A wealth of up-to-date articles, information, reference materials and links are available here for career enhancement and professional development. This health administration website assists healthcare professionals and administrators in finding pertinent resources, both on and off the Internet. Extensive listing of professional books. The **executive toolbox**, offers health services administration topics including, medical legal, health reform, healthcare legislative and compliance updates, professional associations, management strategy, technology, employment and job search services, hospital and practice management tools, human resources, healthcare news and publications, and much more. Has an extensive listing of **Employment, Careers and Jobs Guidebooks,** as well as those on **Job Search Resources: Health & Medical Employment.**

Medical and Health Information Directory, 10 part set, Edition 27, 2012, Gale

This comprehensive guide to organizations, agencies, institutions, services and information sources in medicine and health-related fields provides complete contact information and a description of the organization. Each edition includes more than 33,000 organizations; nearly 20,000 libraries, publications and electronic resources; and more than 40,500 health service providers.

Health Care Careers
www.health-care-careers.org

Resource for education, training, and schools in the medical and allied healthcare fields. Get career information and find degrees offered by many healthcare schools.

Healthlinks.net
www.healthlinks.net

A site for health-care consumers and professionals that provides links to services and products, alternative health, education, dental and medical resources, hospitals, employment, healthcare publications, mental health, and much more.

Human Resources

Best Kept HR Secrets: 400 Most Powerful Tips For Thriving at Work, Making Yourself Indispensable & Attaining Outrageous Success in Human Resources, Alan Collins, 2010, SuccessInHR.com

Lays out the most powerful advice for attaining outrageous success in Human Resources. Over 400 brutal truths, tips, best practices, inspirations, confessions, and expert insights.

HR from the Outside In: Six Competencies for the Future of Human Resources, Dave Ulrich, et al., 2012, McGraw-Hill

This book on HR competencies provides ideas and tools to help HR professionals develop their careers and make their organization more effective.

Never Get Lost Again: Navigating Your HR Career, Nancy E. Glube and Phyllis G. Hartman, 2009

Aimed at experienced HR professionals, this handbook provides practical advice customized for those who wish to strategically develop their careers. Addresses how to avoid common pitfalls and offers counseling from successful HR practitioners and business leaders.

Real-Resumes for Human Resources & Personnel Jobs, Anne McKinney, 2012, CreateSpace Independent Publishing Platform

Resumes and cover letters in this book are for jobs such as Assistant Personnel Administrator, Chief of Personnel Management, Director of Human Services, Employee Relations Manager, Human Resources Analyst, Human Resources Director, and more. An industry-specific resume book.

Unwritten HR Rules: 21 Secrets For Attaining Awesome Career Success In Human Resources, Alan Collins, 2011, Success In HR Publishing

For aspiring professionals or those who are already HR executives, Collins presents the unwritten rules that will take your HR career to the next level. Discover HR career advancement strategies your company doesn't tell you about. You'll learn: the secret to impressing your business leaders as an HR professional; the awful, brutal and unpleasant truth about advancing your career; and more.

Winning Big In HR: 100+ Powerful Strategies For Accomplishing Great Results Faster & Getting Your Clients To Rave About You As A Human Resources Professional!, Alan Collins, 2012

SuccessInHR.com

Billed as an HR career game changer, Collins presents over 110 job success strategies, advice, confessions, stories and insights stolen (and no longer available) from his blog, plus new tricks and tips.

Consultants Forum Referral Directory, SHRM— Society for Human Resource Management

This resource contains contact information on SHRM members who offer HR consulting services. Information in this database is self-reported by SHRM members.

The Directory of Executive & Professional Recruiters 2011-2012, Kennedy Publications
www.kennedyinfo.com

Over 12,000 recruiters in 5,000+ firm locations. Free online access provided. Six indexes include: 84 job function areas (type of job), 120+ industries, services offered, geographical locations (by city and state), retained firms, and an A-Z firm index.

Human Resources Directory
www.hrdirectory.org

This directory is a complete resource for the HR industry— a growing guide of information—everything from employee performance management, to staffing and recruitment solutions—with links and descriptions for every human resource entry.

HumanResourceDirectory.com
www.humanresourcedirectory.com

A destination for anything about or related to employment. Our editorial team makes great effort to evaluate the existence and accuracy of each web site.

Training and Seminar Locators (TASL)
www.tasl.com

TASL is a free education and training resource center/database for career/business. Includes offerings of more than 1,000 of the best universities, industry associations, media, and training companies. An online database of training and seminar providers, searchable by event or service, product or provider.

The Training Registry
www.tregistry.com

A training resources directory. Site has listings of trainers, training companies, consultants, facilities for rent, courses, classes, programs, products and tools, keynote speakers, coaches, books, and more. Covers a wide range of topics, including HR resources, personal & professional development, and organizational development.

Information Technology/High Tech, including eCommerce

ACE the IT Resume, Paula Moreira, 2007, McGrawlHill/Osborne

How to tailor your resume for specific IT specialties. How to make your resume scannable. An objective analysis of why your resume may not be getting you return phone calls and an encyclopedia of resumes tuned to specific IT positions, including database administrator, technical writer, director of IT, and ERP consultant.

Career Launcher: Computers and Programming, 2011, Ferguson Publishing Company

Covers the ground that professionals need to achieve career success. Including handy tidbits of information and statistics, emerging industry trends, a breakdown of key jobs, and much more, this guide also provides an overview and history of this industry. Written with an insider's perspective, this Career Launcher also includes a glossary of industry jargon and a directory of industry resources.

Careers in Focus: Computers, 5th ed., 2010, Ferguson Publishing

Covers 20 careers in this extensive field.

Click Millionaires: Work Less, Live More with an Internet Business You Love, Scott Fox, 2012, AMACOM

Explains how to combine outsourcing, software, and automated online marketing to build recurring revenues, while working less than corporate "success" requires.

E-commerce Get It Right! Essential Step-by-Step Guide for Selling & Marketing Products Online. Insider Secrets, Key Strategies & Practical Tips— Simplified for Start-Ups & Small Businesses, Ian Daniel, 2011, NeuroDigital

Will show you everything you need to know about achieving success with your own e-commerce website and business. Insider secrets, key strategies and practical tips, more.

Find an IT Job: Information Technology Careers From Bioinformatics to Web Design, Paul E. Love, 2012, CreateSpace Independent Publishing Platform

Quick overview of some IT careers; what each job involves, what the job market is like, and which careers may match your interests and qualifications. Each job summary covers the educational or other background needed, as well as the daily tasks and the necessary skills.

How to Succeed in a High-Tech Career: Why Your Reputation and Relationships Matter, Phil Shelton, 2012, Parker/Banks Publishing

Shelton's book is geared towards technical students with degrees, such as computer science or engineering, but the principles apply to anyone's career. Successful people invest time and effort in building their reputations and relationships.

Information Technology Jobs [2012]: Corporate & Government Career Guide (Information Technology Jobs in America: Corporate & Government), 2012, Kindle ed., Partnerships for Community/Amazon Digital

Shows where the jobs are in the U.S. IT Services Sector and in U.S. Federal and State and Municipal government agencies and departments. Also explains how to make contact with this special sector for IT jobs, IT service providers, and how to build a career in the IT services sector.

IT Career JumpStart: An Introduction to PC Hardware, Software, and Networking (Jumpstart), Naomi J. Alpern, et al., 2012, Sybex

To prepare for any kind of certification, IT candidates need a basic understanding of the hardware and software used in a computer network. Alpern strips down a network to its bare basics, and clearly discusses this topic, so IT beginners can confidently gain an understanding of the fundamentals.]

A Quick Start Guide to Online Selling: How to Sell Your Product on e-bay, Amazon, iTunes and Other Online Market Places (New Tools for Business), Cresta Norris, 2010, Kogan Page

New-media marketing specialist Norris covers the fundamentals of online selling, the advantages, what to consider when creating an online shop, and the pitfalls to avoid.

Starting an Online Business All-in-One For Dummies, Shannon Belew and Joel Elad, 2011, For Dummies

Here's everything you need to plan, launch, and maintain a successful online business. From creating a business plan to marketing with Facebook and Twitter, this guide includes coverage of the latest online marketing tools, techniques and trends.

Top Careers in Two Years—Computers and Information Technology, 2010, eBook, Facts on File

Examines professions in this growing field that are available to students with two-year degrees.

The Ultimate Guide To Building And Marketing Your Online Business With Free Tools, Gabriela Taylor, 2012, CreateSpace Independent Publishing Platform

Here are thousands of free solutions that will support your marketing and advertising campaign, with free online tools available that will massively benefit your business.

Major Information Technology Companies of the World, Russ J. Graham, Christine Oddy, David J. Smith and Kate Wilson, eds., 15th ed., 2012, Graham & Whiteside

Covers more than 8,250 of the leading information technology companies worldwide. Entries typically provide: company name; address; telephone, fax numbers; email and website addresses; names of senior management and board members, including more than 45,400 directors and senior executives; description of business activities; brand names and trademarks; subsidiaries and associates; financial information for the previous two years; and more. Includes a comprehensive index and another index listing company names alphabetically by country.

CompInfo Center—The Computer Information Center
www.compinfo-center.com

CompInfo

The one-stop reference resource for corporate IT, computer software, computers and communications, used worldwide for Web-based support resources.

ComputerGraphicsWorld
www.cgw.com

This site has news, conference/event listings, and a free e-newsletter, but not a job board. From the publication *CGW—Computer Graphics World*.

Insurance

(See also the section Banking, Finance, Investing, Securities, Trading, Credit, and Other)

Extreme Producers: Their Insights And Secrets: Quick and easy-to-read ideas that will build your insurance and financial services career, Jerry Hraban, 2010, Xlibris, Corp.

Based on insights from top producers in the field, this book provides quick-and-easy moneymaking ideas.

How to Land a Top-Paying Insurance, Claims Adjuster, Appraisal Manager Job: Your Complete Guide to Opportunities, Resumes and Cover Letters, ... What to Expect From Recruiters and More!, Brad Andrews, 2010, Emereo Pty Ltd

Helpful worksheets make it easier to write about a job experience. This ensures that the narrative will follow a logical structure and reminds you not to leave out the most important points. With this book, you'll be able to revise your application into a much stronger document, to be much better prepared and a step ahead for the next opportunity.

The Insurance Xperience: The Ultimate Guide To Success For Young Insurance Professionals, Matt Brown, et al., 2011, Matt Brown

Provides young insurance professionals with a road map to success. How to develop the right mindset, how to set and accomplish goals, how to increase productivity, how to engage prospects effectively, how to network and connect with others, and more.

Secrets of Successful Insurance Sales, Jack Kinder Jr. and Garry Kinder, 2012, Napoleon Hill Foundation

Based on the principles of success that Napoleon Hill and W. Clement Stone developed.

So You Want To Be An Insurance Agent, Jeff Hastings, 2nd ed., Jan 8, 2009, Farmers Career Center

A tool to a new career that helps you to understand the importance of developing a model, setting goals, creating action plans, and putting processes into place.

The Truth About Insurance Jobs—How to Job-Hunt and Career-Change for Insurance Jobs — The Facts You Should Know, Brad Andrews, 2009, Emereo Pty Ltd

Compiles the information candidates need to apply for their first insurance job, or to apply for a better one. This book is loaded with hundreds of strategies for applying your strengths. Comes filled with useful worksheets that will help you to write the best resume, and cheat sheets to help you get your career organized in a tidy, presentable fashion.

Weiss Ratings
www.weissratings.com

The nation's leading independent provider of research and analysis for the bank and insurance industries, for consumers and professionals alike. **Life & Annuity Insurers**— tracks the financial safety of approximately 875 U.S. life and annuity insurance companies each and every quarter. We then issue the **Weiss Financial Strength Ratings** based on our analysts' review of publicly available information collected by the NAIC, and supplemented by data we collect directly from the companies themselves.

01Web Directory
www.01webdirectory.com/insurance.htm

Has links to institutions providing insurance coverage for all types of risks.

A.M. Best Company
www.ambest.com

A.M. Best Company is a full-service credit rating organization dedicated to serving the financial services industries, including the banking and insurance sectors. Among its publications are Directories of: Actuaries, Adjusters, Attorneys, Auditors, Expert Service Providers, Legal and Claims Professionals, and Third Party Administrators. *See the website for details on products and services.*

A Directory of Insurance and Government Resources, American Insurance Association
www.aiadc.org/aiapub

Information on public policy issues affecting the property and casualty insurance industry via Internet links. This directory of selected organizations' home pages facilitates efficient access to information.

Business Insurance
www.businessinsurance.com

Its website delivers current news and information on a daily basis.

Insurance Broadcasting
www.insurancebroadcasting.com

A next-generation media organization facilitating the exchange of information between 180,000+ insurance industry professionals. Includes **Insurance Newscast**—A daily email newsletter; and **Workplace Benefits Association**—A directory of corporate and individual members that market benefits from: employers to employees; businesses to customers; and organizations to members. **www.workplacebenefits.org.**

InsuranceStates
www.insurancestates.com

Links to insurers by state. Also by category, such as adjusters, aviation insurance, consulting, and much more. The **Directories** link pulls up a large number of directories, information sites, agents, companies, and more.

National Underwriter Company
www.nationalunderwriter.com

Targeted tax, insurance, and financial planning information. The online bookstore has an extensive listing of Print and eBooks. Among them are: **Winning by the Rules: Ethics and Success in the Insurance Profession; How to Sell Long-Term Care Insurance; How to Sell Disability Income Insurance; and The Wedge: How To Stop Selling and Start Winning,** and more.

National Underwriters produces **Kirschner's Agent Source Book,** put out annually. This Source Book has several editions for different regions of the U.S. Each provides thousands of P&C industry listings in a print/digital format. Each edition covers: **Markets (carriers, MGAs and surplus line brokers); Risk Placement Index—coverage and the companies that write them; Agents & Brokers (available online with in the book); Bureaus & Associations; DOI; Insurance Adjusters; Industry Services** and more.

Journalism, including Freelance Writing

(*see also* Publishing)

Ask the Recruiter: Journalism Career Strategies as Published on Poynter Online for Reporters, Photographers and Editors in Newspapers, TV and Magazines, Joe Grimm, 2008, David Crumm Media, LLC

Based on Crimm's years of experience as a newsroom recruiter and staff development editor, plus as a copy desk chief, page-one designer, regional editor and associate editor, he tells how to ace the recruitment process.

A Career as a Foreign Correspondent (Careers Ebooks), Institute For Career Research, 2012

Not all international journalists report from war zones or other hot spots. Capital cities, metropolitan areas, and centers of commerce such as London or Moscow are typical locations. This book presents an overview of the profession.

Career Opportunities in Journalism, 2010, eBook, Facts on File

For writers, reporters, editors or behind-the-scenes producers, directors, photographers, or engineers. Covers more than 70 careers in a variety of contexts, from newspapers and broadcasting to education and new media. Extensive appendixes include listings of related educational programs, professional associations and publications, companies, and internship and scholarship resources.

Do You Belong In Journalism? Eighteen Editors Tell How You Can Explore Career Opportunities In Newspaper Work, Henry Gemmill and Bernard Kilgore, 2012, Literary Licensing, LLC

Additional contributors are John H. Colburn, George W. Healy Jr., Frank H. Bartholomew, and many others.

The Everything Guide To Magazine Writing: From Writing Irresistible Queries to Landing Your First Assignment-all You Need to Build a Successful Career, Kim Kavin, 2012, Kindle ed., Amazon Digital

Provides insider tips and guidance to achieve success. How to write an irresistible query letter; find and keep clients; start a freelance business; negotiate contracts; and get paid for articles.

Excellence in Online Journalism: Exploring Current Practices in an Evolving Environment, David A. Craig, 2010, Sage Publications, Inc.

Helps students develop standards of excellence, based on through interviews with more than 30 writers, editors and producers. It includes dozens of examples of strong work, and provides a framework of concepts to show how the field is evolving.

How To Be A Journalist (Original title: Your Career in Journalism), M.L. Stein and Praguy, 2012, Kindle ed. Amazon Digital

Explore how men and women learn the news business when writing for newspapers, magazines, television and radio, and in public relations. Covers the future for beginners, how to prepare for a journalism job and how to keep it. It tells you how to become a newspaperperson in a foreign country or a special writer for such things as education, sports or space.

How to Work as a Freelance Journalist, Marc Leverton, 2010, How to Books

Covers the tools of the trade—news, views, reviews, opinion pieces, plus feature writing, and more. What it's like to step into the unknown and work for yourself. How to: pitch your ideas successfully to editors; brainstorm original ideas; market yourself as a freelance journalist. Tips and advice from a wide range of successful freelance journalists and editors.

On Your Own: A Guide to Freelance Journalism www.spj.org/freelance.asp

For members of The Society of Freelance Journalists—A 77-page digital guide, addresses a broad range of questions common among new and aspiring freelancers—from bookkeeping to business licenses to branding.

What Can I Do Now? Journalism, 2011, Ferguson Publishing Company

Information on the industry, job profiles, and tips to get started on a career path.

Encyclopedia of Journalism, 2010, Sage Publications

Six-volume Encyclopedia covers all significant dimensions of journalism, including print, broadcast, and Internet journalism; U.S. and international perspectives; history; technology; legal issues and court cases; ownership; and economics. In the A to Z Volumes 1 through 4, both scholars and journalists contribute articles that span the field's wide spectrum of topics, from design to secrecy and leaks. Also covered are recently emerging media such as podcasting, blogs, and chat rooms.

The JournalistDirectory
www.journalistdirectory.com/journalist

For journalists and editors, this is a free way to create a personal profile page with information and optional contact details about you. Relevant information is made available to commission editors who can contact you. You can also create your own press release list and view it in **My Releases.**

Open Directory Project
www.dmoz.org/News/Media/Journalism/ Journalists

This is the largest, most comprehensive human-edited directory of the Web. It is constructed and maintained by community of volunteer editors. The Project has 355 links to journalists, directories, and reports for journalists.

Press Pass
www.presspass.me

Journalists on Twitter—organized by beat, media outlet, & region. Press Pass is an open live directory of journalists and media professionals organized by the outlets they work for and the beats and regions they cover. We track what journalists on Twitter are sharing, and show what they're reading, how they rank compared to others, the topics they care about, who gets their attention, and so on... Who is it for? Every now and then ordinary people need to get the message out to the public. Be it an entrepreneur with a new product, a non-profit that wants to raise awareness for a cause, or a citizen with a great photo of a protest. Press Pass lets you discover reporters interested in your message so they can help you get the word out.

WriterFind.com
www.writerfind.com/journalists

Directory of freelance journalists, feature writers, content writers—all international.

lists professional journalists, commentators and columnists. It includes both specialists and generalist reporters, editorial and feature writers. Most can work globally via email.

Law and Paralegal

Law

100 Plus Pointers for New Lawyers Adjusting to Your Job, Sharon Meit Abrahams Ed.D., 2011, eBook, pdf, First Chair Press

Guides lawyers and law students through what they need to know, from how to work with your new boss to how to keep the copy machine working. Get oriented to the working world through this electronic set of 100+ tailored tips, tactics, and tools for early success in the legal profession.

Careers in Administrative Law and Regulatory Practice, James T. O'Reilly, ed., 2010, American Bar Association

In the first half of the book, an expert describes the field, and outlines optimal entry strategies. The second half contains examples and demands of the careers in administrative law.   *Note: ABA publishes an extensive list of titles on careers in law. See apps.americanbar.org. Some other titles in* the **Careers in...Law** series are: **Animal, Criminal, International, National Security, Sports and Tax.** *See the website for more.*

Changing Jobs: A Handbook for Lawyers in the New Millennium, Heidi L. McNeil Staudenmaier, 3rd ed., 2010, American Bar Association

Helps you design your own route to professional happiness. More than 30 recognized experts in the fields of law and career placement offer valuable insights and guidance to discovering the direction that's right for you.

The Happy Lawyer: Making a Good Life in the Law, Nancy Levit and Douglas O. Linder, 2010, Oxford University Press

Examines the causes of dissatisfaction among lawyers, and then charts possible paths to a happier and more fulfilling career. Maximizing chances for achieving happiness depend on personality types, values, strengths and interests.

The Happy Lawyer Handbook, Mitchell Nathanson, 2012, CreateSpace Independent Publishing Platform

Many young lawyers become unhappy being lawyers, causing them to leave the practice of law or, more often, remain, resigned to spend their entire professional lives working for people they do not like and on issues for which they have no interest. Nathanson offers practical advice for law students and young attorneys on how they can avoid this in their legal careers. He also shows how the combination of new technology and the recent recession has changed the legal employment marketplace forever.

How to Start and Build a Law Practice, Jay Foonberg, 2010, Kindle ed., ABA/Amazon Digital

Practical advice for law students and young attorneys on how they can avoid this in their legal careers.

Make It Your Own Law Firm: The Ultimate Law Student's Guide to Owning, Managing, and Marketing Your Own Successful Law Firm, Spencer M. Aronfeld, 2011, AuthorHouse

Filled with personal anecdotes and practice advice, this book serves as a guide for students and young lawyers who are interested in establishing a law practice.

The New What Can You Do With a Law Degree: A Lawyer's Guide to Career Satisfaction Inside, Outside & Around the Law, Larry Richard Ph.D. and Tanya Hanson J.D., 2012, LawyerAvenue Press

A five-part model for career satisfaction, based on the principle that the better the fit between your career identity and your job, the greater your long-term satisfaction. Contains career exercises, practical career-finding techniques, and a compendium of 800+ ways to use your law degree inside, outside or around the law.

Should You Really Be a Lawyer?: The Guide to Smart Career Choices Before, During & After Law School, Deborah Schneider, 2nd ed., 2012, LawyerAvenue Press

Are you making the right decision to get into—or remain—in law? Here's a unique career-building guide that will help you evaluate and answer this most-basic question facing you now.

Solo by Choice 2011-2012: How to Be the Lawyer You Always Wanted to Be (Career Resources for a Life in the Law), Carolyn Elefant, 2011, LawyerAvenue Press

Covers every aspect of solo practice, from making the gut-wrenching decision to hang out your own shingle to meeting the financial and client-relations demands of a sole practice. It's a detailed and inspirational road map for anyone who wants to succeed in the solo practice of law.

The Young Litigator, 2011, eBook, American Bar Association

This book is a compilation of articles from the ABA Section of Litigation, chosen by young practicing lawyers, that seeks to guide young litigators in their first days, months, and years in the practice of law. Includes: using online social networking sites to make it rain; brief writing; marketing tips for the time-starved lawyer; writing a winning legal argument; and many more.

The Federal Judiciary
www.uscourts.gov

Includes information on federal courts, including employment opportunities. Covers all areas supporting U.S. courts, their services, and areas of responsibilities. Has a glossary of legal terms.

FindLaw Career Center
www.careers.findlaw.com

A tool for reaching legal professionals and for connecting attorneys with people in need of legal representation, as well as information and tips on running a law practice. Site for free legal information on the Internet with more than four million legal consumers visiting each month and the largest legal directory available. FindLaw's law-firm marketing solutions also have websites, online video, online attorney profiles, search engine marketing and Internet advertising.

NALP Directory of Legal Employers, 2012, Online
www.nalp.org

The NALP Directory provides a comprehensive and free solution for researching legal employers throughout the U.S., with information on law firms, government agencies, public interest organizations, and corporations, including lawyer demographics, practice areas, compensation and benefits, diversity and inclusion practices, and other valuable information about legal employers. *The 2011/2012 version is available in print.*

www.Law.com

Law.com connects legal professionals to more than 20 award-winning national and regional legal publications online, and delivers legal news on *The*

Newswire. Through linked information sites, legal professionals can track developments in their practice specialties, research legal technology purchases, access VerdictSearch.com, a verdict and settlement database, use LawJobs.com to conduct national job searches, identify expert witnesses at ALMExperts. com and purchase books, newsletters and other publications at LawCatalog.com.

Lawyers.com
www.lawyers.com
Among other resources, this site provides accurate and reliable profiles of 1 million lawyers and firms worldwide, and consumer-friendly explanations of major areas of law, articles on current legal topics, links to legal resources on the web, a glossary of 10,000 legal terms, and more. Use it to find potential employers and research the profession.

LawyersListings
www.lawyerslistings.com
LawyersListings provides a free listing service to all sole practitioners and law firms desiring a free Internet presence, that includes firm name, address, city, state, and zip code. Also provides the general public with a simple tool to locate a lawyer.

Paralegal

The Everything Guide to Being a Paralegal, Steve W. Schneider, 2011, FW Media
For new paralegals, professionals looking to further or reevaluate their careers, or those considering the profession. Chapters include: Paralegal Career Options; Paralegal Ethics and Professional Responsibility; and Pre-Trial Preparation.

Paralegal Career For Dummies, Scott Hatch and Lisa Hatch, 2006, For Dummies
A practical, hands-on guide to all the basics—from getting certified to landing a job and getting ahead. Includes a CD-ROM with sample memos, forms, letters, and more. Discover how to: Secure your ideal paralegal position. Pick the right area of the law for you.

Paralegal Careers and Salaries: How to Become a Paralegal or Legal Assistant and Find the (Almost Recession Proof) Legal Job of Your Choice, Richard Kaplan, 2012, Kindle ed., Amazon Digital

Learn about this potentially lucrative, new career option. Contents include: What is a Paralegal or Legal Assistant?; How Much Money Can I Make?; Why this Career is Growing So Fast?; and How to Become a Paralegal/Legal Assistant.

Paralegal Today: The Essentials, Roger Miller and Mary Meinzinger Urisko, 2010, Delmar
Using real-world examples, this book offers practical applications of each concept discussed, and has hands-on activities throughout. Covers the basic, key areas of paralegal studies, including careers, legal ethics, litigation procedures, criminal law, legal research and analysis, and legal writing.

The Professional Paralegal: A Guide to Finding a Job and Career Success, Charlsye Smith Diaz and Vicki Voisin, 2012, Prentice Hall
Covers not only how to land a job, but also how to prepare for and build a paralegal career. Explains working in the legal environment, identifies the purpose and payoff to continual professional development, and offers strategies for working collaboratively with attorneys and others drawn into a case.

2012 Job Analysis Report, National Association of Legal Assistants
www.nala.org/jobanalysis.aspx
Summarizes results of a major job analysis for the profession. NALA conducts nationwide utilization and compensation surveys every two years. This survey looks at the duties and responsibilities of paralegals, and ensures that NALA has current information about the roles and responsibilities of paralegals.

Also: **2010 National Utilization/Compensation Survey**— Includes members of NALA, non-members, and members of NALA-affiliated associations. With over 20 years of reports, this regular "look" at the paralegal profession has produced some interesting and valuable data. Findings are divided into four sections: participant background; employers and paralegal duties and responsibilities; billing rates; and compensation levels. Survey is taken every two years.

AAfPE Member Directory, American Association for Paralegal Education
www.aafpe.org/Directory/index.asp
AAfPE's membership includes hundreds of universi-

ties, colleges, and other institutions of higher learning throughout the U.S. and Canada.

National Federation of Paralegal Associations
www.paralegals.org

Publications include: **2012 Legal Hiring and Salary Trends, Charles A. Volkert III, Esq., November 2011** which reports on current trends in the industry. Other career reports are available online.

Paralegal Directory, Online
www.locateparalegal.com

Find paralegals in over 95 practice areas. The Directory contains paralegal listings, paralegal profiles, paralegal books, self-help guides, paralegal articles and important paralegal resources, all with up-to-date paralegal information.

Law Enforcement and Criminal Justice Majors

America's Courts and the Criminal Justice System, David W. Neubauer and Henry F. Fradella, 2010, Wadsworth Publishing

See what its like to be a judge, a prosecutor, a defense attorney, and more. This well-researched text gives a realistic sense of being in the courthouse.

Criminal Justice in America, George F. Cole and Christopher E. Smith, 2010, Wadsworth Publishing

Summarized new career opportunities in criminal justice and true stories of offenders and their experiences within the system. Also learn about the crucial role that public policy plays in the criminal justice system and explore the hot issues that are changing the face of criminal justice today and shaping its future.

Essentials of Criminal Justice, Larry J. Siegel and John L. Worrall, 2011, Wadsworth Publishing

The ins and outs of the criminal justice system. Cutting-edge high-profile cases, current research, detailed career information, and unique myth-busting theme; equips you with a solid understanding of the modern criminal justice system.

Introduction to Criminal Justice, Seventh Edition, Lawrence F. Travis III, 2011, Anderson

This student-friendly introductory text describes the criminal justice process, outlining the decisions, practices, people, and issues involved. It provides a solid introduction to the mechanisms of the system,

with balanced coverage of the issues presented by each facet of the process, including a thorough review of practices and controversies in law enforcement, the criminal courts, and corrections.

Introduction to Law Enforcement and Criminal Justice, Karen M. Hess and Christine Hess Orthmann, 10th ed., 2011, Delmar

Not only examines the role of the police within the larger criminal justice system, but also covers the other components of the system, such as the courts, corrections, and juvenile justice.

Corrections Connection
www.corrections.com

Corrections Connection Network News (CCNN), is an online global community of corrections.

News source committed to improving the lives of corrections professionals and their families. Daily news is the core of our business, with the most comprehensive database of vendor intelligence in corrections.

Criminal Justice USA
www.criminaljusticeusa.com

Helps aspiring criminal justice students and professionals to find the information and resources required to prepare for and ultimately obtain the criminal justice career of their dreams. Free, non-commercial information site that provides relevant and accurate information on criminal justice careers and criminal justice training.

Library and Information Science

The Atlas of New Librarianship, R. David Lankes, 2011, The MIT Press

The library field is searching for solid footing in an increasingly fragmented (and increasingly digital) information environment. Lankes describes a new librarianship based not on books and artifacts, but on knowledge and learning; and he suggests a new mission for librarians: to improve society through facilitating knowledge creation in their communities.

Cybrarian Extraordinaire: Compelling Information Literacy Instruction, Felicia A. Smith, 2011, Libraries Unlimited

Written for every librarian or teacher looking for ways of using active-learning techniques, Smith uses her own experiences to share specific active-learning exercises created to make library instruction more engaging for a wide variety of audiences.

Foundations of Library and Information Science, Third Edition, Richard Rubin, 3rd ed., 2010, Neal-Schuman Publishers

Discussion of the current issues and key technological developments in library and information science. Explores the impact of the World Wide Web. blogs, wikis, and social networks on services, electronic publication including e-books, digital libraries, digital preservation, mass digitization, and digital repositories, and Functional Requirements for Bibliographic Records (FRBR).

Introduction to Information Science and Technology (Asis&T Monograph), Charles H. Davis and Debora Shaw, 2011, Information Today, Inc.

Account of the fundamental issues, with history and theory. Topics include information needs, seeking, and use; representation and organization of information; computers and networks; structured information systems; information systems applications; users perspectives in information systems; social informatics; communication using information technologies; information policy; and the information profession.

Libraries in the Information Age: An Introduction and Career Exploration (Library and Information Science Text Series), Denise K. Fourie and David R. Dowell, 2nd ed., 2009, Libraries Unlimited

Overview of libraries in the era of electronic information. History of libraries, job opportunities, collections, preparing materials for use, circulation, reference service, ethics in the information age, job search basics, and the Internet. References and relevant books, Web sites, and publications at the end of every chapter point to further resources.

Library Services for Children and Young Adults: Challenges and Opportunities in the Digital Age, Carolynn Rankin and Avril Brock, 2012, Facet Publishing

A one-stop resource for working with today's children and young adults. Five sections cover the range of youth librarianship: providing services, keeping up with technology, face-to-face and virtual reference, connecting with users, and evaluating current practices to plan for the future. It contains scenarios, advice, and strategies for innovation and success.

Mid-Career Library and Information Professionals: A Leadership Primer (Chandos Information Professional Series) Dawn Lowe-Wincentsen and Linda Crook), 2011, Chandos Publishing (Oxford) Ltd

Advice on how to become a leader in library and information science during the middle of your career and how to achieve success in the workplace. In addition to tips and tools on leadership, you will find perspectives from others in the field who have advanced to leadership positions, and learn how to make your own career development plan.

The New Information Professional: Your Guide to Careers in the Digital Age, Judy Lawson, et al., 2010, Neal-Schuman Publishers

Covers the opportunities in eight core information fields, including: archives and preservation management, human computer interaction, information analysis and retrieval, information management, information policy, library and information services, records management, and social computing. Chapters are organized by field, and each includes a description, real world profile, education and training programs, sample job titles, illustrated career maps, and online resources for additional exploration.

Reference and Information Services in the 21st Century: An Introduction, Kay Ann Cassell and Uma Hiremath, 2nd ed., 2009, Neal-Schuman Publishers

An updated handbook of library reference work in the U.S. today. A companion Web site (**www.neal-schuman.com/reference21st2nd**) keeps the content up-to-date.

So You Want To Be a Librarian, Lauren Pressley, 2009, Library Juice Press

Answers questions such as: What do librarians do? What are the different types of libraries and professional jobs? What are librarians all about and what hot issues do they discuss in their professional lives? What do I do to become a librarian? What are some important things to know once I'm in a master's program in library science?

What Do Employers Want?: A Guide for Library Science Students, Priscilla K. Shontz and Richard A. Murray, 2012, Libraries Unlimited

For students currently in MLS programs, as well as grads, regardless of what kind of work environment they wish to work in. Guides readers through planning a job search step-by-step in two sections: considering someone's experience and conducting the job search.

What They Don't Teach You in Library School
Elisabeth Doucett, 2010, American Library Association

Practical advice and wisdom that remains between the lines of most library curriculum, while also teaching seasoned professionals a thing or two. Covers library topics relevant to the day-to-day job, such as management, administration, and marketing. Shows how to further a career by using business and organizational skills.

American Association of Law Libraries
www.aallnet.org

Information on the profession, professional development workshops offered by AALL and other organizations, jobs, and other resources.

The American Public Library Handbook, Guy A.
Marco, 2011, Libraries Unlimited

Focuses on all aspects of the American public library experience, providing a topical perspective through comprehensive essays and biographical information on important public librarians. Comprises nearly 1,000 entries addressing all aspects of public library service.

The Library List: Complete Contact Info for All
U.S. Public Libraries, 2010, BearManor Media

Complete contact information for all 50 states is inside, with addresses, links, emails, fax numbers-plus comments from the librarians themselves and why and how they make their book buying decisions.

Libraries of America: a Directory, Robert Charles
Bradley, 2010, Kindle ed., Broad Lea/Amazon Digital

Lists over 17,000 local libraries in all 50 states and D.C., and provides addresses, telephone numbers, and library statistics, including the number of books, periodicals, Internet terminals and even the number of librarians and staff. The book was compiled using the latest data available from Federal sources, and relies on library survey responses.

Strategies for Librarians
www.liscareer.com

An online collection of practical career articles written by information professionals around the world. Lists articles, a wide variety of books about careers for librarians, and LIScareer Consulting Services—for MLS students or new librarians who would like personalized, confidential career advice from an experienced librarian.

World Guide to Library, Archive, and Information Science Associations (3rd Completely Revised Edition), (Ifla Publications), Alexandra Meinhold, 2010, De Gruyter

Associations concerned with the fields of librarianship, documentation, information science and archives. The third, completely revised and expanded edition contains over 600 comprehensive and updated entries from over 130 countries.

Manufacturing

The 12 Principles of Manufacturing Excellence: A Leader's Guide to Achieving and Sustaining Excellence, Larry E. Fast, 2011, Productivity Press; Har/Com edition

A comprehensive, proven approach for delivering world-class performance while cultivating the right culture through leadership and mentoring.

How to Land a Top-Paying Industrial Engineer Machinery Manufacturing Services Job: Your Complete Guide to Opportunities, Resumes and Cover Letters, … What to Expect From Recruiters and More!, Brad Andrews, 2010, EMEREO PTY LTD

Compiles all the information candidates need to apply for their first Industrial Engineer Machinery Manufacturing Services job, or to apply for a better job. Helpful worksheets make it easier to write about a work experience.

Real-Resumes for Manufacturing Jobs, Anne McKinney, 2012, CreateSpace Independent Publishing Platform

Has resumes showing jobs such as machine operator, product design director, production foreman, quality engineer, shipping and receiving manager, tool and die maker, tire builder, welder, team leader, assembler, maintenance supervisor, and many other jobs.

Resume Writing for Manufacturing Careers: The Only 'How To' Guide You Need to Impress Hiring Managers and Get More Interviews, Gary Capone, 2010, CreateSpace Independent Publishing Platform

Customized to the needs of manufacturing professionals, with detailed examples, all tailored to manufacturing careers. Step-by-step example, showing the resume writing process of a hypothetic manufacturing professional. The Resume Assessment shows you how to assess your finished resume. Each of the 30 assessment steps includes a short best practice explanation.

Career Launcher: Manufacturing, 2011, Ferguson Publishing Company

Breakdown of jobs, as well as tips for success, a history of manufacturing, and an overview of the state of jobs in the field today. For recent graduates or seasoned workers. An index, further resources, and helpful boxed features.

Careers in Focus: Manufacturing, 3rd ed., 2010, Facts on File

Covers 21 jobs in this field.

Top Careers in Two Years: Manufacturing and Transportation, 2010, Facts on File

Covers popular careers in the field for students with an associate's degree, comparable certification, and work/life experience.

Manufacturing & Distribution USA, 2010, Gale

Statistics on more than 600 NAICS classifications in the manufacturing, wholesaling and retail industries, compiled from the most recent government publications and includes projections, maps and graphics. More than 30,000 companies are listed with contact information and sales figures. Also included are overviews of 450 distinct industries. Industry sales information, employment figures, payroll, establishment counts, and materials consumed, among others.

Directory Of US Companies, Online, Hoover's
www.hoovers.com/company_directory

Comprises 65,000,000 companies, 85,000,000 people. Search by industry, location & more.

Encyclopedia of American Industries, 6th ed., 2011, Gale
www.gale.cengage.com

Detailed, comprehensive information on a range of industries in every realm of American business. More than 1,000 detailed profiles of the manufacturing and service industries. Volume 1 covers of more than 460 manufacturing industries. Volume 2 presents more than 540 essays on the service and non-manufacturing industries.

Manufacturers' News, Inc.,
Online, Print and CD-ROM
www.manufacturersnews.com

Publisher of state manufacturers directories and databases. Products include: **State Manufacturers Directories and Databases; National Manufacturers Databases by Industry and Metro Area; and International Directories & Databases.**

Manufacturers Resources, National Association of Manufacturers
www.nam.org

NAM offers a variety of manufacturers resources. These range from economic statistics and manufacturing industry data, to the analysis of recent manufacturing-related court cases and policy issue one-pagers.

Reference for Business, Advameg, Inc., Online
www.referenceforbusiness.com

Free online databases: **Encyclopedia of Small Business** is a comprehensive reference for entrepreneurs that demand practical information. Small business owners can browse over the 600 articles that detail information about financial planning, market analysis, sales, business plans, tax planning, human resource issues and more.

Business Biographies contain biographical information of industry leaders worldwide. Over 600 in-depth essays that cover each individual's biographical information, career paths, achievements, leadership strategies and management styles. **Business Plans** section is composed of actual business plans written by entrepreneurs in North America who are seeking financing for their business. Resource for anybody needing examples on how to structure, compose, and write their own business plans.

Encyclopedia of American Industries is a comprehensive guide to industries in every realm of American business. We cover 459 manufacturing industries, and have over 500 essays about non-manufacturing and service industries.

ThomasNet.com
www.thomasnet.com

Among its products are: **Supplier Discovery**—Find over 610,000 qualified manufacturers, distributors, MRO providers and custom manufacturers. **Product Sourcing**—Source over 100 million products with new parametric search technology powered by an engineer-built classification system. **Product News**—Stay informed with this comprehensive collection of innovative products.

Nonprofit

Career Launcher-Nonprofit Organizations, 2011, Ferguson Publishing Company

Featuring behind-the-scenes information, including an overview of the current state of nonprofits, available careers, tips, and fast facts, this resource covers the full scope of this industry and is ideal to jump-start a career.

Careers in Focus—Nonprofit Organizations, 2010, Facts on File

Has 20 career profiles for compassionate job seekers.

Fundraising as a Career: What, Are You Crazy?, Linda Lysakowski, 2010, CharityChannel LLC

Intro to the nonprofit world. Details career options; helps you develop the qualities that will make you a great fundraiser; hints on how to transition into development and how to get started on the right foot once you do; and more.

How To Become A Nonprofit Rockstar: 50 Ways To Accelerate Your Career, Trista Harris and Rosetta Thurman, 2011, lulu.com

A DIY map of how to navigate the nonprofit sector, with the tools to move from entry level to leadership. Walks you through career options; helps develop the qualities to make you a great fundraiser; hints on how to transition into development and how to get started on the right foot once you do; and more.

The Idealist Guide to Nonprofit Careers for First-time Job Seekers, Meg Busse and Steven Joiner, 2010, Hundreds of Heads Books

A comprehensive resource for emerging professionals pursuing their first position. Whether you are a current student, a recent graduate, or someone entering the workforce for the first time, this book will provide you with advice, relevant strategies, and nonprofit-specific resources to strengthen your job search.

The Idealist Guide to Nonprofit Careers for Sector Switchers, Steven Joiner and Meg Busse, 2010, Hundreds of Heads Books

Resource for transitioning professionals pursuing new career options in the nonprofit sector. Advice, relevant strategies, and nonprofit-specific resources. If you are a "mid-career transitioner," a "re-careerer," an "encore careerist," a "bridger," or a "sector switcher" this book is meant for you.

Real-Resumes for Jobs in Nonprofit Organizations, Anne McKinney, 2012, CreateSpace Independent Publishing Platform

Shows resumes and cover letters that worked for real people. Newcomers will learn how to enter the field, and experienced professionals will find help in advancing to choice jobs. Nonprofit professionals often change fields, too, and the book includes resumes of individuals who have successfully transitioned into other areas.

2011 Grantmakers Salary and Benefits Report-Key Findings and Salary Tables, Council on Foundations
www.cof.org

Presents 2011 salaries and compensation trends over a wide range of positions and grantmaking entities-community foundations, private foundations (family and independent), public foundations, and corporate grantmakers.

Foundation Directory Online, **Foundation Center**
www.fconline.foundationcenter.org

Online funding research tool, updated daily. This website has over 108,000 U.S. foundations and corporate donors, over 3 million recent grants, and over half a million key decision makers.

GuideStar
www.guidestar.org

Information about nonprofits. Included in a variety of products are: **GuideStar Premium**— search for individuals by name to find their titles, compensation, and the organizations they are connected with; **GuideStar Nonprofit Compensation Report**—detailed salary ranges and percentile analyses by job category, program area, gender, and geography.

2011 GuideStar Directory of Nonprofit Contractors—compiled from the IRS Forms 990 nonprofits filed for fiscal year 2009, the report lists: 13,000 businesses that provided services to 14,000-plus nonprofits, for a total of $34 billion.

Idealist
www.idealist.org
Connects people, organizations, and resources. Idealist is independent of any government, political ideology, or religious creed. Our work is guided by the common desire of our members and supporters to find practical solutions to social and environmental problems, in a spirit of generosity and mutual respect.

Leadership in Nonprofit Organizations: A Reference Handbook, 2010, Sage Publications
Engages voices on important issues and leadership topics. A major focus of this two-volume reference work is on the specific roles and skills required of the nonprofit leader in voluntary organizations.

National Directory of Nonprofit Organizations, Bohdan R. Romaniuk, ed. 27, 2012, Print and eBook, Taft Group
Provides names, addresses, and annual income figures of more than 260,000 organizations, 180,120 of which have incomes in excess of $100,000. In addition, phone numbers are provided for 100% of listees in the print version. Entries in both volumes cover all 22 of the U.S. Internal Revenue Service 501(c) subsections, as well as IRS sections 501(e), 501(k), and 4947(a)(2), as provided for in the 1954 Internal Revenue Code.

Nursing

201 Careers in Nursing, Joyce Fitzpatrick PhD MBA RN FAAN and Emerson E. Ea DNP APRN-BC CEN, 2011
Career descriptions include educational requirements, core competencies, and required skills. Provides compensation range per degree, certification requirements, and earnings potential for each career.

Advancing Your Career: Concepts in Professional Nursing by Rose Kearney-Nunnery, 5th ed., 2012, F.A. Davis Company
Covers the concepts needed to progress from RN to BSN and beyond. Encourages practicing nurses to master the theories that are changing nursing.

Becoming A Nursing Assistant: Enjoy The Extensive Rewards Of A Certified Nursing Assistant Career, K M S Publishing.com, 2010, CreateSpace Independent Publishing Platform
It takes an extraordinary individual to take on a nursing assistant position, someone with the amazing skills of compassion, dedication, patience, a genuine sincerity to help others, and excellent communication skills. Learn the real secrets of successful nursing assistants.

Fast Facts for Career Success in Nursing: Making the Most of Mentoring in a Nutshell, Connie Vance, 2010, Springer Publishing Company
Practical advice that is useful for nurses starting out. Career transitions of any kind can be difficult, but when the care of others is included, the value of mentorship increases.

A Man's Guide to a Nursing Career, Chad O'Lynn RN PhD, 2012, Springer Publishing Company
A nuts-and-bolts guide for men. Strategies for dealing with a rigorous nursing curriculum, compounded by potential anti-male sentiment. Also considers the obstacles that may result from cross-gender nursing communication and relationships with a focus on teamwork.

Nurses, Jobs and Money: A Guide to Advancing Your Nursing Career and Salary, Carmen Kosicek RN MSN, 2012, CreateSpace Independent Publishing Platform
Using proven techniques and real-life case studies, this book shows exactly how to plan your career for optimal income and success. Looks at the challenges facing nurses today. With tips, scenarios and step-by-step guides to catapult your career.

Nursing Now: Today's Issues, Tomorrow's Trends, 3rd ed., Joseph T. Catalano, 6th ed., 2011
www.fadavis.com
Examines the issues and trends that are shaping the profession of nursing...now and in the future. The author explores the evolution and history, and examines the impact of reform, the legal system, and politics. New information and updates are posted **online annually** to keep you current.

Nursing Programs 2012 (Peterson's Nursing Programs), Peterson's, 2012, eBook
Guide to undergraduate, graduate, and postdoctoral programs in the U.S. and Canada. Profiles more than

3,500 undergraduate, graduate, and postdoctoral options at more than 700 institutions. Latest data on entrance requirements, costs, degrees offered, distance learning options, and more. Includes in-depth articles about degree and career options.

Nursing Today: Transitions and Trends, JoAnn Zerwekh and J. Ashley Garneau, eds., 7th ed., 2011, Saunders Elsevier, Kaplan Publishing

Helps you make a successful transition from student to practicing nurse. Covers the profession's leading issues and opportunities, ensuring that you graduate with career-development skills, including resume writing, finding a job, and effective interviewing. Test-taking tips and strategies prepare you for the NCLEX-RN exam. Information on nursing issues and trends, including health care reform, patient safety, collective bargaining, and emergency preparedness.

Real-Resumes for Nursing Jobs, Anne McKinney, 2012, CreateSpace Independent Publishing Platform

Shows samples of resumes and cover letters that worked for real people. Includes resumes of nurses who have successfully transitioned into pharmaceutical sales and other areas. Nursing professionals will learn how to maximize their career potential, get federal nursing positions, and change fields if they want to.

Your Career in Nursing, Annette Vallano, 2011, Kaplan Publishing

Advice for nurses at any stage of a career as they face the ever-evolving world of health care. Vallano encourages nurses to take a proactive role in managing their careers, and offers advice on clinical skills, career advancement, and practical business tips for entrepreneurial and freelance nurses.

Healthcare Lists and Databases, SK&A www.skainfo.com

Up-to-date information on the industry, including supplemental information such as ownership, organization size, practice specialty, affiliations and more. Our diverse mix of industry information comes from sources such as: company and corporate directories; websites; state licensing information; professional associations, and more. Databases include: physicians; hospitals; pharmacies; nurses; group practices, and more.

Nurse List, SK&A www.skainfo.com/

Lists of nurses connect you with millions of practicing nurses of all types: 4.1 million RNs; licensed practice nurses (915,000 nurse names), and certified nurses aides (412,000 nurse names).

Nursing Business Opportunities: 2012 Franchise Directory for Nurses, Jim Blankenship, 2012, Kindle ed., NursEtAl! Press

Offers resources to quickly realize the opportunities that are available to you as a franchisee of companies that have proven success and a business plan that you can quickly implement to earn your own success.

Pharmaceutical and Medical Sales

Pharmaceutical Sales

A to Z: How to Break into the Pharmaceutical Industry, Daniel Danielian, 2011, CreateSpace Independent Publishing Platform

Using an easy-to-understand, stepwise process of what it takes to break into the pharmaceutical game, you will emerge victorious with a new understanding of what it takes to break into the industry. Learn how to approach each interview and how to prepare for each interviewer. Learn about detailing, visual aids, physician-representative interactions, pharmacy calls, and formulary discussions; with in-depth analysis.

A Day In The Life: Medical Device Sales And Pharmaceutical Sales, Bill Mitchell, 2011, Kindle ed., Amazon Digital

Take an insider's look at medical device sales and pharmaceuticals sales jobs. What do these representatives do on a daily basis? What is the job like? How is the job performed? What expectations are there and what perks do you receive? Get the answers.

Careers in Pharmaceuticals [Paperback], 2011, WetFeet

Consider the pharmaceutical industry: it's fueled by an aging population; the demand for medications continues to grow both in the U.S. and international markets; and so does demand for skilled professionals in the field. This guide looks at this industry overall, and has information on opportunities in areas from sales and marketing to engineering and research.

Insider's Guide to the World of Pharmaceutical Sales, Jane Williams, 9th ed., 2008, Principle Publications

Contains 196 pages of job interview and selling information, including the enhanced PhRMA Code on Interactions with Healthcare Professionals. A complete pharmaceutical sales interview guide on how to gain a pharmaceutical sales position and then excel at it. Features include: 155 pharmaceutical sales interview questions and answers; 26 top company profiles; list of 300 pharmaceutical companies, and more.

Insight into a Career in Pharmaceutical Sales, Anne Clayton, 10th ann. ed., 2008, Print with 2 audio CDs
www.pharmaceuticalsales.com

Clayton covers how to network to obtain that productive interview that includes specific directions every step of the way. Includes exactly what words to use when networking with a representative. It is not about resumes; it's learning to know people and companies by networking: too much emphasis is put on resumes by candidates. Has over 130 questions and answers used in interviews today; over 50 in-depth company profiles that include the company summary, history, annual sales, more. Two audio CDs duplicate interview questions and recommended answers to raise your interview skills to put you at the top 1% of candidates.

Is a Pharmaceutical Sales Career Right For Me?, C G. Schott, 2010, Kindle ed., Xlibris, Corp./Amazon Digital

Within three years of becoming a sales rep, he was G.D. Searle's national "Rep of the Year." Here Schott presents a workbook for success.

Secrets of Successful Pharmaceutical Salespeople, Sarah Taylor, 2010, Taylor Presentations

Look around and you will notice that a small handful of salespeople get exceptional results, year after year. The pharmaceutical industry is filled with some of the best salespeople in the country, and Sarah Taylor has interviewed many of them, compiling their secrets of success into this book!

CoreyNahman.com
www.coreynahman.com/InternetDrugNews.com

This site provides recent pharmaceutical news and information to lay people, academicians, pharmacists and pharmacy students, and other clinicians and scholars, journalists, policy makers and governmental bodies. Pharmaceutical sales jobs are posted worldwide; drug lists; news; female health. Also contains links to pharmaceutical companies' homepages, profiles, news and message boards.

Major Pharmaceutical & Biotechnology Companies of the World, Layla Comstive, Susan Hoernig and Sue Ward, eds., 15th ed., 2012, Print, Graham & Whiteside

Covers over 4,070 of the world's largest pharmaceutical companies, providing essential business profiles of the international leaders in the industry. Entries typically provide: company name; address; telephone, fax numbers; email and website addresses; names of senior management; and more.

Medical Sales

Breaking into Medical Sales: A Climb to the Top, Drue De Angelis, 2012, Kindle ed., Amazon Digital

De Angelis got hired into medical sales without any previous experience back when he was fresh out of college. This book will provide you the information and the techniques that will enable you to make it happen.

A Day In The Life: Medical Device Sales And Pharmaceutical Sales, Bill Mitchell, 2011, Kindle ed.

An insider's look at what it's like to work in medical device sales and pharmaceutical sales. Mitchell has worked in both sales positions for some of the largest companies in the world, as well as for some smaller ones.

From Pharma to Device Sales—A Pocket Guide for Pharmaceutical Sales People Wanting to Move into Medical Device Sales, Samuel D. Lamptey, 2011, Kindle ed.

This straight-to-the-point pocket guide enables pharmaceutical sales people to move into the medical device sales arena. Are you in pharmaceutical sales and are looking to cross over? Wondering what selling medical devices is really like? Do you know the vital differences between selling drugs and devices? Here are all the answers and much more.

How To Get A Medical Device Sales Job: Your best resource to learn the secrets of landing a career in the lucrative medical device sales field, Daniel Riley, 2011, CreateSpace Independent Publishing Platform

Medical device sales jobs are the best-kept secret in business. These jobs generate six figure incomes, are incredibly fun, and are professionally rewarding. Here's how to obtain you first medical device sales job by using the keys and secrets here.

How To Land A High Paying Medical Device Job: An insiders guide to interviewing for a medical device position, Pat Racanelli and Jason Reif,, 2009, CreateSpace Independent Publishing Platform

Interviewing for a medical job and interviewing in general.

Mastering Medical Sales—The Essential Attitudes, Habits & Skills of High-earning Medical Sales Professionals, Mace Horoff, 2010, Healthcare Business Books

A real-world guide to succeeding in the competitive and lucrative world of professional medical sales. The secret to success in medical sales is not just one behavior or idea, but a collection of attitudes, habits, and skills that have been internalized by almost every high-earning medical sales professional.

Medical Device Marketing: Strategies, Gameplans & Resources for Successful Product Management, Terri Wells, 2010, Outskirts Press

You'll learn: how to identify the customer-and why this seemingly simple task is trickier than it sounds; steps to a winning business plan—from conducting insightful market research to making accurate cost projections; keys to product development—along with what to do when the unexpected happens; effective sales support—including what you really need to know about how every sales team operates; and more.

The Healthcare Sales & Marketing Network salesandmarketingnetwork.com

Resources for those in sales, marketing or business development professional in medical devices, pharmaceuticals or biotechnology, including persons who want to enter these fields. Whatever your present

role—field sales, independent sales rep, distributor or senior management—The Network is a repository of continuously updated news and industry data. The site can connect manufacturers and sales management with independent Sales Reps and distributorss.

Top Dog Medical Directory www.topdogmedicalsales.com/directory

This online resource is a human-edited index of medical and medical related websites that helps your site to gain higher search engine results. We accept only medical related websites with topics including allergists, alternative medicine, capital equipment sales, health insurance, medical jobs and employment resources and other healthcare related subjects. All websites are family friendly and organized by category.

Public Relations and Integrated Marketing Communications

Advertising and Promotion: An Integrated Marketing Communications Perspective, George Belch and Michael Belch, 9th ed., 2011, McGraw-Hill/ Irwin

To best communicate with consumers, advertisers must use many tools (advertising, public relations, direct marketing, interactive/Internet marketing, sales promotion, and personal selling); this book reflects the shift from the conventional methods of advertising to the more widely recognized approach of implementing an integrated marketing communications strategy.

Advertising and Public Relations (Career Launcher), Stan Tymorek, 2010, Checkmark Books

Behind-the-scenes information readers need to launch a successful career in these fields, including an overview of the current state of the industry, a breakdown of key jobs within advertising and public relations, fast facts, and tips for effective communications and networking.

Becoming a Public Relations Writer: A Writing Workbook for Emerging and Established Media, Ronald D. Smith, 4th ed., 2011, Routledge

Guide to writing for PR. Realistic examples, easy-to-follow steps and practical exercises. Introduces the various and styles of writing you will encounter as a public relations practitioner. Includes writing for multimedia and social media releases, and websites, blogs, and wikis.

Brand Media Strategy: Integrated Communications Planning in the Digital Era (Advertising Age), Antony Young, 2010, Palgrave Macmillan

From YouTube to Facebook to the iPhone, today's media landscape offers more tools and platforms for the savvy marketer than ever before. And with this rapidly evolving technology comes powerful ways to track what's working, what's not, and how to get the maximum impact for your brand in a shrinking economy. Media and brand expert Antony Young explores how today's most innovative marketers are integrating the latest media tools into a comprehensive strategy to grow their brands and are getting unprecedented results

Career Launcher—Advertising and Public Relations, 2011, eBook, Ferguson Publishing Company

Provides information for launching a successful career in these fields. Includes the current state of the industries, key jobs, fast facts, and tips for effective communications and networking. Lists key publications, websites, schools, and training programs.

Careers in Focus—Public Relations, 2010, Facts on File

Covers 17 careers in this growing field.

Cengage Advantage Books: This is PR: The Realities of Public Relations (Wadsworth Series in Mass Communication and Journalism), Doug Newsom, et al., 2012

For the beginning student or the experienced public relations practitioner. An emphasis on fundamentals, such as history and research, as well as emerging issues such as technology, ethics, and the international aspects.

The Handbook of Strategic Public Relations and Integrated Marketing Communications, Clarke Caywood, 2nd ed., 2011, McGraw-Hill

A comprehensive resource, The Handbook is a gathering of 70 of the brightest, most influential figures in the field. It includes 27 new chapters, as well as 44 new authors addressing the major changes in the field since the last edition: the use of social media in business, demanding and growing stakeholder relationships and a new era of openness and transparency to protect reputations and brands and to prevent crises.

How to Land a Top-Paying Public relations specialists Job: Your Complete Guide to Opportunities, Resumes and Cover Letters, Interviews, Salaries, Promotions, What to Expect From Recruiters and More, Ann Lindsey, 2012, tebbo

Helpful worksheets make it much easier to write about a job, using these outlines. Ensures that the narrative follows a logical structure and important points are included. Cheat sheets help get your career organized in a tidy, presentable fashion.

Marketing in the Round: How to Develop an Integrated Marketing Campaign in the Digital Era (Que Biz-Tech), Gini Dietrich and Geoff Livingston, 2012, Que Publishing

Demolish your silos and sync all your messaging, strategies, and tactics). Optimize every media platform, from iPad and Facebook to TV and direct. Here's a stepwise guide on strategy, tactics, research, metrics, and more.

Cision (formerly Bacon's)
us.cision.com

Cision's PR software and services get you out in front of the story. Plan targeted campaigns. Connect with the right audience. Monitor coverage globally. Analyze results quickly. All delivered through CisionPoint-the on-demand PR software solution.

Cison maintains traditional **Media Database—**-Get access to the world's largest database of media contacts with all of the information you need to uncover the influencers that matter. Who to contact. What to pitch. When to call. And when not to call.

Bacon's Media Directories, annual, the year listing in the title changes every year— Media Directory: Newspaper/Magazine 2012 Edition, Media Directory: Radio/TV/Cable 2012 Edition, as well as Media Directory: Metro California 2012 Edition, and Media Directory: New York 2012 Edition.

2012 O'Dwyer's Directory of PR Firms, annual, Print and Database, O'Dwyer's
www.odwyerpr.com

A directory of PR firms. The 2012 edition contains listings of 1,600 firms in the U.S. and abroad. The directory's exclusive cross-client index is where you can look up a company and determine its outside PR counsel.

O'Dwyer's supplies news of PR and marketing communications. The company also has newsletters, blogs, product listings. Other key resources include:

Public Relations Associations, Clubs & Societies—links to the homepages of these organizations. **O'Dwyer's PR Buyer's Guide, annual, Online**—everything from Annual Reports/Design to Website Development.

Online Public Relations
www.online-pr.com
Online links to media, reference and PR resource sites. Also: **Marketing and PR Sources On-line (www.online-pr.com/markpr.htm)**—lsinks to PR/ marketing directories, U.S. and international associations, plus blogs, and more.

PR.com
www.pr.com
Links to PR agency profiles, and more. Directory of businesses, products and services, a press release distribution service, job search website, and online publication of articles, reviews and celebrity interviews.

PR Media Directories
www.aboutpublicrelations.net/mediadir.htm
Links to media directories for print and broadcast outlets. Search for local, national, and international media markets. Career guides, plus articles, books, news.

Publishing and Writing, including Freelancing

(*see the listing for* Journalism *as many of the career options apply to both*)

102 Ways to Earn Money Writing 1,500 Words or Less: The Ultimate Freelancer's Guide, I.J. Schecter, 2010, Writer's Digest Books
Insider's guide to an often-complex arena, that gives freelancers the knowledge, confidence, and inspiration to recognize, and make the most of, all the opportunities before them.

The Art of Making Magazines: On Being an Editor and Other Views from the Industry (Columbia Journalism Review Books), Victor S. Navasky and Evan Cornog, 2012, Columbia Journalism Review Books
Editors, writers, art directors, and publishers from such magazines as *Vanity Fair, The New Yorker,* and *Harper's* draw on their experiences to explore a range of issues concerning their profession.

Careers in Focus—Publishing, 3rd ed., 2010, eBook, Facts on File
Covers 20 jobs in the exciting field of publishing.

How to Actually Make Money Writing, Jim Brumm, 2012, Kindle ed., Full Moon Publishing/ Amazon Digital
Stepwise method for writing business profiles, which are articles businesses use to market their products or services—a marketing tool, conceived by the author. Such profiles help businesses gain customers by building trust through the telling of their personal story. Writers can create their own jobs and earn a steady income producing business profiles.

How to Make, Market and Sell Ebooks—All for FREE: Ebooksuccess4free, Jason Matthews, 2010, CreateSpace Independent Publishing Platform
eBooks and the devices that read them are the fastest growing sectors in publishing. Learn how to: build and maximize an online platform; use social media wisely with Facebook, Google Plus, Twitter, LinkedIn, YouTube, etc.; design effective eBook covers; format and upload for Amazon, Smashwords, Barnes & Noble, Apple's iBookstore plus other retailers; and more.

How to Write & Sell Simple Information for Fun and Profit: Your Guide to Writing and Publishing Books, E-Books, Articles, Special Reports, Audio Programs, DVDs, and Other How-To Content, Robert W. Bly, 2010, Linden Publishing
Here are Bly's income-generating ideas on creating a variety of saleable written works, with information for researching and writing effective materials, and calling upon a variety of publishing channels, including magazines, traditional book publishers, self-publishing, and the Internet.

Jeff Herman's Guide to Book Publishers, Editors, and Literary Agents, Jeff Herman 2011, 21st ed., Sourcebooks
Gets you past the slush piles and into the right hands. Names and contact information for hundreds of agents and editors, and how to win them over. Insider information to help you get published, plus a guide to writing pitch letters and proposals.

Starting Your Career as a Freelance Editor: A

Guide to Working with Authors, Books, Newsletters, Magazines, Websites, and More, Mary Embree, 2012, Allworth Press

Learn about the requirements in various fields, how to get started, setting up and conducting your services, working with writers and publishers, promoting yourself and your expertise, and determining what to charge. Markets also include articles, dissertations, brochures, reports, editorials, ad copy, and much more.

Starting Your Career as a Freelance Writer, Moira Anderson Allen, 2nd ed., 2011, Allworth Press

Includes a section on the "online writer," covering how to set up your own website, decide whether you need a blog, how to effectively participate in social networking sites, and information on electronic publishing, POD and more.

2013 Guide To Literary Agents, Chuck Sambuchino, ed., annual, Writers Digest Books

Completely updated contact and submission information for more than 1,000 literary agents seeking new clients. Has business and career advice. Includes profiles on literary reps actively building their client list right now.

Literary Market Place 2012: The Directory of the American Book Publishing Industry with Industry Yellow Pages, (LMP), Karen Hallard, Mary-Anne Lutter and Vivian Sposobiec, 2011, annual, Information Today Inc.

The Directory of the American book publishing industry with Industry Yellow Pages, in a two-volume set.

2013 Novel & Short Story Writer's Market, Scott Francis, ed., 2012, annual, Writer's Digest Books

For fiction writers to get their short stories, novellas, and novels published. Offers hundreds of listings for book publishers, literary agents, fiction publications, contests and more. Each listing includes contact information, submission guidelines, and important tips.

2013 Writer's Market, Robert Lee Brewer, annual, Writers Digest Books

Publishing opportunities for writers, including book publishers, consumer and trade magazines, contests and awards, and literary agents; with contact and submission information. Also includes material on the business of writing; plus there's a pay rate chart to see what you can charge. The **2013 Writer's Market Deluxe Edition (Writer's Market Online)**

also lists of professional writing organizations, has sample query letters, and affords a one-year free subscription to **WritersMarket.com.**

Cision (formerly Bacon's)
us.cision.com

Traditional Media Contacts— Database of media contacts. Who to contact. What to pitch. When to call. And when not to call.

Social Media Contacts— Find the digital influencers who make a difference. With Cision Influence Rating as a guide, gain insight about digital influencers.

Editorial Calendars— Search hundreds of thousands of editorial calendars, events and trade show opportunities by industry, geography, outlet, deadline date.

American Book Trade Directory, 58th ed., 2012-2013, Beverley McDonough and Daniel Bazikian, Information Today

Brings together more than 20,000 booksellers, over 800 wholesalers, and hundreds of book-trade service providers and resources from across the U.S. and Canada in one reference tool. Organized geographically, entries include store or company size, specialties, years in business, owner and key personnel, contact information.

Oxbridge Communications
www.oxbridge.com

One of the largest databases of U.S. and Canadian periodicals and catalogs, more than 70,000 titles. All information is online at **MediaFinder database**. Plus **print directories: The Standard Periodical Directory, Oxbridge Directory of Newsletters, National Directory of Catalogs, and the National Directory of Magazines.**

Authorlink
authorlink.monster.com

Online news, information, and marketing service for editors, agents, producers, writers, and readers. Many sections of the site are free.

Media Bistro
www.mediabistro.com

For anyone who creates or works with content, or who is a non-creative professional working in a content/creative industry. Provides opportunities to meet, share resources, become informed of job opportunities and interesting projects and news, improve career skills, and showcase your work.

Real Estate

6 Steps to 7 Figures: A Real Estate Professional's Guide to Building Wealth and Creating Your Own Destiny, Pat Hiban, 2011, Greenleaf Book Group Press

Including a 7-Figure Game Plan at the end of each chapter and an appendix of helpful forms and worksheets, Hiban's book contains all that the tactics that the best real estate agents use to build and promote their businesses. Shows you how you can live the life of your dreams.

Career Opportunities in Real Estate, 2010, eBook, Facts on File

Featuring more than 70 job profiles, this book is a comprehensive resource that spans five categories: real estate sales and leasing, real estate lending, property management, property development, and real estate acquisitions and analysis.

The Honest Real Estate Agent: A Training Guide For a Successful First Year and Beyond as a Real Estate Agent, Mario Jannatpour, 2011, CreateSpace Independent Publishing Platform

Find out what today's buyers and sellers are looking for in their real estate agent, plus containing relevant information, as well as insights to handle different situations.

Less Blah Blah, More Ah Ha: How Social Savvy Real Estate Agents Become Trusted, Preferred, Referred—and Rewarded, Ken Brand, 2011, Less Blah Blah. More Ah Ha.

The strategies in this book will contribute to your ongoing curiosity and desire to excel mentally, creatively, and professionally. Some new ways of thinking and acting that will help catapult you to higher, more tangibly rewarding levels of success

Your First Year in Real Estate, 2nd Ed.: Making the Transition from Total Novice to Successful Professional, Dirk Zeller, 2010, Three Rivers Press

Proven secrets and strategies to enable novices to excel from day one. Guide to: selecting the right company; developing mentor/client relationships; using

the Internet and social networking; setting—and reaching essential career goals; and more.

DirectoryRealEstateAgent.com Online
www.directoryrealestateagent.com

U.S, and international real estate. Find real estate agents or brokers in your region, commercial and residential real estate listings and classifieds, for sale by owner properties and U.S. timeshare, and more.

Real Estate Directory
www.justrealestate.org

A real estate directory with more than 35,000 companies listed from all over the world, updated every month.

U.S. Real Estate Register
www.usrealestateregister.com

Helps real estate, financial, economic/industrial development and corporate real estate executives find the sites, properties and services they need.

CommercialRealEstateDirect.com
www.crenews.com

The only source, in print or otherwise, that keeps close tabs on the entire real-estate capital markets industry. Market intelligence on the mortgage business, equity raising, investment sales and CMBS. The **Property Sales Database**, details more than 4,000 large property transactions; **CMBS Pricing Matrix**, is a weekly pricing survey and the **CMBS Pipeline**, is a calendar of upcoming transactions with historical pricing information. By subscription.

ibsTeam Real Estate Directory
www.ibsteam.net

State-by-state listings of agents and agencies, news, Q&As, new business.

Institute of Real Estate Management, Online Member Directory
www.irem.org

Quick and advanced searches for nonmembers. Site contains news, discussions, conferences, publications and more.

REALS.com Online
www.reals.com

Offers links to a great number of sites and information to real estate related sites. Links include agents & brokers, finance & mortgage, foreclosures, law, property management, construction, and many more.

Retailing

Career Opportunities in the Retail and Wholesale Industry, Shelly Field and John R. Sohigian, 2009, Ferguson Publishing Company

Profiles more than 80 careers in retail and sales. Broken down into key sections—Malls and Shopping Centers; Stores, Shops, and Boutiques; Department Stores; and Automobile Sales. Each entry provides a job overview and description of a likely career path.

How to Start a Home-based Online Retail Business, Nicole Augenti, 2nd ed., 2011, Globe Pequot

Everything you need to know to run a profitable and satisfying online retail business from your home.

Opportunities in Retailing Careers, Roslyn Dolber, 2008, McGraw-Hill

More than 100 opportunities for students and job seekers.

Retail Customer Service Fundamentals, Dianne Miethner, 2010, Kindle ed., DMSRetail/Amazon Digital

For those new to retail customer service and for those who are trying to get a job in the retail or restaurant industries. What to do, what not to do, how to behave in certain situations.

Retail Sales & Customer Service—Volume 1: Getting Retail Service Right!, Carlo Santoro and Carlo G Santoro, 2012, CreateSpace Independent Publishing Platform

Explores the importance of sales and good customer service and outlines the basic principles of sales. Gaining knowledge of these principles and concepts before venturing out will not only make the job easier, but will also lay a foundation for your career.

Retail Truths: The Unconventional Wisdom of Retailing, Chip Averwater, 2012, ABB Press

427 lessons retailers learn the hard way. A compendium of street-smart retailing insights and acumen. Not academic theory—just hard-nosed realities shrewd retailers discover through experience and use to build profitable stores.

Retailing, Patrick M. Dunne, et al., 7th ed., 2010, South-Western College/West

Puts students on the inside track to success. Covers the latest developments and details behind-the-scenes stories. Emphasizes the impact of technology and the Internet. Has exercises on problems small-business managers and owners face daily.

Smart Retail: Practical Winning Ideas and Strategies from the Most Successful Retailers in the World, Richard Hammond, 2012, FT Press

A guide to retail success, with crucial, up-to-date insights—including case studies, ideas, strategies, and tactics from today's best retailers, like TopShop, IKEA, and Best Buy. Learn from past retail pioneers, use data to drive profits and growth, do more with less, use new technology to build store teams.

Retail Tenants Online www.retailtenants.com

An online subscription-based publication that lists information on over 6,000 active retail chains in the U.S. and Canada. Contact information, plus a listing of over 25,000 retail executives.

Sales and Marketing

(*See also* Advertising, including Graphic Art and Design *and* Public Relations and Integrated Marketing Communications)

The Accidental Salesperson: How to Take Control of Your Sales Career and Earn the Respect and Income You Deserve, Chris Lytle, 2nd ed., 2012, AMACOM

Updated to reflect changes in the marketplace, and provides a roadmap to excel in sales. Offers money-generating strategies, humorous yet instructive anecdotes, thought-provoking axioms, and powerful tools. Includes guidance on: selling to people who don't have time to meet; and differentiating between information seekers and genuine prospects. Explains using social media and other online tools; building relationships competitors can't steal.

Advertising, Sales, and Marketing, 2010, Facts on File

For professionals looking for a career change into the fields of advertising, sales, and marketing. Provides insight on how to change careers and features interviews with professionals, as well as self-assessment. Identifies skills or qualities needed to succeed; also has lists of further information, plus trade organizations.

Careers in Marketing— WetFeet Insider Guide, 2011, WetFeet

Turn to this guide to explore: the current hiring climate and typical career paths for marketing professionals; which industries offer the most promising opportunities for marketing candidates; what marketing professionals—from associates to directors—really do; recent trends in the field and their potential impact on job seekers; how social media has transformed reaching and communicating with target audiences; and the lifestyle, hours, and compensation you can expect from a career in this field.

Free Marketing: 101 Low and No-Cost Ways to Grow Your Business, Online and Off, Jim Cockrum, 2011, Wiley

Delivers more than 100 ideas to help any small business owner or marketer generate new revenue—with little or no marketing budget, using both Internet-based and creative offline ideas.

The New Rules of Marketing & PR: How to Use Social Media, Online Video, Mobile Applications, Blogs, News Releases, and Viral Marketing to Reach Buyers Directly, David Meerman Scott, 3rd ed., 2011, Wiley

Business communication has changed. Creative ad copy is no longer enough. This book will bring you up to speed on the changing requirements of promoting products or services in the new digital age. Here's a stepwise action plan for using the Internet to communicate with buyers directly, raise online visibility, and increase sales.

The New Rules of Marketing & PR: How to Use Social Media, Online Video, Mobile Applications, Blogs, News Releases, and Viral Marketing to Reach Buyers Directly, David Meerman Scott, 3rd ed., 2011, Wiley

Business communication has changed. Creative ad copy is no longer enough. This book will bring you up to speed on the changing requirements of promoting products or services in the new digital age. Here's a stepwise action plan for using the Internet to communicate with buyers directly, raise online visibility, and increase sales.

Piece of the Fame: Rockstar Social Media Marketing Strategy for Everyone to Ignite Your Business, Career and Personal Brand, Jaunique A Sealey, 2012, Inkspiration Press

Ultimate insider's view into successful thinking around brand building, leveraging social media and digital platforms to increase your network, influence, reputation, and revenue.

Successful Marketing Plans In a Week A Teach Yourself Guide, Ros Jay and John Sealey, 2012, McGraw-Hill

Teaches you the insider secrets you need to know to create a successful marketing plan. seven straightforward chapters explaining the key points, plus optional questions to ensure you have taken it all in.

Top Careers in Two Years—Retail, Marketing, and Sales, 2010, Facts on File

Geared towards high school grads with an interest in retail, marketing, and sales, this book explores a variety of careers for those with two-year degrees.

Up Your Sales in a Down Market: 20 Strategies From Top Performing Salespeople to Win Over Cautious Customers, Ron Volper, 2011, Career Press

Offers 20 clearly defined selling strategies, plus hundreds of examples and sample dialogs that teach salespeople and sales managers exactly how to: win over cautious customers even in a down market; overcome customer fears and objections so they are ready to buy; avoid and bounce back from a sales slump; and more.

Successful Marketing Plans In a Week A Teach Yourself Guide, Ros Jay and John Sealey, 2012, McGraw-Hill

Teaches you the insider secrets you need to know to create a successful marketing plan. seven straightforward chapters explaining the key points, plus optional questions to ensure you have taken it all in.

Workplace Skills: Marketing, Sales, and Service, 2011, McGraw-Hill

Career information and skills practice to help explore and prepare for these careers. Explores career pathways and jobs, education and training, work environments, and industry trends. Has brief descriptions of current high-growth jobs.

The Zen of Social Media Marketing: An Easier Way to Build Credibility, Generate Buzz, and Increase Revenue: 2012 Edition, Shama Kabani, Chris Brogan (foreword), 2nd ed., 2012, BenBella Books

Social media is a crucial tool for success in business. People are already talking about your business using social media, whether you're using it or not. Kabani teaches you the "zen" of social media marketing: how to access all the benefits of social media marketing without the stress.

Green Book
www.greenbook.org
GreenBook Volume I—Worldwide Directory of Marketing Research Companies and Services

Comprised of over 400 research categories, cross-referenced indexes permit the listed companies to highlight the marketing research services they offer. Includes Internet/Online providers.

GreenBook Volume II—Worldwide Directory of Focus Group Companies and Services

Cross-referenced indexes highlight focus group facilities and qualitative research services such as recruiting, moderating, videoconferencing, Internet broadcasting, usability testing, etc.

www.greenbook.org—The website accesses the entire directory in a user-friendly and interactive format.

Sales Marketing Directory
www.salesmarketingdirectory.com/

Directories provide listings of tens of thousands of businesses across hundreds of categories worldwide. Buyers: browse to find companies. Each company listing now includes a tab describing what the company is doing for the environment. Companies can list for free.

Satellites

Down to Earth: Satellite Technologies, Industries, and Cultures (New Directions in International Studies), Lisa Parks and James Schwoch eds., 2012, Rutgers University Press

A comprehensive overview of the geopolitical maneuvers, financial investments, technological innovations, and ideological struggles that take place behind the scenes of the satellite industry.

Liftoff: Careers in Satellite, the World's First and Most Successful Space Industry (Volume 2), Daniel Fryer, et al., 2012, CreateSpace Independent Publishing Platform

Learn about the industry, the kind of careers it offers, the qualifications required, and the best ways to get a career started.

Satellite Communications (SpringerBriefs in Space Development), Joseph N. Pelton, 2012, Springer

Covers the fundamentals of satellite communications, its technology, operations, business, and economic & regulatory aspects, with key insights into the field's future growth trends and current strategic challenges.

Smaller Satellites: Bigger Business?: Concepts, Applications and Markets for Micro/Nanosatellites in a New Information World (Space Studies), Michael J. Rycroft and Norma Crosby, eds., 2010, Springer

Proc. of Symposium's broad-ranging theme is analyzed and discussed from many viewpoints—engineering, science, policy, law, business, finance and management. Different ways in which small satellites may create larger business opportunities are examined, ranging from telecommunications systems to Earth observation applications and technology demonstrators.

Calendar Of Satellite Events
www.satnews.com/calendar.shtml
Online worldwide satellite events.

The BMO Telecommunications Service, Business Monitor International—Telecommunications Service
www.businessmonitor.com/bmo/telecoms

A data and intelligence tool providing global telecom industry analysis, forecasts and an assessment of company activity and sector trends worldwide.

IHS Jane's Space Systems & Industry 2012-2013, Peter R. Bond, Jane's Information Group

Detailed profiles of thousands of commercial and military space systems in service and under development around the world.

International Satellite Directory, annual, Satnews Publishers
www.satnews.com
Updated annually in two volumes with 16 separate chapters & over 25,000 entries. Includes a CD-ROM containing over 850 EIRP, G/T and SFD maps in full color. A guide to the people, companies, products, services and the market. Also—**Satellite Industry Database** is searchable by company name, country, keyword and category.

Via Satellite's 2012 Satellite Industry Directory, Access Intelligence
www.satellitetoday.com/store/sid
Comprehensive information on global satellite operators and suppliers. Satellite operator profiles are 100% verified and updated for each edition, and contain company and contact information. Market trends and forecasts; brokers & resellers; who's who.

Seniors and Those 40 and Up

Achieving the Good Life After 50: Tools and Resources for Making It Happen, Renée Lee Rosenberg, Five O'Clock Books
www.fiveoclockclub.com
Guides you through the retirement transition process using humor, The Five O'Clock Club methodology and real life stories. Learn about retirement: what to expect, how to plan for it, how to manage its ups and downs, how to stay busy, how to take action and, most importantly, how to enjoy the journey.

Boomer Men Working: Strategies for Staying Employed (and Tackling Unemployment), Norm Crampton, 2012, Wyatt-MacKenzie Publishing
A how-to book with an employment plan in practical steps for men in their late-40s to mid-60s, for those who want to hang on to their present job or find a new one.

BoomerPreneurs: How Baby Boomers Can Start Their Own Business, Make Money and Enjoy Life, Mary Beth Izard, 2010, Achieve Consulting
How to identify a business that fits your needs and those of the marketplace. A four-step method: Step 1—What should baby boomers consider before starting a business?; Step 2—Recognize the opportunity that's right for you and the marketplace; and Step 3—Refine your idea and do your research; and Step 4—determine business viability and get started.

Don't Stop the Career Clock: Rejecting the Myths of Aging for a New Way to Work in the 21st Century, Helen Harkness, 2011, Kindle ed., Career Design Associates/Amazon Digital
Harkness sounds a clarion call for individuals and organizations to create an aging and working paradigm to match the rapidly changing realities of the current age, which is vastly different from any we have known. Presents information, motivation, and tools to begin a new career during this potentially productive period.

Fired at 50: How to Overcome the Greatest Executive Job Search Challenge, Tucker Mays and Bob Sloane, 2011, Optimarket LLC
The nine best ways to overcome the age bias, such as, how to make your age an asset; a proven, month-to-month plan to find your next job faster; and the keys to executive networking success.

Great Jobs for Everyone 50+: Finding Work That Keeps You Happy and Healthy ... And Pays the Bills, Kerry Hannon, 2012, Wiley
Aimed at workers 50+ looking for a new job—-those have been laid off or taken early retirement, or need supplemental income, or want to pursue an encore career—-here is a guide to finding lasting financial security and personal and professional fulfillment. Opportunities abound-—the trick is knowing where to look and what to expect.

Job Hunting After 50, Carol A. Silvis, 2011, Course Technology PTR
Details a plan of action to carry out an effective job search to get the job you want. It covers self-assessment of skills and qualifications, preparing a resume for today's market, dressing with style, using technology to find a job, identifying common mistakes made by job seekers over 50, how to avoid them, and more.

The Job Search Portfolio System for Senior Workers, Steven L. Wetzel, 2012, Kindle ed., Amazon Digital
Prepares you for a successful job search. Emphasis is on organizing the job search, reducing or eliminating the stresses of the job hunting experience, making your effort, time and cost efficient, and most importantly, having a good experience.

Second Career Volunteer: A Passionate, Penny-wise Approach To A Unique Lifestyle, Barbara M. Traynor, 2012, AuthorHouse

Worried about finances? Savings and 401(k) reduced? A solution: organizations that offer free room and board in exchange for your skills, plus how to prepare for retirement with travel on a budget.

Self-Employment Transitions among Older American Workers with Career Jobs, Michael D. Giandrea, Kevin E. Cahill and Bureau of Labor Statistics (BLS), 2012, BiblioGov

This paper looks at the transitions that older workers are making—working longer and changing jobs later in life. Uses the Health and Retirement Study to determine the how many older workers are self-employed or made a job transition later in life, and looks at the factors that determine the choice of wage-and-salary employment or self-employment.

Women Still at Work: Professionals over Sixty and On the Job, Elizabeth F. Fideler, 2012, Rowman & Littlefield Publishers

Everyday stories of professional women and why they're still on the job. Real women, from academia to rehabilitation centers, from business to the arts, talk about the reasons they still work and the impact it has on their lives. Documents the physical and psychosocial benefits and the personal rewards.

AARP
www.aarp.org
The AARP Foundation, through its **WorkSearch** program, supports workers 40+ by offering job and career information, training and related employment services to individuals who are seeking to remain in, or re-enter the workforce. AARP is connected to **SCSEP** (see next listing for a summary of this program).

Senior Community Service Employment Program (SCSEP)
www.doleta.gov/seniors/html_docs/AboutSCSEP.cfm
SCSEP is a community-service and work-based training program for older workers that provides subsidized, service-based training for low-income persons 55 or older who are unemployed and have poor employment prospects.

Approaches and Tactics for Older Workers Who Can't Find a Job

www.quintcareers.com/older_worker_tips.html
Listing of books, links to professional associations, and various websites relating to mature workers.

Small Businesses

Your Great Business Idea: The Truth About Making It Happen, Kate Wendleton, President, The Five O'Clock Club, Five O'Clock Books
www.fiveoclockclub.com
Helps you develop a sound business concept—one that has a good chance of succeeding and is right for your personality. Contains "The One-Hour Business Plan" to help you decide quickly whether your business idea is worth pursuing. A step-by-step guide to get you from square one to a fully operating business. Uses true-to-life examples and success stories.

A Guide to Starting and Developing a New Business (Make Business Your Business), Lord Young of Graffham, 2012, HM Government
A short guide developed by Lord Young, the Prime Minister's adviser on small business and enterprise, to help you turn your business idea into reality. It provides useful hints, advice and further support.

Small Business Big Life for Women, Louis Barajas, Angie Barajas, 2011, Financial Greatness, Inc.
Learn the seven surprising secrets of entrepreneurship. This book will show you how to design a business that will let you create what really matters: a great life with money, time, energy, and health to share with the people you love.

Small Business, Big Vision: Lessons on How to Dominate Your Market from Self-Made Entrepreneurs Who Did it Right, Matthew Toren and Adam Toren, 2011, Wiley
The realities of starting your own business, with insights from some of the world's most successful entrepreneurs. Inspiration and practical advice on everything from creating a one-page business plan to setting up an advisory board.

The Small Business Start-Up Kit: A Step-by-Step Legal Guide, Peri Pakroo, 7th ed., 2012, Nolo
How to launch a business quickly, easily and with confidence: choose the best business structure; write an effective business plan; file the right forms in the right place; price, bid, and bill your projects; draft and use contracts, online and off; and more.

Updated—latest changes to the law, plus all the updated forms, business planning spreadsheets, and the instructions you need to fill them out. Also discussions on using technology.

Start Your Own Business, Fifth Edition: The Only Start-Up Book You'll Ever Need, Entrepreneur Press, 5th ed., 2010

Tap into more than 30 years of small business expertise as you embark on the most game-changing journey of your life—your new business. Offers critical startup essentials and a current, comprehensive view of what it takes to survive the crucial first three years, giving you exactly what you need to survive and succeed.

Takin' Care of Business: The BIG IDEA for Small Business, B. Buffini, 2012, Wiley

Strategies and advice for small business owners to thrive in any market condition, including: the ten most common mistakes small-business owners make; insight on whether or not your business is fundamentally sound; the biggest issue small businesses face— how to create new customers, and more.

Small Business Sourcebook, 29th ed., 2012, print, Gale

Covers over 340 specific small business profiles and 99 general small business topics; small business programs and assistance programs in the U.S., its territories, and Canadian provinces; and U.S. federal government agencies and offices specializing in small business issues, programs, and assistance.

U.S. Small Business Administration
www.sba.gov

SBA offers a variety of programs and support services to help you navigate the issues you face with your initial applications, and resources to help after you open for business. SBA provides assistances primarily through its four programmatic functions: Access to Capital (Business Financing); Entrepreneurial Development (Education, Information, Technical Assistance & Training); Government Contracting (Federal Procurement); and Advocacy (Voice for Small Business).

Summer Jobs and Internships

All Work, No Pay: Finding an Internship, Building Your Resume, Making Connections, and Gaining Job Experience, Lauren Berger, 2012, Ten Speed Press

Land killer internships—and make the most of them. Guide reveals insider secrets to scoring the perfect internship, building invaluable connections, boosting transferable skills, and ultimately moving toward your dream career. Nail the phone, Skype, and in-person interviews, know your rights, use social networking, and more.

College Students Do This! Get Hired!: From Freshman to Ph. D. The Secrets, Tips, Techniques and Tricks you need to get the Full Time Job, Co-op, or Summer Internship position you want, Mark Lyden, 2009, BookSurge Publishing

Learn the best secrets, tips, techniques, and tricks that have been proven to work for students. Covers interviewing, resumes, career fairs, negotiating salary, applying online, and more.

The Best Book on Getting An IBanking Internship: Written By A Former Banking Intern At UBS, JPMorgan, and FT Partners, Erin Parker, 2011, Hyperink

Stepwise advice, from interview preparation to conquering the 90-hour workweek. Tips to give you an unfair advantage over others.

Dream Work Experience—Unconventional Strategies to Land the Internship of Your Dreams, Bill Riddell, 2010, Kindle ed., Amazon Digital

Combines some of the more useful timeless advice with plenty of unconventional strategies that have been successfully tested. For anyone in high school, college or university who wants to kick-start their career with an incredible internship and continue on to a great job.

Guide To Summer Jobs, Dr. Kary Hastings, 2012, Amazon Digital

Strategies for college students to find summer jobs. Has lists and all kinds of suggestions to help get started.

Intern Nation: How to Earn Nothing and Learn Little in the Brave New Economy, Ross Perlin, 2012, Verso

The first no-holds-barred exposé of the exploitative world of internships. Perlin profiles fellow interns, talks to academics and professionals about what unleashed this phenomenon, and explains why the intern boom is perverting workplace practices around the world.

Internship Insider, Gavin Ricketts, 2012, Kindle ed., Napoleon Creative/Amazon Digital

A special report for those trying to break into the film, television and other creative industries. How to find internships, how to make a good impression when applying, what employers will expect and what to expect from them.

Internships, Fellowships, and Other Work Experience Opportunities in the Federal Government—CRS Report, Jennifer E. Manning and Elli K. Ludwigson, 2011, Kindle ed., Congressional Research Service/Amazon Digital

Describes Internet resources on major internship, fellowship, and work experience programs within the federal government. A selective guide for students of all levels: high school, undergraduate, graduate, and postgraduate. Updated annually.

Landing Summer Jobs, Gabriel Ortiz, 2011, Kindle ed., Roosevelt Goose/Amazon Digital

Teen hiring is at its lowest since 1949. Unemployed adults are trying for teen jobs. Special techniques, presented here, are needed for teens to land summer jobs. Find out who's the competition, best time to look for summer jobs (and where), and the one thing you can bring that will make an employer create a job for you.

Lies, Damned Lies & Internships: The Truth About Getting from Classroom to Cubicle, Heather R. Huhman, 2011, Kindle ed., Happy About/Amazon Digital

There are a lot of misconceptions about—and controversies surrounding—internships, mostly negative for both the intern and the employer. In fact, internships have essentially become nothing more than a "necessary evil" to many. Huhman covers: recent controversies surrounding internships; the importance of internships; the characteristics of a good internship program; current problems and possible solutions; and more.

Not A Moment To Lose: A Step-By-Step Guide to Internship Success (OnBoard Yourself), Todd Hudson, 2011, Maverick Institute

Filled with entertaining and instructive illustrations, stories, tips, advice, checklists, exercises and activities to help interns accelerate their learning and progress. Has a plan for the critical first weeks of internship.

The Quintessential Guide to Finding and Maximizing Internships, Randall Hansen and Katharine Hansen, 2012, Kindle ed., Quintessential Careers Press/Amazon Digital

Surveys say 95% of employers want new-grad hires to have experience, and almost half prefer that students get such experience through internships. Eight chapters cover what you need in your internship experience, how to find one, the tools to secure one, how to make the most of your internship experience, how to turn an internship into a job, and internship resources.

Summer Jobs Worldwide: Make the Most of the Summer Break, Susan Griffithl, 43rd ed., 2012, annual, Vacation Work, Crimson Publishing

The only annually updated guide to summer jobs available for anyone taking a gap year or a summer break. Now in its 43rd edition, Summer Jobs Worldwide 2012 is packed with over 50,000 paid and unpaid job opportunities around the world: from crewing yachts in the Caribbean to stewarding at a music festival in Europe.

What Your Boss Will Never Tell You: the Intern's Guide to Getting Ahead, K. A. Patton, 2011, Kindle ed., Amazon Digital

Tells: how to avoid common mistakes; why you should stay out of your boss's office; how to avoid hidden traps of socializing in and out of the office; the best way to get a great reference; and how to improve your chances of turning the internship into a job.

Why Internships Are Good, Dan Gershenson, et al., 2012, Kindle ed., Amazon Digital

Through internships, students are often able to access employers they otherwise could not. Internships are good for students, they are good for teachers, they are good for employers, they are good for parents, for the economy, for society.

Your Last Day of School: 56 Ways You Can Be a Great Intern and Turn Your Internship Into a

Job, Eric Woodard, 2011, CreateSpace Independent Publishing Platform

Gives students specific, actionable advice on how they can be massively successful during an internship. Based on the author's experience as an intern at the White House, and later as a staffer charged with managing interns. Skills to start internships on the right foot and start learning the good stuff from day one.

Work Your Way Around the World: The Globetrotter's Bible, Susan Griffith, 15th ed., 2012, Crimson Publishing

Incorporating hundreds of first-hand accounts, as well as a clear, country-by-country guide to the opportunities available—from selling ice cream in Cape Town to working as a film extra in Bangkok—this working travel handbook reveals how to fund the trip of a lifetime by finding temporary work abroad, both in advance and on the spot while traveling.

About.com Internships
internships.about.com/

Although this is a job board, there are tips and links helpful to carrying out the search.

Job & Internship Guide
career.berkeley.edu/Guide/Guide.stm

This Career Center guide, reviewed and updated each year, is a resource for students during their job search. Downloadable as a pdf. Among the topics covered are Internships, Your Job or Internship Search, and Internship & Job Offers.

Peace Corps
www.peacecorps.gov

Since its founding in 1980, 210,000+ Peace Corps Volunteers have served in 139 host countries to work on issues, ranging from AIDS education to information technology and environmental preservation. Peace Corps Volunteers continue to help countless individuals who want to build a better life for themselves, their children, and their communities.

Telecommunications

The Essential Guide to Telecommunications, (Essential Guides (Prentice Hall), Annabel Z. Dodd,

5th ed., 2012, Prentice Hall

Completely updated for the newest trends and technologies, the Fifth Edition is the world's top-selling non-technical guide to today's fast-changing telecommunications industry. Dodd demystifies today's most significant technologies, standards, and architectures. She introduces the industry-leading providers worldwide, explains where they fit in a fast-changing marketplace, and presents their key strategies.

The Essentials of Telecommunications Management: A Simple Guide to Understanding a Complex Industry, Jayraj Ugarkar, 2011, AuthorHouse

This guide was written by a consultant who has been in the telecommunications industry for nine years.

How to Land a Top-Paying Radio and Telecommunications Equipment Installers and Repairers Job: Your Complete Guide to Opportunities, Resumes and Cover ... What to Expect From Recruiters and More!, Brad Andrews, 2010, tebbo

Worksheets make it easier to write about a job, ensuring that the narrative follows a logical structure and that key points are included. Cheat sheets helps you get your career organized in a tidy, presentable fashion. Andrews successfully challenges conventional job search wisdom to offer radical, but inspired suggestions for success.

Introduction to Communications Technologies: A Guide for Non-Engineers, Second Edition, Stephan Jones, et al., 2nd ed., 2008, Auerbach Publications

The second edition helps students in telecommunications business programs become familiar with and stay abreast of the ever-changing technology surrounding this industry.

Newton's Telecom Dictionary: Telecommunications, Networking, Information Technologies, The Internet, Wired, Wireless, Satellites and Fiber, Harry Newton, 2011, Flatiron Publishing

This dictionary not only defines the terms and the acronyms, but it also tells what the term is, how it works, how to use it, what its benefits are, what its pitfalls are and how it fits into the greater scheme of things. This is not a common dictionary. It's far closer to an encyclopedia.

Major Telecommunications Companies of the World, Heather Bradley, Layla Comstive and Alison

Gallico, eds., Edition 16, 2012, Graham & Whiteside Ltd

Profiles more than 5,950 of the leading telecommunications companies worldwide, including many of the top Internet companies. Each listing typically includes: company name and information; contact information of senior management and board members; description of business activities; and much more.

Plunkett's Telecommunications Industry Almanac 2011: Telecommunications Industry Market Research, Statistics, Trends & Leading Companies, Jack W. Plunkett, Plunkett Research

Key features include industry trends analysis, market data and competitive intelligence; market forecasts and industry statistics; and industry associations and professional societies list.

The Open Directory Project
www.dmoz.org/Business/Telecommunications

The Open Directory Project is the largest, human-edited directory of the web. It is constructed and maintained by a global community of volunteer editors. There are over 4,700 listings for telecommunications, including call centers, carriers, equipment, location and tracking, services, and more. Also, links to 30 associations, software, and more.

Telecommunications Directory, 23rd ed., 2012, eBook, Gale

Comprehensive source of information on the products, services, and related activities of organizations in the telecommunications field. Users can identify and compare traditional telecommunications offerings of established carriers, as well as the many new systems and services under development.

Transportation (Shipping, Marine, Freight, Express Delivery, Supply Chain)

Career in Air Freight — Air Express Transportation, Operation, and Management (Careers Ebooks), 2010, Kindle ed., Institute For Career Research/Amazon Digital

Unbiased information about careers in air freight, based on the latest national surveys— covering: both the attractive and unattractive sides; opportunities; earnings; job descriptions; how to get started; and

including practical advice on what to do now.

Career Opportunities in Transportation, 2010, Facts on File

This industry involves much more than just the movement of people and cargo: It also includes the manufacturing of transportation equipment; development of transportation infrastructure; management and administration of transport systems and networks; the enforcement of transportation laws, regulations, policies and procedures; and scenic and sightseeing transportation. This book examines the most common, and the unfamiliar careers, featuring more than 100 job profiles in ground, air, rail, maritime, pipeline, and other diverse areas of transportation.

Discovering Careers—Transportation, 2012, eBook, Ferguson Publishing Company

Presented in a full-color format, it provides up-to-date information for readers interested in pursuing a career in this diverse field.

How to Land a Top-Paying Cargo and freight agents Job: Your Complete Guide to Opportunities, Resumes and Cover Letters, Interviews, Salaries, Promotions, What to Expect From Recruiters and More, Jean Cooley, 2012, tebbo

Worksheets make it easier to write about a job, ensuring that the narrative follows a logical structure and that key points are included. Cheat sheets helps you get your career organized in a tidy, presentable fashion. Successfully challenges conventional job search wisdom to offer radical, but inspired suggestions for success.

Two similar books are:

How to Land a Top-Paying Logistics specialist Job: Your Complete Guide to Opportunities, Resumes and Cover Letters, Interviews, Salaries, Promotions, What to Expect From Recruiters and More, Gerald Orr, 2012, tebbo

and

How to Land a Top Paying Truck Transportation, Warehousing and Logistics Management Job, Brad Andrews, 2010, Emereo

Real-Resumes for Supply & Logistics Jobs, Anne McKinney, 2012, CreateSpace Independent Publishing Platform

There are samples of resumes and cover letters used by real people to obtain jobs related to supply and logistics. Resumes and cover letters are included that have helped in finding that first job. Also included are sample resumes and cover letters geared to the most-experienced experts, plus samples of the federal "resumix," as well as the write-ups for the Knowledge, Skills, and Abilities (KSAs) often required for government jobs.

Transportation Careers, Jobs and Employment Information, Career Overview www.careeroverview.com/transportation-careers.html

Some careers in transportation require post-secondary education while others require training that can be found through attending a trade school or obtained via on-the-job training. To find out more, a list of links is provided on information on job opportunities, earnings, training requirements and much more.

JOC Sailings
www.jocsailings.com/

Directory of Transportation, published twice yearly, for those in the international trade industry who control the movement of cargo. Key sections include a comprehensive listing of VOCCs (Vessel Operating Common Carriers) and NVOCCs, trucking services, warehousing, shipper's agents, terminal operators, stevedores and rail consolidators and railroads. JOC Sailings also publishes the **Carrier Directory** and the **Vessel Directory.**

LogisticsWorld
www.logisticsworld.com

Directory offers service and contact information from various companies and organizations in the transportation, logistics, and supply chain industry. Directory listings are free.

Lloyd's List Online
www.lloydslist.com

The company provides information, analysis and knowledge for business decision-makers in the global shipping community. It has **Online Directories** of **Ports, Companies** and **Ship Services.**

Transportation Directory
users.rcn.com/lawhughes/index.htm

An edited list of links to nearly all known scheduled public transportation services throughout North

America. This directory is intermodal, with links provided to services by bus, rail, and sea.

Transportation Directory—Accounting, Bookkeeping & Fuel Tax Preparation
www.transport911.com
Covers the industry in Canada.

Travel, Leisure and Hospitality (Including Hotels, Food Service, Travel Agents, Restaurants, Airlines)

Career Launcher—Hospitality, Ferguson Publishing Company, 2011

Hospitality looks at three core sectors of this industry: lodging, restaurants, and gaming. It explains how these businesses work, what opportunities they provide, and what it takes to succeed. Covers the full scope of hospitality careers, including tips for success, an in-depth glossary, and current and future trends.

Career Opportunities in Casinos and Casino Hotels, 2nd ed., 2010, Ferguson Publishing Co.

This book gives readers what's needed to start a career in the growing casino and gaming industry. Features more than 90 job profiles, as well as appendixes covering professional organizations, schools, associations, unions, and casinos.

Career Opportunities in Travel and Hospitality, eBook, Jennifer Bobrow Burns, 2010, Infobase
www.infobasepublishing.com

This *Career Opportunities* guide profiles occupations in a wide variety of areas, including travel and tourism services, hotels and lodging, specialty resorts and cruise ships, recreation, restaurants and culinary, casinos and gaming, and communications. Features more than 75 job profiles, plus appendixes listing educational programs, professional associations, major employers, industry resources, and more.

A Career with Meaning: Recreation, Parks, Sport Management, Hospitality, and Tourism, Cheryl A. Stevens, 2010, Sagamore Publishing LLC

Enables individuals to match their core beliefs and values with opportunities within the leisure industry. Leading experts provide detailed discussions and insight for 11 primary areas related to recreation, parks, sport management, hospitality, and tourism.

Careers in Hotel and Resort Management (Careers Ebooks), Institute For Career Research, 2012, Kindle ed.

Many resort customers never leave the property, preferring to eat all their meals and have all their fun in one place. Such all-inclusive resorts offer hundreds of different career paths, most of which can lead to managerial positions. You can start your career from any number of angles and find your own way to the top. You can tailor your career to your personal specifications.

The Complete Guide to Careers in Special Events (Wiley Event Management), Gene Columbus, 2010, Wiley

How to create a unique and creative approach with a proven plan. Industry professionals provide insight and advice on gaining the appropriate skills, making contacts, networking, and using knowledge to ace job interviews. Includes samples of cover letters and thank you notes.

The Cornell School of Hotel Administration on Hospitality: Cutting Edge Thinking and Practice, Michael C. Sturman, 2011, Wiley

Develop and manage a multinational career and become a leader in the hospitality industry; maximize profits from franchise agreements, management contracts, and leases; understand and predict customer choices; motivate your staff to provide outstanding service; and more.

Culinary Careers: How to Get Your Dream Job in Food with Advice from Top Culinary Professionals, Rick Smilow and Anne E. McBride, 2010, Clarkson Potter

Instead of giving glossed-over, general descriptions of various jobs, *Culinary Careers* features interviews with both food-world luminaries and those on their way up, to help you discover what a day in the life is really like in your desired field.

Culinary Careers For Dummies, Michele Thomas, et al., 2011, For Dummies

Information every culinary novice needs to enter and excel in the food service industry. Guidance on cooking up your career plan; tips and advice on what to study; information on the many career options; plus information on training, degrees, and certificates.

The Everything Guide to Starting and Running a Restaurant: The ultimate resource for starting a successful restaurant!, Ronald Lee, 2nd ed., 2011, Adams Media

Topics include how to: secure financing and find the perfect site; develop an engaging marketing plan to build and keep a patron base; operate an offbeat site like a food truck or rotating restaurant; create an innovative and diverse menu; hire and manage wait, kitchen, and front-end staff; and much more.

Hospitality (Ferguson Career Launcher), Kirsten Hall and Christian Dahl Schulz, 2011, Ferguson Publishing Company

State of the industry, tips for success, talk like a pro, and resources.

Hospitality and Catering Careers (In the Workplace), Cath Senker, 2011, Amicus

Covers a wide range of career choices in various fields, with jobs ranging from restaurant work to cruise ships. Looks at four different topics: How do I find a job? What qualities do I need? What will be my main tasks? and What might I become? With jobs ranging from restaurant work to cruise ships.

Hospitality and Personal Care (Field Guides to Finding a New Career), Adrienne Friedberg, 2010, Ferguson Publishing Company

All-in-one guide to navigating to a new career.

Travel and Transportation, (Field Guides to Finding a New Career), Ferguson Publishing Company

Aimed at students looking to take their career in a new direction, this book explores the ins and outs of this profession and provides readers with the tools necessary to transition to a career in this field. Self-assessment questions, helpful advice, and essential tips for career changers round out this accessible guide.

Hospitality Link Directories
ehotelier.com/company.php

Global Hospitality Directory Links: over 7,500 preselected and categorized hotel-industry website links that are growing daily. Links to directories, including Airlines, Associations, Consultants, Events, Food & Beverage, and much more.

Hospitality Net
www.hospitalitynet.org
Among other resources, there is a suppliers directory,

International Encyclopedia of Hospitality Management, Abraham Pizam, ed., 2nd ed., 2010, Taylor & Francis
Online material makes it up-to-date. Covers all of the relevant issues in hospitality management from both a sectoral level: Lodging, Restaurants/Food service, Time-share, Clubs and Events, as well as from a functional one: Accounting & Finance, Marketing, Strategic Management, Human Resources, Information Technology and Facilities Management. Credible source of core information from experts from around the world.

Veterans

150 Best Jobs for the Military-to-Civilian Transition, Laurence Shatkin, 2012, Jist Works
Lists the most popular jobs for veterans; and jobs in which veteran status confers the biggest earnings advantage. Job descriptions show veterans' earnings vs. those of non-veterans; veterans' employment by economic sector, specific information on for-profit, nonprofit, government, education, and much more.

Battlefield to Business Success, Chad Storlie, 2011, Kindle ed., Amazon Digital
Dedicated to helping individuals understand, apply, and adapt military skills and military Special Operations Techniques for use in their civilian career success. Military skills are especially helpful for business professionals to understand, plan, execute, and improve business plans and operations.

Best Boot Forward: What Veterans Need to Read for Their Transition to Succeed, Deniz Emre, 2012, Poetic Life Publishing
Provides fresh and relatable insight from a much-needed Post/9-11 Era Veteran's perspective. This is a humorous, entertaining guide and companion for our brave men and women of the U.S. Military as they make the difficult adjustment from soldier to civilian.

The Coffee Break Guide for Veterans Seeking Federal Employment, Mark Butler and A. Taoty, 2011, Kindle ed.

Understand the federal employment process, announcements, application of veteran's preference and what veterans can do to get a leg up on the employment process.

Combat Leader to Corporate Leader: 20 Lessons to Advance Your Civilian Career, Chad Storlie, 2010, Praeger
Understand, translate, and apply military and SPEC OPS skills to maintain a strong leadership ethic, excel in execution, and coach and develop employee skills, to succeed in business. Additionally, focuses on preparing and excelling when the unexpected happens.

The Little Green Guide for Veterans: The 8 Principles You Need to Know to Get the Job You Want!, Stephen A. Cleare, 2010, CreateSpace Independent Publishing Platform
This book teaches veterans how to successfully transition into finding jobs in the private sector. Covers: attitude adjustment; defining yourself; resumes; interviewing; and more.

Lock and Load!: 24 Job Interview Questions Military Veterans Must Know! (Volume 3), Tom Stein and Greg Wood CCMP, 2012, CreateSpace Independent Publishing Platform
Learn to highlight your value by conducting a tactical and strategic interview that will greatly enhance your chances of winning the job. But you must rehearse your interview answers: this book will help you prepare and rehearse.

Military to Federal Career Guide: Ten Steps to Transforming Your Military Experience into a Competitive Federal Resume, Kathryn K. Troutman and Emily K. Troutman, ed., 2nd ed., 2010, The Resume Place, Inc.
Critical resume tips on: how to add keywords to match your federal resume to a particular vacancy announcement; highlight your accomplishments so that federal human resources specialists will notice them; and more. Includes samples of Military to Federal Resumes in Outline Format for USAJOBS, CPOL, DONHR, AVUE, Talentlink, and other federal resume builders. Also features a CD-ROM with over ten samples of Military to Federal Resumes.

Networking For Veterans: A Guidebook for a Successful Military Transition into the Civilian Workforce, Michael L. Faulkner, et al., 2012, Pearson Learning Solutions

Teaches transitioning service-members to properly network and build relationships with the people in their community who are most willing and able to help them launch new careers of their own choosing. Includes how to overcome the challenges of making a military transition, properly apply military experience to business, and more.

Out of Uniform: Your Guide to a Successful Military-to-Civilian Career Transition,

Tom Wolfe, 2011, Potomac Books Inc.

Divided into eight sections, covering key matters in roughly the same order that they occur in military-to-civilian transition, plus anecdotes based on actual experiences of soldiers, sailors, airmen, and Marines.

Roadmap to Job-Winning Military to Civilian Resumes, Barbara A. Adams and Lee Kelley, 2011, Career Pro Global Inc.

Learn to write military-to-federal, military-to-defense-contractor, and military-to-corporate resumes that earn job interviews. There is also a Veteran's Toolbox with useful information and resources, including resume samples and easy-to-use templates.

Veteran Employment Tactics!: Packaging Yourself for Job Hunting Success (Volume 1), Tom Stein and Greg Wood CCMP, 2012, CreateSpace Independent Publishing Platform

Covers how the job search system really works and how to use your tactical advantage as a military veteran. Develop a proven strategy for your job search, instead of the "traditional" resume-based approach. For job seekers who are frustrated, discouraged and increasingly fed up.

Veterans: DO THIS! GET HIRED!: Proven Advice For Veterans That Need A Job, Mark Lyden, 2011, CreateSpace Independent Publishing Platform

A no-nonsense guide to help vets get hired, even in this difficult job market—even if nothing else has worked.

VETS—U.S. Dept. of Labor
www.dol.gov/vets

VETS provides resources and expertise to assist and prepare vets to obtain meaningful careers, maximize their employment opportunities, and protect their employment rights. Includes information on broad range of topics, such as job-search tools and tips, employment openings, career assessment, education and training, and benefits and special services available to veterans.

Vocational/No Four-Year College Degree

The Community College Career Track: How to Achieve the American Dream without a Mountain of Debt, Thomas Snyder, 2012, Wiley

Get a good education without massive debt, and enter a field that's actually hiring. In coming years, millions of great jobs will be opening up in growth areas like advanced manufacturing, biotechnology, health care and more. These jobs can pay as well as, or much better than, the average for four-year college graduates. Snyder offers insights on how to save money over a lifetime through an affordable college education that provides high-paying jobs.

Great Careers in 2 Years by Sheila Danzig and Francis Mutulu (Feb 26, 2011), BG Publishing International

A two-year degree has the advantage that student loans are minimal, and the market for jobs is growing. Here's advice and tips, loopholes and pitfalls, with ample contact details to help you on your way to those well-paying jobs. With proven information to give you a jump-start on your career path.

Great Careers with a High School Diploma, Set, 10 Volumes, 2010, Infobase Publishing/Facts on File www.infobasepublishing.com

This set profiles jobs that require no more than a high school diploma or a GED. Each volume explores some of the U.S. Department of Labor's career clusters, examining several careers within each cluster. These career books give students the know-how to find a job in their desired field, as well as insider tips and guidance to career success. Each book examines the on-the-job training that often leads to certification, in addition to the potential for self-employment in a particular field. Covers articles about the job (Is this job right for me?) and employment prospects (What's a typical day on the job).

The ten books cover: **Armed Forces; Communications, the Arts, and Computers; Construction and Trades; Food, Agriculture, and Natural Resources; Health Care, Medicine, and Science; Hospitality, Human Services, and Tourism; Manufacturing and Transportation; Personal Care Services, Fitness, and Education; Public Safety,**

Law, and Security; and **Sales, Marketing, Business, and Finance.**

Teens' Guide to College & Career Planning, 2011, Peterson's

For high school sophomores and juniors who are starting to get serious about their careers. Whether for a two-year or four-year college, a technical school, an apprenticeship, the military, or directly into the workforce-or are still undecided—here's information on the options available.

Top 100 Careers Without a Four-year Degree: Your Complete Guidebook to Good Jobs in Many Fields (Top Careers), Laurence Shatkin and Michael Farr, 10th ed., 2011, Jist Works

Explore 100 careers that don't require a bachelor's. Shows you how to assess which career matches your skills, and get the job you want. Everything needed to research careers is here; learn about pay, the outlook through 2018, education, and skills needed for the 100 jobs; and seven steps to land a good job in less time.

Chronicle Two-Year College Databook: Schools Offering Programs That Result in an Occupational Certificate/Diploma or an Associate Degree (Chronicle Career College & Technology School Databook), 2011, Chronicle Guidance Publications

Find the online school that is right for you.

Open Directory Project
www.dmoz.org/Reference/Education/Subjects/
Vocational

Open Directory Project is a human-edited directory of the Web. Links to a wide variety of directories and business sites under "Vocational" plus more info at other listed sites.

Volunteering

99 Thoughts for Volunteers: Making an Impact Right Where You Are, Danette Matty, 2012, Group Publishing

With her 25 years as a youth ministry volunteer, Matty knows this world: part-time hours, full-time passion and no-time pay. But she also knows that you're an integral part of God's work in the lives of students and in your church's ministry to teenagers. This book will help you discover how to maintain your spiritual vital-

ity, lead from the middle, serve through all the seasons of life, and do what you do best.

Don't Just Count Your Hours, Make Your Hours Count: The Essential Guide to Volunteering & Community Service, Kristin E. Joos Ph.D. and Alana Rush, 2011, Treetop Software Company

Provides basic information about community service, service learning, and volunteering, so students can then focus on the big (and arguably much more important) questions, like: How does what I'm seeing while volunteering connect to the social issues we're studying in class? Has best practices, tips, lists, "How to's", "Don't do's", popular wisdom, academic research, real-life experiences, student volunteer etiquette guides, and more.

Giving Back: Discover your values and put them into action through volunteering and donating, Steven P. Ketchpel Ph.D., 2012, Jonquil Press

Along the way, you'll discover: friends who share your vision; skills you develop while volunteering; opportunities to work together with your family; and more.

The health benefits of volunteering: a review of recent research, U.S. Government, 2011

Yes, there is a significant relationship between volunteering and good health; when individuals volunteer, they not only help their community but also experience better health in later years, whether in terms of greater longevity, higher functional ability, or lower rates of depression.

Second Career Volunteer: A Passionate, Penny-wise Approach To A Unique Lifestyle, Barbara M. Traynor, 2012, AuthorHouse

How about volunteering at organizations that offer free room and board in exchange for workplace or hobby skills? This is a reality. How-to find organizations that offer free room and board in exchange for your skills. How-can college grads find employment and gain experience while remaining independent. How-to prepare for retirement with travel on a budget.

Strategic Volunteering: 50 ingredients to transform your life and career (Volume 1), Mark McCurdy, 2010, CreateSpace

This book that redefines volunteering and how it can help you and your career move to the next level. You will learn new strategies and perspectives in volunteering such as "To help move yourself forward after a mistake," "To free yourself from your fears" and "To develop your leadership."

Volunteer: A Traveller's Guide to Making a Difference Around, Charlotte Hindle, et al., 2nd ed., 2010, Lonely Planet

Much more than a resource directory, *Volunteer* is packed with information and full-color inspiration to get you planning your perfect short- or long-term volunteer experience anywhere in the world.

The Volunteer Traveler's Handbook, Shannon O'Donnell, 2012, Full Flight Press

Guides new and veteran travelers through the challenges of finding, vetting, and choosing their ideal volunteer experience.

Volunteer Vacations: Short-Term Adventures That Will Benefit You and Others, Bill McMillon, et al., 11th ed., 2012, Chicago Review Press

Shows how a short-term stint can transform your life. This fully updated edition is filled with in-depth information and profiles of 150 select organizations, running thousands of quality programs in the U.S. and around the world.

Volunteering & Your Retirement Lifestyle, Jeffrey Webber, 2011, Booklocker.com, Inc.

Volunteering offers you the opportunity to meet new people, engage in challenging activities, travel, and have fun. This book offers specific information on how to expand your horizons during your retirement years.

Volunteering: The Essential Guide, Leonie Martin, 2011, Need-2-Know

Whether you are still in school, retired, out of work, living with a disability or long-term condition, and are not sure where to begin, this guide can help you find an opportunity to fit in with your life.

AmeriCorps
www.americorps.gov

Each year, AmeriCorps offers 75,000 opportunities for adults of all ages and backgrounds to serve through a network of partnerships with local and national nonprofit groups. Whether your service makes a community safer, gives a child a second chance, or helps protect the environment, you'll be getting things done through AmeriCorps.

ServiceSpace
www.servicespace.org

ServiceSpace is an all volunteer-run organization that leverages technology to inspire greater volunteerism. It's a space to learn how outer change is closely tied to our own inner transformation. It's about changing ourselves, to change the world.

Idealist.org

Connects people, organizations, and resources to help build a world where all people can live free and dignified lives. Idealist is independent of any government, political ideology, or religious creed.

Make a Wish
wish.org

Since 1980, the Make-A-Wish Foundation has given hope, strength and joy to children with life-threatening medical conditions.

One Brick
newyork.onebrick.org

One Brick provides support to local non-profit and community organizations by creating a unique, social and flexible volunteer environment. One Brick has brought volunteers to support over 1,200 organizations.

Project America
project.org

A non-partisan organization devoted to providing an online resource to help people understand the state of issues facing this country.

SmartVolunter
www.smartvolunteer.org

SmartVolunteer connects talented professionals with meaningful skills-based non-profit volunteer opportunities.

Teach for America
www.teachforamerica.org

We can provide an excellent education for kids in low-income communities. We recruit a diverse group of leaders with a record of achievement who work to expand educational opportunities, starting by teaching for two years in a low-income community.

VolunteerMatch
www.volunteermatch.org

VolunteerMatch strengthens communities by making it easier for good people and good causes to connect.

Offers a variety of online services to support a community of nonprofit, volunteer and business leaders committed to civic engagement.

Wholesaling and Distributing/Importing and Exporting

5 Fundamentals for the Wholesale Distribution Branch Manager, Second Edition, Jim Ambrose, 2012, Kindle ed., Amazon Digital

This is the Second Edition of the classic step-by-step guide to help branch managers improve their business and leadership skills. The branch manager is the key to success for every wholesaler-distributor according to author Jim Ambrose. "If winning means profitable market share and profitable market share growth, then developing the branch manager is essential to a company's success," he says.

al la Carte Importing—The Definitive Guide to Small Volume Importing from Scratch, Nigel Schulze, 2012, Kindle ed., Amazon Digital

A stepwise guide spelling out the process to get started running your own small importing business beginning with less than $500 in your pocket.

Career Opportunities in the Retail and Wholesale Industry, 2nd ed., 2010, Facts on File

Retail and wholesale trade is a trillion dollar industry that presents a myriad of employment opportunities, from sales and merchandising to IT, marketing, finance, customer service, and much more. Featuring more than 90 job profiles, this *Career Opportunities* volume provides up-to-date information in one accessible resource.

How to Land a Top-Paying Sales Representatives, Wholesale and Manufacturing Job: Your Complete Guide to Opportunities, Resumes and Cover Letters, ... What to Expect From Recruiters and More, Brad Andrews, 2012, tebbo

Worksheets included in this book make it easier to write about a work experience. This ensures that the narrative will follow a logical structure and reminds you not to leave out the most important points. With this book, you'll be able to revise your application into a much stronger document, be much better prepared and a step ahead for the next opportunity. This book successfully challenges conventional job search wisdom and doesn't load you with useful but obvious suggestions (Don't forget to wear a nice suit to your interview, for example).

Similar books are available from tebbo from other authors: **How to Land a Top-Paying Wholesale and retail buyers Job: Your Complete Guide to Opportunities, Resumes and Cover Letters, Interviews, Salaries, Promotions, What to Expect From Recruiters and More,** Teresa Moss, 2012; **How to Land a Top-Paying Wholesale diamond brokers Job: Your Complete Guide to Opportunities, Resumes and Cover Letters, Interviews, Salaries, Promotions, What to Expect From Recruiters and More,** Jerry Harding, 2012; **How to Land a Top-Paying Wholesale ultrasonic equipment salespersons Job: Your Complete Guide to Opportunities, Resumes and Cover Letters, Interviews, ... What to Expect From Recruiters and More,** Joyce Petty, 2012

How to Open & Operate a Financially Successful Import Export Business (Book & CD-ROM), Maritza Manresa, 2010, Atlantic Publishing Group Inc.

Provides readers with an understanding of the basic concepts of international trade and helps navigating the maze of international trade policies and regulations. Learn how to draw up a winning business plan, and more.

How to Start a Wholesale Business: Start Up Tips to Boost Your Wholesale Business Success by Luke Moinert (Sep 12, 2011), Kindle ed., Amazon Digital

Here is a simple and easy-to-apply book in which you will discover the essential first steps to take to start your business on the road to profit, in the shortest time possible. Includes: how to name your business; why 99% of small business owners slip up here and how to avoid "poor name" pitfalls; and the easy way to draw up a business plan—without wasted time and effort.

How and Where to Find Wholesale Suppliers, Young Kim, 2012, Kindle ed., Amazon Digital

Based on Kim's nearly 20 years' experience and information as an active buyer and seller of wholesale merchandise, this guide will show you the places you should search for wholesalers first. With complete sources including websites, phone numbers and photos of over 100,000 different products.

Import/Export Kit For Dummies, John J. Capela, 2012, with CD, For Dummies

Provides entrepreneurs and small- to mid-sized businesses with the critical, entry-point information needed to begin exporting their products around the world and importing goods to sell in the U.S. The bonus CD includes: a printable dictionary of international business and Internet terms to help understand the international marketplace; sample distributor and agent agreement outlines; guidelines and checklists for developing a successful business and marketing plan; and the most up-to-date templates for pricing models, licensing, and shipping.

Import Export Business Plan—How To Import From China Using Other Peoples Money, Perry Belcher, 2011, Kindle ed., Amazon Digital

A guide to the secrets of running a successful business.

Start Your Own Import/Export Business, Third Edition, Krista Turner and Entrepreneur Press, 2010, Entrepreneur Press

Valuable insights and practical advice for tapping into the highly lucrative global markets. Covers every aspect of the startup process, including: choosing the most profitable goods to buy and sell; setting up and maintaining a trade route; using the Internet to simplify your transactions; understanding how the government can help you find products and customers; and learning essential trade law information to keep your business in compliance.

Wholesale Trade and Related Careers Outlook, U.S. Department of Labor, James Williams, 2012, Kindle ed., Amazon Digital

An up-to-date report of the latest career-related information and future economic prospects for the field. Includes an in-depth overview of these careers. Information in this report is taken from the latest government research. This authoritative report is vital for all current and future Wholesale Traders and Related Careers.

American Wholesalers and Distributors Directory, 24th ed., 2011, Gale

Discover more than 27,000 large and small wholesalers and distributors throughout the U.S and Puerto Rico, with the names and addresses, fax number, SIC code, principal product lines, total number of employees, estimated annual sales volume and principal officers.

Daily Trader
www.dailytrader.com

A worldwide online directory of legitimate, genuine and reliable wholesalers, dropshippers, importers, manufacturers, distributors, wholesale suppliers, liquidators, with ex-catalogue, ex-chain and surplus stockists. Also lists hundreds and thousands of up-to-date wholesale supplies, products and offers from nearly every region of the world including UK, U.S., Canada, France, Australia and many other countries.

Global Export Import Directory
globalexport.usaexportimport.com

Usaexportimport.com is searchable by category, such as wholesale distributors, auctions, and wholesale lenders.

Manufacturing Company And Export Information Directory, ExportBureau
www.exportbureau.com

ExportBureau is an export association for manufacturer companies, on the Internet, with the largest international sales agent professional network. ExportBureau provides one of the most popular manufacturing company networks in the world for international import quantity buyer communities.

UBM Global Trade— Directories & Databases
www.cbizmedia.com

Provider of proprietary data, news, business intelligence and analytical content supporting commercial maritime, rail, trucking, warehousing and logistics industries worldwide.

USA Based Wholesale Directory, Diana K. Loera, 2012, Loera Publishing LLC

Directory featuring over 500 U.S.-based sources for buying wholesale. Categories include candles, candies, general merchandise, electronics, as seen on TV, clothing and more. Resource for flea market vendors and any one else wanting to find U.S.-based companies that offer wholesale merchandise.

Wholesale Distributors Directory
www.wholesaledistributorsnet.com/

Said to be used by over 4 million buyers, this directory has links to products, cities, wholesale leads, and much more.

World Exporters & Importers Trade Directory
www.eximdata.com

Worldwide directory of manufacturers, exporters, importers, dealers, distributors, buying agents, traders, and wholesalers. Searchable by company and country, business type, category, and much more. Has a very large number of **links to trade associations worldwide.**

Dialog
www.dialog.com

Dialog, with direct operations in 27 countries, offers online information services that help organizations across the globe to seek competitive advantages in such fields as business, science, engineering, finance and law. Products and services include Dialog and DataStar, which offer the ability to precisely retrieve data from more than 1.4 billion unique records of key information, accessible via the Internet or through delivery to enterprise intranets.

EximData.com

A leading online world trade directory of manufacturers, exporters, suppliers, dealers, agents, importers, distributors for thousands of products and services.

FITA— The Federation of International Trade Associations
www.fita.org/jobs

FITA's International Trade and Compliance Job Career Headquarters offers hundreds of compliance & international career opportunities.

Import Genius
www.importgenius.com

Subscribers have access to lists of all of your competitors' suppliers and all of your suppliers' customers in the U.S. View trade data relevant to your business, find trading partners you can trust, monitor competitors' shipping activities, and connect with sales prospects.

Importers.com
www.importers.com

Importers.com is the world's largest North American-based online B2B platform, dedicated to promoting trusted trade across the globe, with a particular focus on the G20 economies. It allows users to post and browse both company and trade-related information in over 1,200 sub-categories. Our portal is for importers and exporters from across the globe

to interact and conduct business both smoothly, efficiently, and cost-effectively.

JETC
www.jetc.com

JETC.com is used to build a solid global business community, helping small and large businesses to participate in the global economy and to provide tools for sharing resources to support communities around the world.

Kompass
us.kompass.com

Kompass is a comprehensive B-2-B database, with more than 3 million international and domestic companies listed, which link buyers and sellers worldwide.

Made-in-China.com
globalexport.usaexportimport.com

Made-in-China.com Buyer Service Team provides professional support and assistance to its members with the goal of helping global buyers do business with Chinese suppliers. Offer trading related services, such as: trade safely; product sourcing & recommending; and premium buyers membership upgrade.

Zepol
www.zepol.com

Online trade tools generate competitive advantages for over 1,300 businesses from around the world. With our products, TradeIQ, TradeView, and ComplianceIQ, clients gain essential information on a daily basis that helps drive their businesses. From competitive intelligence to supplier sourcing and lead generation, we help those dealing with the opportunities and perils of global trade.

Section III:
International Careers and Cross-Cultural Business, including Wholesaling and Distributing/ Importing and Exporting

Note: For North American Industry Classification System (NAICS), official U.S. Census Bureau listing of all NAICS, see www.census.gov/epcd/naics02/. In the section, Professions Industries/Interests, many of the resources contain information on international companies and job sources. See this listing for additional information. The Science, Industry, and Business Library (SIBL) of the New York Public Library has an extensive listing of international directories. The list is too specific and too long to include here. For details, see www.nypl.org, go to Locations and Hours, and click on Science, Industry, and Business Library (SIBL) and search International Directories.

See Sections I and II for sources that contain information on international operations.

The $10 Trillion Dollar Prize: Captivating the Newly Affluent in China and India, Michael J. Silverstein, et al., 2012, Harvard Business Review Press

Here is a comprehensive profile of the emerging middle class, primed to transform the global marketplace. Already the world's biggest buyers of cars, mobile phones, appliances, and more, these consumers are eager for more products and services. It's estimated that by 2020, consumers in China and India will generate about $10 trillion of total annual revenue for companies selling to them. This book explains who these consumers are—what they buy and why, how they think and shop, and how their needs and tastes are changing.

The 30 Day MBA in International Business: Your Fast Track Guide to Business Success, Colin Barrow, 2011, Kogan Page

Gives the reader guidance on many hot topics: global business strategy, international marketing strategy, finance and accounting, managing the international organization, human resource management, selecting global strategic partners, ethics, entrepreneurship, growth plans and budgets.

42 Rules for Sourcing and Manufacturing in China: A practical handbook for doing business in China, special economic zones, factory tours and manufacturing quality, Rosemary Coates, 2012, Super Star Press

Doing business in China is tougher than you think. Not only is the culture vastly different, but also China's experience in manufacturing is still developing. It will be a few years before the majority of manufacturers are up to world standards. Based on over 20 executive interviews, Coates captures the essence of sourcing and manufacturing in China.

Business Leadership in China: How to Blend Best Western Practices with Chinese Wisdom, Frank T. Gallo, 2011, Wiley

Ideal for any international manager who wants to better understand how to blend the best practices of Western leadership with traditional Chinese wisdom. Covers major areas of cultural differences such as teamwork, decision-making and employee motivation.

Career Diplomacy, Second Edition: Career Diplomacy: Life and Work in the US Foreign Service, Harry W. Kopp and Charles A. Gillespie, 2011, Georgetown University Press

An insider's guide that examines the foreign service as an institution, a profession, and a career. Based on their own experiences and through interviews with over 100 current and former foreign service officers and specialists, the authors lay out what to expect in a foreign service career, from the entrance exam through mid-career and into the senior service—how the service works on paper, and in practice.

The Cultural Intelligence Difference: Master the One Skill You Can't Do Without in Today's Global Economy, David A. Livermore, 2011, AMACOM

There is a deep cultural intelligence (CQ) required to thrive in our multicultural workplaces and global world. Now everybody can tap into the power of CQ to enhance their skills and capabilities. This book gives readers CQ, a scientifically validated instrument for measuring their personal CQ score.

Doing Business in India, Pawan S. Budhwar and Arup Varma, 2010, Routledge

Both the shortcomings and opportunities associated with the Indian business environment are covered. Critical skills are revealed for negotiation and incentives for foreign investors, including case studies of Italian companies that have entered the Indian market in different ways. Shows the business culture in India, including particular customs and etiquette.

Doing Business With China: Avoiding the Pitfalls by Stewart Hamilton and Jinxuan (Ann) Zhang, 2012, Palgrave Macmillan

Presents a series of detailed cases to illustrate what went wrong and why, drawing on extensive interviews with both Chinese and Western executives. This guide will help Western companies and executives avoid the common mistakes and assist their understanding of what is required to make a success of venturing into China, and vice-versa, as Chinese companies and executives are coming onto the world stage.

Go Global! Launching an International Career Here or Abroad, Stacie Nevadomski Berdan, 2012, SNB Media LLC

A resource that reveals how job seekers can tackle the exciting, yet daunting challenge of developing the necessary skills to land a job in an increasingly global world. Practical advice conveying everything from preparing yourself for the global marketplace—here or abroad—to landing your first big job.

How To Work Overseas—The Recent Grad's Guide To Landing An International Job Fast By Teaching English Abroad, Dylan Alford, 2012, Kindle ed., Amazon Digital

This guide is designed to help recent college graduates land an international job as fast as possible. Working abroad can be one of the most rewarding ways to kick-start a young career.

India—Culture Smart!: The Essential Guide to Customs & Culture, Becky Stephen, 2010, Kuperard

It highlights the subtle and not so subtle changes that are taking place in Indian society, describes and explains those areas of life where traditional attitudes and practices continue to prevail, and offers original insights, practical tips, and vital human information to guide you through the pitfalls and delights of this complex, vibrant, and increasingly important country.

The India Way: How India's Top Business Leaders Are Revolutionizing Management, Peter Cappelli, et al., 2010, Harvard Business Press

The Wharton School India Team unveils these companies' secrets: looking beyond stockholders' interests to public mission and national purpose; drawing on improvisation, adaptation, and resilience to overcome endless hurdles; identifying products and services of compelling value to customers; and investing in talent and building a stirring culture.

Inside a U.S. Embassy: Diplomacy at Work, The Essential Guide to the Foreign Service, 3rd ed., Shawn Dorman, 2011, Potomac Books Inc.

Widely recognized as the essential guide to the Foreign Service, this all-new third edition takes readers to more than 50 U.S. missions around the world, introducing Foreign Service professionals and providing detailed descriptions of their jobs and firsthand accounts of diplomacy in action. In addition to diplomats, there are day-in-the-life accounts from more than 20 countries, each describing an actual day on the job.

International Business, John J. Wild and Kenneth L. Wild, 6th ed., 2011, Prentice Hall

Presents international business in a comprehensive, yet concise framework with unrivaled clarity. Real-world examples and engaging features help bring the concepts to life and make international business accessible to all readers. Captures and explains the influence of the global credit crisis and the recent recession on international business,

International Business, John Daniels, et al., 2010, Prentice Hall

An effective balance between authoritative theory and meaningful practice.

International Business, Charles W. L. Hill, 8th ed., 2010, McGraw-Hill/Irwin

The standard for international business textbooks. The text explores the pros and cons of economic theories, government policies, business strategies, organizational structures, etc.

International Business: The Challenge of Global Competition The Challenge of Global Competition, Michael S. Minor, 13th rev. ed., 2012, McGraw Hill Higher Education; Global

This is a current, objective and thorough treatment of international Business. The author has firsthand international business experience, specializing in international management, finance, law, global strategy, and marketing.

International Business: The New Realities (2nd Edition), S. Tamer Cavusgil, et al., 2nd ed., 2011, Prentice Hall

A complete learning system that seamlessly integrates cases, exercises, and videos.

Rewriting the Rules of Borderless Business, Hiroshi Mikitani, 2013, Palgrave Macmillan

Mikitani argues for an alternate model that benefits vendors, customers, and communities alike by empowering players at every step in the process.

He envisions retail "ecosystems," where brick-and-mortar businesses around the world partner with e-retailers to maximize their customer bases and service capabilities, and he shows why emphasizing collaboration over competition, customization over top-down control, and long-term growth over short-term revenue are by far the best use of the Internet's power.

Work Your Way Around the World: The Globetrotter's Bible, Susan Griffith, 2012, Vacation Work

Griffith incorporates hundreds of first-hand accounts from people who have actually done the jobs as well as a clear, country-by-country guide to the opportunities available—from selling ice cream in Cape Town to working as a film extra in Bangkok this working travel handbook reveals how to fund a trip of a lifetime by finding temporary work abroad both in advance and on the spot while traveling.

Asia's 10,000 Largest Companies, 2010, GAP Books

This volume covers 10 key countries in the Asia-Pacific region: China, Hong Kong, Indonesia, Japan, Malaysia, Philippines, Singapore, South Korea, Taiwan, and Thailand.

Bernan
www.bernan.com

Bernan is a leading distributor of essential publications from the U.S. government and intergovernmental organizations, and a publisher of reference works based on government data. Bernan provides access to a world of government and international agency books, journals, and CD-ROMs for academic and public libraries in the U.S.; as well as to law and corporate libraries. The company distributes more than 45,000 publications.

Uniworld
www.uniworldbp.com

Through our **Uniworld Online**, we offer two unique directories to unravel the maze of "who operates where" and "who owns whom" regardless of whether you're sourcing, building your business, selling, tracking competitors, or seeking employment with a multinational firm. Uniworld Online has contact information for headquarters, branches, subsidiaries, and affiliates of the multinational firm. All of the firms we list are multinational firms.

Directories: American Firms Operating in Foreign Countries and **Foreign Firms Operating in The United States.** Covering over 200 countries and 20,000 industries, our corporate contact information is more comprehensive and accessible than any other such contact product; online or in-print.

Encyclopedia of Associations: International Organizations, annual—*See listing in Section I.*

Encyclopedia of Global Industries, 5th ed., 2011, Print and eBook, Gale

The fully updated 5th edition chronicles the history, development and current status of the world's most lucrative and high-profile industries. Includes comprehensive, international coverage organized by industry, providing a blend of overview and outlook. Consists of approximately 125 detailed profiles of major global industries, including rankings; size and nature of the work force; and a bibliography of further reading sources.

Euromonitor International
www.euromonitor.com

A world leader in strategy research for consumer markets, providing comprehensive international coverage and leading edge innovation, for companies locally and worldwide. Its content covers every region, country, category and channel. A network of strategic analysts in 80 countries provides the depth of global, national and local business information required in today's increasingly international business environment. Products include—Market research by industry, geography, company, or consumer; or by surveys, integrated research systems, and more. **Statistical Reference Handbooks— yearbooks** and **directories** are a starting point for international market research.

F&S Index-Europe, 2009 edition, Thomson Gale
F&S Index-International, 2008, Gale

F&S Indexes offer a compilation of company, product and industry information from financial publications, business-oriented newspapers, trade magazines and special reports. Each F&S Index contains information on corporate acquisitions and mergers, new products, technological developments and social and political factors affecting business.

The Handbook on International Corporate Governance: Country Analyses (Elgar Original Refer-

ence), **2nd ed.,** Christine A. Mallin, 2011, Edward Elgar Pub

Offers extensive analysis of the development of corporate governance across a broad range of countries including, Australia, China, Germany, India, Italy, Japan, Poland, Russia, South Africa, Spain, Turkey and the UK. Additional coverage in this second edition includes Brazil, Hungary, Malaysia, and Norway. The Handbook reveals that while the stage in the corporate governance life cycle may vary from country to country, there are certain core features that emerge such as the importance of transparency, disclosure, accountability of directors and protection of minority shareholders' rights.

Hoover's Handbook of World Business, Margaret L. Harrison, et al., 17th ed., 2010, Hoover's Inc. **www.hooversbooks.com**

This resource contains hard-to-find information on 300 of the most influential public, private and state-owned enterprises across the world, from Canada and Europe, to Asia and South America. Includes lists of the top global companies from Fortune and other publications. Indexes are organized by headquarters location, industry and company executives.

Major Companies of the World, Graham & Whiteside **www.gale.cengage.com**

Updated annually, this series covers **26 industries, worldwide.** For example, M**ajor Chemical and Petrochemical Companies of the World** covers more than 8,500 of the leading chemical and petrochemical companies worldwide. Coverage includes companies involved with general chemicals, petrochemicals, industrial gases, agricultural chemicals, specialty chemicals, fertilizers and oil refining. Entries typically provide: company name; address; telephone, fax numbers; names of senior management and board members, including more than 44,000 senior executives, and more.

Industry Sector Directories provide information on the main sectors of industry and commerce including, pharmaceuticals, telecommunications and finance. Titles include: Major Food and Drink Companies of the World 2011, Major Energy Companies of the World 2011, Major Financial Institutions of the World 2011; and more.

The **Gale Directory Library** is an online source of directory information. With expanded data and state-of-the-art search and export features, works like the Graham & Whiteside Major Companies Series and Gale's Encyclopedia of International Organizations are transformed into research tools for students, companies and professionals of all kinds. Accesses about 58 directories and more soon to be added.

The Major Companies Directories provide top quality company information on the leading businesses worldwide. They are packed with essential facts and contacts, including addresses, phone and fax numbers, email and web addresses together with listings of companies activities, executive names, financial information for the previous two years, parent company and associates, agents and trade names. Major Companies of Europe 2012, NEW—Major Companies of Asia and Australasia 2012, and more.

Trade Associations and Professional Bodies of the UK and Eire, 6th ed., 2013, Graham & Whiteside

Information on more than 4,500 trade associations and professional bodies in the UK and Ireland. Typical listings include name; address; telephone and fax numbers; e-mail and Web site addresses;

Trade Shows Worldwide, 31st ed., 2013, annual, Gale **www.gale.cengage.com**

Includes listings for more than 10,000 trade shows; approximately 6,000 trade-show sponsoring organizations; and more than 5,900 facilities, services and information sources on trade shows and exhibitions held in the U.S. and around the globe.

Yearbook of International Organizations, annual, Print, Online and Streaming, Union of International Associations **www.uia.be**

Contains entries on about 66,000 civil society organizations in 300 countries and territories, in every field of human endeavour. Profiles international non-governmental (INGOs) and intergovernmental organizations (IGOs).

Volume 6: Who's Who in international organizations, 2012-2013

Lists over 24,000 presidents, general secretaries, executive directors, chairmen and other officers active in every field of human endeavor. Some 15,300 international organizations are represented. Information on career, personal and educational, and addresses for each person.

World Directory of Business Information Sources, 2010, Euromonitor International
www.euromonitor.com

This 2-volume set lists full contact details for 22,000 providers of business information for a range of industries in 82 countries. These are the same information sources that Euromonitor International's network of analysts use when starting new research projects. Browse this directory to find brand new sources of information.

The Global Yellow Pages www.globalyp.com

Links to international phone directories, toll-free and unlisted numbers, and more.

LexisNexis Corporate Affiliations
www.corporateaffiliations.com

Corporate Affiliations offers insight on nearly one million parent and subsidiary businesses worldwide, and has recently expanded coverage to include additional in-depth details on directors, executives and their professional interactions, to help you build relationships that encourage business success. A selective focus on the public and private companies, in the U.S. and internationally that drive the global economy.

World Trade and Industrial Enterprise
www.worlddirectory.com

This digital information network and the first-ever World directory that will help your business grow beyond your marketplace. Database which contains **Business directories** covering the world are updated daily, enable making worldwide business-to-business marketing connections.

The
Five
O'Clock
Club®

PART SIX

What Is
The Five O'Clock Club?

FIND YOUR PERSONAL PATH IN
JOB SEARCH AND CAREER SUCCESS

How to Join the Club

The Five O'Clock Club:

Find your personal path in job search and career success

"One organization with a long record of success in helping people find jobs is The Five O'Clock Club."

Fortune

- Weekly Job-Search Strategy Groups
- Private Coaching
- Books, Audio CDs and audio downloads
- Membership Information
- When Your Employer Pays

> **THERE *IS* A FIVE O'CLOCK CLUB NEAR YOU!**
> For more information on becoming a member, please fill out the Membership Application Form in this book, sign up on the web at: www.fiveoclockclub.com, or call:
> **1-800-538-6645**
> (or 212-286-4500 in New York)

The Five O'Clock Club Search Process

The Five O'Clock Club process, as outlined in *The Five O'Clock Club* books, is a targeted, strategic approach to career development and job search. Five O'Clock Club members become proficient

at skills that prove invaluable during their entire working lives.

Career Management

We train our members to manage their careers and always look ahead to their next job search. Research shows that an average worker spends only four years in a job—and will have 12 jobs in as many as 5 career fields—during his or her working life.

Getting Jobs . . . Faster

Five O'Clock Club members find more satisfying jobs, faster. The average professional, manager, or executive Five O'Clock Club member who regularly attends weekly sessions finds a job by his or her 10th session. Even the discouraged, long-term job searcher can find immediate help.

The keystone to The Five O'Clock Club process is teaching our members an understanding of the entire *hiring* process. A first interview is primarily a time for exchanging critical information. The real work starts *after the interview*. We teach our members how to *turn job interviews into offers* and to negotiate the best possible employment package.

Setting Targets

The Five O'Clock Club is action oriented. *We'll help you decide what you should do this very next week to move your search along.* By their third session, our members have set definite job targets by industry or company size, position, and geographic area, and are out in the field gathering information and making contacts that will lead to interviews with hiring managers.

Our approach evolves with the changing job market. We're able to synthesize information from hundreds of Five O'Clock Club members and come up with new approaches for our members. For example, we discuss temporary placement for executives, how to use voice mail and the Internet, the use of LinkedIn and other social media, and how to network when doors are slamming shut all over town.

The Five O'Clock Club's Weekly Small Group Strategy Sessions

The Five O'Clock Club weekly meeting includes you, 6 to 8 peers (people at your same salary level) and a senior Five O'Clock Club career coach who has been certified by us. The meeting is a carefully planned *job-search strategy program where participants go away with an assignment to help them get more interviews in their target markets or turn those interviews into offers.* We provide members with the tools and tricks necessary to get a good job fast—even in a tight market. Networking and emotional support are also included in the meeting.

Participate in 10 *consecutive* small-group strategy sessions to enable your group and career coach to get to know you and to develop momentum in your search.

Weekly Presentations via Audio CDs or audio Downloads

Prior to each week's teleconference, listen to the assigned audio presentation covering part of The Five O'Clock Club methodology. These are scheduled on a rotating basis so you may join the Club at any time.

Small-Group Strategy Sessions

During the first few minutes of the teleconference, your small group discusses the topic of the week and hears from people who have landed jobs. Then you have the chance to get feedback and advice on your own search strategy, listen to and learn from others, and build your network. All groups are led by trained career coaches with years of experience. The small group is generally no more than six to eight people, so everyone gets the chance to speak up.

Let us consider how we may spur one another on toward love and good deeds. Let us not give up meeting together, as some are in the habit of doing, but let us encourage one another.

HEBREWS 10:24-25

Private Coaching

You may meet with your small-group coach—or another coach—for private coaching by phone or in person. A coach helps you develop a career path, solve current job problems, prepare your résumé, or guide your search.

Many members develop long-term relationships with their coaches to get advice throughout their careers. If you are paying for the coaching yourself (as opposed to having your employer pay), please pay the coach directly (charges vary from $100 to $175 per hour). Private coaching is not included in The Five O'Clock Club seminar or membership fee and the Club gets no portion of whatever you pay the coach. For coach matching, see our website or call 1-800-538-6645 (or 212-286-4500 in New York).

From the Club History,
Written in the 1890s

At The Five O'Clock Club, [people] of all shades of political belief—as might be said of all trades and creeds—have met together.... The variety continues almost to a monotony.... [The Club's] good fellowship and geniality—not to say hospitality—has reached them all.

It has been remarked of clubs that they serve to level rank. If that were possible in this country, it would probably be true, if leveling rank means the appreciation of people of equal abilities as equals; but in The Five O'Clock Club it has been a most gratifying and noteworthy fact that no lines have ever been drawn save those which are essential to the honor and good name of any association. Strangers are invited by the club or by any members, [as gentlepeople], irrespective of aristocracy, plutocracy or occupation, and are so treated always. Nor does the thought of a [person's] social position ever enter into the meetings. People of wealth and people of moderate means sit side by side, finding in each other much to praise and admire and little to justify snarlishness or adverse criticism. People meet as people—not as the representatives of a set—and having so met, dwell not in worlds of envy or distrust, but in union and collegiality, forming kindly thoughts of each other in their heart of hearts.

In its methods, The Five O'Clock Club is plain, easy-going and unconventional. It has its "isms" and some peculiarities of procedure, but simplicity characterizes them all. The sense of propriety, rather than rules of order, governs its meetings, and that informality which carries with it sincerity of motive and spontaneity of effort, prevails within it. Its very name indicates informality, and, indeed, one of the reasons said to have induced its adoption was the fact that members or guests need not don their dress suits to attend the meetings, if they so desired. This informality, however, must be distinguished from the informality of Bohemianism. For The Five O'Clock Club, informality, above convenience, means sobriety, refinement of thought and speech, good breeding and good order. To this sort of informality much of its success is due.

Fortune, The New York Times, Black Enterprise, Business Week, The TODAY Show, NPR, CNBC and ABC-TV are some of the places you've seen, heard, or read about us.

The Schedule

See our website for the specific dates for each topic. All groups use a similar schedule in each time zone.

Fee: $49 for LIFETIME membership (includes Beginners Kit, a LIFETIME subscription to *The Five O'Clock News*, and LIFETIME access to the Members Only section of our website), plus session fees based on member's income (the price for the Insider Program includes audio-CD lectures, which retail for as much as $150).

Reservations are required for your first session. Unused sessions that you paid for (as opposed to employer-paid programs) are transferable to anyone you choose or will be donated to members attending more than 16 sessions who are having financial difficulty.

The Five O'Clock Club's programs are geared to professionals, managers, and executives from a wide variety of industries and professions, and also recent graduates. Most earn from $30,000 to $500,000 per year. Half of the members are employed; half are unemployed. You will be in a group of your peers.

> **To register, please fill out form on the web (at www.fiveoclockclub.com)**
> or call 1-800-538-6645
> (or 212-286-4500 in New York).

Lecture Presentation Schedule

- History of the Five O'Clock Club
- The Five O'Clock Club Approach to Job Search
- Developing New Targets for Your Search
- Two-Minute Pitch: Keystone of Your Search
- Using Research and Internet for Your Search
- The Keys to Effective Networking
- Getting the Most Out of Your Contacts
- Getting Interviews: Direct/Targeted Mail
- Beat the Odds when Using Search Firms and Ads
- Developing New Momentum in Your Search
- The Five O'Clock Club Approach to Interviewing
- Advanced Interviewing Techniques
- How to Handle Difficult Interview Questions

- How to Turn Job Interviews into Offers
- Successful Job Hunter's Report
- Four-Step Salary-Negotiation Method

Audio excerpts from many of these presentations can be found on our website in the "How to Get a Job" section.

All groups run continuously. Dates are posted on our website. The textbooks used by all members of The Five O'Clock Club may be ordered on our website or purchased at major bookstores.

> The original Five O'Clock Club was formed in Philadelphia in 1883. It was made up of the leaders of the day who shared their experiences "in a spirit of fellowship and good humor."

Questions You May Have about the Weekly Job-Search Strategy Group

Job hunters are not always the best judges of what they need during a search. For example, most are interested in lectures on answering ads on the Internet or working with search firms. We cover those topics, but strategically they are relatively unimportant in an effective job search.

At The Five O'Clock Club, you get the information you really need in your search—*such as how to target more effectively, how to get more interviews, and how to turn job interviews into offers.*

What's more, you will work in a small group with the best coaches in the business. In these strategy sessions, your group will help you decide what to do, this week and every week, to move your search along. You will learn by being coached and by coaching others in your group.

We find ourselves not independently of other people and institutions but through them. We never get to the bottom of our selves on our own. We discover who we are face to face and side by side with others in work, love, and learning.

ROBERT N. BELLAH, ET AL., *Habits of the Heart*

Here are a few other points:

- For best results, attend on a regular basis. Your group gets to know you and will coach you to eliminate whatever you may be doing wrong—or refine what you are doing right. Our research shows that if

you attend only once a month, the group will have little or no impact on your search results.

- The Five O'Clock Club is a members-only organization. To get started in the small-group teleconference sessions, you must purchase a minimum of 10 sessions.
- The teleconference sessions include the set of 16 audio-CD presentations on Five O'Clock Club methodology. In-person groups do not include CDs.
- After that, you may purchase blocks of 5 or 10 sessions.
- We sell multiple sessions to make administration easier.
- If you miss a session, you may make it up any time. You may even transfer unused time to a friend.
- Although many people find jobs quickly (even people who have been unemployed a long time), others have more difficult searches. Plan to be in it for the long haul and you'll do better.

Carefully read all of the material in this section. It will help you decide whether or not to attend.

- The first week, pay attention to the strategies used by the others in your group. Soak up all the information you can.
- Read the books before you come in the second week. They will help you move your search along.

To register:

1. Read this section and fill out the application.
2. After you become a member and get your Beginners Kit, call to reserve a space for the first time you attend.

To assign you to a career coach, we need to know the following:

- your current (or last) field or industry
- the kind of job you would like next (if you know)
- your desired salary range in general terms

For private coaching, we suggest you attend the small group and ask to see your group leader, to give you continuity.

The Five O'Clock Club is plain, easy-going and un-conventional.... Members or guests need not don their dress suits to attend the meetings.

(FROM THE CLUB HISTORY, WRITTEN IN THE 1890s)

What Happens at the Meetings?

Each week, job searchers from various industries and professions meet in small groups. The groups specialize in professionals, managers, executives, or recent college graduates. Usually, half are employed and half are unemployed.

The weekly program is in two parts. First, listen to a lecture on some aspect of The Five O'Clock Club methodology. Then, job hunters meet in small groups headed by senior full-time professional career coaches.

The first week, get the textbooks, listen to the lecture, and meet with your small group and the senior coach who is leading the group. During your first session, listen to the others in your group. You learn a lot by listening to how your peers are strategizing their searches.

By the second week, you will have read the materials. Now we can start to work on your search strategy and help *you* decide what to do next to move your search along. For example, we'll help you figure out how to get more interviews in your target area or how to turn interviews into job offers.

In the third week, you will see major progress made by other members of your group and you may notice major progress in your own search as well.

By the third or fourth week, most members are conducting full and effective searches. Over the remaining weeks, you will tend to keep up a full search rather than go after only one or two leads. You will regularly aim to have 6 to 10 things *in the works at all times*. These will generally be in specific target areas you have identified, will keep your search on target, and will increase your chances of getting multiple job offers from which to choose.

Those who stick with the process find it works.

Some people prefer to just listen for a few weeks before they start their job search and that's okay, too.

How Much Does It Cost?

It is against the policy of The Five O'Clock Club to charge individuals heavy up-front fees. Our competitors charge $4,000 to $6,000 or more, up front. Our average fee is $360 for 10 sessions (which includes audio CDs (or downloads) of 16 presentations for those in the teleconference program). Those in the $100,000+ range pay an average of $540 for 10 sessions. For administrative reasons, we charge for 5 or 10 additional sessions at a time.

You must have the books so you can begin studying them before the second session. (You can purchase them on our website, at Amazon.com, or ask for them at your local library.) If you don't do the homework, you will tend to waste the time of others in the group by asking questions covered in the texts.

Is the Small Group Right for Me?

The Five O'Clock Club process is for you if:
- You are truly interested in job hunting.
- You have some idea of the kind of job you want.

- You are a professional, manager, or executive— or want to be.
- You want to participate in a group process on a regular basis.
- You realize that finding or changing jobs and careers is hard work, but you are absolutely willing and able to do it.

If you have no idea about the kind of job you want next, you may attend one or two group sessions to start. *Then see a coach privately for one or two sessions,* develop tentative job targets, and return to the group. You may work with your small-group coach or **contact us through our website or by calling 1-800-538-6645** (or 212-286-4500 in New York) for referral to a private coach.

How Long Will It Take Me to Get a Job?

Although our members tend to be from fields or industries where they expect to have difficult searches, the average person who attends regularly finds a new position within 10 sessions. Some take less time and others take more. During the worst recessions, our average professional, manager and executive still found employment in an average of 16.4 weeks (as opposed to the 35 weeks that the population as a whole was taking—assuming they didn't give up on searching).

One thing we know for sure: **Research shows that those who** regularly **attend the small-group strategy sessions get more satisfying jobs faster and at higher rates of pay than those who search on their own,** only **work privately with a career coach, or simply take a course**. This makes sense. If a person comes only when they think they have a problem, they are usually wrong. They probably had a problem a few weeks ago but didn't realize it. Or the problem may be different from the one they thought they had. Those who come regularly benefit from the observations others make about their searches. Problems are solved before they become severe or are prevented altogether.

Those who attend regularly also learn a lot by paying attention and helping others in the group.

This *secondhand* learning can shorten your search by weeks. When you hear the problems of others who are ahead of you in the search, you can avoid them completely. People in your group will come to know you and will point out subtleties you may not have noticed that interviewers will never tell you.

Will I Be with Others from My Field/Industry?

Probably not, but it's not that important. If you are a salesperson, for example, would you want to be with seven other salespeople? Probably not. You will learn a lot and have a much more creative search if you are in a group of people who are in your general salary range but not exactly like you. Our clients are from virtually every field and industry. The *process* is what will help you.

We've been doing this since 1978 and understand your needs. That's why the mix we provide is the best you can get.

Career Coaching Firms Charge $4,000-$6,000 Up Front. How Can You Charge Such a Small Fee?

1. We have no advertising costs, because 90 percent of those who attend have been referred by other members or an association you belong to. (Be sure to ask your alumni or trade association to contact us for a special rate for its members.).

   A hefty up-front fee would bind you to us, but we have been more successful by treating people ethically and having them pretty much *pay as they go.*

   We need a certain number of people to cover expenses. When lots of people get jobs quickly and leave us, we could go into the red. But as long as members refer others, we will continue to provide this service at a fair price.

2. We focus strictly on *job-search strategy,* and encourage our clients to attend free support groups if they need emotional support. We

focus on getting *jobs that fit in with your career goals*, and that reduces the time clients spend with us and the amount they pay.

3. We attract the best coaches, and our clients make more progress per session than they would elsewhere, which also reduces their costs.

4. We have expert administrators and a sophisticated computer system that reduces our overhead and increases our ability to track your progress.

May I Change Coaches?

Yes. Great care is taken in assigning you to your initial coach. However, if you want to change once for any reason, you may do it. We don't encourage group hopping: It is better for you to stick with a group so that everyone gets to know you. On the other hand, we want you to feel comfortable. So if you tell us you prefer a different group, you will be transferred immediately.

What If I Have a Quick Question Outside of the Group Session?

Some people prefer to see their group coach privately. Others prefer to meet with a different coach to get another point of view. Whatever you decide, remember that the group fee does not cover coaching time outside the group session. Therefore, if you wanted to speak with a coach between sessions—even for *quick questions*—you would normally meet with the coach first for a private session so he or she can get to know you better. *Easy, quick questions* are usually more complicated than they appear. After your first private session, some coaches will allow you to pay in advance for one hour of coaching time, which you can then use for quick questions by phone (usually a 15-minute minimum is charged). Since each coach has an individual way of operating, find out how the coach arranges these things.

What If I Want to Start My Own Business?

The process of becoming a consultant is essentially the same as job hunting and lots of consultants attend Five O'Clock Club meetings. However, if you want to buy a franchise or existing business or start a growth business, you should see a private coach. Regardless of the kind of business you want to have, be sure to read our book: *Your Great Business Idea: The Truth About Making It Happen.*

How Can I Be Sure That The Five O'Clock Club Small-Group Sessions Will Be Right for Me?

Before you actually participate in any of the small-group sessions, you can get an idea of the quality of our service by listening to all 16 audio CDs that you purchased. If you are dissatisfied with the CDs for any reason, return the package within 30 days for a full refund.

Whatever you decide, just remember: **Research shows that those who** regularly **attend the small-group strategy sessions get more satisfying jobs faster and at higher rates of pay than those who search on their own,** only **work privately with a career coach, or simply take a course**. If you get a job just one or two weeks faster because of this program, it will have more than paid for itself. And you may transfer unused sessions to anyone you choose. However, the person you choose must be or become a member.

The Five O'Clock Club's Job-Search Buddy System

Do you wish you had someone to talk to—fairly often and informally—about the little things? "Here's what I'm planning to do today in my search? What are *you* planning to do? Let's talk tomorrow to make sure we've done it." You and your job-search buddy could keep each other positive and on track, and encourage each other to do what you told your small group you were going to do: Make that call, send out those letters, write that follow-up proposal, focus on the most important things that should be done—rather than (for example) spending endless hours responding to job postings on the Web.

With your buddy, practice your Two-Minute Pitch, get ready for interviews, bounce ideas off each other. Some job-search buddies talk every day. Some talk a few times a week. Most of the conversation is by phone and e-mail.

Sometimes, people match themselves up as buddies. Just pick someone you get along with in your small group. Sometimes, your coach can match you up. However you do it, stay away from negative people who talk about how bad it is out there. They will drag you down.

The small group changes over time: people get jobs; new people come in. If you lose one buddy who got a job, get another buddy.

Your buddy does not have to be in your field or industry. In fact, being in the same field or industry could keep you focused on the industry rather than on the process. But you do have to get along! The relationship may last only a month or two, or go on for years. Some buddies become friends.

Of course, you should see your Five O'Clock Club career coach privately for résumé review, target development, salary negotiation, and job interview follow-up. It's usually best to get professional coaching advice for these areas. And nothing beats the weekly small-group strategy sessions for making progress in the job search itself. Those who regularly attended the small group got jobs in half the time.

Using The Five O'Clock Club
From the Comfort of Your Home

A man who found the Five O'Clock Club books at his library near Denver calls to ask if there is a local branch. A woman in Seattle who bought the books on Amazon wants to know if she can attend our weekly seminars. A man in Phoenix who received *Targeting a Great Career* from his daughter also wants to attend. And an HR executive wants to know whether we can help her employees in an office closing in Miami.

In our early years, the reach of The Five O'Clock Club—because of the popular Club books—exceeded its presence, but systems have been in place for the past ten years to allow people anywhere to access the Club seminars and coaching by phone and computer.

The Launch of the Insider Groups

Teleconferencing has long come into its own, and for ten years we have offered weekly Club meetings on a nationwide basis. Our Insider Groups (via teleconference) were launched in February 2000, and the first teleconference group included executives from California, North Dakota and Maryland. Prior to the conference call, each person listens to the topic of the week on his or her audio CD or reads the topic in the books. They can listen to the "topic of the week" at their leisure and are then ready for the weekly teleconference.

Following the conference, participants can stay on the line and chat with each other—and most do. In addition, they can browse our LinkedIn Group and network with the almost 1,000 Five O'Clock Clubbers who participate. They can "reply all" to the emails sent to members of their small group and stay in touch with each other that way. And they can talk daily to their Job-Search Buddies, offering advice and encouragement that follow The Five O'Clock Club's methodology. What's more, they can talk to their private coach about a specific interview coming up, get advice on turning a job interview into an offer, or get help negotiating their compensation.

Website as a Public Service

Anyone can wander through the various areas of www.FiveOClockClub.com and tap into vast amounts of useful information—without being a member! For example, click on How To Get a Job to find a menu of 13 substantive articles that represent the heart of the Five O'Clock Club methodology. These articles cover job targeting, interviewing and salary negotiations—and how to start out on the right foot on your new job. There is also a free mini-course to help you assess the **quality** of your job search. Sure, you're working hard, but are you doing the right things?

Remember, The Five O'Clock Club is the ONLY organization devoted to conducting research on behalf of job hunters. We are the only organization with a research-based methodology for you to use rather than the vanilla job-search techniques that everyone else uses. We are the ONLY organization that has books and audios that document the methodology you should use in your job search.

In the Free Articles section you can access hundreds of articles that have appeared in our monthly magazine, *The Five O'Clock News*.

The Weekly Small-Group Strategy Sessions

You are assigned to a small group of your peers (same salary level). Each session is moderated by a certified Five O'Clock Club coach, lasts for an hour, and is guided by the same principles and techniques presented in our books and audios. These are not general discussions on job-search topics; each session moves you forward in your search by helping you to identify steps to take during the coming week. You leave the session with an assignment and proactive coaching on how to do it.

"Our group coach expects us to recap what we've done and we get an assignment. The momentum you get with The Five O'Clock Club makes the big difference," reports one Clubber.

One California Insider member said, "It's really been neat. I've been involved with other job-hunting groups, but they don't have the full breadth of job-search regimen that you have with The Five O'Clock Club. Reading the books and listening to the audios ahead of time helps keep us focused. Our coach expects us to recap what we've done and we get an assignment. The momentum you get with The Five O'Clock Club makes the big difference. I've stagnated with other groups." And he finds that there is a benefit in working with a group whose members are in California, Florida, Massachusetts and New Jersey. "It gives us a different perspective on issues. We have great rapport on the phone and we email and call each other after the session is over."

Reach Out and Touch Someone

ch for private one-on-one coaching. Most of these match-ups result in telephone sessions—the coach may be in Maryland or Chicago, the client

in California or Maine. Many clients want an hour or two of private coaching to help them determine goals and targets. You can find a sampling of coach bios and photos on our website.

Our coaches are trained in The Five O'Clock Club method and are committed to our ethical standards. At other such firms, a newly hired coach with experience is up and running that day. At The Five O'Clock Club, a coach with experience must go through our four-month certification program, un-learn what they thought they knew about job search, and master the methodology.

Seasoned career coaches are attracted to our certification program. Candidates for the Guild must study our 250-page training manual and pass exams to be admitted; they must do two "before" and "after" résumés so they don't give you a cookie-cutter résumé; they must observe 10 small-group coaching sessions and write an essay on what they have learned; and they must do an audition on some aspect of The Five O'Clock Club methodology so they can again prove that they have mastered it. With some 50 coaches in training, in addition to our certified coaches, we are in a position to meet the volume of coaching requests that may come our way in the future.

Be sure to tell your friends about us, and tell your employer that you want The Five O'Clock Club as your outplacement provider!

When Your Employer Pays

Does your employer care about you and others whom they ask to leave the organization? If so, ask them to consider The Five O'Clock Club for your outplacement help. The Five O'Clock Club puts you and your job search first, offering a career-coaching program of the highest quality at the lowest possible price to your employer.

Over 25 Years of Research

The Five O'Clock Club was started in 1978 as a research-based organization. Job hunters tried various techniques and reported their results back to the group. We developed a variety of guidelines so job hunters could choose the techniques best for them.

The methodology was tested and refined on professionals, managers, and executives (and those aspiring to be) from all occupations. Annual salaries ranged from $30,000 to $400,000; 50 percent were employed and 50 percent were unemployed.

Since its beginning, The Five O'Clock Club has tracked trends. Over time, our advice has changed as the job market has changed. What worked in the past is insufficient for today's job market. Today's Five O'Clock Club promotes all our relevant original strategies—and so much more.

As an employee-advocacy organization, The Five O'Clock Club focuses on providing the services and information that the job hunter needs most.

Get the Help You Need Most: 100 Percent Coaching

There's a myth in outplacement circles that a terminated employee just needs a desk, a phone, and minimal career coaching. The new trend is to provide job hunters with databases of fake job openings and other online help and call it "outplacement." The price is ridiculously low, but then an employer can claim that it is providing outplacement to all employees.

<u>**Our experience clearly shows that downsized workers need qualified, reliable coaching more than anything else.**</u> Most traditional outplacement packages last only 3 months. The average executive gets office space and only 5 hours of career coaching during this time. Yet the service job hunters need most is the career coaching itself—not a desk and a phone.

Most professionals, managers, and executives are right in the thick of negotiations with prospective employers at the 3-month mark. Yet that is precisely when traditional outplacement ends, leaving job hunters stranded and sometimes ruining deals.

It is astonishing how often job hunters and employers alike are impressed by the databases of job postings claimed by outplacement firms. Yet only 10 percent of all jobs are filled through ads and another 10 percent are filled through search firms. Instead, direct contact and networking— done The Five O'Clock Club way—are more effective for most searches.

For the latest information on our
outplacement services, go to our
website, www.fiveoclockclub.com, and
look in both the "For Employers"
and "For Employees" sections.

You Get a Safety Net

Imagine getting a package that protects you for a full year. Imagine knowing you can come back if your new job doesn't work out—even months later. Imagine trying consulting work if you like. If you later decide it's not for you, you can come back to The Five O'Clock Club.

We can offer you a safety net of one full year's career coaching because our method is so effective that few people actually need more than 10 weeks in our proven program. But you're protected for a year.

You'll Job Search with Those Who Are Employed—How Novel!

Let's face it. It can be depressing to spend your days at an outplacement firm where everyone is unemployed. At The Five O'Clock Club, half the attendees are working, and this makes the atmosphere cheerier and helps to move your search along.

What's more, you'll be in a small group of your peers, all of whom are using The Five O'Clock Club method. Our research proves that those who attend the small group regularly and use The Five O'Clock Club methods get jobs faster and at higher rates of pay than those who only work privately with a career coach throughout their searches.

So Many Poor Attempts

Nothing is sadder than meeting someone who has already been getting job-search help, but the wrong kind. They've learned the traditional tech-niques that are no longer effective. Most have poor résumés and inappropriate targets and don't know how to turn job interviews into offers.

You'll Get Quite a Package

You'll get up to 14 hours (or more, depending on the package) of private coaching—well in excess of what you would get at a traditional outplacement firm. You may even want to use a few hours after you start your new job.

And you get one full year of weekly small-group career coaching. In addition, you get books, audio CDs, and other helpful materials.

To Get Started

The day your human resources manager calls us authorizing Five O'Clock Club outplacement, we will immediately ship you the books, CDs, and other materials and assign you to a private coach and a small group.

Then we'll monitor your search. Frankly, we care about you more than we care about your employer. And since your employer cares about you, they're glad we feel this way—because they know we'll take care of you.

What They Say about Us

The Five O'Clock Club product is much better, far more useful than my outplacement package.

SENIOR EXECUTIVE AND FIVE O'CLOCK CLUB MEMBER

The Club kept the juices flowing. You're told what to do, what not to do. There were fresh ideas. I went through an outplacement service that, frankly, did not help. If they had done as much as the Five O'Clock Club did, I would have landed sooner.

ANOTHER MEMBER

When Your *Employer* Pays for The Five O'Clock Club, *You* Get:

- **Up to 14 hours (or more, depending on the package) of guaranteed private career coaching** to determine a career direction, develop a résumé, plan salary negotiations, etc. In fact, if you need a second opinion during your search, we can arrange that too.
- **ONE YEAR of weekly small-group strategy sessions via teleconference** (average about 5 or 6 participants in a group) headed by a senior Five O'Clock Club career consultant. That way, if you lose your next job, you can come back. Or if you want to try consulting work and then decide you don't like it, **you can come back**.
- **LIFETIME membership** in The Five O'Clock Club: Beginners Kit and two-year subscription to The Five O'Clock News.
- **The complete set of our four books** for professionals, managers, and executives who are in job search.
- **A boxed set of 16 audio CDs** of Five O'Clock Club presentations.

COMPARISON OF EMPLOYER-PAID PACKAGES

Typical Package	Traditional Outplacement	The Five O'Clock Club
Who is the client?	The organization	Job hunters. We are employee advocates. We always do what is in the best interest of job hunters.
The clintele	All are unemployed	Half of our attendees are unemployed; half are employed. There is an upbeat atmosphere; networkng is enhanced.
Length/type of service	3 months, primarily office space	1 year, exclusively career coaching
Service ends	After 3 months—or before if the client lands a job or consulting assignment.	After 1 full year, no matter what. You can return if you lose your next job, if your assignment ends, or if you need advice after starting your new job.
Small group coaching	Sporatic for 3 months Coach varies	Every week for up to 1 year; same coach
Private coaching	5 hours on average	Up to 14 hours guaranteed (depending on level of service purchased)
Support materials	Generic manual; web-based info	• 4 textbooks based on over 25 yrs. of job-search research • 16 40-minute lectures on audio CDs • Beginners Kit of search information • LIFETIME subscription to the Five)'Clock Club magazine, devoted to career-management articles
Facilities	Cubicle, phone, computer access	None; use home phone and computer

The Way We Are

The Five O'Clock Club means sobriety, refinement of thought and speech, good breeding and good order. To this, much of its success is due. The Five O'Clock Club is easy-going and unconventional. A sense of propriety, rather than rules of order, governs its meetings.

J. Hampton Moore, *History of The Five O'Clock Club*
(written in the 1890s)

Just like the members of the original Five O'Clock Club, today's members want an ongoing relationship. George Vaillant, in his seminal work on successful people, found that "what makes or breaks our luck seems to be... our sustained relationships with other people." (George E. Vaillant, *Adaptation to Life,* Harvard University Press, 1995)

Five O'Clock Club members know that much of the program's benefit comes from simply showing up. Showing up will encourage you to do what you need to do when you are not here. And over the course of several weeks, certain things will become evident that are not evident now.

Five O'Clock Club members learn from each other: The group leader is not the only one with answers. The leader brings factual information to the meetings and keeps the discussion in line. But the answers to some problems may lie within you or with others in the group.

Five O'Clock Club members encourage each other. They listen, see similarities with their own situations, and learn from that. And they listen to see how they may help others. You may come across information or a contact that could help someone else in the group. Passing on that information is what we're all about.

If you are a new member here, listen to others to learn the process. And read the books and listen to the presentations so you will know the basics that others already know. When everyone understands the basics, this keeps the meetings on a high level, interesting, and helpful to everyone.

Five O'Clock Club members are in this together, but they know that ultimately they are each responsible for solving their own problems with God's help. Take the time to learn the process, and you will become better at analyzing your own situation, as well as the situations of others. You will be learning a method that will serve you the rest of your life, and in areas of your life apart from your career.

Five O'Clock Club members are kind to each other. They control their frustrations—because venting helps no one. Because many may be stressed, be kind and go the extra length to keep this place calm and happy. It is your respite from the world outside and a place for you to find comfort and FUN. Relax and enjoy yourself, learn what you can, and help where you can. And have a ball doing it.

There arises from the hearts of busy [people] a love of variety, a yearning for relaxation of thought as well as of body, and a craving for a generous and spontaneous fraternity.

J. Hampton Moore, *History of The Five O'Clock Club*

Lexicon Used at The Five O'Clock Club

The LEXICON—to help you talk about your search

The Five O'Clock Club lexicon is a short-hand—a way to quickly analyze your search and to clearly speak about your search to other Five O'Clock Clubbers. We all speak the same language so we can help each other. Our counselors across the country also speak the same language.

Whether you are in a group or working privately with a Five O'Clock Club career counselor, you can learn our language and analyze your search. After you read the summary below, study our books "as if your were in graduate school." You will learn to better express where you are in your job search, and be better able to figure out what to do next.

The average person who attends The Five O'Clock Club regularly has a new job within just ten weekly sessions–even those who have been unemployed up to two years. Follow our method and you will increase your chances of getting a better job faster.

The following questions will help you to pinpoint what is wrong with your search.

I. Overview and Assessment

How many hours a week are you spending on your search?

Only two or three hours a week, you say? The good news is that you have not yet begun to search. That's why you're making so little progress. To develop momentum in your search, spend 35 hours a week on a full-time search; if you are employed, spend 15 hours a week for a solid, part-time search.

What are your job targets?

If your job targets are wrong, everything is wrong. A target includes:
- industry or organization size,
- the position you want in that industry, and
- your targeted geographic area.

For example, let's say you want to target the health care industry. That's not a good target. It needs to be better defined. For example, perhaps you would consider hospitals. In the metropolitan New York area, for example, there are 80 hospitals. Let's say you're a marketing person, and you would consider doing marketing in a hospital in the NY area. That's one target: Hospitals is the industry, marketing is the position, and NY area is the geographic area. You could also target HMO's. Let's say there are 15 HMO's that you consider appropriate in the NY area. You could do marketing for them. That's a second target. You could also work for a consulting firm in the NY area that does health-care consulting. That's your third target.

But let's say you and your spouse have always loved Phoenix. You think you may like to investigate all three of those industries in the Phoenix area. That's three more targets. The reason you divide your search into targets is so you can have control over it, and tell what's working and what isn't. You make a list of all of the organizations in each of your targets–we call that your "Personal Marketing Plan." Then you find out the names of the people you need to contact in each of those targets–the hiring managers of the departments or divisions you are interested in.

That's the start of an organized search. At the very beginning of your search, you can assess how good your targets are and whether you stand a chance getting a job within a reasonable time-frame. Take a look at "Measuring Your Job Targets" in our books.

How does your resume position you?

The average resume is looked at for only ten seconds–regardless of length. When someone looks at your resume, will they pick up the most important information that you want them to know about you? The summary and body should make you look appropriate to your target. We recommend that the first line of your summary tell the reader exactly how they should see you, e.g., as an "Accounting Manager" or whatever. They will want to stereotype you anyway, so why not help them see you the way you want to be seen?

The second line should differentiate you from your competition: How are you different from all of those other Accounting Managers out there? Your second line could say, for example, "Expert in Cost Accounting."

That is followed by three or four bulleted accomplishments–the most important things you want them to know about you. That way, if they spend only 10 seconds on your resume, they will see what you want them to see. For the complete Five O'Clock Club approach, see our Resume book. It contains summaries related to over 100 industries and professions.

What are your back-up targets?

Decide at the beginning of the search before you start your first campaign. Then you won't get stuck later when things seem hopeless.

Have you done the Assessment?

If you have no specific targets, you cannot have a targeted search. Do the Assessment exercises in our books. You could see a counselor privately for two or three sessions to determine possible job targets. When a person joins the Club, we want them to do the exercises even if they are perfectly clear about what they want to do next. Doing the assessment helps a person to do better in interviews and helps them to have a better resume. Do not skip the assessment, especially the Seven Stories Exercise and the Forty-Year Vision.

II. Getting Interviews

How large is your target area (e.g., 30 companies)? How many of them have you contacted?

When you know your targets, you can research them and come up with a list of all of the companies in your target areas. Figure out how large your target market is. If you have contacted only a few companies in your target area, contact the rest. If you haven't contacted any, contact them all. That's a thorough–and fast–search.

How can you get (more) leads?

You will not get a job through search firms, ads, networking or direct contact. Those are techniques for getting interviews–job leads. Use the right terminology, especially when speaking to someone who has already landed a job. Do not say: how did you get the job, if you really want to know where did you get the lead for that job. In our books, you will find cover letters and approaches for each of these techniques. A good search does not rely on just one technique. We want our members to consider all four techniques for getting interviews in your target markets.

Do you have 6 to 10 things in the works?

When a job hunter is going after only one position–and hoping they will get an offer–that is a weak search. Our research shows that a good job hunter has 6 to 10 things in the works at all times. This is because five will fall away through no fault of your own: Maybe the company decides to hire a finance person instead of a marketing person, or maybe they decide to hire their cousin!

Do not put all of your eggs in one basket. When one offer falls through, you will have lost months in your search because you have to gear up all over again. To avoid losing momentum, make sure you have 6 to 10 things in the works at all times–through search firms, ads, networking or direct contact. It's not as hard as it sounds. Just follow our approach.

If you have 6 to 10 things going at once, you are more likely to turn the job you want into an offer because you will seem more valuable. Don't go after only one job.

How's your Two-Minute Pitch? (Who shall we pretend we are?)

A Two-Minute Pitch is the answer to the question, "So, tell me about yourself." Practice a tailored Two-Minute Pitch. Tell the group–or a friend–the job title and industry of the pretend hiring manager. You will be surprised how good the group is at critiquing pitches. Do it a few weeks in a row until you have a smooth presentation.

Practice it again after you have been in search a while, or after you change targets. Make sure your pitch separates you from your competition.

You seem to be in Stage One (or Stage Two or Stage Three) of your search.

Know where you are in the process. If you are in Stage One–making initial contacts you will recontact later–make lots of contacts so at least 6 to 10 will move to Stage Two: the right people at the right levels in the right companies. You will get the best job offers in Stage Three–talking to 6 to 10 people on an ongoing basis about real jobs or the possibility of creating a job.

Are you seen as insider or outsider?

Are people saying: "I wish I had an opening for someone like you." You are doing well in meetings. If your target is good, it's only a matter of time.

III. Turning Interviews into Offers

Want to go through the Brick Wall?

The brainiest part of the process is turning your job interview into an offer. First, make sure you want the job. If you do not want the job, perhaps you want an offer, if only for practice. If you are not willing to go for it, the group's suggestions will not work.

Who are your likely competitors and how can you kill them off?

"Outshine and outlast your competition" does not mean dirty tricks, but reminds you that you have competitors. You will not get a job simply because "they liked you". The issues are deeper. Ask: Where are you in the hiring process? What kind of person would be your ideal candidate?

What are your next steps?

The "next step" means: what are you planning to do if the hiring manager doesn't call by a certain date, or what are you planning to do to assure the hiring manager does call you.

Can you prove you can do the job?

Most job hunters take the "Trust Me" approach. Instead, prove to them that you can do the job, often by doing additional research or by writing a "proposal" of how you would handle the job.

Which job positions you best for the long run? Which job is the best fit?

Don't decide only on salary. Since the average person has been in his or her job only four years, you will have another job after this. See which job looks best on your resume, and makes you a stronger candidate next time. Take the job that positions you best for the long run.

In addition, find a fit for your personality. If you don't "fit," it is unlikely you will do well there. The group can give feedback on which job is best for you.

> **"Believe me, with self-examination and a lot of hard work with our coaches, you can find the job... you can have the career... you can live the life you've always wanted!"**
>
> **Sincerely,
> Kate Wendleton**

Membership

As a member of The Five O'Clock Club, you get:

- A LIFETIME subscription to *The Five O'Clock News*—10 issues a year filled with information on career development and job-search techniques, focusing on the experiences of real people.
- LIFETIME access to the *Members Only* section of our website containing, for example, all of our basic worksheets, our 111-page bibliography of research resources, and many other items.
- Access to reasonably priced weekly seminars featuring individualized attention to your specific needs in small groups supervised by our senior coaches.
- Access to one-on-one coaching to help you answer specific questions, solve cur-

rent job problems, prepare your résumé, or take an in-depth look at your career path. You choose the coach and pay the coach directly.
- An attractive Beginners Kit containing information based on over 25 years of research on who gets jobs... and why... that will enable you to improve your job-search techniques—immediately!
- The opportunity to exchange ideas and experiences with other job searchers and career changers.

> **All that access, all that information, all that expertise for the one-time membership fee of only $49, plus seminar fees.**

How to become a member— by mail or Email:

Send your name, address, phone number, how you heard about us, and your check for $49 (made payable to "The Five O'Clock Club") to our headquarters address: The Five O'Clock Club, 300 East 40th Street, New York, NY 10016, or sign up at www.fiveoclockclub.com. Or call us at 1-800-538-6645.

We will immediately mail you a Five O'Clock Club Membership Card, the Beginners Kit, and information on our seminars followed by our magazine. Then, call 1-800-538-6645 (or 212-286-4500 in New York) or email us (at info@fiveoclockclub.com) to:

- reserve a space for the first time you plan to attend, or
- be matched with a Five O'Clock Club coach.

Index

About the Author

Kate Wendleton is a nationally recognized authority on career development. She founded The Five O'Clock Club in 1978 and developed its methodology to help job hunters, career changers and employees of all levels, making The Five O'Clock Club the only organization to conduct ongoing research on behalf of employees and job hunters.

Kate was a nationally syndicated columnist for eight years and a speaker on career development, having appeared on the *Today Show*, CNN, CNBC, Larry King, National Public Radio and CBS, and in *The Economist, The New York Times, The Chicago Tribune, The Wall Street Journal, Fortune* magazine, *Business Week* and other national media.

For the past two years, Kate has spent every Saturday with young adults who have aged out of foster care, trying to give them the opportunity to make the most of their lives. This organization, Remington Achievers, is a not-for-profit arm of The Five O'Clock Club.

Kate also founded Workforce America, a not-for-profit Affiliate of The Five O'Clock Club, that served adults in Harlem who were not yet in the professional or managerial ranks. For ten years, Workforce America helped each person move into better-paying, higher-level positions as each improved in educational level and work experience.

Kate founded, and directed for seven years, The Career Center at The New School for Social Research in New York. She also advises major corporations about employee career-development programs.

A former CFO of two small companies, she has twenty years of business-management experience in both manufacturing and service businesses.

Kate attended Chestnut Hill College in Philadelphia and received her MBA from Drexel University. She is a popular speaker with groups that include associations, corporations, and colleges.

While living in Philadelphia, Kate did long-term volunteer work for the Philadelphia Museum of Art, the Walnut Street Theatre Art Gallery, United Way, and the YMCA. Kate currently lives in Manhattan with her husband, has a number of children, including young men who have aged out of foster care.

Kate is the author of The Five O'Clock Club's five-part career-development and job-hunting series for professionals, managers and executives as well as *Your Great Business Idea: The Truth About Making It Happen, WorkSmarts (co-editor)* and The Five O'Clock Club's boxed set of sixteen lectures on audio CD's as well as via downloads.

About The Five O'Clock Club and the "Fruytagie" Canvas

Five O'Clock Club members are special. We attract upbeat, ambitious, dynamic, intelligent people—and that makes it fun for all of us. Most of our members are professionals, managers, executives, consultants, and freelancers. We also include recent college graduates and those aiming to get into the professional ranks, as well as people in their 40s, 50s, and even 60s. Most members' salaries range from $30,000 to $400,000 (one-half of our members earn in excess of $100,000 a year). In addition to attending the weekly small-group strategy sessions at the Club, The Five O'Clock Club Book Series contains all of our methodologies—and our spirit.

The Philosophy of The Five O'Clock Club

The "Fruytagie" Canvas by Patricia Kelly, depicted here, symbolizes our philosophy. The original is actually 52.5" by 69". It is reminiscent of popular 16th century Dutch "fruytagie," or fruit tapestries, which depicted abundance and prosperity.

I was attracted to this piece because it seemed to fit the spirit of our people at The Five O'Clock Club. This was confirmed when the artist, who was not aware of what I did for a living, added these words to the canvas: "The garden is abundant, prosperous and magical." Later, it took me only 10 minutes to write the blank verse "The Garden of Life," because it came from my heart. The verse reflects our philosophy and describes the kind of people who are members of the Club.

I'm always inspired by Five O'Clock Clubbers. They show others the way through their quiet behavior... their kindness... their generosity... their hard work... under God's care.

We share what we have with others. We are in this lush, exciting place together—with our brothers and sisters—and reach out for harmony. The garden is abundant. The job market is exciting. And Five O'Clock Clubbers believe that there is enough for everyone.

About the Artist's Method

To create her tapestry-like art, Kelly developed a unique style of stenciling. She hand-draws and hand-cuts each stencil, both in the negative and positive for each image. Her elaborate technique also includes a lengthy multi-layering process incorporating Dutch metal leaves and gilding, numerous transparent glazes, paints, and wax pencils.

Kelly also paints the back side of the canvas using multiple washes of reds, violets, and golds. She uses this technique to create a heavy vibration of color, which in turn reflects the color onto the surface of the wall against which the canvas hangs.

The canvas is suspended by a heavy braided silk cord threaded into large brass grommets inserted along the top. Like a tapestry, the hemmed canvas is attached to a gold-gilded dowel with finials. The entire work is hung from a sculpted wall ornament.

Our staff is inspired every day by the members of The Five O'Clock Club, and our mantra, which is to "always do what is in the best interests of the job hunter." We all work hard—and have FUN! The garden is abundant—with enough for everyone.

We wish you lots of success in your career. We—and your fellow members of The Five O'Clock Club—will work with you on it.

—Kate Wendleton, President

The original Five O'Clock Club was formed in Philadelphia in 1883. It was made up of the leaders of the day, who shared their experiences "in a spirit of fellowship and good humor."

 THE GARDEN OF LIFE IS abundant, prosperous and magical. ❦ **In this garden, there is enough for everyone.** ❦ **Share the fruit and the knowledge** ❦ **Our brothers and we are in this lush, exciting place together.** ❦ **Let's show others the way.** ❦ **Kindness. Generosity.** ❦ **Hard work.** ❦ **God's care.**

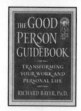